The Development of Competition Law

Global Perspectives

Edited by

Roger Zäch

Europa Institut, University of Zurich, Switzerland

Andreas Heinemann

Europa Institut, University of Zurich, Switzerland

Andreas Kellerhals

Europa Institut, University of Zurich, Member of the Swiss Competition Commission

ASCOLA COMPETITION LAW
The Third ASCOLA Workshop on Comparative Competition Law

Edward Elgar

Cheltenham, UK • Northampton, MA, USA

Published by
Edward Elgar Publishing Limited
The Lypiatts
15 Lansdown Road
Cheltenham
Glos GL50 2JA
UK

Edward Elgar Publishing, Inc.
William Pratt House
9 Dewey Court
Northampton
Massachusetts 01060
USA

A catalogue record for this book
is available from the British Library

Library of Congress Control Number: 2009937922

ISBN 978 1 84844 446 1

Printed and bound by MPG Books Group, UK

Contents

Contributors

Josef Bejček
Professor of Law; Director of the Department of Commercial Law, Masaryk University Brno; Member of the Appellate Committee of the Czech antitrust authority in Brno, Czech Republic

Srinivasan Chakravarthy
Civil servant, competition expert, consultant to World Bank, ADB etc., India

Paulo Furquim de Azevedo
Commissioner at Conselho Administrativo de Defesa Econômica (CADE), Brazil and Professor of Economics at Getúlio Vargas Foundation – FGV-EESP, São Paulo, Brazil

Rainer Geiger
Professor of International Economic Law; Senior regional advisor, OECD, Paris, France

Warren S. Grimes
Professor, Southwestern Law School, Los Angeles, CA., Senior Fellow, American Antitrust Institute, Washington, D.C., USA

Andreas Heinemann
Professor of Law, Member of the board of the Europa Institute, University of Zurich, Switzerland

Alexandre Lauri Henriksen
Conselho Administrativo de Defesa Econômica (CADE), Brazil

Yong Huang
Professor of Law, Director of the Economic Law Department, University of International Business and Economics, Beijing, P.R. China

Shan Jiang
Economic Law Department, University of International Business and Economics, Beijing, People's Republic of China

Andreas Kellerhals
Professor of Law, Director at the Europa Institute, University of Zurich, Member of the Swiss Competition Commission, Switzerland

Adrian Künzler
Dr.iur., District Court of Zurich, Switzerland

Giorgio Monti
Reader in Law, Law Department, London School of Economics, UK

Iwakazu Takahashi
Professor of Law, Faculty of Law, Meiji University, Tokyo, Japan

Wouter P.J. Wils
Member of the Legal Service of the European Commission, Brussels, Belgium, Visiting Professor at King's College London, UK

Roger Zäch
Professor of Law em., Director at the Europa Institute, University of Zurich, Switzerland

Daniel Zimmer
Professor of Law, University of Bonn, Institute for Commercial Law, Member of the German Monopolies Commission, Bonn, Germany

Preface

Competition law has substantially changed since 1990. The worldwide tendency towards market-based economic systems has induced many countries to adopt competition rules. On the other hand, in those countries with a long-standing competition law tradition, the foundations of competition policy have undergone considerable change. The third conference of the Academic Society of Competition Law (ASCOLA) in Zurich took this development as a starting point for a deeper analysis. In the contributions collected in this book, the focus is on three main topics. As regards methodology, the relationship between law and economics has become blurred. This is not only true for US antitrust law, which always has been relatively open for economic thinking, but also for Europe where the transition to a more economic approach animates the debate. The discussion is not only theoretical but has an enormous impact on the formulation of substantive law.

The second issue is the competition law experience in selected countries (Japan, India, China, Czech Republic, Brazil). No matter if the competition law tradition is rather long or more recent, competition law has to adapt to the political, economic, geographic and socio-cultural conditions of states. The institutional framework heavily influences the outcome of competition policy. The variety of selected countries gives a fascinating insight into the specific problems which may occur.

Thirdly, the perspectives of competition law are explored. Competition law has never been so international. What impact does this fact have on the global level? In most parts of the world, competition law is enforced by administrative authorities. Should there be more space for private enforcement and criminal sanctions? And, finally, what should be the role of economics for competition policy in the future?

The Zurich ASCOLA conference would not have been possible without the support of the Europa Institute Zurich (EIZ). The editors especially would like to thank Daniela De Marco, Marietta Zürcher and Robert Lesjak for their constant and most valuable support, as well as Fabio Babey for the preparation of the manuscript. We are very grateful to Peter Behrens, Ulrich Immenga, Joël Monéger and Rolf H. Weber who moderated the lively discussions which are reflected in the contributions to this volume.

Zurich, April 2009

Roger Zäch, Andreas Heinemann, Andreas Kellerhals
Europa Institut at the University of Zurich

PART I

The methodological foundations of competition law

1. EC Competition Law: The Dominance of Economic Analysis?

Giorgio Monti*

1 INTRODUCTION

Nobody can doubt that the most noticeable trend in EC competition law since 1990 has been the increased use of economics by the EC Commission. This is manifested at a range of levels: personnel in Directorate General for Competition (DG Competition) (e.g. creation of the post of Chief Economist, an increase in economists working in the DG); decisions with increased economic sophistication;[1] legal instruments designed by reference to economic studies; and general policy ambitions (e.g. the liberalisation drive that began in the early 1990s affecting utilities and other sectors shielded by state legislation; the plan to reform Article 82 EC; prosecutorial focus on hard-core cartels and away from less significant vertical restraints). Even the Commission's sternest critic for many years, Valentine Korah, has acknowledged that there has been an improvement in this respect if one compares the concluding chapter in the Fifth and Ninth editions of her well known 'yellow book'.[2] In the earlier edition she criticised the paucity of economic analysis, while in the latest edition she notes a dramatic improvement over the last decade, although identifying discrete areas of concern. Thus, this chapter shall not call into question the fact that there is more economic analysis in EC competition law today than there was in the past, nor provide a detailed account of how economic analysis is applied in all aspects of competition enforcement.[3] Instead we examine the

* Reader in Law, Law Department, London School of Economics, UK.

1 E.g. COMP/34.579 *Europay (Eurocard-MasterCard)* 9 December 2007, where the Commission even cited an economics journal at footnote 846.

2 Korah, V. (1994), *An Introductory Guide to EC Competition Law and Policy* 5th edition, London: Sweet & Maxwell; Korah, V. (2007), *An Introductory Guide to EC Competition Law and Policy* 9th edition, Oxford: Hart Publishing.

3 *See* Monti, G. (2007), *EC Competition Law*, Cambridge: Cambridge University Press for an overview.

extent to which economics plays a role and ask questions, such as whether the use of economics is legitimate and about how economics is used. While the scope of issues covered is too wide to allow for detailed discussion of each point, an overview that joins up a variety of themes can offer a helpful critical evaluation of the role of economics in EC competition law.

It helps to break down three dimensions of the decision-making function in a regulatory sphere: the design of rules, the application of rules to a given scenario, and their enforcement.[4] This allows us to examine the extent to which economics plays a role in each of these three stages. The bulk of this chapter (sections 2 and 3) is concerned with the first function because if economics plays no role at that stage, then it can hardly play a meaningful role in the other stages. Having demonstrated that there is a significant, but limited, role for economics in the formulation of legal rules in EC competition law, and that there are arguments that legitimise this role, we next look at some instances of the interaction of economics with competition law in section 4 to question the extent to which the two disciplines are as well integrated as a cursory glance might suggest at first. Having noted these limitations, we turn (in section 5) to examine whether the proposed shift towards greater private enforcement of EC competition law (a trend that also began meekly in the early 1990s but might see more bold legislative action soon) might affect (or be affected by) the increased role of economics in EC competition law.

2 A 'MORE' ECONOMICS-BASED APPROACH

This is how the competition Commissioner summarised the aim of competition enforcement under the more economics-based approach:

> to protect competition in the market as a means of enhancing consumer welfare and ensuring an efficient allocation of resources. An effects-based approach, grounded in solid economics, ensures that citizens enjoy the benefits of a competitive, dynamic market economy.[5]

This statement contains three important assumptions and conclusions: it blurs the line between positive and normative economic analysis, it sets out a welfare paradigm based on distributive considerations, and it signals

---

4 Along similar lines, *see* Brunt M. (1998), 'Antitrust in the Courts: The Role of Economics and Economists' Fordham Corporate Law Institute 357 (Hawk ed 1999).

5 Kroes, N. (2005), 'European Competition Policy: Delivering Better Markets and Better Choices', speech of 15 September). The same distinction is found in Guidelines on Article 81(3) [2004] OJ C101/97 para 21.

a commitment to eliminate the consideration of other goals when enforcing competition law. An important qualification about the economics-based methodology that the Commission makes regularly is that it is a 'more' economics-based approach,[6] which is ambiguous because it may either mean that it is not an exclusively economic approach, or that more economics is used today than in the past. These official statements are scrutinised below.

2.1 Positive and Normative Economics

There is an important distinction between a positive economic analysis, which explains the economic consequences of certain events (e.g. why monopoly prices are high) and a normative economic analysis, which prescribes action (e.g. that monopolies should be broken up). Often, when one speaks of economics in competition law this distinction is blurred. Typically one starts with the fundamental measure of economic performance from a positive perspective, efficiency, which is defined as a situation where the economy cannot increase the welfare of anyone without harming someone else. This measure of performance however, is quickly turned into the goal to be pursued by competition law, so one moves from the positive to the normative without questioning whether efficiency ought to be the sole goal of competition law enforcement. Thus, one of the major United States (US) economics textbooks proclaims: 'in recent years, under the prodding of economists, antitrust policy has been evolving away from the "big is bad" philosophy and toward the economic approach to antitrust. Emphasising the intrinsic rivalry of oligopolists, the economic approach holds that the most powerful incentives for large business to reduce prices and improve quality occur in a deregulated world . . . antitrust policy should be reserved for the worst abuses of market power.'[7] This approach uses economics both in the positive sense (studying the performance of markets) and in the normative sense (regulating markets based on efficiency). The same can be seen in the Commissioner's statement quoted above.[8]

---

6 *A Pro-active Competition Policy for a Competitive Europe* COM(2004) 293 final, para 3.1.

7 Samuelson, P.A. and W.D. Nordhaus (1998), *Economics* 16th edition, Boston: Irwin McGraw Hill, p. 313.

8 Similarly Gerber, D. J (2008), 'Two Forms of Modernisation in European Competition Law', *Fordham International Law Journal*, **31**, 1235 and 1240 noting how the more economics-based approach 'posits that neo-classical economics provides not only the goals of competition law, but also its standards and methods'.

One criticism of this kind of reasoning is that it ignores that, from a normative perspective, society might not wish for competition law to be enforced with an economic approach that focuses only upon whether the actions of firms are inefficient. From a positive perspective, it may well be true that inefficient outcomes are rare, and that open markets and free trade tend to make markets contestable, but this is not enough to say that society should not demand that antitrust law enforcement serves other goals. It follows that, strictly speaking, a normative economics approach to competition law could be consistent with the design of rules to protect vulnerable people in society, or to promote employment, or to sustain an industrial policy. Furthermore, the economic approach summarised above owes a lot to the so-called Chicago School of antitrust analysis, which insists upon efficiency as the sole goal of antitrust enforcement. In contrast, other economists have suggested a wider range of normative goals for economic regulation: progress, full employment (especially of human resources), and an equitable distribution of income.[9] This chapter is not the place to decide what the goals of competition law should be, but in what follows it is important to note that the EC Commission views the economic approach summarised above as relevant both as a matter of positive and normative economics, so that efficiency is both a measure of performance and the test for legality.

2.2 Economic versus Consumer Welfare

Almost all economists say that the basic norm of economics is the maximisation of the overall wealth of society, not a concern about a selected group, e.g. consumers.[10] For example, the reason economists object to monopsony power is that it reduces overall wealth, while a consumer welfare standard might decide that if the exercise of monopsony power (by say supermarkets) leads to lower consumer prices, then there is no reason for competition law to intervene. Conversely, if price discrimination allows sellers to extract more money from consumers willing to pay more, a consumer welfare standard might require intervention even if the action of the price discriminator is efficient. In spite of this, very few competition authorities say that their aim is to maximise total welfare.[11] Instead, competition law is normally about

---

[9] Scherer, F.M. and D. Ross (1990), *Industrial Market Structure and Economic Performance* 3rd edition, Boston: Houghton Mifflin Company, p. 4.

[10] Buccirossi, P. (2008), 'Introduction' in P. Buccirossi (ed.) *Handbook of Antitrust Economics*, Cambridge, MA: MIT Press, pp. xv–xvii.

[11] Two exceptions are said to be Canada and New Zealand. Motta, M. (2004), *Competition Policy*, Cambridge: Cambridge University Press. However this is not

consumer welfare, and it is so in the EC as evidenced by Commissioner Kroes' statement above. Dennis Carlton offers two reasons why this is so.[12] The first reason is the 'monitoring of antitrust policy.' By this he means that focusing on the anticipated short run effects on consumers allows third parties (even courts) to check whether the agency has done its job properly by seeing if prices fall after a prohibited transaction. Instead, a total welfare standard is less easily susceptible to scrutiny given the greater number of variables and also the long term justifications for allowing certain practices – e.g. a merger to monopoly that is said to be good for long term innovation. A second reason which is hinted at by Carlton is that the cost of running a total welfare standard is much greater than examining the effects of a practice under a consumer welfare standard, because one has to examine the impact over a larger range of players in the economy. A third reason we might offer is that although in theory the consumer welfare focus prioritises allocative over productive efficiency, clashes (e.g. a merger to monopoly that would lead to lower costs) are rare so the choice of consumer welfare over total welfare does not yield different outcomes frequently. Consumer welfare then is a proxy for total welfare.[13] But this does not seem to be quite what the EC Commission has in mind. Returning to Commissioner Kroes' statement, competition enhances consumer welfare and ensures an efficient allocation of resources.[14] By distinguishing allocative efficiency and consumer welfare this means that in addition to the loss of economic welfare resulting from output restrictions, the enforcement of competition law also looks at the money transfers from consumers to producers. While this might be criticised as simplistic (producers are firms owned by shareholders, their extra profits result in benefits to society unless there is a monopoly when there is a risk the extra profits are invested in rent-seeking activities), this distributive concern is at the heart of EC competition law.[15]

---

so if one looks at the statutes: Commerce Act 1986, s. 1 provides that the purpose is to 'promote competition in markets for the long-term benefit of consumers within New Zealand'; Canada's Competition Act 1985, s. 1 includes a range of purposes beyond efficiency including ensuring 'that small and medium-sized enterprises have an equitable opportunity to participate in the Canadian economy and in order to provide consumers with competitive prices and product choices'.

[12] Carlton, D. (2007), 'Does Antitrust Need to be Modernized?' EAG 07-3 January, available at: http://papers.ssrn.com/sol3/papers.cfm?abstract_id=956930 (accessed 18 June 2009).

[13] Bishop, S. and M. Walker (2002), *The Economics of EC Competition Law* 2nd edition, London: Thomson Sweet & Maxwell, p. 25.

[14] *See* above, n 5.

[15] The efficiency defence in Article 81(3) and the Merger Regulation requires that the benefits of efficiency are passed on to consumers.

Furthermore, the quote above from the Commissioner raises another issue: whether by focusing on consumer welfare one can sensibly consider static and dynamic efficiencies and make the right policy call between these two kinds of efficiency: should an agency tolerate harmful effects for consumers today in exchange for benefits to consumers in the future? The issue was looked at in brief in the Microsoft decision by the Commission and although the CFI took the view that the discussion was unnecessary for the decision, it is still worth noting that the Commission is sceptical of the view that there may be instances where dominance should be tolerated to allow for increased dynamic efficiency.[16] In a recent case considering parallel trade in pharmaceuticals, the Grand Chamber of the ECJ refused to get involved in this kind of argument in spite of counsel pressing the Court to address the question of how dynamic efficiencies affect the interpretation of Article 82 EC.[17]

One difficulty with the consumer welfare standard is that while in many cases it is easy to see how consumers are hurt by anticompetitive practices, there are instances where putting the standard into operation is complex. Consider a typical vertical restraint that leads to higher prices but greater visibility for the product. The effect of this is that new consumers find out about the good and buy it, but those who already bought it before the restraint now pay higher prices.[18] How do you apply a consumer welfare standard to this kind of behavior? Do you take into account the losses of the consumers who pay a higher price? (No, an economist would say, but yes say antitrust agencies); does one ask whether consumers as a whole are better off? According to Carlton US agencies and courts look at overall consumer welfare, although he qualifies this by noting that 'technically under the Clayton Act, antitrust harm to any substantial consumer group could provide a basis to enjoin a merger.'[19] In the EU, it seems one must also look at the welfare of all consumers.[20] For example the Guidelines on Article 81(3) state that in order to establish that an anticompetitive practice merits exemption

---

16 Case T-201/04 *Microsoft v Commission* judgment of 17 September 2007.

17 Case C-468/06 à C-478/06 *Sot. Lélos Kai Sia E.E. (and others) v GlaxoSmithKline* judgment of 16 September 2009, para 70. The issue may be confronted in Case C-501/06 P *GSK v Commission* [2007] OJ C42/11.

18 Similarly, RBB 'Art or Science? Assessing efficiencies under the Commission's Article 81(3) Notice' RBB Brief N.14 (July 2004) p. 3, available at: http://www.rbbecon.com/publications/downloads/rbb_brief15.pdf (accessed 18 June 2009).

19 *See* Carlton above, n 12, p. 3.

20 Case C-238/05 *Asnef Equifax v Ausbanc* judgment of 23 November 2006, para 70.

because it benefits consumers, one looks at the 'overall impact' on consumers affected by the agreement.[21] So if before the vertical restraint 100 consumers bought the good, and after the restraint there are 200 new customers, the overall effect is positive and the practice benefits from Article 81(3). Yet it may not be easy to do this kind of calculation at all (it will necessarily be an ex ante assessment in that one will want to enjoin the restraint before it has a significant market impact), and when comparing qualitative improvements and price increases the Commission acknowledges that this will be a matter of 'value judgment.'[22] Some have criticised this as an attempt to compare apples and pears,[23] while others suggest that the Commission has some way to go to clarify what it understands as consumer welfare.[24]

2.3 Non-competiton Considerations

So far I have argued that the commitment to consumer welfare stymies the dominance of the total welfare approach that economists favour, injecting a distributive consideration. A second observation is that there are other legitimate, non-efficiency related objectives that could be pursued and this affects the application of competition law. This could lead to the non-enforcement of competition law, so in the EC context an anticompetitive agreement may be said to satisfy the conditions of Article 81(3), or be found not to restrict competition at all. Likewise if the vitality of a given industry is valued, more generous rules might be designed for it. On the other hand, competition law might be enforced in a particular manner as a means to achieve a goal unrelated to efficiency.[25] An illustrative example of this is the way the EC has regulated car distribution, and we focus on the aftermarket for car repairs.[26] Car manufacturers that set up a distribution system for their vehicles must comply with a number of conditions in order to be exempted from liability under Article 81, among these is an obligation to supply technical information

---

[21] Guidelines on Article 81(3) above, n 5, para 87.

[22] *Ibid.* para 103.

[23] *See* RBB above, n 18.

[24] Van den Bergh, R.J. and P.D. Camesasca (2006), *European Competition Law and Economics: A Comparative Perspective* 2nd edition, London: Thomson Sweet & Maxwell, pp. 43–45.

[25] This proposition is supported by Case 14/68 *Walt Wilhelm v Bundeskartellamt* [1969] ECR 1, para 4.

[26] For a brief overview of the regulation of this sector, *see* Monti above, n 3, pp. 384–390.

and other relevant assistance to independent repairers. This is a duty to deal akin to that applied in the so-called ‘essential facilities doctrine’ and it is applied with little analysis of what the market conditions are like, seemingly protecting small garage owners rather than consumers. For example, in adopting a commitment decision (under Article 9 of Regulation 1/2003) whereby Daimler Chrysler agreed to improve access to independent repairers, the Commission’s focus was on the significant price differences between the cost of repair at a garage affiliated with the car manufacturer and an independent repairer. The fact that in the market for repair the Daimler Chrysler affiliated garages had ‘very high market shares’[27] and did not have a stranglehold on the aftermarket, which is a necessary condition for the application of the refusals to deal doctrine under Article 82,[28] was irrelevant. So this market is regulated aggressively even though, strictly speaking from an economic perspective, there was no loss of total welfare, and probably the Commission had an eye to protecting small businesses.

Furthermore, many say that, at least traditionally, EC competition law has been enforced to ‘protect competitors, not competition’.[29] This misleading shorthand phrase refers to the fact that competition is seen by some as a ‘process’, and the protection of such an ‘institution’ is the key to competition enforcement. This approach draws on literature normally grouped together under the label of ‘ordoliberalism’.[30] While it is perhaps overly simplistic to equate EC competition law with the approach of the ordoliberals, some of the case law of the European Courts can be interpreted as demonstrating a concern over the economic freedom of market participants that are harmed by the practices of other firms, and that this foreclosure (actual or potential) often suffices

---

[27] *Daimler Chrysler* [2007] OJ L 317/76, para 5.

[28] Case C-7/97 *Oscar Bronner v Mediaprint* [1998] ECR I-7791.

[29] For a critique of the use of this phrase, *see* Schweitzer, H. (2008), ‘The History, Interpretation and Underlying Principles of Section 2 Sherman Act and Article 82 EC’ in C.D. Ehlermann and M. Marquis (eds) *European Competition Annual 2007: A Reformed Approach to Article 82 EC*, available at: www.ssrn.com (accessed 18 June 2009).

[30] There is little literature about ordoliberalism written in English by those intimately involved with this school of thought. Möschel, W. (1989), ‘Competition Policy from an Ordo Point of View’ in H. Willgerodt and A. Peacock (eds) *German Neo-Liberals and the Social Market Economy*, London: Macmillan is a helpful introduction. Cf. Vanberg, V.J. (2001), *The Constitution of Markets*, London: Routledge, pp. 46–49, who places more of a focus on the view that according to these scholars competition should serve the interests of consumers.

to raise antitrust concerns, regardless of the actual impact on consumer welfare.[31] Interestingly some US commentators say similar things about their antitrust laws.[32]

A 'more economics' oriented approach might suggest that some of these non-efficiency based considerations will have less prominence or are eliminated altogether. For example, the Commission is eager to restrict the role played by non-economic policy factors in Article 81(3) exemptions.[33] Likewise, some hope that the 'economic freedom' basis of some Article 82 doctrines will be abandoned by the use of efficiency-based standards.[34] More economics, in this light, means less policy. (This aphorism again, blurs the line between positive and normative economics.) To test whether there has been a real reduction in considerations other than efficiency, one might examine the application of Article 81(3) since 2004, the year when the Guidelines on Article 81(3) were issued, which seemed to shrink that provision to include only economic efficiency defences or non-economic defences that may be subsumed under the efficiency rubric.[35] No decision under Regulation 1/2003 has yet to find that an agreement that restricts competition under Article 81(1) benefits from an exemption under Article 81(3) – on efficiency grounds or otherwise. That said, absent the notification procedure, the vast majority of Article 81 cases taken up have been hard-core cartels where exemptions are not normally granted. There is one decision where there is a detailed consideration of the efficiency arguments brought up by the parties, but these were rejected as unproven.[36] However, a small number of commitment decisions have been issued under Article 9 of Regulation 1/2003 whereby the Commission decided not to take further action once the parties under investigation undertook to remove the restrictions to competition. In some of these the agreement was redesigned so that had a formal decision

---

31 *See* Lovdhal Gormsen, L. (2006), 'Article 82 EC: Where Are We Coming From and Where Are We Going To?', *Competition Law Review*, **5**, 2(2).

32 E.g., Sullivan, L.A. and W.S. Grimes (2000), *The Law of Antitrust: An Integrated Handbook*, St Paul, Minnesota: West Publishing, pp. 9–10, describing the overriding goal as maintaining 'public confidence in the market mechanism by deterring and punishing instances of economic oppression'.

33 Past cases are reviewed in Monti, G. (2002), 'Article 81 EC and Public Policy', *Common Market Law Review*, **39**, 1057.

34 Ahlborn, C. and C. Grave (2006), 'Walter Eucken and Ordoliberalism: An Introduction from a Consumer Welfare Perspective', *Competition Policy International*, **2**, 197.

35 Guidelines on Article 81(3) above n 5, para 42.

36 *See* above, n 1.

been taken, the conditions in Article 81(3) would have been satisfied.[37] Thus, commitment decisions have become the functional equivalent of exemptions. One concern over this is the lack of transparency: while these decisions are published, the reasons for the Commission considering that the agreement restricts competition and that the amendments suffice to render it compatible with the common market are set out in a sketchy manner, so it is not obvious whether non-economic considerations have played any role in these decisions. One of the settlements has involved the sale of broadcasting rights to football matches, and here it seems to me that the solution accepted by the Commission is designed to foster non-economic considerations, not least an industrial policy in favour of facilitating the growth of new broadcasting technologies by requiring the sale of online content.[38]

In place of the Commission's silence it is worth noting the remarks of the ECJ in *Asnef-Equifax v Ausbanc*. Spanish banks had agreed to set up an electronic register of credit information that would disclose the credit history of potential customers. The effect is that each bank is aware of each potential client's credit history and takes this into account when negotiating further loans. The Court held that it was unlikely that this agreement would restrict competition, but also added some reflections on how one might go about analysing the consumer benefit test in Article 81(3). It suggested that two groups of consumers benefit: those who get loans on better terms, and those who do not get loans because of their bad credit scores, and this is a benefit because it avoids over indebtedness.[39] So resolving the social problem of over indebtedness is a factor that counts in favour of an exemption, suggesting the Court is happy to continue to consider a broad range of justifications under Article 81(3).

To summarise, there are good reasons for the Commission to insist in its public communications that its approach is only about using more economics, because contemporary EC competition law is governed by: a distributive concern about ensuring consumer welfare (which is very difficult to implement in certain instances); other non-economic values; a policy choice (at present at least) in favour of efficiency in the short term over long term dynamic efficiencies; and a wish to see the law enforced to

[37] Most clearly the *Premier League settlement* (COMP/38.173) which is on very similar terms to the decision of the Commission in UEFA Champions League, similarly the pending *Skyteam settlement* (COMP37.984) mimics previous airline alliance exemption decisions.

[38] Monti above, n 3, pp. 105–110.

[39] Above, n 20, para 67.

protect the process of competition.[40] So what economic analysis is used is subject to these boundaries. One might legitimately question whether the use of economics within such a framework is at all possible.

3 THE LEGITIMACY OF ECONOMIC ANALYSIS

Having considered critically the Commission's announcement about the use of economics, it may be worth exploring whether the choice to use economics can be justified. To address this question one usually looks first at the legal text and at the legislative history of that text. In reading the Treaty literally, one could argue that no economist would ever have written Articles 81 and 82 in the way that they have been, so this might counsel against an economic approach. I have taken this view in the context of Article 81(1) and (3) suggesting that no economist would be able to understand a legislative scheme that prohibits restrictions of competition in one paragraph and then exempts efficient agreements in another. If there is efficiency, then there is no restriction to competition in an economic sense, so a restriction of competition for the purposes of Article 81(1) must have a non-economic meaning.[41] Accordingly, Professor Drexl has rightly noted that a restriction of economic freedom is an 'indicative test for the existence of a restriction of competition.'[42] While this interpretation fits well within the scheme of Article 81, it can be argued that it does not serve a helpful interpretative basis because every contract restricts economic freedom, and it cannot be that every contract between undertakings is presumptively unlawful,[43] so one might argue that a literal interpretation leads to undesirable results and so should not be followed. Another relevant consideration in looking at the text of the statute literally is that illegality is defined in terms of what is 'incompatible with the common market' (this is

---

[40] Contra Roller, L-H (2005), 'Economic Analysis and Competition Policy Enforcement in Europe' in P.A.G. van Bergeijk and E. Kloosterhuis *Modelling European Mergers*, Cheltenham: Edward Elgar, who thinks that the connotation 'more' is misleading and that the question is how to best use economics.

[41] Monti above, n 33.

[42] Drexl, J. (2006), 'Competition Law as Part of the European Constitution' in A. von Bogdandy and J. Blast (eds) *Principles of European Constitutional Law*, Oxford: Hart Publishing, p. 649.

[43] As Justice Brandeis recognised: 'the legality of an agreement or regulation cannot be determined by so simple a test, as whether it restrains competition. Every agreement concerning trade, every regulation of trade, restrains. To bind, to restrain, is of their very essence'. *Chicago Board of Trade v United States* (1918) 246 US 231, 238.

the common standard in Articles 81 and 82 EC and Article 2 of the Merger Regulation).[44] Accordingly, economic activity is to be judged against a set of ambitions which are wider than just economic efficiency. (Though here the counter argument is that by focusing on efficiency in enforcing competition law one contributes to the other Community aims indirectly.) Another interesting literal analysis of Article 81 and the EC Merger Regulation suggests that while efficiencies may be taken into consideration, they must benefit the consumer, and the activity in question must not eliminate competition. The implications are twofold: the process of competition prevails over efficiencies; the interests of consumers are placed ahead of anyone else. This prevents the consideration of efficiencies that a Chicagoan might recommend,[45] and as noted above justifies the retention of a distributive concern as well as scepticism over dynamic efficiency claims.

Legislative history has not been used by the ECJ as an interpretative tool in competition cases, neither when interpreting the Treaty, nor when interpreting secondary legislation. Indeed in the latter case the ECJ once refused to bow to legislative intent.[46] My understanding is that there is a consensus that the reports that led to the Rome Treaty are not to be utilised as authoritative sources, moreover the Spaak Report (the preliminary document outlining the issues to be considered by the draftsman of the Rome Treaty, which is the only source publicly available) gives us very little sense of the role of competition policy in the Treaty aside from broad generalisations. Nor can one read much in the motives behind that deletion of the phrase 'free competition' from Article 3(3) of the Lisbon Treaty.[47]

The upshot, from the perspective of community law as a whole, is that the European courts become the interpreters of the Treaty.[48] The courts'

---

44 The Treaty of Lisbon will update the text of Articles 81 and 82 (renumbered Articles 101 and 102) to refer to the internal market. Consolidated versions of the Treaty on European Union and the Treaty on the functioning of the European Union [2008] OJ C115/1.

45 This point is nicely explored by Ghidini, G. (2006), 'Comment; A short note on the generation of efficiencies in the context of the "constitutional' principles of European Competition Law' in H. Ullrich (ed) *The Evolution of European Competition Law*, Cheltenham: Edward Elgar, pp. 357–359.

46 Joined Cases C-68/94 and 30/95 *France v Commission* [1998] ECR I-1375, ruling that the Merger Regulation applies to collective dominance scenarios in spite of evidence that this had been deliberately omitted by the draftsman.

47 Discussed in Chalmers, D. and G. Monti (2008), *European Union Law – Updating Supplement*, Cambridge: Cambridge University Press, pp. 153–155.

48 Stone Sweet, A. (2004), *The Judicial Construction of Europe*, Oxford: Oxford University Press, for a convincing account of the powerful role of the ECJ in interpreting the Treaty and engineering market integration.

pronouncements are more significant in determining the legitimacy of an economics-approach than legislative history. In this vein, Professors van den Bergh and Camesasca have stated 'economic analysis is required by the European courts.'[49] They cite passages from the *Tetra Laval* judgment of the CFI to support this.[50] However I am not certain that the court's ruling can support such a broad proposition: as the Commission had set out to prove the anticompetitive effects of a conglomerate merger by economic standards, then it had to offer convincing economic evidence that the effects would materialise. The court does not say that the Commission must use economic evidence all the time. The court has merely legitimised the use of economic analysis, it has not required it. To prove the position embraced by van den Bergh and Camesasca one would need an appeal where the Commission analysed a merger without a shred of economic evidence and ruled that the merger should be blocked for industrial policy reasons, and a Court saying that this is not allowed. In contrast what we have is authority for the proposition that the interests of employees are relevant in merger cases. In an appeal against the Nestlé/Perrier merger clearance the court said that within the scheme of the EC Merger Regulation 'the primacy given to the establishment of a system of free competition may in certain cases be reconciled . . . with the taking into consideration of the social effects of that operation if they are liable to affect adversely the social objectives referred to in Article 2 of the Treaty.'[51] This passage sets out a soft duty on the Commission, but it goes the other way – the Commission may need to look at employment consequences in addition to consumer welfare effects and render a decision that takes both repercussions into account.

To a certain extent, it is understandable that the court has not required the use of economic analysis because the Commission has considerable interpretative latitude in the sphere of competition law. Professor Majone has argued that the Commission's relationship with the Council ranges from being an agent to being a trustee. In politics, appointing an agent is helpful to signal commitment to a given policy

---

49 Van den Bergh and Camesasca above n 24, p. 2.

50 *See* for example, Case C-12/03 *Tetra Laval v Commission* [2005] ECR I-987, para 39. Van den Bergh and Camesasca (above n 24 at p. 1) also refer to paragraph 14 of *Walt Wilhelm* (above n 25) but there is nothing there to support the proposition for which it is cited; it is a paragraph making an order on costs. On the contrary, paragraph 4 seems to support the view that non economic considerations may be relevant in competition cases.

51 Case T-96/92 *Comité d'Entreprise de la Société Générale des Grades Sources v Commission* [1995] ECR II-1213, para 28, *see also* paras 29–30.

so that governments do not make short term politically expedient decisions. A trustee has greater powers than an agent in that he has a property right in the object he manages. While a trustee is accountable, he also has discretion on how to manage the object. So in whether as agent or trustee, the Commission has political latitude to interpret the rules.[52] As Professor Hartley put it, the Commission 'gives expression to the Community interest.'[53] This allows the Commission to review its interpretative stance if it considers that a different paradigm is necessary to interpret the competition rules and to contribute to the goals set out in the Treaty.

Obviously, the court may have some say in controlling the Commission's policy choices though as has been noted it has not yet compelled the use of economic analysis. The interaction between the court and Commission in the sphere of rule making is a significant issue and worth looking at in closer detail. The European courts hear competition cases through two routes: appeals from Commission decisions (Article 230 EC) or references from national courts normally in the context of private litigation (Article 234 EC). In the former, the CFI's role to review the decision and the grounds are limited: lack of competence; infringement of an essential procedural right; misuse of power; infringement of the EC Treaty or any rule of law relating to it. The court has no formal power to substitute its views for those of the Commission provided that the Commission makes its case with convincing evidence. There are exceptions, however: Professor Gerber has noted that some judgments in the merger field have seen the court play the role of economic expert by relying on its own understanding of economics and what evidence is sufficient to establish the anticompetitive effects.[54] In these cases the court acts as economic expert in the way the facts are handled by the Commission. What is more relevant for this chapter however are instances where the court acts as economic expert in deciding how the rule should be designed in the first place. An example is the AKZO judgment where the court favoured a cost-based approach to examine predatory pricing, in contrast to the Commission's focus on threats and eliminatory intent.[55] But the general approach in Article 230 cases has been one of deference to the judgment

---

52 Majone, G. (2001), 'Two Logics of Delegation: Agency and Fiduciary Relations in EU Governance', *European Union Politics* 2(1), 103.

53 Hartley, T.C. (2003), *The Foundations of European Community Law* 5th edition, Oxford: Oxford University Press, p. 11.

54 Gerber, D.J. (2003), 'Courts as Economic Experts in European Merger Law' Fordham Corporate Law Institute 475 (Hawk ed 2004).

55 Case C-62/86 *AKZO v Commission* [1991] ECR I-3359.

of the Commission. Instead the court has a potentially more significant role as economic expert in Article 234 references. The court is offered a sketch of the facts under dispute and asked to interpret the competition rules. In this context the court can be much more creative and influential, this is so with respect to EU constitutional law, for example.[56] Given that the bulk of competition judgments arise through the Article 230 procedure this limits the potential for the court to dominate the direction of competition policy. This has two implications. One is for the reform of the abuse of dominance doctrine – one of the puzzles has been how to reform the Commission's overly aggressive case law when the court has normally accepted the Commission's approach. Is the Commission somehow 'bound' by its current approach?[57] This puzzle is probably one of the reasons why the December 2005 *Discussion Paper on Exclusionary Abuse* was so disappointingly ambiguous. However, if one accepts the analysis above, it seems that provided the ECJ has not rendered a judgment where it acts as expert in determining how economic analysis should be carried out, its judgments have merely ratified the Commission's approach and its margin of appreciation. So while in the context of refusals to deal there is significant case law emanating from the ECJ that prevents a change of direction by the Commission,[58] the same is not so for rebates (the one field where the Commission is keen on significant reform). The rebate case law merely sees the European courts ratifying the reasoning of the Commission and not necessarily rejecting a less aggressive stance.[59] The second implication of the above is that, unless the court has intervened in setting out the rules, it is up to the Commission to do so and it is able to revise its approach.

Accordingly the question of whether the more economics based approach is legitimate can be framed in a different manner: is the Commission's role as guardian of the Treaty best discharged by deploying an economic analysis to competition cases? The source of legitimacy then becomes functional, and here there is a consensus that competition law is best enforced by the application of economics both in its positive and normative sense. Along similar lines for instance, both Hebert Hovenkamp and the Australian Supreme Court took this view noting that antitrust is an economic, not a moral enterprise and it is defensible only if intervention in the market is

---

56 Starting with Case 26/62 *Van Gend en Loos* [1963] ECR 1, and *see* Stone Sweet above n 48.

57 *See* Gerber above, n 8, p. 1261 suggesting Article 82 reform might be the forum where the legitimacy of the economic approach is tested.

58 E.g., *Oscar Bronner* above, n 28.

59 E.g., Case C-95/04 *British Airways v Commission* [2007] ECR I-2331.

economically justified.[60] Moreover, the stronger economic performance in the US was said to result in part from less aggressive antitrust enforcement.[61] In addition, decentralised enforcement of EC competition law is helped by having a simpler standard for judging anticompetitive practices to rein in the discretion of national competition authorities and prevent them favouring national firms. In Gerber's words, 'procedural modernisation helped to foster substantive change.'[62] Taking these three considerations into account, the choice of an economics-based paradigm as means of testing the legality of undertakings' activities can be legitimised.

4 THE APPLICATION OF ECONOMICS

Let us consider the application of the economics-based approach. Four concerns arise: the instability of economic analysis, the need for simple rules, the problem of miscommunication, the risk of the rogue economist. The first two are well-known so emphasis will be placed on providing an example of the third and outlining the fourth.

4.1 Choosing Economics

The Commission claims that it intends to apply 'mainstream economics' to analyse the disputes that come to its attention. It is not particularly clear that there is such a body of knowledge which is sufficiently precise and uncontroversial to amount to 'mainstream economics.' There is some consensus over certain practices (e.g. the standard to predict coordinated effects in mergers; cartels) but there is much controversy surrounding even practices that have seen hundreds of economic journal articles: consider for instance resale price maintenance, predatory pricing, or tying. This does not mean that economics is useless, but that we cannot expect to be able to reach for an economic textbook and find an answer to how to deal with a given practice. My sense is that all an agency can do is 'choose' an economic analysis among those available and run with it.[63] This choice matters and can be informed by ideology: one wanting an aggressive antitrust policy against predatory pricing will more readily try to incorporate

---

60 Hovenkamp, H. (2005), *The Antitrust Enterprise*, Cambridge, MA: Harvard University Press, p. 10; *Queensland Wire Industries Pty Ltd v Broken Hill Proprietary Company Limited* (1989) 167 CLR 177 Per Deane J, para 2.

61 Gerber above, n 8, p. 1250.

62 *Ibid.*, p. 1258.

63 For detail on this, *see* Monti above, n 3, ch. 3.

modern economic theories that suggest various means through which predatory pricing may occur, while one more inclined to believe that predation is rarely tried and rarely successful will opt for more restrictive rules. As noted above, the European courts are not likely to call into question the economic theory as such, although they might require a higher standard of proof if they find the theory is not plausible. So the court has allowed the Commission to set out a rule that prohibits conglomerate mergers, but because the court has taken the view that these mergers are rarely harmful, it has asked for particularly strong evidence for a prohibition to prevail.[64] As Gerber has noted the effects of stringent review are several: it increases the Commission's costs, it leads to unpredictability of outcomes, and it may deter the Commission from taking certain cases fearful of the court substituting its own expertise.[65] As he notes it is not particularly clear why the court should have a better sense of the economic plausibility of the rule proposed by the Commission, and it may well be argued that as competition policy design is in the hands of the Commission, it should be free to determine which style of economic analysis it prefers, provided the theory has not been falsified.

4.2 Administration v Correctness

In his dissenting opinion in *Leegin* Justice Bryer said: 'antitrust law cannot, and should not, precisely replicate economists' (sometimes conflicting) views.'[66] This sentiment embodies an important lesson about how to design antitrust rules. Even in circumstances when we have economic consensus over how to analyse a given practice, running a full scale economic analysis might be so costly as to outweigh the benefits of the final decision. Accordingly, an enforcement structure with formalistic 'black lists', 'white lists' and 'filters', is actually the 'expression of sound economic reasoning.'[67]

Black lists (or per se rules to the Americans) serve to identify behavior that is normally anticompetitive and allows an agency to dispense with economic analysis, merely requiring proof that that practice has taken

---

[64] *Tetra Laval* above, n 50.

[65] Gerber above, n 54, pp. 491–492.

[66] *Leegin Creative Leather Products v PSKS* (2007) 551 US 877 at p. 8, available at: http://www.supremecourtus.gov/opinions/06pdf/06-480.pdf (accessed 18 June 2009).

[67] Gavil, A.J. (2005), 'Competition Policy, Economics, And Economists: Are We Expecting too Much?', Fordham Corporate Law Institute 575, 590 (Hawk ed 2006).

place. Cartels fall within this list – even if the cartel members have designed it badly so that it is likely that the cartel has had no effect on price, the behavior can be condemned. This is not because there is a concept of 'attempts' in competition law, but because it is rational to punish all collusion because most such practices harm economic welfare. Strictness also prevents appeals and strengthens the deterrent value of the law.

White lists (or safe harbours to the Americans) serve the opposite purpose: excluding from competition law scrutiny practices which may be anticompetitive if judged by a thorough economic analysis, because generally such practices are not anticompetitive. Above-cost predatory pricing is a good example of this: while economists concede that in certain circumstances this behavior is anticompetitive, it is so unlikely to obtain that it makes more sense to allow above cost discounts lest one chills price competition.[68]

Filters allow agencies to use certain markers to determine whether to pursue a more full scale economic inquiry. For example merger guidelines in both the EC and the US begin by requiring a calculation of market shares and certain thresholds trigger deeper analysis. Filters create a safe harbour for firms whose size falls below a given threshold, as in the Block Exemption for Vertical Restraints.

These three processes look like formalistic approaches to applying competition law. However, it makes economic sense not to utilise the full gamut of economic expertise in each and every case that an agency has because to do so would cost too much, reduce the scope of work the agency can do, and thereby under enforce the law. Of course there are difficult questions about what goes in the white and black lists and what filters we want to adopt, but it might be preferable to have that debate at a general policy level (perhaps revisiting the formalistic rules on a regular basis) than hold this debate every time a case is litigated.[69] Perhaps one criticism that might be made of EC competition policy in this respect is the reluctance to allow for white lists – even in vertical restraint cases, there is always a risk that the benefit of the block exemption may be withdrawn, and in merger cases, there is no safe harbour market share, nor are there any safe harbours in the Article 82 case law, on the contrary a dominant firm has a special responsibility not to harm the competitive process and the low dominance threshold places many firms under possibly unnecessary scrutiny.

---

[68] Motta above, n 11, p. 446.

[69] For a more subtle suggestion, *see* Christiansen, A. and W. Kerber (2006), 'Competition Policy with Optimally Differentiated Rules Instead of Per se v Rule of Reason', *Journal of Competition Law & Economics* **2**, 215.

4.3 Miscommunication between Lawyers and Economists

In an interesting reflection on the role of economics, Andrew Gavil noted the problem of economics that gets 'lost in translation', which has two manifestations: first when there is uncertainty among economists as to how to best design the rule then a particular rule may never be applied; the example he gives is predatory pricing where the Courts have not yet decided what relevant cost measure should be utilised with the upshot that the predatory pricing is effectively per se legal. The second manifestation is when the judge is unable to apply the economic theory in any meaningful way and so rejects the argument ab initio. I want to suggest a third 'lost in translation' story, which can be assessed by looking to the reform of the Merger Regulation.[70] As is well known, the substantive test changed from one where proof of dominance was necessary, to one where intervention is justified if the merger may substantially impede effective competition. However, it is not clear that lawyers and economists saw eye to eye on this reform. The ostensible concern was that unilateral effects might arise even when the merged entity is not dominant, but gains enough power to raise prices. However, to put it bluntly, if dominance is defined as the ability to act independently of rivals and we find a merger where the firm is able to raise prices unilaterally (i.e. not caring how rivals respond), then this seems to me to be a merger that creates a dominant position. The real policy issue that lawyers had in mind was to distinguish the application of merger rules from the application of Article 82, and the policy was to allow the Merger Regulation to tackle manifestations of market power that would not be sufficiently worrisome under Article 82, so that only firms holding *significant* market power would have duties under Article 82. The way to achieve this was to reword the Merger Regulation and remove the dominance requirement. However, economists in my view had two other concerns in wishing to opt for a substantial impediment of effective competition test. The first is that a structural analysis that begins with market shares is not always the best way to prove that a merger will have anticompetitive effects. The second is that the new test allows the Commission to look at the overall effects of a merger on the market. This second point helps explain the otherwise puzzling conclusion in a paper co-authored by the former Chief economist where he said that the one merger case at the time where the new standard had been applied was a vertical merger where the overall impact

---

[70] This section draws heavily on Monti, G. (2008), 'The New Substantive Test in the EC Merger Regulation: Bridging the Gap Between Economics and Law?' WPS 10-2008 August, available at: http://www.lse.ac.uk/collections/law/wps/wps.htm (accessed 18 June 2009).

Table 1.1 Market shares in the T.Mobile Austria/Tele.ring merger

T-Mobile	Tele.ring	Mobilkom	ONE	H3G
[20–30%]	[10–20%]	[35–45%]	[15–25%]	[< 5%]

on the wholesale and retail markets was considered.[71] This is not a conclusion to be criticised, but it is significant that a reform discussion conducted exclusively with examples of horizontal mergers should then be justified by an economist with reference to a vertical merger!

There is also a risk that the new standard leads to an unnecessarily aggressive policy. This is exemplified in the one case the Commission itself considered to be one that could not have been dealt with under a dominance test: *T-Mobile Austria/Tele.ring*. Here, the Commission devised a novel theory, considering that a merger in a differentiated product market that eliminates the most important competitive force is anticompetitive even if no dominant firm results, and even if there is no tacit collusion (although in a belt-and-braces approach the Commission does examine the risk of co-ordinated effects as well).[72] The competition concerns occurred in the market for mobile telecommunications services, where the market shares in 2005, measured by customers were as set out in Table 1.1.

The merged entity would not become dominant, but the Commission noted several features which suggested that unilateral effects would occur. First, that Tele.ring had almost doubled its market share in the last three years, while Mobilkom and T-Mobile had lost market shares in that period. Second, ONE was developing a different commercial strategy, selling higher value services and H3G faced an uncertain future given the regulatory framework. Third, Tele.ring was the main reason why Mobilkom and T-Mobile were cutting prices, and its elimination as a market player would reduce the incentive on the two larger firms to reduce prices. Significantly, the Commission did not say that post merger prices would rise, merely that they would not fall as fast as before the merger:

> Even if prices do not rise in the short term, the weakening of competitive pressure as a result of tele.ring's elimination from the market makes it unlikely that prices will continue to fall significantly as in the past.[73]

---

[71] Röller, L.-H. and M. de la Mano, (2006), 'The Impact of the New Substantive Test in European merger Control', *European Competition Journal* **2** (1), 9 (the decision is Case M.3696 *O.EON/MOL* 21 December 2005).

[72] Case M.3916 *T.Mobile Austria/tele.ring* 26 April 2006.

[73] *Ibid.*, para 125.

In spite of this risk, the Commission cleared the merger subject to commitments that facilitated H3G's expansion in the near future, in the expectation that it would become the new maverick player in the Austrian market. The decision seems to use the acquired firm's disruptive presence on the market as the key indicator of anticompetitive harm,[74] but it is unclear what combination of factors in addition to it will lead the Commission to reach the same conclusion, nor what sort of evidence suffices to describe a target firm as a maverick.[75] Moreover, while ONE had deployed a different commercial strategy pre-merger, the Commission should probably have considered more fully that firm's ability to reposition itself to become a direct competitor of the merged entity.[76] There are two further worrying aspects of the decision: first, given the passage quoted above it is not clear why the merger should substantially impede effective competition given that prices would have continued to fall; second the remedy prescribed suggests that the problems in the mobile telecommunications market in Austria had more to do with a defective regulatory regime than with the merger, so the Commission stepped in to regulate a market, not to prevent anticompetitive harm. In sum, this first decision where the Commission felt the dominance test would have prevented the application of the ECMR is one where the Commission appears to stretch its powers significantly. It is not clear that in this bout of law reform lawyers and economists understood each other's concerns.

4.4 Minimising the Risk of the Biased Economist

In the above sections I assumed that economists were scientists working in a Popperian fashion, seeking to falsify conclusions that others have reached. However, one should note the risk that competition law litigation probably encourages economists to overstep their scientific independence. This was a risk that Ronald Coase noted in 1972, when he said that antitrust has turned economists into 'economic statesmen'.[77] By this he meant

---

[74] A similar theory of harm was explored in Case M.4523 *Travelport/Worldspan* (21 August 2007) paras 106–128 but found that the target was not a maverick because: (i) target was not charging lower prices; (ii) target had been losing market share; (iii) the target and acquirer were not each other's closest competitors.

[75] Killick, J. and A. Schulz (2007), 'Horizontal and vertical mergers' in Amato and Ehlermann (eds) *EC Competition Law – A Critical Assessment*, Oxford: Hart Publishing, p. 467.

[76] Horizontal Merger Guidelines [2004] OJ C31/5 para 30.

[77] Coase, R.H. (1988), *The Firm, the Market and the Law*, Chicago: University of Chicago Press, p. 66.

that they were willing to provide definite answers even though methodologically no such answers were available. Moreover, this led to economists looking for a monopoly explanation for the behavior they observed, facilitating prosecutions while not necessarily looking at economically relevant evidence. Coase's main point was that the study of economics had lost its way; and there is another implication, which is that economists become advocates for a given proposition because it supports their clients. A similar concern was aired in passing by George Stigler who suggested that the influence of direct employment is 'neither negligible nor large.'[78] More recently Gavil has noted the risk of agencies and courts being affected by what he calls 'legonomic commentary'. This is represented by lawyers and sometimes economists who have acted in a given case and who write to explain why the decision was wrong (if they lost) or correct (if they won). Reliance on this kind of commentary is risky because it is not driven by a scientific purpose.[79]

These risks are managed well in private litigation in the US because the admissibility of economic evidence is subject to strict procedural standards (the so-called *Daubert* standard), and it has even been argued that similar standards should apply to the workings of US antitrust agencies.[80] The strength of the US rules is such that it deters economists from acting as economic statesmen – disqualification of their evidence leads to a loss of future income and reputation. Similar kinds of safeguards need to be deployed in EC competition law as well, whether enforcement is public or private.

5 PUBLIC VERSUS PRIVATE ANTITRUST REGULATION

One might assume that, if economics guides competition law, then public enforcement is superior to private enforcement. If so, the Commission's current interest in legislating to facilitate private litigation might be counterproductive. These two assumptions are defended below.

---

78 Stigler, G.J. (1982), *The Economist as Preacher*, Oxford: Basil Blackwell, p. 51. For an interesting case study noting these kinds of risks, *see* Dumez, H. and A. Jeunemaître (1998), 'The unlikely encounter between economics and a market: the case of the cement industry' in M. Callon (ed) *The Laws of Markets*, Oxford: Blackwell.

79 Gavil above, n 67, p. 595.

80 Werden, G.J. (2005), 'Making Economics More Useful in Competition Cases: Procedural Rules Governing Expert Opinions', Fordham Corporate Law Institute 601 (Hawk ed 2006).

Public bodies do not necessarily act in the public interest all the time. Some studies in the US have indicated that enforcement is often not dictated by the wish to maximise efficiency but by the staff's career goals or by internal conflicts.[81] It is likely that this is so for any regulator anywhere to a greater or a lesser extent. Moreover, as Professor Neven has noted in an important paper, the Commission's procedures are inquisitorial with a prosecutorial bias and this tends to lead to the Commission ignoring alternative viewpoints and pursuing an economic assessment which is unsatisfactory.[82] The upshot is that public enforcers design weak rules and apply them to individual cases poorly. However, it might be argued that the use of economics in antitrust serves to abate these two concerns. First because in announcing an economics based standard say through guidelines, the agency exposes itself to ex ante evaluation/criticism of its policy. Self-interest would dictate that the agency will not draft Guidelines that subject it to severe criticism for its failure to use economic advice accurately. After all, one of the major reasons for adopting an economics-based approach was precisely to gain greater credibility among antitrust agencies. Second, because in individual disputes the agency knows that its use of economics will be subjected to critical scrutiny by the other side and an appeal to the courts will make an agency reluctant to take a case where the economic evidence is weak. A good example in the EC context is the *Airtours* judgment of the CFI where, while the court accepted the broad theory of coordinated effects that the Commission had applied, it rejected the Commission's handling of the economic evidence.[83] The repercussions of this and other judgments at around the same time led to considerable internal reforms in DG Competition to avoid future errors, although as has been noted above this leads to a risk of under-enforcement because the standard for judicial review is too high.

However, even if imperfect in the ways suggested above, public enforcement also has certain comparative advantages over private enforcement. In the context of cartel-busting it is impossible to say that private enforcement could reach the same results as public enforcement – the

---

[81] Shughart II, W.F. (1996), 'Monopoly and the Problem of the Economists' in F.S. McChesney (ed) *Economic Inputs, Legal Outputs: The Role of Economists in Modern Antitrust*, Chichester: John Wiley & Sons; Mackay, R.J., J.C. Miller III, B. Yandle (eds) (1987), *Public Choice and Regulation – A View from Inside the Federal Trade Commission*, Hoover Institution Press: Stanford: Stanford University Press, esp. chs. 9 and 10.

[82] Neven, D. J. (2006), 'Competition Economics and Antitrust in Europe', *Economic Policy*, **743**.

[83] Case T-342/99 *Airtours v Commission* [2002] ECR II-2585.

tools at the hands of agencies (discovery powers, leniency, fining and settlement policies) combine to give them a much stronger role in fighting the supreme evil of antitrust; in the context of other infringements, the Commission's superior experience and expertise places it at an advantage in interpreting economic evidence. Neven makes the point that there are a lot more economists working at economic consultancies than there are in the Commission, and this is of concern when the Commission prosecutes. But private litigation would merely exacerbate this issue as one side would have access to infinitely greater resources than the other. Consider the *Chester City Council v Arriva* case: the claimants alleged predatory pricing but failed on market definition. The point to note is that the defendant multinational recruited a highly respected economic consultant while the claimant could only afford to recruit someone with very little formal economics training who, the judge found, had 'sufficient expertise, no doubt largely absorbed in the college of life, to entitle him to offer his opinion to the court on the matters in question.'[84] In this setting it is obvious who is going to prevail. This echoes the concern of Ulf Boge who said that the risk of requiring considerable economic evidence of plaintiffs could deter litigation and undermine the Commission's policy to increase the role of private litigation.[85]

Turning to private enforcement, one might argue that since agencies suffer from regulatory capture, private enforcement ensures that antitrust action is taken in the right cases. However, there is no empirical verification that this is so. What we have evidence of is that many antitrust cases are brought between contracting parties pleading that an agreement is void because anticompetitive (pursuant to Article 81(2) EC) and consequently absolving the claimant from any contractual liability – the so-called Euro defence. In the US, because damages for breach of the antitrust laws are trebled, there is a good amount of litigation where breach of competition law is pleaded with the hope that it will result in a windfall for the claimant. The risks that antitrust litigation is likely to be used strategically to undermine competition has been noted before, but has led to little reform.[86] This risk is amplified by the approach of the European Court of Justice in both *Crehan* and *Manfredi* where it was held that 'anyone' who suffers from an anticompetitive practice is entitled

---

84 *Chester City Council v Arriva* [2007] EWHC 1373 (Ch), para 147.

85 Boge, U. (2005), 'Panel Discussion', Fordham Corporate Law Institute 86 (Hawk ed 2006).

86 Baumol, W.J. and J.A. Ordover (1985), 'Use of Antitrust to Subvert Competition', *Journal of Law and Economics,* **28**, 247.

to sue for damages.[87] The *Crehan* case is particularly unhelpful because it encourages litigation among parties to a vertical restraint where the likelihood of anticompetitive effects is very small. Could this lead the Court to devise antitrust standards with an eye to safeguarding the interests of traders and customers instead of focusing on the economic consequences of a given practice as a whole? Furthermore, if private litigation is to contribute in a complementary manner to deter anticompetitive practices, then it is surprising that the White Paper's legislative package does not try and press for those measures which are most likely to yield a substantial increase in litigation. A recent Editorial in the *Common Market Law Review* for example suggests that the White Paper failed to propose the three measures that the Commission considered to be those most likely to lead to an effective private enforcement regime: double damages, lax discovery rules, and giving national courts the power to issue cost orders to favour losing plaintiffs.[88]

6 CONCLUSIONS

By way of summary, my central arguments are that economics does not yet dominate competition policy, and the use of economics in EC competition law is problematic. If economics dominated, a total welfare standard would apply that took into consideration dynamic efficiencies. As things stand the EC applies a consumer welfare standard which is not always easy to implement, and is unlikely to trade off allocative for dynamic efficiencies. Furthermore, an unspecified range of non-competition considerations may impact on the assessment of the behavior of firms. The upshot of this is that it is not clear how one can design rules that have an economic content that fit within the EC system. Even if we surmount this (e.g. by suggesting that the competition authority should first run an economic analysis of a practice and only then explore whether non-economic considerations justify a different result from that prescribed by economics), there are certain difficulties in the application of economics: in many fields there is no consensus upon what the correct economic approach is so the Commission's choice of a given economic standard signals a political commitment of some sort (the alternative answer strongly suggested

---

87 Case C-453/99 *Courage v Crehan* [2001] ECR I-6297; Joined Cases C-295/04 to C-289/04 *Manfredi v Lloyd Adriatico Assicurazioni* [2006] ECR I-6619.

88 Editorial (2008), 'A little more action please! – The White Paper on damages actions for breach of the EC antitrust rules', *Common Market Law Review*, **45**, 609.

by Easterbrook is that if there is no mainstream economic consensus then there should be no antitrust enforcement at all is not one that the Commission is likely to accept);[89] sometimes the best implementation of economics is to design simple non-economic rules that optimise the costs of enforcement; there are risks that economists and lawyers do not understand each other and rules are designed that are imperfect; the presence of rogue economists needs to be controlled, this is a particular issue with regard to the potential growth of private enforcement. Finally, the relationship between the use of economics and the policy to foster private enforcement is an uneasy one: on the one hand too high an economic standard might deter good antitrust plaintiffs, on the other hand, private litigation may risk stimulating anticompetitive lawsuits, undermining the emergent economics-based approach.

One final reflection: in the US antitrust experience more economics has, so far, led to less liability. This has been argued is the result of the Supreme Court adhering too closely to the Chicago School paradigm.[90] There is a similar risk in the EU, but for different reasons: the significant mismatch between the economic capacity of defendants and of the Commission, combined with the court's tougher standard for review could make the Commission less likely to bring controversial cases that apply new economic theories. Paradoxically, this can stifle the development of new antitrust theories and reduce the impact of economics in competition law, by undermining enforcement efforts.

---

89 Easterbrook, F.H. (1984), 'The Limits of Antitrust' *Texas Law Review*, **65**, 1.

90 *See* Grimes, W. (2008) in this volume and R. Pitofsky (ed.) (2008), *How the Chicago School Overshot the Mark*, New York: Oxford University Press.

2. Fifteen Years of Supreme Court Antitrust Jurisprudence: The Defendant Always Wins*

Warren S. Grimes**

1 INTRODUCTION

In June of 1993, the Supreme Court decided *Eastman Kodak Co v Image Technical Services, Inc* in a manner favourable to private plaintiffs.[1] A year later, in *Hartford Fire Insurance Co v California*, in an enforcement proceeding brought by US States and private parties, the court handed down another decision largely favourable to plaintiffs. That was to be the last Supreme Court decision favourable to plaintiffs in any sort of antitrust suit in a 15-year period extending through today. The clock is still ticking.[2]

Examining only the private suits decided in the 16 years since *Kodak*, all 13 of them have been decided adversely to plaintiffs. In addition, in the only post-*Kodak* decision involving a claim brought by a Federal agency, the court in 1999 ruled unfavourably for the Federal Trade Commission.[3] The purpose of this chapter is to provide an overview of the Supreme Court's approach to antitrust issues involving the 15 post-*Kodak* decisions, all but one of them favouring defendants.[4]

* The title recalls Justice Potter Stewart's famous remark in his dissent in *United States v Von's Grocery Co* 384 US 270, 301 (1962), that the 'sole consistency' to be found in merger litigation was that 'the Government always wins'.

** Professor, Southwestern Law School, Los Angeles, CA, Senior Fellow, American Antitrust Institute, Washington, DC, USA.

1 504 US 451 (1992).

2 The court is currently reviewing yet another antitrust private suit, reviewing the decision in *LinkLine Communications, Inc v SBC California, Inc* 503 F3d 876 (9th Cir 2007) and is expected to rule in that suit by the end of the current term (June of 2009).

3 *California Dental Association v FTC* (1999) 526 US 756.

4 Prior to publication of this chapter, the Supreme Court decided *Pacific Bell Telephone Co. v LinkLine Communications, Inc.*, 555 US (2009), the 14th consecutive ruling adverse to private plaintiffs.

Some conclusions are evident. A majority of the court has taken opportunities to limit the scope of antitrust substantive and procedural law. In all but one of the 13 private cases, the federal antitrust agencies have filed friend-of-the-court briefs on the side of defendants, making it easier for the court to rule as it did. Some of the decisions were relatively non-controversial. A few, however, have been harshly criticised. In some of these cases, the criticism is directed not at the holding, but at the logic and analysis that accompanied the court's decision.

The court's apparent agenda to limit the scope and reach of antitrust enforcement appears motivated in part by a view that private enforcement is excessive. Some members of the court may also hold general views that government intervention into the commercial sphere is unwise or overreaching. While substantial parts of the court's recent jurisprudence are likely to endure, there are a number of areas where a reexamination of the court's reasoning is in order.

After reviewing 15 years of Supreme Court antitrust jurisprudence, I offer three general conclusions. The first is that the court's current polarised membership, when coupled with the certiorari process by which the court selects a small number of cases to review, is skewing antitrust away from the mainstream goals of competition policy. The second conclusion is that the court decisions over the past 15 years have often abandoned genuine empiricism in favour of Chicago School aphorisms that have little or no connection with the facts before the court. These statements are picked up by lawyers who advocate and judges who decide; they are becoming unspoken rules for the per se legality of conduct that may have serious anticompetitive effects. The third conclusion, closely related to the second, is that the court has failed in its role to carefully examine economic policy arguments because of the unprincipled way in which it mixes arguments based on *stare decisis* or precedent with economic analysis. This last shortcoming is a reflection of the stylised way in which American lawyers have long made legal arguments. Law professors, who instruct law students on the nuances of legal argument, are complicit in this shortcoming.

2 THE UNITED STATES SUPREME COURT

The United States Constitution provides that members of the Supreme Court shall be nominated by the President and approved by the United States Senate. There is no limit on the term that a justice may serve and no mandatory retirement age. A justice may voluntarily step down at any time, but cannot be forced out of office except through use of the cumbersome impeachment process.[5] Although members of Congress have occasionally threatened to initiate impeachment proceedings against a disfavoured justice, and one justice was actually tried on impeachment charges in 1805, no justice has ever been convicted and removed.[6] The drafters of the Constitution apparently saw secure tenure as a way of insulating justices from popular opinion or pressures from other branches of government.

With no mandatory retirement age, and no limit on the number of years that a justice may serve, members of the court commonly serve well into their 70s or 80s.[7] As Presidents seek to fill the court with justices that fit a particular ideology, gamesmanship in the appointment process involves finding a relatively young candidate in the hopes that the appointee can serve three decades or more. For example, President Bush has chosen Samuel Alito (56 years old when nominated) and John Roberts (51 years old when nominated) for his appointees.

Total insulation of the court from outside influence is impossible and almost certainly undesirable. In addition to Presidential and Senate control over the appointment of justices, other outside influences on the court include the court's dependence on the Congress for annual appropriation of funds needed for its operation. Criticism from

---

[5] The impeachment process is commenced by the House of Representatives, which must approve articles of impeachment by a majority vote. US Constititution Article I, § 2, cl. 5. The impeachment trial occurs in the Senate, where a 2/3 majority is required to convict and remove a federal official; US Constititution, Article I, § 3, cl. 6.

[6] Justice Samuel Chase was tried by the United States Senate on impeachment charges, but was not convicted or removed. A number of lower court judges have been removed through the impeachment process. For a recounting of the history of judicial impeachments, *see* Grimes, W. (1991), 'Hundred-Ton-Gun Control: Preserving Impeachment as the Exclusive Removal Mechanism for Federal Judges', *UCLA Law Review*, **38**, 1209, at 1212–1216.

[7] As of 30 June 2008, the ages of serving justices were: Chief Justice Roberts – 53; Justice Stevens – 88; Justice Ginsburg – 75; Justice Scalia – 73; Justice Kennedy – 71; Justice Breyer – 69; Justice Souter – 68; Justice Thomas – 60; and Justice Alito – 58. *Supreme Court Historical Society*, available at: http://www.supremecourthistory.org/02_history/subs_current/02_b.html (accessed at 18 June 2009). Former Chief Justice William H. Rehnquist served on the Court for 33 years and was 80 years old in September 2005 when he died in office. No recently retired justice has been less than 75 years old at the point of retirement. Justice Blackmun retired at 85; Justice White at 76; and Justice O'Connor at 75. *Supreme Court of the United States*, available at: http://www.supremecourtus.gov/about/members.pdf (accessed 18 June 2009). In April of 2009, Justice Souter, then 69, announced his retirement effective at the end of the Court's term in June of 2009.

the popular media and in scholarly commentary can also impact the justices.

President Franklin Roosevelt, for example, inherited from his predecessors a court that, by a five to four vote, nullified on constitutional grounds a number of key regulatory initiatives that the President thought necessary to address the economic depression of the 1930s. The President responded by proposing to increase the number of justices – new Roosevelt appointees would likely have been more sympathetic to his policies. This failed initiative, known as Roosevelt's 'Court-packing' proposal, was widely condemned at the time as an overreaching effort to manipulate the court.[8] But popular support for Roosevelt's programs may have had the desired impact on the court. Shortly after Roosevelt's re-election in 1936, one of the nine sitting justices, for reasons that may have been known only to him, switched his position on regulatory issues, a switch that gave a five-member majority to justices who were willing to uphold the constitutionality of the President's initiatives.[9] The Roosevelt example is one of many in the court's history that demonstrates the interplay between the Court and contemporaneous political events.

The political nature of the court is perhaps less evident when the court is dealing with statutory provisions that are precise and comprehensive. In common law areas (not governed by statute) or when a statute employs general terms and is therefore open to interpretation, the court's discretion invites consideration of policy. Both the Sherman Act 1890 and the Clayton Act 1914 are written in general terms that encourage the court to entertain policy arguments in interpreting the language.

The Supreme Court is accustomed to issuing majority and dissenting opinions. This allows students of the Court to analyse the decision patterns of individual justices. Today's Supreme Court may be one of the most polarised in the court's two-century history. A study by Landes and Posner reached this conclusion after rating the decisions of 43 past and current justices on a 'liberal' to 'conservative' scale.[10] The analysis showed that four of the court's current nine members are among the five most conservative justices to serve during the 70-year period 1937 to 2006. A

---

[8] Hofer, Peter Charles, Williamjames Hull Hofer and N.E.H. Hull (2007), *The Supreme Court: An Essential History*, Kansas: University Press of Kansas, pp. 252, 264.

[9] *Ibid.,* at p. 264.

[10] Landes, W.M. and Posner, R.A. (2008), *Rational Judicial Behavior: A Statistical Study, National Bureau of Economics Research*; John M. Olin, *Law and Economics Working Paper No 404*, available at: http://ssrn.com/abstract=1126403, (accessed 18 June 2009).

fifth justice is among the ten most conservative to serve.[11] On the opposite side of the ideological spectrum, none of the current justices are among the five most liberal to serve, but the remaining four justices on today's court are each identified among the 15 most liberal justices.[12] This suggests that, although the entire court has shifted markedly in a conservative direction (as compared to the court in the 1960s and 1970s), polarisation is pronounced. There is no strong ideological middle to anchor the court.[13]

The ideological spectrum measured in the Landes and Posner study is based on justices' decisions on a broad variety of issues. Although it need not apply to a narrow area like antitrust, an examination of the 15 antitrust decisions from 1993 to 2007 suggests that the broader characterisations of the study do apply. Four of the conservative justices cast no vote in favour of the plaintiffs' position in any of the target cases (Justices Scalia, Kennedy, Roberts, and Alito).[14] Justice Thomas is the sole conservative justice to have authored or joined a concurring or dissenting opinion favourable to plaintiffs.[15] On the liberal side of the court, all of the current justices have cast votes for the defendants' position in multiple cases, and all have drafted at least one majority opinion favourable to defendants. But these four justices, particularly Justice Stevens, occasionally have written or joined concurring or dissenting opinions favourable to the plaintiffs' position.[16] These outcomes are consistent with the trends demonstrated in the Landes and Posner study – that the entire court has

---

11 Justice Anthony Kennedy, often considered to be a 'swing' vote on today's court, is rated as the tenth most Conservative justice to serve during this 70 year period. The other four justices in the conservative block are each among the five most conservative justices to serve during this period (Clarence Thomas, Antonin Scalia, John Roberts (the current Chief Justice) and Samuel Alito). Former Chief Justice William Rehnquist, who died in office in 2006, is rated as the second most conservative justice in the study. *Ibid.* at p. 46.

12 *Ibid.* (In order of their 'liberal' rank, the justices are Ruth Bader Ginsburg, John Paul Stevens, Stephen Breyer, and David Souter.)

13 According to the study, Justices Byron White and Harry Blackmun, who resigned from the court in 1993 and 1994, respectively, occupied positions in the middle of the ideological spectrum. *Ibid.*

14 In *Hartford Insurance*, the opinion of Justice Scalia (joined by Justice Kennedy and others) contains a favourable interpretation of insurance law for the plaintiff's side, but would have dismissed the plaintiff's claim against foreign reinsurance firms. *Hartford Fire Insurance Co* (1993) 509 US at 800–811.

15 Justice Thomas dissented in *Credit Suisse Sec v Billing* (2007) 127 S.Ct. 2383, 2398, joined Justice Stevens' dissent in *Volvo Trucks North America, Inc v Reeder-Simco GMC, Inc*, (2006) 546 US 164, 183 and joined Justice Stevens' concurring opinion in *Verizon Communications v Trinko, LLP* (2006) 540 US 398, 416.

16 *See* Table 2.1.

shifted to the conservative side of the spectrum at the same time as the more conservative justices have become more strident and doctrinaire in their approach, leading to polarisation.

2.1 The Certiorari Process

The court now renders decisions in only around 100 cases during each term, a small fraction of the cases in which Supreme Court review is sought.[17] The court controls the number of cases it decides by granting or denying petitions for certiorari. For the majority of cases, a party wishing to obtain Supreme Court review of a decision by a court of appeals can do so only through the certiorari petition. If four of the nine justices vote to grant the petition, the case will be heard by the court. Failing these four affirmative votes, certiorari is denied and no Supreme Court review is available.

The certiorari process allows the court to pick a small number of cases from a much larger sample. Traditionally, the court has been more receptive to granting certiorari when there is a conflict among the courts of appeal or when the issue is of overriding importance. For antitrust cases, the court has been selecting cases that give it an opportunity to limit the substantive or procedural scope of antitrust law. The *Kodak* case, decided in 1992, involved facts that made a favourable ruling for the plaintiff more likely.[18] Many of the 15 cases that have been selected for review over the past 15 years have involved facts far less attractive for the plaintiff's side. Still, in its push to limit private litigation, the court has not hesitated to choose cases for review even when the facts were favourable to the plaintiffs (see the discussion of the vertical restraints cases below).

A petition for certiorari is accompanied by a brief in support of the petitioner's request for review. Other parties are allowed to file briefs in opposition. Outside parties may file friend-of-court briefs (amicus briefs) either supporting or opposing the grant of certiorari. In *Leegin Creative Leather Products v PSKS, Inc*,[19] the court's 2007 decision overturning the per se rule against resale price maintenance, the losing party in the court of appeals (the manufacturer/defendant found guilty of resale price maintenance) filed a petition for certiorari with the court. The plaintiff (the prevailing party in the

---

17 Hofer, *supra* n 8, at 454–55 (reporting a drop in the number of reviewed cases from 200 to 100 per year during the tenure of Chief Justice Rehnquist).

18 For an assessment of the *Kodak* case, *see* Grimes, Warren S. (2001) 'Antitrust and the Systemic Bias Against Small Business: Kodak, Strategic Conduct, and Leverage Theory', *Case Western Reserve Law Review*, **51**, 231, at 249–253.

19 127 S.Ct. 2705 (2007).

lower courts) filed a brief in opposition. Although the vote of individual justices is not disclosed, at least four of the justices must have voted to grant the petition, probably because these justices welcomed an opportunity to overturn the per se rule. Thus, even before the *Leegin* case was briefed or argued, there seemed a strong likelihood that the court would grant the relief petitioners sought (overturn the per se rule against resale price maintenance).

2.2 Changes in Court Membership

During the 15-year period, a total of 13 justices served on the nine-member court. Five of these justices served for the entire period.[20] Four others were replaced after they resigned or died.[21] Of the 13 justices, all but three were nominated by Republican Presidents. The exceptions were President Kennedy's appointment of Byron White and President Clinton's appointment of Ruth Bader Ginsburg and Stephen Breyer. The political party of the nominating President, however, does not necessarily reflect the policy preferences of the justice. Justice Stevens and Justice Souter, both considered members of the Court's more 'liberal' block, were appointed by Republican Presidents. Some justices may adapt or change their views after appointment. Justice Harry Blackmun, considered a conservative when he was appointed, wrote the majority opinion in *Eastman Kodak* in 1992, perhaps the most significant pro-enforcement antitrust decision of the past three decades.

Among the nine members of the court today, there are varying degrees of expertise and interest in antitrust law. John Paul Stevens has had a long-standing interest that predates his appointment to the court (he taught antitrust law at Northwestern University and the University of Chicago). Stevens, appointed to the court in 1975 by Republican President Gerald Ford, must be regarded as the court's most consistent champion of competition laws. Stevens is also the oldest and longest serving justice on the Court.[22] During the 15-year period, Justice Stevens was the most active antitrust opinion-writer, authoring one majority opinion, two concurring

---

[20] John Paul Stevens, Anthony Kennedy, Atonin Scalia, David Souter, and Clarence Thomas. Supreme Court of the United States, available at: http://www.supremecourtus.gov/about/members.pdf (accessed 18 June 2009).

[21] Byron White resigned in 1993 and was replaced by Ruth Bader Ginsburg; Harry Blackmun resigned in 1994 and was replaced by Stephen Breyer; Chief Justice William Rehnquist died in 2005 and was replaced by Chief Justice John Roberts; and Sandra Day O'Connor resigned in 2005 to be replaced by Samuel Alito, Jr. in January of 2006. *Ibid.*

[22] Stevens had his 88th birthday in April of 2008. The Supreme Court Historical Society, available at: http://www.supremecourthistory.org/02_history/subs_current/images_b/003.html (accessed 18 June 2009).

opinions, and three dissenting opinions.[23] Justice Stephen Breyer, like Justice Stevens a former professor, wrote about antitrust issues at Harvard Law School before his appointment to the court.[24] Justice Breyer has authored three majority opinions (each favourable to the defendants' point of view) and two significant dissents (favourable to the plaintiffs) over the same period. Overall, Breyer's opinions have been markedly less friendly to plaintiffs than those of Justice Stevens. Justice Antonin Scalia, yet another professor before his appointment to the court, has also demonstrated a strong interest in antitrust. Scalia, probably the most strident in seeking to limit the reach of antitrust, wrote a majority opinion, a concurring opinion, and a dissent during the period, each favouring the defense side of the litigation.[25]

Two of the least ideological justices on the court, Justice Souter and Justice Kennedy, have authored respectively three and two majority opinions. Perhaps because of his pivotal 'swing' vote status, Justice Kennedy wrote the majority opinion in two of the most controversial decisions of this period: *Brooke Group* and *Leegin Creative Leather Products*.

2.3 The Role of the Chief Justice

To fill the Chief Justice's position, the President must nominate and the Senate must approve the individual chosen, even if the nominee is already a justice serving on the court. Most Presidents do not have an opportunity to nominate a chief – the current Chief Justice, John Roberts, is only 53 years old and may well occupy his position through several future presidencies. Because of the pivotal role exercised by the Chief Justice, the 15 antitrust cases can be subdivided into those decided before 2005 (eight cases), the date of Chief Justice Rehnquist's death, and those decided after John Roberts assumed the Chief Justice's mantle (seven cases). The Chief Justice can exercise leadership in a number of ways. The Chief chairs the conferences at which the justices discuss and debate outcomes of the cases and has the important power to assign opinions. The Chief may pressure his colleagues, for example, to work toward a consensus outcome that would avoid concurring and dissenting opinions. Chief Justice Roberts

---

23 *See* Table 2.1 Supreme Court Antitrust Decisions (1993–2007).

24 The Supreme Court Historical Society, available at: http://www.supremecourthistory.org/02_history/02.html (accessed 18 June 2009).

25 Justice Scalia's opinion in *Hartford Insurance* is listed as a dissenting opinion, although a portion of that opinion (dealing with boycott issues) was the opinion of the court and was favourable to the plaintiffs. *Hartford Fire Insurance Co* (1993) 509 US at 800–811.

Table 2.1 Supreme Court antitrust decisions (1993–2007)

Case Name	Cite	Type of Action	Government Amicus	Outcome Favours	Vote	Majority Opinion	Concur Opinion	Dissent Opinion
Spectrum Sports (1993)	506 US 447	Private	Supports defendant	Defendants	9–0	White		
Brooke Group (1993)	509 US 209	Private	None	Defendants	6–3	Kennedy	Stevens	
Hartford Fire (1993)	509 US 764	State/ Private	Supports plaintiff	Plaintiffs	5–4	Souter/ Souter	Scalia	Scalia
State Oil Co (1997)	522 US 3	Private	Supports defendant	Defendants	9-0	O'Connor		
Nynex Corp (1998)	525 US 128	Private	Supports defendant	Defendants	9–0	Breyer		
California Dental (1999)	526 US 756	FTC	None	Defendant	5–4	Souter	Breyer	
Verizon Comm (2004)	540 US 398	Private	Supports defendant	Defendants	9–0	Scalia	Stevens	
Hoffman-La Roche (2004)	542 US 155	Private	Supports defendant	Defendants	8–0	Breyer	Scalia	
(Transition from the Rehnquist to the Roberts Court)								
Volvo Trucks (2006)	546 US 164	Private	Supports defendant	Defendants	7–2	Ginsburg	Stevens	
Texaco Inc (2006)	547 US 1	Private	Supports defendant	Defendants	8–0	Thomas		
Illinois Tool (2006)	547 US 28	Private	Supports defendant	Defendants	8–0	Stevens		
Weyerhaeuser (2007)	549 US 312	Private	Supports defendant	Defendants	9–0		Thomas	
Bell Atlantic (2007)	550 US 544	Private	Supports defendant	Defendants	7–2	Souter	Stevens	
Credit Suisse (2007)	551 US 264	Private	Supports defendant	Defendants	6–1	Breyer	Stevens	Thomas
Leegin Prods (2007)	551 US 877	Private	Supports defendant	Defendants	5–4	Kennedy		Breyer

has expressed support for consensus opinions, and three of the first four antitrust opinions issued after his appointment were unanimous opinions. However, given the polarisation of the court, that goal may be difficult to achieve. In its important *Leegin Products* decision in 2007, the court was split five to four.

Tradition dictates that the Chief may write the opinion of the court whenever the Chief votes with the majority. If the Chief does not write the opinion, the tradition is to offer it to the other justices on the majority side in order of seniority. There is, however, some flexibility in the assignments, perhaps necessary to assure that opinion writing responsibilities do not fall disproportionately on any single justice. The choice of who writes the opinion may make it easier to gather a majority of votes in a particular case. For example, in *Leegin Products*, Justice Kennedy wrote the opinion. This assignment might have been a strategic move to assure Justice Kennedy's vote (needed to create the five to four majority).

The pace of antitrust decisions has accelerated since Chief Justice Roberts' arrival on the bench. Seven antitrust decisions in two years (with an eighth decision issued in 2009) vastly exceeds the pace during the Rehnquist years (eight cases in thirteen years). In pursuit of a more aggressive 'limit-antitrust' agenda, it would appear that Chief Justice Roberts and Justice Alito have been willing to vote with other conservatives to grant certiorari in antitrust cases in which their predecessors (Chief Justice Rehnquist and Justice O'Connor) might not have done so.

2.3.1 The role of the federal agencies

The federal agencies have played a significant role in Supreme Court antitrust cases. Although the Justice Department was not a party to any of the 13 private cases, it filed an amicus brief in all but one of them.[26] The Federal Trade Commission (FTC) joined in most of these amicus filings. In the first eight years there were three amicus interventions in support of defendants and one in support of plaintiffs.[27] This pattern became more pronounced after the election of President George W. Bush in 2000 – the

---

[26] The exception was *Brooke Group* decided in 1993.

[27] In *Hartford Fire Insurance,* the Justice Department's 1992 amicus supported the State claims of jurisdiction. Brief for the United States as Amicus curiae Supporting Respondents, *Hartford Fire Insurance Co v California*, (1993) 509 US 764 (No 91-1111). In *California Dental*, the Justice Department filed no amicus brief, but filed a brief on behalf of the FTC. Brief for the Respondent, *California Dental Association v FTC* (1999) 526 US 756 (No 97-1625).

record of amicus interventions in favour of defendants is 9–0 since that year.[28]

The two federal agencies have not always seen eye to eye in their positions offered to the Supreme Court. For example, in the most recent case to be accepted for Supreme Court review, the FTC refused to join the Antitrust Division in recommending the grant of certiorari.[29] In a case involving an allegedly collusive settlement of drug industry patent litigation, the FTC sought certiorari to review an adverse ruling by a court of appeals, only to have the Justice Department recommend against review. The Supreme Court followed the Department's recommendation.[30]

In assessing the performance of the federal agencies in their amicus role, it is not sufficient to look only at the position the agency advocates. For example, in advocating the elimination of a per se rule, it is important to know what, if anything, the agency urged be substituted in order that litigation might proceed smoothly and relatively efficiently. The mode of argument is also critical – whether or not the agency is presenting a balanced position that fairly presents policy arguments on both sides of the issue. In their amicus role, the federal agencies have a responsibility to the court and the antitrust community to present a comprehensive picture that might not be presented in the briefs of the private parties.

2.3.2 The 15 cases analysed

To facilitate discussion of the Court's 15 decisions, they are grouped into convenient categories: (1) Cases involving the international reach of the Sherman Act 1890; (2) Cases involving unlawful horizontal conspiracies under the Sherman Act 1890, s. 1; (3) Cases involving vertical restraints; (4) Cases involving Predatory Conduct under the Sherman Act 1890, s. 2; and (5) Cases involving the interaction of the antitrust laws with other regulatory schemes.

---

[28] In another private suit in which the defendant sought Supreme Court review, the Justice Department filed an amicus brief in opposition to the defendant's petition for certiorari (the court apparently followed this advice and denied certiorari). Brief for the United States as Amicus curiae, *3M v LePage's Inc* (2004) 542 US 953 (No 02-1865). In cases in which certiorari has been granted, since 2000 the Department has uniformly supported the defendants' position.

[29] *Pacific Bell Telephone Co. v LinkLine Communications, Inc.*, Brief for the United States as Amicus Curiae on Petition for Writ of Certiorari, available at www.usdoj.gov/atr/cases/f233500/233594.htm.

[30] *Schering-Plough v FTC* (2006) 548 US 919 (denying FTC petition for certiorari).

2.3.2.1 Application of the Sherman Act to extra-territorial conduct There were two cases in this category. One of them, *Hartford Fire Insurance v California*, involved the only Supreme Court decision favourable to plaintiffs during the past 15 years. This suit was initiated by 19 State Attorneys General and numerous private plaintiffs against American-based insurance and reinsurance companies and reinsurers based in London. In the trial court, the London-based reinsurers were dismissed from the suit based in part on their claim that the Sherman Act should not apply because the reinsurers' activity was in conformity with the laws of the United Kingdom. The dismissal was reversed by the court of appeals. The Supreme Court granted certiorari and a divided court held that the suits against defendants could proceed. On the important question of whether the Sherman Act claims could be brought against the British reinsurers, the court was split five to four.[31] Justice Souter wrote for the majority that the Sherman Act applied and that no comity analysis – or balancing of interests between US and Britain – was required because there was no direct conflict between the Sherman Act and the laws of the United Kingdom. British law did not prohibit the reinsurers' conduct, but neither did it expressly authorise it. Justice Scalia (joined by three other justices) wrote in dissent that a comity analysis was required and that, under this analysis, the claims against the British reinsurers should be dismissed.

There is controversy surrounding both the majority holding of Justice Souter and the dissent of Justice Scalia. The *Hartford* case, however, involved a number of US defendants and a rather clear case of potential injury to US businesses who purchased liability policies from the defendants. The question of when extraterritorial applications of the Sherman Act require a comity analysis was revisited 11 years later in *F. Hoffman LaRoche Ltd v Empagran, SA.*[32] This time, the suit was a solely private action with substantially weaker connections with the United States. A number of purchasers of vitamins sought damages from participants in a world-wide vitamin cartel. The defendants, both US and foreign firms, moved to dismiss all foreign plaintiffs (customers who had purchased vitamins for delivery outside the United States) from the action. A divided

---

[31] *Hartford Insurance* also involved interpretation of the McCarran Ferguson Act 1945, a statute that grants the domestic insurance industry limited immunity from the antitrust laws. *Hartford Fire Insurance Co (1993)* 509 US at 800–811. These aspects of *Hartford* are discussed in Chapters 5 and 14 of Sullivan, L. and W.S. Grimes (2006), *The Law of Antitrust: An Integrated Handbook*, 2nd edition, St. Paul, Minnesota: Thompson West.

[32] (2004) 542 US 155.

court of appeals had ruled that the motions to dismiss should be denied. In an opinion by Justice Breyer, the Supreme Court ruled unanimously that a comity analysis was required in this instance. Applying that analysis, the foreign purchasers were dismissed from the law suit. The ruling was based on the failure of the plaintiffs to establish a nexus between the injury suffered by foreign purchasers and injury in the United States. The plaintiffs argued unsuccessfully that damage remedies for foreign buyers in US courts are necessary to deter international cartel conduct that will injure US consumers. Limiting damages to US customers would, in plaintiffs' view, have left defendants free to profit from cartel activity because many nations have insufficient remedies for cartel conduct.[33]

Although *Hoffman-LaRoche* is consistent with the pattern of rulings against plaintiffs, the fault lines in the controversy surrounding this decision do not fall cleanly into a Chicago versus post Chicago dichotomy.

2.3.2.2 Horizontal conspiracy under section 1 of the Sherman Act *California Dental Association v FTC* is a controversial holding addressing the standard to be applied to horizontal restraints.[34] In this five to four ruling, the court held that the FTC could not rely on the 'quick-look' doctrine to condemn an arrangement among California dentists to proscribe advertising of discounts or other features that might be attractive to dental patients. The dental association defended its restrictions on the ground that such advertising could be misleading to patients. In rejecting this defense, the FTC found that, although per se condemnation was inappropriate because the conduct involved self-regulation by professionals, the conduct could nonetheless be condemned under the 'quick look' doctrine, which governed horizontal restraints limiting price or output.[35] Application of the quick look doctrine was approved by the Ninth Circuit, but disapproved by the five-member majority of the Supreme Court. Justice Souter wrote that an 'enquiry meet for the case' is required.[36] On these facts, Justice Souter concluded that 'a less quick

---

33 For a detailed analysis, *see* Klevorick, Alvin K. and Alan O. Sykes (2007), 'United States Courts and the Optimal Deterrence of International Cartels: A Welfarist Perspective on Empagran' in Eleanor Fox and Daniel Crane (eds) *Antitrust Stories*, New York: Foundation Press, p. 361.

34 (1999) 526 US 756.

35 The historical roots for the quick look doctrine were two prior Supreme Court cases, *FTC v Indiana Federation of Dentists* (1986) 476 US 447 and *National Collegiate Athletic Association v University of Oklahoma* (1984) 468 US 85 (1984).

36 *California Dental Association*, 526 US at p. 781.

look was required for the initial assessment of the tendency of these professional advertising restrictions'.[37] In his dissent for four members of the Court, Justice Breyer wrote that the court of appeals' affirmance of the Commission's order was unexceptional. The Association's rule in practice precluded all advertising that rates were 'low, reasonable, or affordable', all advertising of across the board discounts, and all quality claims, more than an adquate basis for determining that this conduct unreasonably restrained trade.[38]

On remand, apparently after a cost/benefit analysis of retrying the case, the FTC decided to drop its enforcement action against the association. The *California Dental* decision is consistent with a pattern of decisions that make a plaintiff's path to success more difficult. Critics of the decision believe that it substantially clouded and confused the law surrounding the quick look doctrine, which was an apparently sound way to reduce the costs of litigation without significant compromise of a defendant's opportunity to mount a meritorious defense.

Two other cases decided by the court will narrow the scope of the per se rule governing horizontal conduct. In *NYNEX Corp v Discon, Inc*, Justice Breyer wrote for a unanimous court that a supplier's conspiracy with a customer to preclude a rival of the supplier from making sales was a vertical, not a horizontal, conspiracy and thus would not be considered per se unlawful.[39] The clarity of the issue was clouded because of evidence the firms involved in the conspiracy had violated New York regulatory law governing the telephone industry, raising the issue of whether regulatory law should preempt application of the Sherman Act. *NYNEX* does not preclude a plaintiff from pursuing Section 2 monopolisation claims, nor does it preclude a vertical restraints claim based on the rule of reason. It does deprive plaintiffs of the advantageous per se rule in cases in which, although the effects of the conspiracy are horizontal, the participants consist only of two firms in a vertical relationship.

The third case in this group, *Texaco v Dagher*, was again a unanimous ruling by the Court that conduct would not be considered subject to the per se rule governing classic cartel conduct.[40] Two large integrated oil companies had entered into a joint venture to distribute petroleum products in the western United States. The joint venture would bear all the

---

[37] *Ibid.*
[38] *Ibid.*, at p. 783.
[39] (1998) 525 US 128.
[40] (2006) 547 US 1, 8.

risk and garner all the profits from this business, regardless of whether the products were sold under the Shell or the Texaco brand. As a part of the agreement, the firms agreed to set uniform prices for sales under either brand name. In a unanimous opinion by Justice Thomas, the court held that the Sherman Act, s. 1 did not apply because the corporation created by the joint venture was a single entity. The decision seems consistent with the principle that an efficiency-enhancing joint venture should be assessed under the rule of reason.

The fourth and final case in this group is *Bell Atlantic Corporation v Twombly*.[41] The case dealt not with the substantive law of horizontal restraints, but with the adequacy of the private plaintiffs' complaint that initiated this action. A 7–2 majority opinion of Justice Souter concluded that plaintiffs had not made an adequate factual pleading to survive the defendants' motion to dismiss. The complaint alleged that the defendant telephone companies, who were not direct competitors but operated in distinct territories that were sometimes adjacent to one another, had conspired not to enter one another's territories in violation of the Sherman Act, s. 1. Justice Souter noted that this result might have been the product of perfectly lawful independent decisions by individual defendants. Some more specific factual allegations of a conspiracy were necessary for this litigation to move forward. In Justice Souter's words, 'because the plaintiffs here have not nudged their claims across the line from conceivable to plausible, their complaint must be dismissed.'

What is novel about the court's holding is not the conclusion that parallel conduct, by itself, does not violate section 1 of the Sherman Act, but rather the court's willingness to dismiss this suit before any discovery commenced. As Justice Stevens wrote in dissent, the plaintiffs had alleged a conspiracy. The parallel conduct, Stevens argued, was consistent with either an unlawful conspiracy or with lawful parallel conduct. The allegation of a conspiracy, under past Supreme Court precedents, would have sufficed to get past the motion to dismiss and into the discovery phase of the case. Justice Souter and the majority impose a tougher pleading standard on plaintiffs at least in part because of their desire to prevent the initiation of expensive discovery. To get that result, the majority had to aggressively find its way around past precedent as well as statutory language. All of this led to Justice Stevens' conclusion that the majority had ignored 'the intentions of the drafters of three important sources of law – the Sherman Act, the Telecommunications Act of 1996, and the Federal Rules of Civil Procedure'.

41 (2007) 550 US 544.

2.3.2.3 Vertical cases Vertical restraints are a focus in the debate between Chicago and post Chicago scholars. The Supreme Court decided three vertical restraints cases during the past 15 years. In each case, the Court accepted certiorari with the evident purpose of overturning a rule that made it easier for a plaintiff to prosecute a vertical case successfully. In each case, the rule was overturned despite facts that could have warranted a holding that the restraint was anticompetitive.

In *State Oil Co v Khan*, a unanimous Court overturned the per se rule that had governed vertical maximum price-fixing.[42] The Justice Department and the FTC urged this result in their amicus brief. Eliminating the per se rule also had support from most antitrust theorists who had addressed the issue. A key point in Justice O'Connor's reasoning was that an upstream monopolist that has the power to dictate a maximum price to retailers might do so in a manner that would benefit consumers – to prevent price gouging activity by retailers. The holding was controversial primarily because it did not acknowledge that genuine competitive harm can result from a powerful seller's efforts to squeeze the margin of a downstream seller. [43] A retailer purchasing from a monopolist or who is in a dependent relationship with the supplier (a franchisee could fit this description) might be forced to resell a product at a lower margin that could result in distorted market incentives (for example, the retailer might raise its prices on other products that impede an efficient allocation of those products). If the retailer is forced to absorb the loss of a reasonable margin, incentives for the retailer to expand or continue its business would be distorted. The court's response to this concern was that a producer would also be harmed by such a decision, 'making it unlikely that a producer would set such a price as a matter of business judgment'.[44] The court cites no empirical support for this statement. Maximum prices are set when the supplier exercises power over its downstream customers. The power-wielding producer will frequently find it advantageous to squeeze the margin of downstream retailers. Although a powerful seller is unlikely to squeeze the resale margin to the point of driving the retailer out of business, this limitation on the seller still leaves ample latitude for abusive conduct.

---

[42] (1998) 522 US 3.

[43] *See* criticism of the case in Grimes, Warren S. (1998), 'Making Sense of *State Oil Co v Khan*: Vertical Maximum Price-Fixing Under the Rule of Reason', *Antitrust Law Journal*, **66**, 567; Roszkowski, Mark E. (1998), 'State Oil Company v Khan and the Rule of Reason: The End of Intrabrand Competition?', *Antitrust Law Journal*, **66**, 613.

[44] *Khan*, 522 US at p. 17.

The court's failure to address these issues left potential plaintiffs with no roadmap for bringing legitimate maximum price-fixing cases.

In *Illinois Tool Works v Independent Ink, Inc*, the Supreme Court seized an opportunity to eliminate another rule governing vertical restraints that favoured plaintiffs.[45] Earlier Supreme Court holdings had concluded that a tying seller has market power in a patented tying product for purposes of determining the legality of the tie. This rule had been criticised as overreaching since a large percentage of patents have little or no economic value. The rule had its defenders, who pointed out that most patents that were the target of litigation do have market power (except when the litigation is undertaken for strategic reasons).[46] When certiorari was granted, however, it was widely assumed that the Court would eliminate the market power rule. That's precisely what occurred in an 8–0 opinion authored by Justice Stevens.

The Justice Department and Federal Trade Commission joined in an amicus brief that supported eliminating the market power rule. It was apparently of no concern to the federal agencies, nor to a unanimous Supreme Court, that the underlying requirements tie in this case was transparently anticompetitive. Over a period of 90 years, the Supreme Court has condemned a series of requirements ties, a circumstance that plaintiffs suggested warranted a presumption that such ties are unlawful.[47] These points were preemptorily dismissed in Justice Stevens' opinion.[48] The Court focused single-mindedly on the task of removing the market power rule.

The final vertical restraints decision was the court's highly controversial 5–4 holding in *Leegin Creative Leather Products v PSKS, Inc*[49] that resale price maintenance would no longer be per se unlawful. As with most high profile court cases, amicus briefs were filed by a variety of parties on both sides of the issue. Among those arguing that the per se rule should be retained were the State Attorneys General, the American Antitrust Institute, Consumers Union (a prominent consumer advocacy organisation) and a large discounting retail chain. As in the two previous vertical cases, the Justice Department filed an amicus brief in support of the defendant and urging that the per se rule

---

45 (2006) 547 US 28.

46 Sullivan and Grimes, *supra* n 31, at § 8.3d9.

47 Grimes, Warren S. and Lawrence A. Sullivan (2007), 'Illinois Tool Works, Inc v Independent Ink: Requirements Tie-Ins and Intellectual Property Illinois Tool', *Southwestern Journal of Law and Trade in the Americas*, 13, 335.

48 *Illinois Tool Works Inc* (2006) 547 US at p. 45.

49 127 S. Ct. at p. 2705.

be overruled. There are, however, a number of factors that differentiate *Leegin* from the prior two vertical cases. Although the FTC joined in the Government's amicus brief, two of the five Commissioners dissented from this decision, and one issued a public statement in support of the per se rule.[50]

The precedent that the Supreme Court overturned had a century-long pedigree.[51] Although United States policy towards resale price maintenance has vacillated between tolerance and prohibition during the ensuing century, the Congress had spoken on the issue in adopting legislation in 1975 that reestablished the per se rule, and in subsequent years to withhold appropriated funds that the Department of Justice threatened to use in support of overturning the per se rule.[52] Finally, unlike the two prior vertical cases in which there was arguably a consensus among theorists favouring elimination of a rule that favoured plaintiffs, there was no consensus favouring elimination of the per se rule governing resale price maintenance.

Leegin involved a leather goods producer that manufactured women's purses and other high end leather accessories. Products sold under this label had a reputation for quality. The manufacturer apparently restricted distribution of its products and discouraged retailers from offering the brand at discount prices. PSKS was a retailer in Texas that prominently carried and promoted Leegin products, earning a substantial share of its revenues from sales of the brand. But PSKS and the manufacturer disagreed about the retailer's sale of Leegin products at discount prices. Leegin terminated PSKS as a dealer. The dealer then brought suit alleging resale price maintenance and a per se violation of section 1 of the Sherman Act. After the Court of Appeals affirmed a decision favouring PSKS, Leegin sought and obtained certiorari from the Supreme Court.

In a majority opinion drafted by Justice Kennedy, the court overruled a century-old precedent – *Dr. Miles Medical Co v John D. Park & Sons, Co*,[53] and held that the rule of reason should govern resale price mainte-

---

50 Brief for the United States et al. As Amicus Curiae Supporting Petitioner, *Leegin Creative Leather Products v PSKS, Inc* (2007) 127 S.Ct. 2705 (No 06-480). The FTC voted 3–2 to join the Justice Department's brief, available at: www.ftc.gov/opa/2007/01/fyi0711.shtm (accessed 18 June 2009).

51 *Dr. Miles Medical Co v John D. Park & Sons Co* (1911) 220 US 373.

52 This history is documented in Brunell, Richard M. (2007), 'Overruling Dr. Miles: The Supreme Trade Commission in Action', *Antitrust Bulletin*, **52**, 475.

53 (1911) 220 US 373.

nance. In some respects, the majority opinion appears more balanced and comprehensive than the rather perfunctory opinions in *Khan* and *Illinois Tool*. The Kennedy opinion discusses at some length the possibility that resale price maintenance can be associated with cartel conduct at the producer or dealer level. It also recognises that widespread use of Resale Price Maintenance (RPM) in an industry may be cause for more careful scrutiny of RPM.[54] But any illusion of a comprehensive or balanced opinion is quickly destroyed. The majority does not carefully and fairly canvass the literature on RPM, instead focusing on the writings of theorists who argue that RPM is usually procompetitive.[55] Nor does the majority fairly assess the anticompetitive potential of RPM. For example, the likelihood that RPM is associated with deceptive or misleading promotion[56] is not mentioned in the opinion. Although the majority opinion concedes the possibility of cartel conduct, the opinion also suggests that these outcomes are unlikely. In support of this view, Justice Kennedy cites studies by Ippolito and Overstreet that conclude that collusion was not likely in RPM cases that were litigated,[57] but ignores a fundamental criticism of these studies (that litigants had no need to allege or prove horizontal collusion under the per se rule governing RPM).[58] Finally, the majority opinion, while stressing the potential benefits of RPM, fails to mention that other promotion techniques (such as contractual promotion allowances and non-price vertical restraints) may be more effective in achieving legitimate promotion objectives and usually have fewer anticompetitive effects.

---

[54] *Leegin*, 127 S.Ct. at pp. 2716–17.

[55] In the opinion, the court on multiple occasions cites the work of theorists who have consistently argued for relaxed treatment of resale price maintenance, including Robert Bork, Richard Posner, Frank Easterbrook, Howard Marvel, and Benjamin Klein. Some of the most prominent opponents of RPM, including Robert Pitofsky and Basil Yamey, are not cited at all. Others whose writings have been supportive of the per se rule are cited selectively – for example, when the writer recognised that RPM could occasionally be procompetitive (writers in this category include Robert Steiner, F.M. Scherer, and Philip Areeda and Herbert Hovenkamp). *See* the majority opinion, 127 S. Ct. at pp. 2714–2725.

[56] This story is told in Grimes, Warren S. (1992), 'Spiff, Polish, and Consumer Demand Quality: Vertical Price Restraints Revisited', California Law Review, **80**, 815, 834–836 (1992). See Areeda, Philip E. and Herbert Hovenkamp (2004), *Antitrust Law*, 8, 1614a–d, at 165–71 (dealer good will not a justification for RPM because multi-brand dealer's promotion of a brand leads to deception).

[57] *Leegin* (2007) 127 S.Ct. at p. 2717.

[58] *Ibid.*, at p. 2732 (dissent of Justice Breyer).

The decision has already sparked substantial commentary among theorists.[59] Justice Kennedy had to deflect stare decisis arguments (since *Dr. Miles* and its progeny had applied the per se rule). To accomplish this, the majority opinion relied on a line of cases beginning with *Continental TV, Inc v GTE Sylvania Inc*[60] (which held that vertical non-price restraints were to be assessed under the rule of reason). Kennedy argued that resale price maintenance, like vertical non-price restraints, could have procompetitive consequences. On this point, the majority suggested, there was a consensus among economists.

Most economists who have studied RPM agree that it can have procompetitive consequences. There is less agreement, however, on how widespread or how frequently these procompetitive effects occur. It might equally be said that a majority of economists agree that RPM can have anticompetitive effects and that these anticompetitive effects are likely to be more frequent and more pronounced than would occur with non-price vertical restraints. The procompetitive effects of RPM can often be obtained through tools that involve no vertical restraints (such as contractual promotion allowances) or through vertical non-price restraints that have fewer anticompetitive effects. I have argued that RPM is most pernicious when it is imposed in open distribution systems (in part because it is more likely to be emulated and will have greater restraining effects on downstream, efficient retailers).[61] As compared to RPM, restraints that limit distribution (such as exclusive territories or dealer location clauses) are more likely to promote dealer investment, more likely to limit free-riding retailers, and less likely to have systemic competition-dampening effects on retailers.[62]

Justice Breyer, joined by three other Justices, wrote a lengthy dissent. Breyer criticised the majority for inappropriate judicial activism in two respects: (1) ignoring longstanding and venerable precedents of the Court; and (2) ignoring Congressional intent as expressed in a variety of legislative initiatives since 1975. The Breyer dissenters were not persuaded that

---

59 For critical commentary, *see* Brunnell, *supra* n 52 (criticising the *Leegin* court's judicial activism, disregard of legislative intent, and failure to honour stare decisis); Grimes, Warren S. (2008) 'The Path Forward After Leegin: Seeking Consensus Reform of the Antitrust Law of Vertical Restraints', Antitrust Law Journal, **75**, 467. For supportive commentary, *see* Gifford, Daniel J. and E. Thomas Sullivan (2007), 'The Roberts Antitrust Court: A Transformative Beginning', *Antitrust Bulletin*, **52**, 435, 439–445.

60 (1977) 433 US 36.

61 Grimes, *supra* n 59.

62 *Ibid.*

the evidence favours a relaxed standard for judging resale price maintenance, and suggested that the removal of the per se rule will create a great deal of uncertainty for counselors and courts.

One striking feature of the Kennedy majority opinion is its heavy reliance on *Sylvania* maxims that are misleading at best and had little or no relation to the facts before the Court. Four such aphorisms are addressed here: (1) that vertical restraints promote interbrand competition; (2) that protection of interbrand competition is the primary goal of the antitrust laws; (3) that manufacturers will generally act to protect consumer interests in efficient distribution; and (4) that vertical restraints prevent or discourage free-riding by retailers. Each of these maxims has an element of truth, but each operates perversely, or not at all, in the context of a vertical restraint such as resale price maintenance. For example, most vertical restraints probably promote the sale of a particular brand, and in this sense do promote interbrand competition. But the promotion fostered by vertical restraints increases brand identity, allowing a brand seller to increase the price charged to consumers for that brand. As brand identity (promoted through vertical restraints) becomes more pronounced, interbrand competition is *reduced*, not increased. Consumers tend to shop among retailers for a favoured brand, heightening the importance of intrabrand competition at the retailer level.

To take a simple example, if an Acme brand television set is favoured by consumers, they will be willing to pay more to obtain that brand. Consumers are also more likely to shop around for the best price on the brand. In the absence of effective interbrand competition, intrabrand price competition for Acme television sets at the retailer level becomes an important competitive discipline benefitting consumers. Thus, even if the primary goal of antitrust is protection of interbrand competition, that goal is already compromised by the brand promotion associated with some vertical restraints. When assessing the competitive impact of resale price maintenance, because this restraint tends to decrease interbrand competition, it becomes *more important, not less important*, to measure the impact on retail intrabrand competition.

The third maxim relied upon by *Leegin* majority, that suppliers will act to protect consumer interests in efficient distribution, also can be misleading. It is true that producers have an interest in minimizing distribution costs, thereby bringing their products to consumers at low prices. But retail price maintenance is a vertical restraint most often associated with a relatively weak brand. Suppliers of weak brands often must act in response to downstream dealer power, and thus are not in a strong position to protect the consumer desire for efficient distribution. Application of this maxim to vertical maximum price-fixing makes more sense – because suppliers who invoke this restraint usually possess substantial power in their relationships with dealers.[63]

The fourth aphorism relied upon by the *Leegin* majority, that resale price maintenance may be employed to reduce the incidence of dealer free-riding on pre-sale services, also is not appropriately invoked. When there are many retailers selling a supplier's brand, free-riding by a percentage of those retailers can be a legitimate issue for the supplier. But note that if the supplier's brand is a strong one, the supplier is likely to be relatively unconcerned about such free-riding. Each dealer will have an incentive to carry the producer's product (because it is one that consumers demand and one that will draw customers into the store). Resale price maintenance is more likely to be employed by suppliers of weaker brands – as an incentive for dealers to carry the brand. If presale services are important in convincing a customer to buy a product, the dealer will have a built-in incentive to provide these services. Nonetheless, if there is open distribution, there will likely be some retailers who will not offer the presale services and hope to capture a higher margin.[64] Resale price maintenance will not end this sort of free-riding. If the supplier genuinely is concerned about free-riding dealers, there are two tools available that are likely to be more effective than resale price maintenance. The first is the contractual promotion allowance – offering dealers a contractual incentive for supplying presale services. The second is restricted distribution – through exclusive territories or dealer location clauses – that lessens the opportunity for free-riding.[65]

What is perhaps most striking about the invocation of the free-rider argument in *Leegin* is that there were no facts indicating that free-riding occurred in that case. PSKS was apparently a loyal retailer of Leegin products, earning a high percentage of its revenues from Leegin sales and advertising the brand widely. The crux of the dispute between Leegin and

---

63 Even with respect to vertical maximum price-fixing, whether suppliers will act in consumer interests is still open to question. A powerful supplier might act to suppress the dealer's margin so that it might maximise monopoly revenue, not in order to reduce prices to consumers.

64 Klein, Benjamin and Kevin M. Murphy (1988), 'Vertical Restraints as Contract Enforcement Mechanisms', *Journal of Law & Economics*, **31**, 265, 266 ('retailers may merely take the additional money created by the vertical restraint and continue to free ride'). The authors argue that the combination of vertical minimum price-fixing and contractual restraints creates an atmosphere best suited to prevent free riding.

65 For a more detailed analysis of free riding, see Grimes, *After Leegin*, *supra* n 59.

PSKS was discounting (and possibly undermining the brand image), not free-riding.[66]

The *Leegin* opinion also provides a clear example of the deficiencies in the stylized opinion writing by the United States Supreme Court. The court mixes arguments involving stare decisis (precedent) and economic policy in an indiscriminate manner that does not produce sound legal analysis. Stare decisis is a fundamental principle of jurisprudence in common law systems (and to some extent in civil law systems as well). Adhering to precedents provides certainty and predictability in the law. When a past precedent is overruled, the change is usually incremental, producing less disruption to those who have acted in reliance on past court decisions. To many critics, the court's ruling in *Leegin* is an unwarranted departure from stare decisis. At the same time, the court has invoked stare decisis arguments in support of policy positions in a manner that obscures or confuses the policy analysis.

An example of this indiscriminate mixture of stare decisis and economic analysis is the following language from Justice Kennedy's opinion:

> The justifications for vertical price restraints are similar to those for other vertical restraints. See *GTE Sylvania*, 433 US at pp. 54–57. Minimum resale price maintenance can stimulate interbrand competition – the competition among manufacturers selling different brands of the same type of product – by reducing intrabrand competition – the competition among retailers selling the same brand. See ibid. at pp. 51–52. The promotion of interbrand competition is important because 'the primary purpose of the antitrust laws is to protect [this type of] competition.' (*Khan*, 522 US at p. 15.)[67]

The quoted language is a policy discussion, yet it cites no evidence from the case and no theorist who has studied the issues. Instead, it operates to foreclose the policy discussion by citing analysis from past cases. Stare decisis is being invoked to end the policy discussion, yet neither of the two

---

66 *Leegin* (2007) 127 S. Ct. at p. 2711. There was evidence that Leegin wanted its dealers to promote its 'Brighton' products, but evidence suggests the dealer did so ('Once it began selling the brand, the store promoted Brighton. For example, it ran Brighton advertisements and had Brighton days in the store.') This is not the first time the Supreme Court has invoked the free-rider aphorism in a vertical restraints case that showed no evidence of free riding. *See* the discussion of *Business Electronics Corporation v Sharp Electronics Corporation* (1988) 485 US 717 in Grimes, Warren S. (2008), 'The Sylvania Free Rider Justification for Downstream-Power Vertical Restraints: Truth or Invitation for Pretext?' in Robert Pitofsky (ed.) *Where the Chicago School Overshot the Mark: Effect of Conservative Economic Analysis on US Antitrust*, Oxford: Oxford University Press, p. 181.

67 *Leegin (2007)* 127 S. Ct. at p. 2715.

cases cited involved vertical minimum price-fixing, and neither of them offered a comprehensive analysis of RPM (or of vertical price restraints in general) that could fairly be deemed preclusive.

The majority opinion similarly invokes a stare decisis argument to cut off any meaningful discussion of free-riding – the Court cites *GTE Sylvania* as authority for the proposition that resale price maintenance helps to prevent free riding by retailers.[68] This mode of analysis is not a genuine policy discussion. There is no empirical evidence or reference to scholars who have performed this analysis.[69] This mode of argument is particularly disturbing when the facts of the case do not suggest that free-riding was present or the basis for the defendant's imposition of the vertical restraint.

2.3.2.4 Predatory conduct During the 15-year target period, the Court decided five cases involving alleged predatory conduct under section 2 of the Sherman Act or under the Robinson Patman Act 1936 (addressing price discrimination). Each decision was favourable to the defendants.

In *Spectrum Sports, Inc v McQuillan*, a terminated regional distributor of a shock-absorbing plastic product useful in medical, athletic and equestrian products sued the patent-holder and manufacturer for attempted monopolisation. The distributor had used the patented plastic to develop a horseshoe pad. Relying on language from a 1905 Supreme Court case involving attempted monopolisation[70] and Ninth Circuit interpretation of that language,[71] the distributor argued that no showing of power in the relevant market was required and that a showing of the defendant's unfair or predatory conduct would satisfy both the specific intent and the dangerous probability elements of the offense. Verdict was entered for the distributor and the Ninth Circuit affirmed. The Supreme Court reversed and remanded. The court held, in line with the larger number of circuits, that a showing of intent did not obviate the need to establish a dangerous probability of monopolisation. In remanding the case to the circuit, the court did not challenge the lower courts' conclusion that the defendant

---

68 *Ibid.*

69 One sentence later, *ibid.*, the court cites Posner, Richard (2nd edition 2001) *Antitrust Law* pp. 172–73, but Posner's musings contain no empirical studies and are challenged by theorists (unmentioned by the court) who have a different view of resale price maintenance.

70 *Swift & Co v United States* (1905) 196 US 375.

71 *Lessig v Tidewater Oil Co*, 327 F.2d 459 (9th Cir.), *certiorari denied* (1964) 377 US 993.

had engaged in predatory conduct, but merely the test applied to reach that conclusion.

Spectrum Sports was the first of five predatory conduct cases and perhaps the least controversial of the five. *Brooke Group Ltd v Brown & Williamson Tobacco Corporation*,[72] also decided early in the 15-year period, is one of the most important, and also one of the most controversial, of the Court's decisions. The suit was initiated by Liggett, then the fourth largest US cigarette manufacturer, against the third largest firm, Brown & Williamson (B&W). The complaint alleged that B&W had priced its generic cigarettes (with black and white packaging and no brand identification) at predatory prices and thereby caused competitive injury to Liggett, which had introduced the generic line of cigarettes. Although the jury was persuaded that B&W had violated both section 2 of the Sherman Act and section 2(a) of the Robinson Patman Act, the district court ruled against Liggett as a matter of law, an outcome that was affirmed by the court of appeals. In a 6–3 opinion by Justice Kennedy, the court affirmed the dismissal of the complaint.

The *Brooke* majority recognised two requirements for a plaintiff bringing a predatory pricing action: (1) a demonstration that the defendant has priced its product below some measure of cost (the court did not specify the appropriate measure of cost); and (2) a demonstration that the defendant has a likelihood of recouping its losses after the below-cost prices cease. The court held that the plaintiffs had introduced sufficient evidence of below-cost pricing, but had failed to demonstrate the required likelihood of recoupment.[73] The court found that recoupment was unlikely because B&W had a relatively small market share (less than 12%) of the overall domestic cigarette market. In order to recoup its losses, B&W would have to rely on the co-operation (tacit or express) of the two largest cigarette producers (R.J. Reynolds and Philip Morris), and this outcome was deemed unlikely. The majority was guided in its analysis by an aphorism – that 'predatory pricing schemes are rarely tried, and even more rarely successful.'[74] The court offered no empirical support for this conclusion, which it lifted from language in an earlier Supreme Court opinion.[75]

In his dissent (joined by Justices Blackmun and White), Justice Stevens emphasised that the cigarette industry was highly concentrated, highly

---

72 509 US at p. 209.

73 *Ibid.*, 509 US at pp. 231–232.

74 *Ibid.* at p. 226.

75 *Matsushita Electric Industrial Co v Zenith Radio Corporation* (1986) 475 US 574, 589.

profitable, and had a long-established pattern of oligopoly pricing that made recoupment by B&W quite probable. Thus, the aphorism, even if it were generally accurate, was not consistent with the history of this industry. As in the vertical restraints cases, the court was invoking a premise with no apparent link to the case before it.

Brooke Group has been heavily analysed and criticised. There are a substantial group of theorists in the United States that believe that predatory conduct is far more likely than the *Brooke* majority suggests. Criticism focuses on the two part test announced by the majority, which many find too strict.[76]

Verizon Communications, Inc v Trinko, a unanimous decision of the court in 2004, is the second court decision involving a section 2 Sherman Act complaint.[77] The plaintiff was a law firm that claimed that Verizon, the dominant local exchange carrier (LEC) had failed to provide prompt access to the local network for rival LECs that sought to offer local telephone service to the plaintiff and other class members. Although three concurring justices (in an opinion by Justice Stevens) would have disposed of this case on antitrust standing grounds, the court, after addressing the merits, concluded that no valid claim had been stated under Section 2 of the Sherman Act. In response to claims that rival LECs required access to Verizon's local exchange network, the court distinguished older cases that imposed a duty on a monopolist to deal with a rival. The court then cautioned that despite lower court applications of an essential facilities doctrine, there was 'no need either to recognise it or to repudiate it here.'[78] The court concluded that access to the network was governed by 1996 federal legislation that assigned regulatory supervision to the FCC, a circumstance that ruled out any application of the essential facilities doctrine. This conclusion was bolstered by the court's concern that any 'forced access' ordered by the courts might create intractable problems of court supervision and deter innovative or efficient conduct.[79]

Justice Scalia's majority opinion in *Verizon* contains aphorisms that have become characteristic of the Court's rulings during this period. When discussing the law governing section 2 monopolisation cases, Justice Scalia

---

[76] For a summary of literature critical of the Chicago view of predatory pricing, *see* Baker, Jonathan (1994), 'Predatory Pricing After Brooke Group: An Economic Perspective', *Antitrust Law Journal*, **62**, 585, 589–592 (1994). Another critique of the Chicago view is offered in Bolton, Patrick et al. (2000), 'Predatory Pricing: Strategic Theory and Legal Policy', *Georgetown Law Journal*, **88**, 2239.

[77] (2004) 540 US 398.

[78] *Ibid.* at p. 411.

[79] *Ibid.*

offers the view that 'the opportunity to charge monopoly prices – at least for a short period – is what attracts "business acumen" in the first place; it induces risk taking that produces innovation and economic growth.' Later in the opinion, the court offers this view: 'The cost of false positives counsels against an undue expansion of § 2 liability.'[80] Although either of these statements is defensible as part of a comprehensive and balanced analysis of section 2, there is not even the slightest attempt to achieve balance here. There is, for example, no mention of the well-documented evidence that monopolists frequently wield their power to stifle innovation and new entry. Nor is there any mention of the costs to society of 'false negatives,' interpretations of the antitrust law that allow anticompetitive conduct to continue unabated.[81]

Weyerhaeuser Co v Ross-Simmons Hardwood Lumber Co[82] is the third and most recent of the court's section 2 decisions. The case is an important precedent involving alleged predatory-bidding – a monopsonist's high bids for an item in short supply that could have the effect of driving rivals of the monopsonist out of business. The plaintiff was a lumber mill in competition with Weyerhaeuser for alder logs used to make finished lumber. After the plaintiff was forced to pay high prices for the input lumber, it went out of business and brought suit for alleged predatory bidding. In a unanimous decision written by Justice Thomas, the Court reversed decisions of the two lower courts and dismissed the suit. The Court held that the plaintiff had failed to satisfy the tests for predatory pricing announced in *Brooke Group*, and that these same tests applied in the predatory bidding contest: (1) the plaintiff must demonstrate that the high prices paid for the input caused it to lose money when the finished product was sold below cost; and (2) the plaintiff must demonstrate the likely recoupment of these losses.

In the course of reaching its conclusions, the court repeats a key aphorism of *Brooke Group* – that 'predatory pricing schemes are rarely tried, and even more rarely successful'.[83] As in the earlier decision, there is no empirical evidence offered to support this conclusion. Predatory bidding – or buying power issues in general – are an evolving area for competition law. There was active debate on these issues at the time the court decided *Weyerhaeuser*.[84] The court's rather blithe treatment of these issues is

---

80 *Ibid* at p. 414.

81 Gavil, Andrew, (2004), 'Dominant Firm Distribution: Striking a Better Balance', *Antitrust Law Journal,* **72**, 3, 30–51.

82 (2007) 549 US 312.

83 *Ibid.* at p. 75 (quoting *Matsushita*, 475 US at 589).

84 (2005) 'Symposium: Buyer Power and Antitrust', *Antitrust Law Journal*, **72**, 505.

remarkable, but perhaps aided by the Justice Department's amicus brief, which similarly gave scant regard for the active debate. Given the controversy surrounding *Brooke Group*, and given the distinction in the way buyer and seller power operate, a more cautious and balanced approach was warranted.

Volvo Trucks North America Inc v Reeder-Simco is the final decision in this group.[85] The plaintiff was a dealer of Volvo heavy-duty trucks that alleged that Volvo was charging higher prices to it than to other Volvo dealers. This strategy, the plaintiff alleged, was in furtherance of Volvo's efforts to eliminate a large number of dealerships, including the plaintiff. The plaintiff offered evidence that other Volvo dealers were sold Volvo trucks at larger discounts than were made available to the plaintiff. In a majority decision written by Justice Ginsburg, a 7–2 majority held that the Robinson Patman Act did not apply because the discrimination did not involve an effort to sell to the same retail customer. Volvo dealers were sold trucks only after they had won a competitive bid to a customer, and the bulk of the plaintiff's evidence involved separate bids made to different customers. The court saw the price discrimination protections of the Act as applying primarily when the plaintiff could show that it paid a discriminatory price for trucks that would be sold as a part of the same transaction. If the Robinson Patman Act was to apply in a competitive bidding context, a more comprehensive statistical analysis of disriminatory pricing would be required. The court's opinion once again relies on aphorisms, quoting from *Sylvania* the statement that the primary purpose of the antitrust laws is to protect 'interbrand competition.'[86] Whatever merit that statement might have in other contexts, it makes little sense when interpreting the Robinson Patman Act, which deals *directly* with discriminatory pricing of the *same* brand.

Justice Stevens, joined by Justice Thomas, dissented. The dissent takes note of the jury's verdict that price discrimination had occurred, a verdict that had been upheld by both the district court and the court of appeals. Justice Stevens expresses his own skepticism about the policy underlying the Robinson Patman Act, hinting that its focus on individual competitors may place it in conflict with the broader goals of competition policy.[87] In the end, despite these policy concerns, the dissenters have little sympathy for the defendant. The dissenters point to evidence that could have influenced the jury's verdict – that Volvo was systematically pricing higher to

---

85 (2006) 546 US 164 (2006).

86 *Ibid.* at p. 180 (quoting *Continental TV, Inc* (1977) 433 US 36, n 19).

87 *Ibid.* at p. 187.

the plaintiff in an effort to get out from under its contractual dealership obligations.

2.3.2.5 Interaction between antitrust and regulatory schemes Here, the lead case is *Credit Suisse Securities LLC v Billing*.[88] In an opinion by Justice Breyer, a 7–1 majority ruled that the federal antitrust laws do not apply to underwriting firms that form syndicates to facilitate the issuance of new securities (initial public offerings). The plaintiffs, buyers of the new securities, alleged that the syndicates agreed to various conditions that 'artificially inflated' the share prices.[89] In reversing a court of appeals ruling that the claims should not be dismissed before discovery, the majority addressed the question whether comprehensive regulation of the syndicate's conduct by the Securities and Exchange Commission (SEC) precluded application of the antitrust laws.

The court concluded that the conduct challenged in the complaint was a violation of the SEC's rules. Allowing an antitrust challenge to the conduct would not, therefore, be inconsistent with securities law regulation. Nonetheless, the majority concluded that the antitrust laws do not apply because of a variety of factors: 'the fine securities-related lines separating the permissible from the impermissible; the need for securities-related expertise (particularly to determine whether an SEC rule is likely permanent); the overlapping evidence from which reasonable but contradictory inferences may be drawn; and the risk of inconsistent court results.'[90]

In a separate concurring opinion, Justice Stevens argued that the conduct described in the complaint was a procompetitive joint venture that did not violate the antitrust laws. On this narrower basis, the complaint should have been dismissed.

Justice Thomas dissented, arguing that the antitrust laws, by their terms, applied to the conduct in question. The majority's extended logic, needed to reach a conclusion that the antitrust laws do not apply, was inconsistent with a 'savings' clause that preserved other remedies (outside the securities laws) for injured persons.

Verizon v Trinko, described in the section dealing with predatory conduct of a monopolist, also involved regulatory overlap issues. Although Justice Scalia conceded that a savings clause in the telecomunications legislation that expressly preserved 'antitrust' remedies was dispositive of the question

---

88 551 US 254.

89 *Ibid.* at p. 2389.

90 *Ibid.* at p. 2395.

of implied immunity, he nonetheless relied on regulatory overlap issues in developing policy arguments against the application of the antitrust laws.

Both *Credit Suisse* and *Verizon* reached results that are relatively non-controversial. In reaching those results, however, the Court applied more sweeping language and analysis than was necessary to conclude that the complaint should be dismissed.

2.3.3 Conclusions

For many years, conservative legal scholars in the United States have been highly critical of the United States Supreme Court for what is known as 'judicial activism.' Although judicial activism has no precise definition, it is understood to be inappropriately aggressive court interpretations that are beyond the accepted role of a court in a democratic state. Thus, a Supreme Court that ignores past precedents or legislative intent expressed through statutory language or legislative history, a court that reaches for a broad interpretation when a narrow one would have disposed of the case, or a court that uses the certiorari process to pursue an ideological agenda, might be deemed an inappropriately activist court. The favourite target of this criticism was the Warren Court (the Supreme Court under the leadership of former Chief Justice Earl Warren during the period 1953 to 1969).

Although one's view on 'judicial activism' tends to change depending on whether that activism serves or does not serve the desired policy goals, there is no doubt that judicial activism is the appropriate word to describe a number of the Court's recent antitrust decisions. For example, the recent decision in *Leegin* has been criticised both for ignoring strong past precedents and the intent of the Congress.[91] Justice Stevens offered the same criticism of the majority opinion in *Bell Atlantic v Twombly*.

It is no accident that the Supreme Court has decided the last 14 private cases in a manner favourable to defendants. The court chose most of these cases precisely because it sought opportunities to limit private enforcement. To some theorists, the court has done nothing more than clear away the various precedents that do not fall cleanly within a Chicago School paradigm of antitrust law.[92] Read narrowly, some, perhaps most of these holdings are unobjectionable. Antitrust theorists with differing fundamental views on antitrust law would probably agree on the need to curtail mar-

---

91 Richard Brunell, supra n 52.

92 This is the view, for example of Gifford, Daniel J. and E. Thomas Sullivan (2007), 'The Roberts Antitrust Court: A Transformative Beginning', *Antitrust Bulletin*, **52**, 435, 466–469.

ginal private enforcement initiatives. The pattern and stridency of these decisions is, however, a matter of substantial concern. In the interests of a forced and false intellectual consistency, the court has strayed from the empiricism that was a hallmark of earlier Chicago School criticism of populist antitrust decisions of the 1960s and 1970s.

By choosing to review only cases that allow the court to limit antitrust enforcement, the court's last 16 decisions provide a distorted jurisprudence. The risk of one-sided precedents would be minimal if the court were an ideologically balanced court, with a strong middle-of-the road profile. The court would be more likely to render a just decision on the facts before it, less likely to pursue a preconceived ideological agenda. A more balanced court would be approaching difficult issues with more openness – with centrist justices willing to be persuaded to rule either way based on the evidence. But that is not today's Supreme Court. The court is picking cases solely because they present an opportunity for limiting the law. In so doing, the court is systematically eliminating or restricting rules of decision that have been in place for decades – such as per se rules or the 'quick look' doctrine. In place of these rules that make it easier for counselors to render advice, for plaintiffs to bring meritorious cases and for judges to try them, the court is leaving, at best, a sea of doubt, or, at worst, a disingenuous paradigm based on indiscriminately invoked free-market maxims that may have little or no bearing on the facts before the court.[93]

It is indeed the lack of measured empiricism that is the most disturbing failure in recent antitrust decisions. In the vertical restraints area, the court rotely repeats statements from its 1977 decision in *Continental TV v GTE Sylvania*,[94] regardless of their bearing on the case before it. A free market maxim invoked with no anchor to the facts becomes a rule of per se legality.

The lack of empiricism is also fostered by the stylistic way in which the court writes its opinions, mixing stare decisis arguments with economic policy arguments. The examples of this use of stare decisis to squelch an economic policy analysis are from the *Leegin* case, but the problem

---

93 A court preoccupied with limiting private enforcement opportunities can, in the course of this endeavor, alter the substantive antitrust law in ways that make all enforcement efforts, including those undertaken by state and federal enforcers, more difficult. The court's decision in *Leegin* provides a prime example. Both the FTC and state enforcers have been active over the past two decades in bringing cases that challenge resale price maintenance. *Leegin* potentially will make those enforcement efforts more costly and more difficult.

94 (1977) 433 US 36.

extends well beyond that case. Courts at all levels and lawyers who write briefs engage in the same indiscriminate mixing of policy and precedent.

There are possible solutions to some of these concerns. Changing the manner in which Supreme Court Justices are selected might mitigate ideological imbalance, but such a change would probably require a controversial (and difficult to ratify) amendment to the Constitution.[95] Without altering the Constitution, one could change the way in which cases are brought before the court. Perhaps the court should be required to review cases in which the Justice Department or the FTC requests review, making case selection less susceptible to an ideological clique of justices.

Lawyers often write briefs with seamless transitions between policy and stare decisis arguments. They do so because the briefs sound persuasive and often are persuasive to a judge who fails to read the submissions in a disciplined fashion. American legal education can play a role in ending a pattern of writing briefs that has developed over generations. Both the Justice Department, in the briefs that it files with the court, and the court itself, can foster a more disciplined dichotomy between stare decisis and policy arguments. Perhaps a Supreme Court rule that requires lawyers to make stare decisis arguments and policy arguments in separate sections of the brief would set a paradigm that the court itself would follow when drafting its opinions.

---

[95] Imposing term limits and/or a mandatory retirement age on Court Justices might reduce the President's incentive to engage in gamesmanship to appoint the youngest possible ideologically approved candidate to the court. The Justices themselves can be a part of this gamesmanship, seeking to time their retirement so that a replacement is chosen by a President with views compatible with the retiring justice.

3. Freedom to Compete or Consumer Welfare: The Goal of Competition Law according to Constitutional Law

Roger Zäch* and Adrian Künzler**

1 INTRODUCTION

Under the basic constitutional provisions of the USA, the EU and many European countries, the overall purpose of legal rules against private restraints on competition is to favour economic prosperity, which includes consumer welfare.[1] However, legal rules against private restraints on competition are not aimed at creating economic prosperity directly. This is rather brought about indirectly, by protecting the freedom to compete of actors on markets, and can even occur against their will.[2] The reason for this is that freedom to compete generally leads to competition and competition leads to an efficient allocation of resources and thus to consumer welfare. The goal of competition law, therefore, is to ensure the freedom to compete of individuals and thus to safeguard the competitive process.

Due to the influence of the so called 'more economic approach' in the EU legal rules have recently been enacted and opinions expressed that could result in future scenarios in which restraints on competition are assessed directly under the aspect of consumer welfare, efficient allocation

* Professor of Law em., Director at the Europa Institute, University of Zurich, Switzerland.

** Dr.iur., District Court of Zurich, Switzerland.

1 Article 3 lit. g and Preamble to the EC Treaty; *see* for example also Articles 94, 96 and 27 of the Swiss Federal Constitution.

2 Zäch, R. and A. Künzler (2006), 'Individualschutz und Institutionsschutz als Aufgaben des Kartellrechts' in R. Zäch, C. Breining-Kaufmann, P. Breitschmid, W. Portmann, A. Thier, W. Ernst and P. Oberhammer (eds) *Individuum und Verband. Festgabe zum Schweizerischen Juristentag 2006*, p. 295; cartel bans are a very clear example of this. To mention are the paradigmatic provisions of section 1 of the Sherman Act 1890 and Article 81, para 1 of the EC Treaty. The primary purpose of such bans is to uphold the market actors' freedom of action; it is a secondary goal thereby to promote competition as an institution and hence economic welfare in society.

of production factors or, in short, their economic outcomes.[3] The direct purpose of rules against private restraints on competition would consist solely or essentially of maximizing consumer welfare. Therefore, competition restraints should be assessed with reference to their impacts on consumer welfare.[4] If consumer welfare is diminished, then the practice

---

[3] EC Merger Regulation Article 2, Recital No 29; Guidelines on the assessment of horizontal mergers under the Council Regulation on the control of concentrations between undertakings, ABl 2004 C 31/03 Rz 31, 5-18; Guidelines on the application of Article 81 (3) of the EC Treaty, ABl 2004 C 101/08 Rz 13, 33. With regard to the reform of the procedural rules, the Commissioner responsible at the time, Mario Monti gave a speech entitled 'EU competition policy after May 2004' at the Fordham Annual Conference on International Antitrust Law and Policy in which he stated: 'In making this revision, we have shifted from a legalistic based approach to an interpretation of the rules based on sound economic principles', available at: http://ec.europa.eu/comm/competition/speeches/index_speeches_by_the_commissioner.html (accessed 18 June 2009); *see* also Schmidtchen, D. (2005), 'Effizienz als Leitbild der Wettbewerbspolitik: Für einen "more economic approach"' in P. Oberender (ed.) *Effizienz und Wettbewerb*, 9 ff.; Whish, R. (2009), *Competition Law*, 19–25.

[4] *See* above all Schmidtchen, *supra* n 3, 9 ff.; Hellwig, M.(2007), *Wirtschaftspolitik als Rechtsanwendung: Zum Verhältnis von Jurisprudenz und Ökonomie in der Wettbewerbspolitik*, Preprints of the Max Planck Institute for Research on Collective Goods, available at: http://www.coll.mpg.de/pdf_dat/2007_19online.pdf (accessed 18 June 2009) 34 ff; von Weizsäcker, C.C. (2007), 'Konsumentenwohlfahrt und Wettbewerbsfreiheit: Über den tieferen Sinn des "Economic Approach"', *Wirtschaft und Wettbewerb,* 1078 ff.; *see* also Amstutz, M. and M. Reinert (2004), 'Vertikale Preis- und Gebietsabreden – eine kritische Analyse von Article 5 Abs. 4 KG' in W.A. Stoffel and R. Zäch (eds), *Die Kartellgesetzrevision 2003 – Neuerungen und Folgen*, 69, 77 f. and Amstutz, M. and M. Reinert, Erfasst (2005), *Article 4 Abs. 2 KG auch die überragende Marktstellung und die relative Marktmacht?*, 547 ff. with references to literature supporting the same view; against such tendencies Möschel, W. (2003), 'Juristisches versus ökonomisches Verständnis eines Rechts der Wettbewerbsbeschränkungen' in E. Keller, C. Plassmann and A. von Falck (eds) (2003), *Festschrift für Winfried Tilmann*, 716 ff; Immenga, U. (2006), 'Ökonomie und Recht in der europäischen Wettbewerbspolitik', *Zeitschrift für Wettbewerbsrecht* 346 ff.;. Mestmäcker, E.J (2005), 'Die Interdependenz von Recht und Ökonomie in der Wettbewerbspolitik' in Monopolkommission (ed) (2005), *Zukunftsperspektiven der Wettbewerbspolitik. Colloquium anlässlich des 30-jährigen Bestehens der Monopolkommission am 5 November 2004 in der Humboldt-Universität zu Berlin,* 19 ff.; Mestmäcker, E.J. (2007), in U. Immenga and E.J. Mestmäcker, *EG-Wettbewerbsrecht* Einleitung Rz 3; Zimmer, D. (2007), *Der rechtliche Rahmen für die Implementierung moderner ökonomischer Ansätze, Wirtschaft und Wettbewerb*, 1198 ff.; Zimmer, D. (2005), 'Kommentar: Ende gut, alles gut? – Bemerkungen zur 7', GWB-Novelle, *Wirtschaft und Wettbewerb* 715; Dreher, M. and M. Adam (2006), 'The more economic approach to Article 82 EC and the legal process', *Zeitschrift für Wettbewerbsrecht* 259 ff.; *see* also Basedow, J., (2007), 'Konsumentenwohlfahrt und Effizienz – Neue Leitbilder der Wettbewerbspolitik?', *Wirtschaft und Wettbewerb* 712 ff.; Schmidt, I. (2008), 'More Economic Approach: Der performance-Test als "invitation to nonenforcement"' in

under assessment should be prohibited; however, if welfare is increased or if there is welfare-economic neutrality (or indeed uncertainty) the practice must be declared permissible.[5]

Thus the role of competition law under the 'more economic approach' – in contrast to the traditional paradigm – is no longer thought to consist of upholding a 'regulatory framework' by formulating certain 'rules of play' and thereby ensuring just process or fair play.[6] Instead, according to the 'new competition policy', competition law should rather be aligned to the criterion of just outcomes, such as the welfare effects of anti-competitive practices or particular ideas about which market players are more protection-worthy or more efficient. From a Swiss point of view the more economic approach would reintroduce the notorious 'balance sheet-method' abandoned by the Swiss legislator in 1995.[7]

Advocates of the 'more economic approach', believing that the latest advances in scholarly thought confirm their approach as correct,[8] pursue a

---

Grusevaja, M. et al (ed), *Quo vadis Wirtschaftspolitik? Festschrift für Norbert Eickhof*, 67 ff; Dreher, M. (2008), 'Die Zukunft der Missbrauchsaufsicht in einem ökonomisierten Kartellrecht', *Wirtschaft und Wettbewerb* 23; Beijček, J. (2010), 'Transition Countries Facing Transitory Competition Rules (Alias "Moving Shooter" Taking Aim at a "Moving Target")' in Heinemann, A., A. Kellerhals and R. Zäch (eds) *The Development of Competition Law*, 7.

5 Amstutz and Reinert (2004), *supra* n 4, 77 ff; Amstutz and Reinert (2005), *supra* n 4, 547–549; *see* also Emch, D. and M. Saurer (2008), *Wettbewerber in der Zwangsjacke von Article 5 Abs. 4 KG. Gefahr kontraproduktiver Wirkungen der Wettbewerbspolitik bei vertikalen Abreden*, 335 ff.

6 Vanberg, V.J.(2005), *Marktwirtschaft und Gerechtigkeit. Zu Hayeks, F.A., Kritik am Konzept der 'sozialen Gerechtigkeit', Freiburger Diskussionspapiere zur Ordnungsökonomik*, available at: http://www.walter-eucken-institut.de/publikationen/05_11bw.pdf (accessed 18 June 2009) 7; *see* also Trechsel, S. (2000), 'Gerechtigkeit im Fehlurteil', 118 *Schweizerische Zeitschrift für Strafrecht*, 1 ff.

7 DG Discussion Paper on the application of Article 82 of the Treaty to exclusionary abuses (2005), available at: http://ec.europa.eu/comm/competition/antitrust/art82/discpaper2005.pdf (accessed 18 June 2009) Rz 54; Zäch, R. (2005), *Schweizerisches Kartellrecht* (2005) Rz 335 f.

8 Röller, L.H. (2005), 'Economic Analysis and Competition Policy Enforcement in Europe' in P.A. van Bergeijk and E. Kloosterhuis (eds) *Modelling European Mergers: Theory, Competition Policy and Case Studies*, 11 ff.; Röller, L.H. (2005), 'Der ökonomische Ansatz in der europäischen Wettbewerbspolitik' in Monopolkommission (ed), *Zukunftsperspektiven der Wettbewerbspolitik. Colloquium anlässlich des 30-jährigen Bestehens der Monopolkommission am 5 November 2004 in der Humboldt-Universität zu Berlin*, 37; *see* also Schmidt, A. (2006), *Wie ökonomisch ist der 'more economic approach'? Einige kritische Anmerkungen aus ordnungsökonomischer Sicht. Freiburger Diskussionspapiere zur Ordnungsökonomik*, available at: http://www.eucken.de/publikationen/06_10bw.pdf (accessed 18 June 2009), 3 ff., 14.

competition policy whereby restraints on competition are made dependent on their actual effects on the relevant markets; competitive strategies are assessed with regard to their actual impacts on economic welfare.[9] They endeavour to arrive at the correct outcome, either by confirming their rulings empirically and/or by applying proven models from (economic) research. Yet the search for an 'economically correct competition policy'[10] or a 'more objective approach'[11] is fundamentally viewed as a desirable goal – even (and most specifically) when matters regulated by legislative norms are thereby identified as incorrect and need to be radically reinterpreted as a result.[12]

This chapter first sets out the view that in the USA, the EU and Switzerland the freedom of individuals to compete is protected by constitutional law and that the goal of competition law is not to promote consumer welfare directly by this legislation. Therefore the legislator had to ensure that undue restrictions of the freedom to compete are outlawed (2). In a second part the question will be raised whether the judiciary may change the goal of competition law. This question deals with the boundaries of the judiciary's powers (3). Since constitutional law for the economic order may be changed, finally *de constitutione ferenda* the epistemological and legal implications of an approach based on market-outcomes will be outlined. Particular attention will be drawn to the fact that paradigms of competition are axiomatic in character, so that there is no such thing as the 'correct' competition policy. The scope and significance of the terms 'welfare' and 'consumer welfare' cannot be determined with scientific objectivity. For practical competition policy, a goal should therefore be defined which is compatible with other basic rulings in constitutional law (4). The chapter concludes with a summary of findings (5).

---

[9] Drexl, J. (2004), 'Die neue Gruppenfreistellungsverordnung über Technologietransfer-Vereinbarungen im Spannungsfeld von Ökonomisierung und Rechtssicherheit', *GRUR Int*, 716, 717.

[10] Drexl, J. *supra* n 9, 723; Albers, M., *Der 'more economic approach' bei Verdrängungsmissbräuchen: Zum Stand der Überlegungen der Europäischen Kommission,* available at: http://ec.europa.eu/comm/competition/antitrust/art82/albers.pdf (accessed 18 June 2009), who talks of 'correct application of law'; *see also* Hellwig, *supra* n 4, who talks of 'factually true and false statements'.

[11] Drexl, J., R.M. Hilty, B. Conde Gallego, S. Enchelmaier, M.O. Mackenrodt and M. Feil (2004), 'Comments on the Draft Technology Transfer Block Exemption Regulation', *International Review of Intellectual Property and Competition Law*, 187, 190.

[12] *See* Amstutz and Reinert (2004), *supra* n 4, 106.

2 THE RULING CONSTITUTIONAL AND STATUTORY LAW

2.1 Legal Situation in the USA

In consideration of the origins of competition law, US law has been the model legislation for many jurisdictions. The development of competition law began in the USA with the enactment of the Sherman Act in 1890. This was followed in 1914 by the Clayton Act. After 1945, under pressure from the USA, effective provisions against private restraints on competition were introduced in Europe: in 1951 within the European Coal and Steel Community and in 1958 in what was then West Germany and in the European Economic Community.

In the United States, the Sherman Act of 1890 was an instrument for democratic control of economic power because such power was perceived as a threat to the individual liberties guaranteed by the constitution.[13] Senator Sherman explained:

> This bill, as I would have it, has for its single object to invoke the aid of the courts of the United States [. . .] in dealing with combinations that affect injuriously the industrial liberty of the citizens. [. . .] It is the right of every man to work, labor, and produce in any lawful vocation. [. . .] This is industrial liberty and lies at the foundation of the equality of all rights and privileges.[14]

Anti-trust legislation came to be viewed as a charter of freedom on a par with the Bill of Rights. The constitutional status of American anti-trust legislation is emphasized in the paradigmatic arguments of the US Supreme Court ruling in the case of *United States v Topco Associates*:

> Antitrust laws in general, and the Sherman Act in particular, are the Magna Carta of free enterprise. They are as important to the preservation of economic freedom and our free enterprise system as the Bill of Rights is to the protection of our fundamental personal freedoms. And the freedom guaranteed each and every business, no matter how small, is the freedom to compete – to assert with vigor, imagination, devotion, and ingenuity whatever economic muscle it can muster. Implicit in such freedom is the notion that it cannot be foreclosed with respect to one sector of the economy because certain private citizens or groups believe that such foreclosure might promote greater competition in a more important sector of the economy.[15]

---

13 Peritz, R.J. (1996), *Competition Policy in America, 1888–1992. History, Rhetoric, Law*, 13 ff. supporting evidence.

14 Quoted according to Peritz, *supra* nn 13 and 14.

15 *United States v Topco Associates* (1972) 405 US 596, 610.

In order to achieve these goals, both the Sherman and Clayton Act prohibit restraints of competition by contracts, monopolisation and trusts if the effect is to 'substantially reduce competition' (Sherman Act, ss. 1 and 2, Clayton Act, s. 7). The goal of this legislation is to protect the individual's freedom to compete. In contrast, consumer welfare as such is not mentioned. Thus the legislation correctly implemented the constitutional mandate.

2.2 Legal Situation in the EU

Today EU competition law is the model regulatory framework for competition law in Europe and beyond.[16] The Treaty Establishing the European Community (EC Treaty) contains major parts of the written constitution of the EU. The competition rules in Articles 81 and 82 of the treaty, like the provisions of the Sherman Act in the USA, have constitutional status and form the Magna Carta of European competition law.

According to the fundamental constitutional provisions of the EC Treaty, the primary purpose of the European Community is to promote the objectives set out in Article 2 of the EC Treaty (sustainable economic development, high level of employment and social protection, the raising of the standard of living and quality of life). Each of these objectives is an element of economic and social welfare, which also comprises consumer welfare. Article 3 para 1(c) EC Treaty states that the means for achieving these objectives include the establishment of a Common Market and an Economic and Monetary Union. According to Article 14 para 2 of the Treaty, the Common Market should have the features of a genuine internal market and should work in accordance with the principles of an open market economy with free competition.[17] This is to be achieved by

[16] This applies also to the new antitrust law in China, *see* Owen, B.M., S. Sun and W. Zheng (2004), 'Antitrust in China: The Problem of Incentive Compatibility', *Stanford Institute for Economic Policy Research,* available at: http://papers.ssrn.com/sol3/papers.cfm?abstract_id=595801 (accessed 18 June 2009), 4 ff.; Xiaoye, W. (2004), 'Recent Development in Chinese Antitrust Law', Speech to ABA on 5 October 2004, available at: http://www.abanet.org/antitrust/at-committees/at-ic/pdf/programs/speech_to_aba_on_oct.5-1.pdf (accessed on 18 June 2009) 6 ff.; *see* also Kellerhals, A. (2008), 'Neues Wettbewerbsrecht in China – Bedeutung für schweizerische Unternehmen', *Jusletter* 17 März, Rz 8 f.

[17] Article 4, para 1, 81 ff., 98 sentence 2, 105 para 1 sentence 3 and 157 Abs. 1 para 2 EC Treaty; Mestmäcker, E.J. and H. Schweitzer (2004), *Europäisches Wettbewerbsrecht*, § 2; *see* also Emmerich, V. (2006), *Kartellrecht*, § 3 Rz 1.

establishing a system of undistorted, i.e. free competition.[18] The objectives specified in Article 2 EC Treaty should be achieved by protecting the competition process and thus ensuring the freedom of individuals to compete.[19]

This is confirmed and concretized in Article 98 EC Treaty, under which the Member States and the Community shall act 'in accordance with the principle of an open market economy with free competition, favouring an efficient allocation of resources'. This provision makes it clear that the goal of competition policy is free competition. Free competition can only be realised by promoting the interests and freedoms of individuals. In contrast, a competition paradigm that makes economic efficiency the primary or essential goal of competition policy does not necessarily take into account restrictions of the freedom to compete. Such an economic policy would not be compatible with the wording of Article 98 EC Treaty. Moreover, the wording of Article 98 EC Treaty makes it clear that safeguarding competition is the primary goal of competition policy. It is by means of competition that an efficient allocation of resources is achieved. Article 98 EC Treaty is thus at odds with a paradigm of competition that makes consumer welfare the primary goal of competition policy. Under the ruling law, consumer welfare has to be achieved indirectly by ensuring free competition and hence by upholding market actors' freedom to compete.[20]

The same applies in relation to the provisions of Articles 81 and 82 EC Treaty. Article 81 para 1 EC Treaty deals with agreements which may have as their object or effect the prevention, restriction or distortion of competition. Analysis of market outcomes is therefore at odds with the clear wording of Article 81 EC Treaty. It is enough for restraint on competition to be intended or effected. As soon as a business plan incorporates practices which restrain competition, even if they are not systematically and strictly implemented, it is reasonable to dispense with the examination

---

[18] *See* Zäch and Künzler, *supra* n 2, 291 and 297; in detail Künzler, A. (2008), *Effizienz oder Wettbewerbsfreiheit? Zur Frage nach den Aufgaben des Rechts gegen private Wettbewerbsbeschränkungen*, § 8 A. III. 3.

[19] Schröter, H. (2003), in H. Schröter, T. Jakob and W. Mederer (eds) *Kommentar zum Europäischen Wettbewerbsrecht*, Vorbemerkungen zu Articles 81–89 Rz 9 ff.; *see* also Mestmäcker and Schweitzer, *supra* n 17, § 2 Rz 74, 81 and Emmerich, *supra* n 17, § 3 Rz 2.

[20] Basedow, *supra* n 4, 714; Dreher, M. (1998), 'Der Rang des Wettbewerbs im europäischen Gemeinschaftsrecht', *Wirtschaft und Wettbewerb*, 658; di Fabio, U. (2007), 'Wettbewerbsprinzip und Verfassung. Der freie Wettbewerb und die Verantwortung des Staates', *Zeitschrift für Wettbewerbsrecht*, 275.

of concrete market outcomes.[21] This has been confirmed by consistent rulings at the European Court of Justice: The actual effects of an agreement need not be ascertained if interference with competition is found to be the purpose.[22] If no anti-competitive purpose to the agreement is found, then it is time to examine whether collusion is restraining competition on the basis of its actual or potential effects. So where the purpose of the agreement is not to restrain competition, the definitive criterion is its actual or likely effect on competition in the Common Market, particularly the consequences that the agreement has on the possibilities of market access.[23] Hence the view of advocates of the 'more economic approach', that the notion of agreements restricting competition should be examined with regard to its effects on market outcome, is not compatible with the wording of Article 81 EC Treaty nor with the rulings of the European Court of Justice.[24] This also holds true in relation to Article 82 EC Treaty, the wording of which prohibits any abuse of a dominant position by one or more undertakings, and thus precludes a market outcome analysis.

Rules with the direct purpose of maximizing consumer welfare do not exist in the EC Treaty.[25] Such rules would also conflict with the constitutional assumptions of a relationship between economic welfare, or consumer welfare, and of free competition as a means to achieving this end.

With reference to the competition provisions of Article 81 EC Treaty the following has to be taken into consideration: If one accepts the view that the welfare effects of anti-competitive agreements can be offset against one another, 'balance sheet' fashion, and the final balance determines the

---

21 *See* Mestmäcker and Schweitzer, *supra* n 17, § 10 Rz 60 supporting further evidence. *See* also Mestmäcker and Schweitzer, *supra* n 17, § 10 Rz 65 ff. and Emmerich, V. in Immenga and Mestmäcker, *supra* n 4, Article 81 Abs. 1 Rz 147 f.

22 EuGH 30.1.1985 Slg. 1985, 391 Rz 22 BNIC/Clair: 'It must be pointed out in that respect that for the purposes of Article 85 (1) [today Article 81 para 1 EC Treaty] it is unnecessary to take account of the actual effects of an agreement where its object is to restrict, prevent or distort competition'; EuGH 27.1.1987 Slg. 1987 405 Rz 39 Verband der Sachversicherer/Kommission; *see* also EuG 6.4.1995 Slg. 1995 II 1197 Rz 32 ff. ILRO/Kommission; EuG 12.7.2001 Slg. 2001 II 2035 Rz 73 Tate & Lyle/Kommission: 'Therefore, once the anti-competitive nature of the purpose [. . .] has been established, it is no longer necessary to verify whether the agreements also had any effects on the market.'

23 EuGH 28.2.1991 Slg. 1991 I 935 Rz 20 ff. Delimitis; EuGH 30.4.1998 Slg. 1998 I 2055 Rz 50 Cabour; *see also* Emmerich, V. in Immenga and Mestmäcker, *supra* n 4, Article 81, Abs. 1 Rz 145.

24 Regarding Swiss law *see* Borer, J. (2005), *Kommentar zum schweizerischen Kartellgesetz*, Article 5 Rz 6 22; Zäch, *supra* n 7, Rz 379.

25 *See* also Article 153 of the EC Treaty.

application of Article 81 EC Treaty, then one is confronted with a boundary problem between Article 81, para 1 and Article 81, para 3 of the EC Treaty. Advocates of the 'more economic approach' suggest reserving the sphere of Article 81 para 3 EC Treaty for difficult cases requiring particularly complex balancing and forecasting decisions.[26] They also find it conceivable to reserve Article 81, para 3 of the EC Treaty for the broad field of non-competition-based justification of anti-competitive agreements, e.g. for social or industrial-political reasons.[27] It is evident, however, that this proposed solution can hardly be compatible with Article 81 of the EC Treaty. In view of the already difficult task of balancing positive and negative welfare effects, it is impossible to make the distinction between 'simple cases' and 'difficult cases requiring particularly complex balancing and forecasting decisions'.[28] Furthermore, it is fundamentally accepted that the assessment of restraints on competition must be made exclusively on the basis of competition-based criteria.[29] Under the Swiss Cartels Act, for example, the exceptional authorisation of a restraint on competition on non-competition-based criteria is explicitly confined to the special exceptional provisions of Article 8 and Article 11 KG (Kartellgesetz, KG).

Moreover, agreements or concerted practices in the sense of Article 81, para 1 of the EC Treaty necessarily entail a restraint on the freedom to compete of parties to the agreement. They restrict the parties' freedom to utilise competition parameters at will in order to close a business deal.[30] This restraint can, for its part, influence the scale of competition to which the parties and other market participants are exposed. The scale of competition can be reduced but it can also be amplified. The latter is the case, for instance, when some restraint of the colluding parties' freedom to compete puts them in a position to start competing with competitors at

---

[26] Leupold, H. and G. Weidenbach (2006), 'Neues zum Verhältnis von Article 81 Abs. 1 und Article 81 Abs. 3 EG-Vertrag? Zugleich ein Beitrag zum O2-Urteil des EuG', *Wirtschaft und Wettbewerb*, 1009 ff.

[27] Caspar, U. (2001), *Wettbewerbliche Gesamtwürdigung von Vereinbarungen im Rahmen von Article 81 Abs. 1 EGV. Ein Beitrag zur Auslegung des Tatbestandsmerkmals der Wettbewerbsbeschränkung im europäischen Kartellverbotsrecht*, 32 ff.

[28] *See* Section 4.2 below; *see* in detail Künzler, *supra* n 18, § 6 D.

[29] *See* on this problem Mayer, C (2005), *Ziele und Grenzen des Kartellverbots im Recht der EG und der USA. Zur Rechtfertigung wettbewerbsbeschränkender Vereinbarungen unter Berufung auf wettbewerbsfremde Gesichtspunkte*, 40 ff.; *see* also Emmerich, V. in Immenga and Mestmäcker, *supra* n 4, Article 81 Abs. 1 Rz 145; Zäch, *supra* n 7, Rz 335 f.

[30] RPW 2002/4 768 E. 12.3 Obergericht Luzern, X/Y; Borer, *supra* n 24, Article 5 Rz 6; Zäch, *supra* n 7, Rz 350.

all or to compete more successfully.[31] If, on the other hand, welfare effects are the sole criteria, this ignores the fact that one market player's freedom to compete is always protected at the expense of another's, regardless of which way the ruling goes.[32] If freedom to compete is precluded as an assessment criterion, and given the poor prospects of proving welfare effects adequately, many cases are placed beyond the scope of cartel law.[33] This would contravene the intention of the legislator, which is to encompass all competition agreements, particularly in the context of concerted practices.[34]

Article 81 of the EC Treaty therefore alludes to restraints on freedoms to compete with a bearing on competition. This corresponds to the fundamental constitutional decision to adopt a paradigm of competition oriented to freedom of competition, or competition as such. It ensures that key types of restraint on competition are not excluded from the application of law. The definitive criterion by which restraints on freedom of action can be assessed as anti-competitive derives (according to Article 81 of the EC Treaty) from their effects on the conditions of competition – and particularly on the market counterpart's options and alternatives – and not from their effects on market outcomes. Consequently the law in force is not ambiguous with regard to its determined goal. In fact, in so far as the determined goal of competition law is up for discussion, it can only be observed that the current law and its constitutional foundations are clear.

2.3 Legal Situation in Switzerland

Swiss law is mentioned here because protecting the freedom of competition has always been central in Swiss constitutional law. Since 1874 the Swiss Federal Constitution (Bundesverfassung, BV) has explicitly safeguarded economic freedom, the freedom to compete as a right of all citizens (Article 27 BV) and furthermore, since 1999, explicitly requires that all state authorities shall ensure that the freedom to compete shall be respected, where appropriate, in relations among private parties (see Article 35, para 3 BV). This concept was developed in a landmark ruling

---

31 Zäch, *supra* n 7, Rz 350.

32 For a detailed account on this problem, *see* Zäch and Künzler, *supra* n 2, 294 f.

33 *See* in detail on this problem Künzler, *supra* n 18, § 8 A and B; this is why Ingo Schmidt calls the 'more economic approach' an 'invitation to nonenforcement', see Schmidt, *supra* n 3.

34 *See* EuGH 6.1.2004 Slg. 2004 I 23 Bayer/Kommission; EuG 26.10.2000 Slg. 2000 II 3383 Bayer/Kommission.

by the Swiss Federal Court on the case of the *baker Vögtlin* in 1896, six years after the enactment of the Sherman Act. Safeguarding free competition is thus considered a means for achieving economic welfare, particularly consumer welfare. For the direct protection of consumers, pursuant to Article 97, para 1 BV the Federation is obliged to take special measures, if needed. The mandate of the Swiss Constitution thus imposes the obligation to ensure free competition and hence the individual's freedom to compete.

The provisions of the Swiss Cartels Act of 1995/2003 correspond to Articles 81 and 82 of the EC Treaty and hence to the European model. In the same way as the provisions of the EC Treaty, their goal is to protect the individual's freedom to compete. It is worth mentioning that the Cartels Act (Kartellgesetz, KG) explicitly states that consumer protection organisations of national or regional significance may participate in the investigation of a restraint on competition (Article 43, para 1(c) KG). Furthermore, they are entitled to submit a complaint pursuant to Article 26, para 1 KG.

2.4 Conclusions

The ruling constitutional and statutory laws in the USA, the EU and Switzerland lead to the following conclusions:

(1) The goal of competition law is to protect the freedom of individuals to compete. The goal of competition law is not to promote consumer welfare directly.
(2) The decisive adjudication principle is an undue competition restriction and not consumer welfare.
(3) Consumer welfare is a goal of the legal order. This goal shall be achieved primarily by an undistorted competition process and – if needed – by special consumer protection measures.

3 CHANGING THE GOAL OF COMPETITION LAW BY THE JUDICIARY?

3.1 Current Tendencies and Consequences

Given the current legal situation, the question that arises is whether the judiciary has the power to change the goal of competition law to the effect that consumer welfare becomes the decisive adjudication principle instead of commercial actors' freedom to compete. Tendencies which suggest that this could happen cannot be overlooked: Since the 1980s the Chicago School has exercised a growing influence on antitrust policy in the USA,[35] on competition law in the European Union[36] and on the scholarly community in general.[37] Some scholars dealing with competition matters seem to ignore the fact that in constitutional states, which are based (among others) on the principle of separation of power (Montesquieu), human behavior has to be adjudicated by the judiciary according to the ruling law. Therefore, at least in constitutional states, the propositions are not grounded, 'that, unless the Court has intervened in setting out the rules, it is up to the Commission to do so'[38] and that 'competition law is "best" enforced by the application of economics'.[39] In light of this statement, it seems appropriate to point out the limits of the power of the judiciary. The following case should serve as a starting point:

> Producer P distributes his products within the EU, but only supplies dealers that accept to resell his products within a geographically limited market, e.g. only within Germany. As dealer D in Germany also sells P's products in France, producer P refuses to supply dealer D. Dealer D sues producer P for delivery.[40]

There are several possibilities for a court to adjudicate on such a case:

(1) If the purpose of competition law is to safeguard the individual's freedom to compete and thus the competitive process a court could identify P's agreements with the other distributors as agreements that restrict the freedom of his dealers to compete, with the object to share markets among his dealers and thus to restrict competition in the sense of Article 81, para 1(c) of the EC Treaty. A court could further find no justification for such agreements under Article 81, para 1(3) of

---

[35] Peritz, *supra* n 13, 236 ff. especially 240 f.; *see* also Mueller, D.C. (1986), 'Das Antitrustrecht der Vereinigten Staaten am Scheidewege', *Wirtschaft und Wettbewerb*, 533 ff.

[36] *See* above under n 1.

[37] *See* above under n 1.

[38] Monti, G. (2009), *EC Competition Law: The Dominance of Economic Analysis?* or as Giorgio Monti put it in his speech at the 3rd ASCOLA Conference: 'Absent Court intervention [sc. the] Commission is free to design and redesign its competition policy', slide no 9.

[39] Monti, *supra* n 38, Draft, p. 6; against such tendencies see the literature quoted *supra* note 4; see also Heinemann, A. (2008), 'Die Relevanz des "more economic approach" für das Recht des geistigen Eigentums', *GRUR* 7; Beijček, *supra* n 4, 7.3.

[40] *See* EuGH 13.7.1966 Slg. 1966, 457 Consten and Grundig/Commission.

the EC Treaty and therefore would have to declare these agreements illegal, with the consequence that dealer D will be supplied by P, eventually on order of the court.

As a consequence of this adjudication we can note: The freedom of dealer D to compete with others and the freedom of dealers to sell where they want to and where they can is sustained. Those who want to restrict this freedom – by using their own freedom – have no right to do so. The question in such cases is not which party's freedom prevails but which party's action restricts the competitive process in an undue way. Therefore it is the concept of free competition that limits the freedom of action of competitors or market actors.[41]

(2) On the other hand, if the purpose of competition law is to promote consumer welfare directly, a court could read into Article 81, para 1 of the EC Treaty that this provision does not apply to all competition restrictions, but only to those that in fact decrease consumer welfare. A court could further argue that it cannot be established that P's agreements with the other distributors will in fact decrease consumer welfare in the future and that therefore these agreements would not fall within the scope of Article 81, para 1 of the EC Treaty and thus could not be declared illegal. Therefore, the court could not order P to deliver to dealer D. In this way in the Béguelin Import-Case the European Court of Justice introduced the appreciability requirement ('Spürbarkeitskriterium') as an unwritten assessment criterion into Article 81, para 1 of the EC Treaty.[42]

As a consequence of this adjudication we can note: The scope of application of Article 81, para 1 of the EC Treaty would substantially be reduced. In many cases it will not be possible to determine whether such agreements will in fact decrease consumer welfare. In those cases the freedom of individuals to compete, which has to be protected according to the ruling law in all three jurisdictions, will not even be taken into account. At stake is not the freedom to compete of the

---

41 Mestmäcker, E.J. (2008), '50 Jahre GWB: Die Erfolgsgeschichte eines unvollkommenen Gesetzes', *Wirtschaft und Wettbewerb* 13-16; Merz, H., 'Kartellrecht – Instrument der Wirtschaftspolitik oder Schutz der persönlichen Freiheit?' in H. Coing, H. Kronstein and E.J. Mestmäcker (eds), *Wirtschaftsordnung und Rechtsordnung*, Festschrift zum 70. Geburtstag von Franz Böhm, Karlsruhe 1965, 227–259 quoted according to Mestmäcker (2008) *Wirtschaft und Wettbewerb*, 13.

42 EuGH, Slg. 1971, 960 Rz 16/18 Béguelin Import/G.L. Import-Export; *see* Emmerich, V. in Immenga and Mestmäcker, *supra* n 4, Article 81 Abs. 1 Rz 185 ff.; in European legal methodology this is referred to as teleological reduction of a legal provision, see Kramer, E.A. (2005), *Juristische Methodenlehre*, 192 f.

two or more parties and thus the competitive process but consumer welfare.

According to the traditional approach, which protects the individual's freedom to compete, the adjudicative body has to take into account the restriction of D's freedom to compete – due to P's agreements with his dealers – against the freedom of P to do so and the restriction of the competitive process caused by the restriction of the freedom to compete of one or the other party. The adjudicative body has to decide against the party whose exercise of freedom appreciably restricts the competitive process. Also, if it comes to adjudicate a cartel agreement that restricts the freedom to compete of the cartel members, the court has to decide on whether the restriction of the freedom to compete on which the cartel members agree restricts the competitive process appreciably.

In contrast, if the goal of competition law – in accordance with the 'more economic approach' – consists essentially in the maximisation of consumer welfare, then the adjudicative body has to assess whether P's contracts with his dealers will lower or raise consumer welfare in the future. According to this approach the adjudication of a case can be carried out without even taking into consideration the restriction of the freedom to compete and thus the restriction of competition itself.

3.2 Limits of the Judiciary

In applying legal provisions to a concrete case, in addition to the wording of legal provisions and other criteria, competition authorities and courts must give consideration to constitutional law. This is especially the case when fundamental rights are at issue and the constitutional mandate is clear. Interpretation of the law in conformity with the constitution means that where several variant interpretations are possible, preference has to be given to the one that corresponds most closely with constitutional law. Such an interpretation is justified because the process of constitutional legislation functions in such a way as to involve the widest possible range of political interests, so that constitutional provisions are developed with broad democratic support. Decisions from authorities applying the law have no similar legitimation basis.[43] Application of law serves the purpose of ruling on disputes in individual cases. A plaintiff faces a respondent and the substance of the argument is confined to the case to be ruled upon. The authorities applying the law therefore have to apply the law currently in

---

[43] *See* Künzler, *supra* n 18, § 8 B. III. 2.

force. Due to the strongly persuasive nature of constitutional arguments and the special degree of democratic legitimation they possess, when it comes to interpreting legal provisions there are strong grounds for interpretation in conformity with the constitution.[44]

This applies not only to the actual interpretation of competition rules but equally to the procedure of elaborating law, i.e. the justification of a decision which actually constitutes an amendment of the competition rules. In these cases the authorities applying the law are functionally acting as legislators. As such they must primarily consider constitutional law. If a ruling can be said to harmonise with a constitutional provision, then it is safe to assume that many people will find that argument convincing.[45] On the other hand, a ruling which conflicts with constitutional law will often meet with poor acceptance. For – it bears repeating – the fundamental values of a legal community as codified in a constitution carry strong persuasive force. Therefore the justification of a decision with constitutional values also carries great persuasive force. If the justification of a decision ignores fundamental constitutional values, it is questionable from the perspective of the rule of law, because in these cases the activity of the authorities applying the law is no longer covered by a democratically legitimated mandate.[46] In particular, basic rights – one being the freedom of action and competition for enterprises, a freedom enshrined in the current economic constitution – must always be borne in mind by the authorities applying the law.[47]

3.3 Conclusions

In order to adjudicate competition litigations the judiciary and competition authorities do not have to apply economic theories but the provisions of the ruling law. By doing so, they have to take into consideration, among the texts of legal provisions and other criteria, the constitution, especially when fundamental rights are at issue and the constitutional

---

44 For the standard account, *see* Zäch, R. (1989), 'Der Einfluss von Verfassungsrecht auf das Privatrecht bei der Rechtsanwendung', *Schweizerische Juristen-Zeitung* 1 ff.; *see* also Zäch, R. (2008), 'Competition Law Should Promote Economic and Social Welfare through Ensuring the Freedom to Compete – A Lawyer's View' in Drexl, J., L. Idot and J. Monéger (eds), *Economic Theory and Competition Law*; regarding the significance of economic analysis in the application of the law, *see* Künzler, *supra* note 18, § 8 B. III.

45 Zäch (1989), *supra* n 44, 10.

46 *See* Künzler, *supra* n 18, § 8 B. III. 2.

47 Zäch (1989), *supra* n 44, 10.

mandate is clear. Interpreting in accordance with constitutional law means choosing out of various possible interpretations the one that fits constitutional law best. Elaborating (new) law is the function of the legislator. However, the judiciary has the power to create new law when the existing law is incomplete. In elaborating new law the judiciary acts as legislator and therefore has to act first of all in accordance with constitutional provisions. If the existing law is not incomplete, there is no room for the judiciary to create new law. In so far as the goal of competition law is at stake, the existing law and its constitutional base are clear. Altering the goal from protecting freedom to compete and thus the competitive process to promoting consumer welfare would thus be an interpretation *contra legem et contra constitutionem* and would be illegal.

4 THE ECONOMIC CONSTITUTION DE CONSTITUTIONE FERENDA

4.1 Protecting Freedom of Competition or Consumer Welfare?

If 'de constitutione ferenda' consumer welfare should become the decisive assessment criterion for competition law, then business practices with a bearing on competition could only be prohibited if the practice in question were found to have negative effects on welfare. Restraints of the freedom to compete of market actors and thus the competitive process would no longer be necessarily subject to scrutiny. As a result, the fact that individuals want to have freedom to compete would be ignored. Nevertheless, this is the very reason why individual freedom to compete is protected as a basic right. In the assessment of concrete cases, therefore, infringements of this right should be scrutinised by the authorities applying the law and, where found, prohibited. Moreover, free competition is in the public interest, for experience shows that free competition is the best means of promoting economic and social welfare. This is why substantial restraints on competition are outlawed. The ultimate consequence of the 'more economic approach' would be that competitors, by engaging in competition, would no longer be serving their own freely chosen purposes but, instead, a collective economic purpose, consumer welfare. At this point, the constitutionally guaranteed freedom of competition would be instrumentalised. Instances of the instrumentalisation of fundamental basic rights tend to be found in societies organised on socialist principles and/or in centrally planned economies where governmental agencies have to decide which economic behavior will in the future have positive results for society (result-oriented approach).[48] For instance, the constitution of the German Democratic Republic (GDR) of 1968/74 provided, in Article 19, para 3:

> Free from exploitation, oppression, and economic dependence, every citizen has equal rights and diverse opportunities to develop his abilities to the full and to expend his efforts freely and unimpeded for the good of society and for his own benefit in the socialist community.

Instrumentalisation of that nature is not compatible with a freedom-based paradigm of competition: it is inconceivable to adopt the viewpoint that competitors engaging in competition might be dedicated solely to consumer welfare, yet simultaneously to emphasise that in doing so, competitors were only pursuing their own, freely chosen ends.[49] An approach that is compatible with a freedom-based competition paradigm, however, is to prohibit practices that restrain freedom. In other words, the rights of freedom must not be limited by particular stipulations of purpose, but only by the prohibition of particular kinds of practice.[50]

4.2 Conclusions from Economics

If, as advocates of the 'more economic approach' postulate, competition policy should be informed by more recent epistemological principles, justice must be done to the fact that – as recent research has found – macro-social problems such as economic and social systems, ongoing economic and social processes and ongoing economic and social policy, come into the category of 'complex organised phenomena'.[51] These involve the interdependent actions of millions of agents, whose behavioral structures are not constant but variable in space and time. The relevant data in these fields is so diverse and complex that it can never be captured in its entirety.[52] Therefore, market processes can only be conceived of as open-ended historical processes, to be described and recognised not with reference to

---

[48] Beijček, *supra* n 4, 4.2, 5.

[49] *See* on this problem Künzler, *supra* n 18, § 8 C.

[50] Hangartner, Y. (1981), 'Materielle Voraussetzungen von Freiheitsbeschränkungen' in U. Häfelin, W. Haller, G. Müller and D. Schindler (eds) *Festschrift zum 70. Geburtstag von Hans Nef*, 150.

[51] Weaver, W. (1967), 'Wissenschaft und Komplexität', 18 ORDO *Jahrbuch für die Ordnung von Wirtschaft und Gesellschaft* 163 ff. distinguishes between simple, unorganised-complex and organised-complex phenomena; for a detailed account, *see* Künzler, *supra* n 18, § 6 D.

[52] von Hayek, F.A. (1972), *Die Theorie komplexer Phänomene*, 25 f.

their outcomes but with reference to their preconditions.[53] This insight must be taken into account by practical competition policy if it proposes to work with facts and not with hypotheses. Competition can therefore be grasped as 'a procedure for the discovery of facts [. . .] which, if it did not exist, [would] either remain unknown or, at the very least, never be used'.[54]

If competition is understood as a discovery procedure then, by definition, the outcomes of discovery are not predictable. The institution of competition is justified by the fact that the essential circumstances determining the actions of competitors are not known.[55] For, obviously, there would be no point in arranging a competition if the winner were known in advance. So competition is only important because, and as long as, its outcomes are not predictable and not exactly what anybody might have tried to bring about consciously.[56]

Attempting to determine the welfare effects of anti-competitive practices or making consumer welfare a direct assessment criterion for competition law is irreconcilable with this insight. From an economic and an epistemological perspective, this goal is therefore eliminated as a legal goal.

If – counter to the above points – the assessment of anti-competitive practices is made dependent upon market outcomes, i.e. if competition authorities are only allowed to intervene in the market mechanism if the practice in question has demonstrably negative welfare effects, this amounts to a lowering of the legal relevance threshold.[57] For the reasons set out, it is impossible to deliver empirical proof in the field of economics. Such an undertaking would fall at the first hurdle of needing to capture all the data necessary for the assessment of a concrete case. It would be presumptuous indeed to assume that the welfare effects of anti-competitive practices can be assessed with sufficient certainty.

As advocates of the welfare-economic approach to assessing restraints on competition would concede, there will hardly ever be a definitive answer to

---

53 Hoppmann, E. (1967), 'Wettbewerbs als Norm der Wettbewerbspolitik', 18 ORDO *Jahrbuch für die Ordnung von Wirtschaft und Gesellschaft*, 77, 84.

54 von Hayek, F.A. (2003), 'Der Wettbewerb als Entdeckungsverfahren', printed in M.E. Streit, *Friedrich A. von Hayek. Rechtsordnung und Handelsordnung. Aufsätze zur Ordnungsökonomik*, 132 ff.

55 Von Hayek, *supra* n 54, 133.

56 Von Hayek, *supra* n 54, 132.

57 Immenga, *supra* n 4, 355; Schmidt, *supra* n 3, 72 f.; Schmidt, I. (2006), 'More Economic Approach: Ein wettbewerbspolitischer Fortschritt?' in I. Brinker, D.H. Scheuing and K. Stockmann (eds) *Recht und Wettbewerb, Festschrift für Rainer Bechtold zum 65. Geburtstag*, 409, 412; Zäch (2008), *supra* n 44; *see* also Drexl, *supra* n 9, 719, 722; F.A. von Hayek, *Die Anmassung von Wissen* (1996) 1 ff.

the question of whether restricting competition reduces economic welfare and is therefore impermissible. In relation to the control of abuse pursuant to Article 82 of the EC Treaty (Article 7 KG) for instance, it is postulated: 'most of the practices investigated under Article 7 KG are double-faceted [. . .] i.e. they can be generally welfare-enhancing or welfare-reducing. [. . .] [Therefore] the aim should not be to examine as many cases as possible under Article 7 KG, but only those which give rise to an expectation of welfare losses (i.e. a reduction of output or supracompetitive prices) with sufficient certainty. Most often those are cases in which a high degree of market dominance is evident. In the other cases, the remaining competition from third parties can be expected to force the company concerned to act in harmony with society's welfare interests.'[58]

If, in light of this, one takes the view that 'in case of doubt' there should be no intervention in the market mechanism, this is to overlook the fact that – as many believe – non-rulings are not value-neutral:[59] The postulate mentioned would make many concrete cases impossible to adjudicate. Such non-rulings would be tolerable if these only favoured the companies whose practices were investigated. But that is not the case: non-rulings can be or often are rulings in favour of companies who are possibly practising illegal restraint of competition. At the same time, they may be rulings to the detriment of third parties, be they economic agents or consumers, who are affected by illegal restraints of competition.[60] Such non-rulings are problematic from a legal perspective, for the individual also plays a central role in the economic sphere. Individual economic freedom is not just a means to an end, but an end in itself.[61] If individuals have a right to economic freedom, they must also be able to make use of this right here and now. It is therefore the task of the legal regime to protect the individual from misuse of power or discriminatory practices by others in the economic sphere. This task has its basis in individual constitutional economic freedom (e.g. Article 27 of the Swiss Constitution). In the face

---

[58] Amstutz and Reinert (2005), *supra* n 4, 547, 548 f.; against such tendencies Schmidt, *supra* n 3, 72 f.

[59] Zäch, R. (2007), *Gewährleistung von Wettbewerb im Spannungsfeld von Auslegung und Rechtsfortbildung*, available at: http://rwiweb.uzh.ch/zaech/home.htm (accessed 18 June 2009) 53; Zäch (2008), *supra* n 44; with detailed justification Künzler, *supra* n 18, § 8 A. II. and § 8 B. II.

[60] Kerber, W. and U. Schwalbe (2007), in G. Hirsch, F. Montag and F.J. Säcker, *Münchener Kommentar zum Europäischen und Deutschen Wettbewerbsrecht (Kartellrecht)*, Einleitung Rz 1391; Vezzoso, S. (2007), *Zur Beurteilung vertikaler Beschränkungen in der europäischen Wettbewerbspolitik aus evolutionsökonomischer Sicht*, 178 ff.; Beijček, *supra* n 4, 7.3; *see* in detail Künzler, *supra* n 18, § 15 C. I. 3.

[61] Zäch (1989), *supra* n 44, 1, 8.

of this, fobbing-off the injured party with assurances of the self-healing powers of competition would constitute a denial of justice.

Furthermore, large numbers of cases would be likely to present problems of this nature. For example, companies in the OECD countries have long realised that their great problem is no longer the production of goods but their distribution. Against this economic backdrop, most cases of non-supply – whether based on collusion (exclusivity agreements) or unilateral steps – are suspect under competition law. Since companies rely totally on distributing their products, instances of non-supply often can only be explained in terms of intentional or incidental restraints on competition. Hence it is justified in such cases – apart from trivial offences – to conduct an official investigation.[62]

Bearing in mind this economic background, and given that it is often impossible to predict future welfare losses with sufficient certainty, it is incomprehensible to postulate – no doubt with due regard and consideration to particular interest groups – that only cases involving 'a high degree of market dominance' should be subjected to examination by the authorities.[63] Such a paradigm leads to regulatory loopholes and undesirably limits the scope of application of laws against restraints on competition, particularly the control of abuse.

4.3 On the Role of Economic Objectives in Competition Law

The traditional paradigm of competition assumes that it is fundamentally impossible to predict how entrepreneurial behavior will affect future economic welfare, whereas experience shows that effective competition results in economic welfare, and effective competition can normally be brought about by upholding market actors' freedom to compete – a practical and realizable objective. From these insights, rules against restraints on competition under the traditional paradigm of competition protect the freedom to compete of economic actors, giving rise to effective competition and hence economic welfare as a consequence.

Advocates of the 'more economic approach' believe that unlike the traditional paradigm, their approach to competition policy is based on scientific evidence and is, in that sense, 'objective'. This gives rise to the question of whether competition paradigms have a basis in scholarly

62 Hangartner, Y. (2006), 'Das Verhältnis von Verwaltungs- und zivilrechtlichen Wettbewerbsverfahren', *Aktuelle juristische Praxis*, 43, 45 f.

63 Amstutz and Reinert (2005), *supra* n 4, 548 f.

knowledge at all, or whether in fact they are based on a priori assumptions, on axioms.[64]

The 'more economic approach' presupposes, among other things, that people generally agree on the meaning of consumer welfare, and that it is possible to predict whether commercial behavior will promote or impede consumer welfare in the future. Therefore, one question to be addressed is whether the concept of consumer welfare used by supporters of the 'more economic approach' can be proved 'true'. This is possible only if the concept of consumer welfare is a report expressing an element of scientific knowledge, but not if the concept is an a priori assumption, an axiom. Note that reports can refer to the fact of a certain linguistic usage, or to reality.[65]

Traditionally, consumer welfare is defined in terms of freedom of competition, whereas under the 'more economic approach' it is defined essentially in terms of economic efficiency. This alone shows that there is no firmly bounded linguistic usage denoting the concept of consumer welfare, which could be verified in the sense of a report on its meaning. For this reason a report with regard to reality is also impossible, because any such report presupposes an axiomatic definition of economic welfare. A verifiable definition of economic welfare is only possible if an axiom already precisely circumscribes the material to be investigated, as for instance if consumer welfare were clearly defined by linguistic usage. As we have seen, however, there is no sufficiently clear linguistic usage regarding the concept of 'consumer welfare'. Thus no report on reality is possible.

It follows that the concept of consumer welfare is based on a prescientific decision. More generally, it is accurate to say: competition paradigms are axiomatic in character, meaning they should not be judged on their truth but on their effectiveness in terms of the conclusions they permit to be drawn.[66] This 'pragmatic' interpretation of competition policy presupposes a level-headed debate in a spirit of tolerance. It is not conducive to such a debate when each faction tries to 'disprove' the other's views and insists on the rightness of its own position. The decisive issue is rather to understand the approach underlying a particular view, and to think through the consequences, i.e. the advantages and disadvantages of each proposed solution. In other words, it is necessary to inquire where a particular theory will lead, what its consequences are. Crucially, it must

---

64 *See* on the following with detailed justification Künzler, *supra* n 18, § 9–12; *see* also von Hayek, *supra* n 57, 1 ff.; Mestmäcker (2008), *supra* n 41, 12–14.

65 *See* in detail Künzler, *supra* n 18, § 11.

66 Künzler, *supra* n 18, § 11; *see* also Heinemann, *supra* n 39, 7.

have the power to solve particular theoretical or practical problems. This means abandoning a value-free approach. For when it comes to the question of which consequences of a competition policy are desirable or undesirable, it is inevitable that value judgments have to be made or value judgments imposed by the legal regime have to be respected.[67]

Starting from this understanding of competition policy, it makes no sense to ask whether an anti-competitive practice 'in fact' leads to an increase in welfare or not. This kind of report cannot be confirmed scientifically, but does lead to irreconcilable controversy. What is worth asking is whether or not, under certain conditions, an anti-competitive practice is desired. The competition policy adopted on a trial basis must above all be assessed for its system compatibility, i.e. for whether it can be reconciled with the rest of the legal context and whether it is in tune with the core ideas of the desired competition culture. Of primary importance among these core ideas, as discussed, is the constitutionally protected right of individuals to compete.

4.4 Conclusions

Economic objectives are not truths but a priori assumptions. Therefore, the paradigm of competition put forward by advocates of the 'more economic approach' is not predetermined, unlike good or bad weather for instance or the effect of the law of gravity on a falling stone. Rather, choosing one of the possible paradigms is justifiable. In making this choice, paradigms of competition should be assessed on the basis of whether they are compatible with fundamental social and legal decisions; in the present case, the freedom of competition in particular. In the sphere of law, a goal should therefore be defined which is reconcilable with other fundamental decisions of constitutional law. In the countries examined, the freedom of the individual represents a fundamental core value of social coexistence. Therefore, the economic constitution in force in these countries should not be changed.

5 SUMMARY

This chapter deals with the main question of whether the goal of competition law should be to protect the individual's freedom to compete, that

---

[67] *See* on the whole problem with detailed justification Künzler, *supra* n 18, § 11 B.

is, the competitive process or whether the goal of competition law should rather be consumer welfare. The findings and conclusions are as follows:

(1) In the USA, the EU and Switzerland, the mandate of the constitution is to protect competition law directly by the individual's freedom to compete and thus the free competitive process. By doing so, consumer welfare is – as long lasting experience shows – promoted indirectly.
(2) In constitutional states the judiciary and other adjudicative bodies are in principle bound to apply the ruling law and may not substitute it, e.g. by economic theories. As the ruling competition law is complete and clear, altering the goal of competition law from protecting freedom to compete to promoting consumer welfare would be an interpretation 'contra legem et constitutionem' and would therefore be illegal.
(3) As all economic theories are not 'truths' but a priori assumptions there is no necessity to implement in competition law one concept rather than another one. In such a situation it is reasonable to choose a concept that is consistent or more consistent with fundamental constitutional decisions, like the constitutionally protected economic freedom of individuals. Therefore the conclusion is: It is not the promotion of consumer welfare which should become the goal of competition law. Instead, the freedom of individuals to compete and thus the free competitive process should remain the goal, especially since this concept promotes consumer welfare indirectly in an effective way.
(4) Therefore, restrictions of the individual's freedom to compete and thus the free competitive process should remain the decisive adjudication principle, especially when applying Article 81(1) EC Treaty. Consumer interests and efficiency arguments play an important role when it comes to adjudicating cases that fall within the scope of Article 81(1) under Article 81(3) EC Treaty or when merger cases are at issue.

PART II

The diversity of competition law regimes

4. The Development of Competition Law for the last 15 Years in Japan: Progress or Setback?

Iwakazu Takahashi*

1 INTRODUCTION

This chapter will analyse the recent changes brought about by the Anti-Monopoly Act in Japan (hereinafter referred to as the 'AMA'). It will highlight the positive and negative aspects of the law.

2 OUTLINE OF THE JAPANESE ANTI-MONOPOLY ACT

2.1 History of the Law

The AMA was introduced in 1947. It is based on the antitrust legislation of the United States. The numerous revisions to it have given it a distinctive flavour of its own, but the framework of the basic system has remained the same. The AMA's purpose was 'the promotion of fair and free competition' by which it aimed at the promotion of 'the democratic and wholesome development of the national economy' as a final goal (Article 1). The AMA, at the same time, had an underlying policy of maintaining the outcomes of the economic democratisation policies of the Allied Powers.[1] Those policies dissolved the big financial combines and the excessive concentration of economic power in the late 1940s to the first half of the 1950s in the Japanese economy. Some examples were: the

* Professor of Law, Faculty of Law, Meiji University, Tokyo, Japan.

[1] *See* for a comparison of the economic democratisation policies in Japan and Germany, Takahashi, Iwakazu (1997), *Doitsu Kyousouseigen-kinshihou no Seiritsu to Kouzou (The Establishment and Structure of Antimonopoly Act in Germany)* Sanseido, pp. 54–59.

provisions prohibiting the establishment of a pure holding company of any size (Article 9), the holding of shares of another corporation (Article 10), the company mergers at any size with some limited exceptions (Article 15), and the restriction on banks etc. holding more than 5 per cent of stock in other banks or companies (Article 11). These strict regulations were gradually modified. One of the most important changes in 1953 was allowing stockholding between corporations as far as it did not cause a substantial restraint of competition in any particular field of trade. Some big financial combines such as Mitsubishi, Mitsui and Sumitomo were reorganised in the 1960s with mutual cross shareholding between the bank, insurance company, trading company and other manufacturing companies, which did not compete in the same field of trade.

Today the business community formed by industrial companies has acknowledged the value of fair and free competition in a modern economic society. Consumers in general (in the form of the consumer movement) and small- and medium-sized enterprises have become strong advocates for supporters of the AMA in the 1960s. It may be concluded that nowadays competition law and policy has been firmly established in Japanese society.

2.2 Structure of the Japanese Anti-Monopoly Act

The AMA is quite comprehensive, even by international standards. The principal provisions of it are as follows: (1) a prohibition of unreasonable restraint of trade (Article 3 2nd part); (2) a prohibition of private monopolisation (Article 3, first part); (3) a prohibition of unfair trade practices (Article 19); (4) limitations on the formation of enterprise groups (Articles 9–18); (5) particular exemptions, such as the exercise of intellectual property rights (Article 21), acts of co-operative society (Article 22) and acts of resale price maintenance (Article 23); (6) administrative sections on the organisation and procedures of the Fair Trade Commission (Articles 27–76).

One of the major provisions of the AMA is the prohibition of cartels. Considering the history of Japan's market economy, in which cartels have been used as a method for industrial control, this prohibition marked the first step in a switchover to a market economy based on the principle of fair and free competition. The AMA, Article 3 (second part) prohibits 'unreasonable restraint of trade', which is defined as follows (Article 2, paragraph 6):

> any entrepreneur, by contract, agreement or any other concerted actions, irrespective of its name with other entrepreneurs, mutually restrict or conduct their

> business activities in such a manner as to fix, maintain, or increase prices, or to limit production, technology, products[,] facilities, or customers or suppliers, thereby causing, contrary to the public interest, a substantial restraint of competition in any particular field of trade.

The meaning of 'mutually restrict or conduct their business activities' covers not only explicit cartel activity, but also implicit concerted action as well. Under Article 3 (second part), the requirement of competition infringement is 'a substantial restraint of competition in any particular field of trade'.

The AMA, Article 3 (first part) prohibits 'private monopolization', which is defined as follows (Article 2 paragraph 5):

> any entrepreneur, individually or by combination or conspiracy with other entrepreneurs, or by any other manner, excludes or controls the business activities of other entrepreneurs, thereby causing, contrary to the public interest, a substantial restraint of competition in any particular field of trade.

Under Article 3 (first part), the requirement of competition infringement is 'a substantial restraint of competition in any particular field of trade'. The AMA Article 19 prohibits 'unfair trade practices', which are defined as follows (Article 2, paragraph 9):

> any act falling under any of following items, which tends to impede fair competition and which is designated by the Fair Trade Commission:
>
> (i) Unjustly treat other entrepreneurs in a discriminatory manner;
> (ii) Dealing with unjust consideration;
> (iii) Unjustly inducing or coercing customers of a competitor to deal with oneself;
> (iv) Dealing with another party on such conditions as will unjustly restrict the business activities of the said party;
> (v) Dealing with another party by unjust use of one's bargaining position;
> (vi) Unjustly interfering with a transaction between an entrepreneur in competition with it in Japan with oneself or a corporation of which oneself is a stockholder or an officer and another transaction counterparty; or, in case such entrepreneur is a corporation, unjustly inducing, instigating, or coercing a stockholder or an director of such corporation to act against the interests of such corporation.

The 'Designation of Unfair Trade Practices' (18 June 1982), which is designated by the Fair Trade Commission of Japan (hereafter referred to as the 'JFTC'), covers the following 16 activities as 'unfair trade practice': (1) Concerted Refusal to Deal; (2) Other Refusal to Deal; (3) Discriminatory Pricing; (4) Discriminatory Treatment on Transaction Terms, etc.; (5) Discriminatory Treatment in a Trade Association, etc.; (6) Unjust Low

Price Sales; (7) Unjust High Price Purchasing; (8) Deceptive Customer Inducement; (9) Customer Inducement by Unjust Benefits; (10) Tie-in Sales, etc.; (11) Dealing on Exclusive Terms; (12) Resale Price Restriction; (13) Dealing on Restrictive Terms; (14) Abuse of Dominant Bargaining Position; (15) Interference with a Competitor's Transaction; and (16) Interference with Internal Operations of a Competing Company.

Regarding the relationship between 'unfair trade practices' and 'private monopolization' the prohibition of 'unfair trade practices' is intended as a preventative measure aimed at activities which, if left unfettered, could eventually develop into 'private monopolization'. Because of this reason, under Article 19, the requirement of competition infringement is that it 'tends to impede fair competition'. Article 19 is also concerned with consumers' rights and regulates misrepresentation concerning products and services, and the imposition of unreasonable premiums (Designation of Unfair Trade Practices Articles 8 and 9).

The AMA prohibits merger, stockholding and interlocking directorships, which may substantially restrain competition in any particular field of trade (Articles 10, 13 and 15). These prohibitions are designed to prevent the formation of oligopolistic market structures limiting price competition, etc.

The AMA also contains a provision prohibiting the establishment of any corporation causing excessive concentration of economic power (Article 9) as well as a provision for restrictions on the level of shareholding by a financial company (Article 11). These regulations are intended to prevent the formation of corporation groupings of giant enterprises ('zaibatsu' in Japanese) and the exertion of economic control by such groupings.

The AMA includes provisions about the JFTC and its independent exercise of the law. The JFTC is the body charged with enforcing the AMA. It comprises a chairman and four commissioners. The chairman and commissioners must be at least 35 years of age and possess academic or occupational experience in the area of law or economics. They are appointed by the Prime Minister and must be confirmed by both houses of the Diet. The chairman and commissioners each serve five-year terms, and they may not be dismissed except for reasons designated by law. They are guaranteed remuneration during their terms of service. The chairman and commissioners of the JFTC perform their duties independently. Ensuring the independent exercise of authority by the chairman and commissioners, the AMA guarantees that the decisions of the JFTC, acting as a collegiate body, are arrived at autonomously and free of the influence of any directives from high-ranking organisations (AMA Articles 27–44).

If the JFTC issues a recommendation, but the violating party does not comply with it, a hearing procedure is instigated. The parties involved in the hearing are the hearing panel (the commissioners or the hearing examiner), the respondent, the investigator, and other participants, such as interested third parties, government agencies, and public organisations. The hearing procedure begins with the official decision to begin the hearing and continues with the procedures preceding the settlement date (serving of written decision to begin hearing, submission of written defense, preparations), initial procedures, investigation of the evidence, final summation, and finally the drafting, serving, and handing down of the decision (AMA, Articles 45–76).

Decisions of the JFTC are equivalent to the decisions of a court of first instance. The decisions have the status of quasi-legal judgments handed down after a hearing procedure. The right of first judgment for suits to quash such decisions rests with the Tokyo High Court. The Third Special Division of the Tokyo High Court, which is a panel of five judges, is a specialist division dealing only with cases involving decisions by the JFTC and other matters related to the application of the AMA. This specialist division has been established in view of the special nature of economic crimes involving violations of the AMA (AMA Articles 77–88).

The measures available for implementing the AMA are: (1) administrative dispositions: cease and desist orders issued in response to violations, measures against a monopolistic situation to restore competition, and the issuing of surcharge orders; (2) criminal sanctions; and (3) civil measures (assessing of compensation for damages, etc.). Of these, the issuing of cease and desist orders by the JFTC occupies the central role. However, the use of criminal sanctions has been increasing in recent years. As to criminal enforcement, the AMA stipulates that: (1) for violations, such as private monopolisation, unreasonable restraint of trade, or collusion by trade associations in substantial restraint of competition, the penalty shall be penal servitude for not more than three years or a fine of not more than five million yen; (2) for violations involving illegal international agreements, or collusion by trade associations not covered by (1) above, or violation of confirmed decisions, the penalty shall be penal servitude for not more than two years or a fine of not more than three million yen; (3) for offences such as violation of the restrictions on stockholdings or cross-directorships, the penalty shall be penal servitude for not more than one year or a fine of not more than two million yen; (4) in cases where an employee of a corporate body has committed a violation in connection with his duties as an employee, the employee who performed the prohibited act may be punished and the corporate body fined, the fine to be not more than 100 million yen in cases of private monopolisation and unreasonable restraint of trade (AMA, Articles 89–100).

The measures to prohibit cartels are mostly administrative dispositions to order the elimination of cartel agreements, but criminal penalties are sometimes imposed. In the case of price collusion, surcharges are imposed. The surcharge order is issued to firms engaged in cartels pertaining to the price of goods or services or in cartels affecting the price by limiting the supply etc. The JFTC orders the firm to pay to the Treasury as a surcharge the amount arrived at by multiplying by the legal rates (3 per cent for retail, 2 per cent for wholesale, and 10 per cent for others). The 'sales amount of such goods or services' for the period from the date on which the firm was engaged in the 'business activities as implementation of such conduct' to the date on which the firm ceased to engage in such business activities (AMA, Articles 7–12).

2.3 AMA Article 19, Article 3 contrasted with Article 82 of EU Competition Law

The AMA, Articles 19, 3 (first part) may have a similar function with Article 82 of EU competition law subject to the qualification that there is no specific independent provision prohibiting the abuse of market dominant position.

The AMA, Article 19 prohibits 'unfair trade practices'. As the meaning of 'unfair' is reasonably equivalent to the concept of 'abuse', Article 19 includes the conduct covered by Article 82 of the EU Competition Law. The 'unfair trade practices' relating to the vertical restraints on transactions in manufacturing and in distribution are: 'abuse of a dominant bargaining position', 'dealing with exclusive terms', 'resale price maintenance', 'refusal to deal', 'discriminatory treatment on transaction terms', 'tie-in sales', (AMA, Article 2, para 9, items 1, 4 and 5; Designation of Unfair Trade Practices, Articles 1, 2, 3, 4, 10, 11, 12 and 14). The 'unfair trade practices' relating to the horizontal restraints of competition are 'unjust low price sales' and 'interference with a competitor's transaction' (AMA, Article 2, para 9, items 2 and 6; Designation of Unfair Trade Practices, Articles 6 and 15). Under Article 19, the requirement of competition infringement is that it 'tend to impede fair competition'.

The AMA, Article 3 (first part) prohibits 'private monopolisation', which includes conduct covered by Article 82 of EU Competition Law as well. The word 'exclusion' can cover a range of different conduct, typically: 'refusal to deal', 'discriminatory treatment on transaction terms', 'tie-in sales', 'dealing with exclusive terms' and 'unjust low price sales' (dumping) etc. Under Article 3, the requirement of competition infringement is 'a substantial restraint of competition in any particular field of trade'.

3 SOME CHARACTERISTICS OF THE JAPANESE ANTI-MONOPOLY ACT

The AMA has two characteristics which reflect the Japanese economic structure and can be traced back over a period 60 years. Firstly, the AMA struggled with an industrial policy which restricted price competition and new entrants to the market for over 50 years. It finally ended in a victory for competition law and policy in the 1990s. Secondly, the AMA promoted the competitiveness of small- and medium-sized enterprises by applying a provision prohibiting abuse of bargaining position in transactions between a main subcontracting entrepreneur (a parent company) and a subsidiary company in the field of production, distribution, and financing, etc. (AMA, Article 19, para 5). This has been complemented by the Subcontract Act introduced in 1956.

3.1 Competition Law Struggled with Industrial Policy over 50 years

Industrial policy is a system for accomplishing rationalisation, organisation and international competitiveness of specific industrial sectors. Governments use several methods to achieve these outcomes, one of which is restricting competition. This can cause conflict between competition policy and industrial policy.

In Japan, the AMA caused fierce opposition from traditional Japanese economic interests. For over 50 years until the 1990s, there has been continuing friction between the advocates for rebuilding 'the cartel state' and those pursuing a 'competitive market economy'. The result of this 50-year conflict is quite clear: a victory for 'competition law and policy'.

With the end of the occupation in 1953, the AMA lost the supreme supporting influence that had been exerted by the occupation forces. Industry began to pursue a system involving allied enterprises grouping together as well as collusion between companies within specific business sectors. The amendment of the AMA in 1953 added the exemptions in the form of depression cartels (Article 24-3), rationalisation cartels (Article 24-4) and resale price maintenance contracts (Article 24-2). Moreover, through the 1950s and 60s, depression cartels, rationalisation cartels and cartels to prevent excessive competition were authorised under several statutes independent of the AMA. There was also administrative guidance regarding raising or reducing prices, or the like, which restricted competition in a similar way to the cartel.[2]

Through the amendment to the AMA in 1953, regulations on stock ownership, and corporate mergers were also relaxed. This was intended to create large corporate groups which resulted in a combination of bank and trading companies on a grand scale. According to the industrial reorganisation policy as a part of industrial policy, companies that had been split up by the Act on Elimination of Excessive Concentration of Economic Power (1948), such as Yawata Iron & Steel Co, Ltd. and Fuji Iron & Steel Co, Ltd., re-amalgamated in the 1960s. Although the merger between Yahata and Fuji was impeached for violating Article 15 of the AMA by JFTC, it was allowed finally with some measures to transfer some factories and technologies to competitors etc.

Despite this overall trend, competition between enterprises became increasingly fierce. It is important to pay due attention to the government intervention to make adjustments to deal with such 'excessive competition.' But, these interventions had limited success. In the *Sumitomo Metals* case, Sumitomo Metal refused to follow administrative guidance to limit the amount of steel they produced. The Law for Temporary Measures to Promote Designated Industries in which reorganisation of some key industries were attempted was also a failure. The competitive urge that had been released among companies by the breakup of the elimination of excessive concentration of economic power was very powerful.

In the 1960s and 1970s, Japan's competition law and policy were in fierce conflict with the industrial policy as mentioned above. From the 1980s onwards, international trade friction grew quite intense especially between Japan and the United States. Economic negotiations were held between both countries in the late 1980s. Contentious issues were the opening of the Japanese market, as well as reforms aimed at making the Japanese economic structure more competitive. The AMA was identified as one of the principal tools to be used for achieving these changes, and as a result, the regulation standards were raised and the application of the AMA was made tougher.

In 1994, the Supreme Court sentenced a petroleum price-fixing cartel to be illegal (Decision of the Supreme Court on 24 February 1994). In this 1973 case, the defendants were 12 petroleum companies. They pleaded

[2] There were cases in which JFTC approved the recommendations by Ministry of International Trade and Industry to cut-off operations in the textiles industry and in the iron industry in the 1950s and 1960s, although these joint operations are thought to violate Article 3 of the AMA.

not guilty, because they raised prices of kerosene jointly according to the administrative guidance by MITI (Ministry of International Trade and Industry). The MITI had asked the defendants to make a submission on prices. The court rejected this defense. The defendants were held to have breached Article 3 (2nd part) of the AMA because they raised the price of kerosene to the upper limit of their plan and fixed it at the highest price level. It had the effect that the defendants' conduct removed the opportunity for price competition among them; they had taken advantage of MITI's request for self-regulation by fixing an artificially high price level.[3]

After this decision, the JFTC issued 'Guidelines Concerning Administrative Guidance under the Antimonopoly Act' (30 June 1994), saying that the administrative guidance poses a problem under the AMA (Articles 3, 8(i), (iv) and (v) and 19). One example that would be in breach of the Act and would be illegal is: 'Guidance regarding raising or reducing prices, stating specific figures relating to amount, percentage (or range), or the like, which would serve as standards. Such administrative guidance may tempt firms acting together or their trade association to decide to raise or lower prices to the level of the stated standards. To decide in this context may mean not only an explicit decision or agreement but also tacitly agreeing or colluding on a common purpose'.

As to the industrial policy, regulations covering surcharges and criminal penalties regarding mainly cartels were strengthened in 1992, and since that time the administrative staff of the JFTC has been increased. In 1999–2000 under revisions to the AMA, exemptions for depression cartels and rationalisation cartels were scrapped. Systems such as depression cartels, rationalisation cartels, and cartels to prevent excessive competition recognised under separate legislation in the 1950s and 60s have been gradually phased out with fewer such systems remaining today.[4]

The role of industrial policy is historically important. It has had some success in sector-specific regulation in several industries, including the iron industry, the petrochemical industry and the semi-conductor industry by using cartels and promoting merger and acquisition. But it has so far failed in other industries such as agriculture, distribution, construction and car manufacturing industries. Today industrial policy has only a

---

[3] *See* Takahashi, Iwakazu (1997), *Gyosei-shido to Seisan-tyousei (Administrative guidance and Production Adjustment)*, Jurist Special Edition No 141, pp. 100–101.

[4] There still remain the rationalisation cartel in liquor and retail industries, the cartels to prevent excessive competition for small- and medium-sized business, the export cartels for trade industry, the transportation cartels for transportation industry, the insurance cartel for insurance industry.

complementary role to the competition policy in the fields of research and development of technology, international trade, education, and small- to medium-sized enterprises. In those areas, industrial policy should not restrict fair and free competition.

3.2 Competition Law Promoting the Competitiveness of Small- and Medium-sized Enterprises

Considering Japan's economic structure, where small and medium-sized enterprises make up more than three-quarters of its corporate landscape, it is clear that Japan has used the AMA as a means of regulating transactions between large corporations and the small and medium-sized enterprises in many industrial fields in the last 60 years. The purpose has been to bring about a competitive order in which the small and medium-sized enterprises are not merely the object of governmental protection, but they can exist as the enterprises acquiring a competitive power by their own efforts in the free market economy. Fostering these small and medium-sized businesses by promotion of 'fair competition' would have been, in this sense, one of the most important achievements of Japan's antimonopoly law.

It is common for business relationships between manufacturers (or department stores) and their subcontractors (or suppliers) to be long-term associations lasting a decade or more in Japan. Examples include the business relationships between manufacturers of finished products and the companies that supply their parts, or the business relationships between manufacturers of primary components and manufacturers of secondary components. In cases such as these, the manufacturer of finished products may use its superior bargaining position to the subcontractor to force the latter to agree to transaction conditions that are unfavourable. For example, payment to the subcontractor that is substantially below the prevailing market rate for the goods or services provided, or late or partial payment. Another example would be refusing to accept parts that had been previously ordered, the return of unnecessary parts, or the request for frequent delivery in small lots at the expense of the subcontractor.

3.2.1 Prohibition of the abuse of a dominant bargaining position: Article 19, Article 2, para 9, item 5 of the AMA

Such trade practices by manufacturers (or department stores) were recognised as an abuse of a dominant bargaining position and an article to regulate it was introduced into the AMA when it was amended in 1953.

Article 19 of the AMA, prohibits many types of unfair trade practices and bans an abuse of a dominant bargaining position as well. Designation of Unfair Trade Practices (the Fair Trade Commission Notification No.

11 of 1953 amended in 1982, hereinafter refered to as 'the Designation') designated by Article 19 of the AMA provides:

> Taking any act specified in one of the following paragraphs, unjustly in the light of the normal business practices by making use of one's dominant bargaining position over the other party: (1) Causing the said party in continuous transaction to purchase a commodity or service other than the one involved in the said transaction; (2) Causing the said party in continuous transaction to provide for oneself money, service or other economic benefits; (3) Setting or changing transaction terms in a way disadvantageous to the said party; (4) In addition to any act coming under the preceding three paragraphs, imposing a disadvantage on the said party regarding terms or execution of the transaction; or (5) Causing a company which is one's other transacting party to follow one's advanced directions, or to get one's approval, regarding the appointment of officers of the said company.

Article 14[5] of the Designation requires the conduct comprising (1) to (5) (above) made by using one's dominant bargaining position, and the infringement of competition which is 'unjustly in the light of the normal business practices', being equivalent to '(any act . . . which) tends to impede fair competition' of Article 2, para 9 of the AMA. Article 14 requires the use of 'one's dominant bargaining position over the other party'. Using a retailer,[6] by way of an illustration. The retailer will be in a dominant bargaining position over its suppliers in such cases where the suppliers are obliged to accept the retailer's requests even if they are excessively disadvantageous to the suppliers, since discontinuance of transaction with the retailer would significantly damage the suppliers' business. In making this finding, comprehensive consideration is to be given to such factors as 'degree of dependence on the retailer', 'changeability of customer', 'position of the retailer in a market', and 'supply and demand forces of the product'.[7]

The 'making use of (one's dominant bargaining position over the

---

[5] About the requirement of Article 14, *see* Takahashi, Iwakazu (2006), *Yuetsuteki-chii no Ranyo (An Abuse of a dominant bargaining position)*, Kanai et. edt. Dokusen-kinshi-ho [Dai 2 Han](Anti-Monopoly Act [2nd edition]), Kobundo, pp. 313–321.

[6] In addition to Article 14 of the *Designation of Unfair Trade Practices* (the Fair Trade Commission Notification No 11 of 1953 amended on 1982), *Specific Unfair Trade Practices in the Department Store Industry* (Fair Trade Commission Notification No. 7 of 2005) shall apply to the acts of large-scale retailers such as department stores and supermarkets having no less than a certain number of square meters of sales area and selling a large variety of goods for ordinary use to general consumers vis-a-vis their suppliers.

[7] The explanation below is according to Guidelines concerning Distribution System and Business Practices (JFTC, 11 July 1991).

other party)' means the obligation to the suppliers to accept the retailer's requests above mentioned, by which the retailer infringes the freedom in transaction of its suppliers who have lost their independence.[8]

As to the requirement of infringement of competition, the words 'unjustly in the light of the normal business practices', which is equivalent to '(any act . . . which) tends to impede fair competition' (Article 2, para 9 of the AMA), means that the retailer is able to gain unfair profit through such practices. This will give it a competitive advantage over rival companies and at the same time, the suppliers who are the victims of such unfair practices are put into a disadvantageous position relative to their competitors. The competition which relies on such retailer's practices can be considered the 'competition with unfair method'.[9]

Article 14 of the Designation has been applied typically to transactions between manufacturers and their subcontractors and department stores or large supermarkets and suppliers. It has also been applied to transactions between banks and borrowers and transactions between licenser and licensee.

In relation to distribution, there is the *Mitsukoshi Department Store* case.[10] Mitsukoshi department store, having a very successful brand image, was the second largest department store in Japan with other department stores holding only a small percentage of the market. Mitsukoshi had long term suppliers for its store. It asked each supplier to buy goods and services provided by the department at a certain amount for each, or to bear the cost of the renewal of retail space within the department store. The suppliers accepted the proposal from Mitsukoshi department store because they feared they would lose business with the store. It was accepted that the Mitsukoshi department store was the suppliers' main transaction partner and it would be very difficult for the suppliers to establish business connections with other department stores. Consequently Mitsukoshi department store had a dominant bargaining position in transactions with suppliers; it had used its bargaining power, and the suppliers were dependent on

---

8 As to the relationship between freedom of decision and disturbance of competition, refer to Takahashi, Iwakazu (2002), *Yuetsuteki-chii no Ranyo to Kosei-kyoso-sogaisei (An Abuse of a Dominant Bargaining Position and the Tendency to impede Fair Competition)* Kousei Torihiki (Fair Trade) No 626, pp. 2–7.

9 About the situation of academic theories on this point, refer to Takahashi, Iwakazu (2006), *Yuetsutekichii no Ranyo to Dokkinhou (An Abuse of a Dominant Bargaining Position and Anti-Monopoly Act)* Nippon keizaiho Gakkai Nenpou (Annual Report of Japan Academy of Economic Law) No 49, pp. 1–20.

10 *Mitsukoshi Department Store* case (1982) Consent degree by JFTC, 17 June.

Mitsukoshi department store for their business, and were forced to accept the proposals by Mitsukoshi department store.

In relation to banking cases, there is the *Mitsui-Sumitomo Bank* case.[11] Mitsui-Sumitomo Bank, whose market share of deposits was less than 10 per cent, forced smaller borrowers to buy a financial product of an interest rate swap as a condition of its providing finance. There is also a case of *Gifu Credit Cooperative*,[12] which required applicants for a loan to deposit funds as a condition for a loan. This was a private suit with the Supreme Court decision given in favour of the borrowers.

In relation to licences, Article 14 may apply to the abuse of the dominant bargaining position in a transaction between licensor and licensee. The application of the Article 14 of the Designation is possible in a situation in which a licensor is enjoying a dominant bargaining position with respect to the licensees and unjustifiably imposes disadvantageous conditions on licensees at the time of granting licenses to them. In addition, Article 14 is applicable to the conduct, to which other articles of the Designation will be primarily applied, such as (1) 'Inhibiting the Use of Technology'; (2) 'Limiting the Scope of the Use of Technology (Licensing Rights in Part, Restrictions in relation to Manufacturing, Restrictions in relation to Export, Sub-licensing)'; (3) 'Imposing Restrictions in relation to the Use of Technology (Restrictions on Raw Materials and Parts, Restrictions on Sales, Restrictions on Sale and Resale Prices, Restrictions on Manufacturing and Sale of Competing Products or on Transactions with Competitors, Best Effort Obligations, Obligations to protect Confidentiality of Know-how, No-contest Obligation)'; (4) 'Imposing other Restrictions (Unilateral Termination Provisions, Setting of Royalties without relation to the Use of Technology, Restrictions after Extinction of Rights, Bundle Licensing, Addition of Functions to Technology, Obligations of Non-assertion of Rights, Restrictions on Research and Development Activities, Obligations to hand over Improved Technology or to grant Exclusive Licenses for improved Technology, Obligations to grant Non-exclusive Licenses for Improved Technology, Obligations to report Obtained Knowledge and Experience)'.[13]

The vertical integration between large corporations and small and medium-sized enterprises in distribution and manufacturing ('keiretsu' in Japanese), is affected by Article 19. Article 19 of the AMA prohibits the

---

11 *Mitsui-Sumitomo Bank* case (2005) Decision by JFTC, 26 December.

12 *Gifu Schoko-kumiai Jiken* (Gifu Credit Cooperative Case) (1977) Decision of Supreme Court, 20 June.

13 JFTC, *Guidelines for the Use of Intellectual Property under the Antimonopoly Act* (2007).

exclusive sales arrangements and the limitation of sales regions, when that conduct is likely to impede fair competition, in which exclusive sales rights were extended to a wholesaler for a limited sales region, and the wholesaler was restricted from handling competing products, or a retailer was required to buy stock only from a specified wholesaler. Since that conduct often has the purpose of maintaining resale price directly or indirectly, Article 19 of the AMA prohibits the resale price maintenance as well. It is also possible to prohibit the exclusive sales arrangements, the limitation of sales regions and the resale price maintenance by Article 19 of the AMA as an abuse of a dominant bargaining position.

3.2.2 Prohibition of the abuse of a dominant bargaining position (2) – Subcontract Act of 1956, amended 2003

The abuse of a dominant bargaining position is alternatively dealt with by using corrective measures authorised under the Act Against Delay in Payment of Subcontract Proceeds, etc., to Subcontractors (Act No. 120 of 1 June 1956, amended 2003, hereinafter referred as 'the Subcontract Act'). This is a law that was enacted as a complement to the AMA in order to permit immediate action by JFTC.

With reference to the relationship of the Subcontract Act to the AMA, the Subcontract Act, Article 8 provides that in the case the JFTC has rendered a recommendation to the main subcontracting entrepreneur, to the extent that the entrepreneur has complied with the recommendation, Article 20 of the AMA (Elimination measures against unfair trade practices) shall not apply to the act of that entrepreneur. If the main subcontracting entrepreneur does not take the measures to protect the interests of the subcontractor against the recommendation, JFTC may order the entrepreneur to cease and desist from the said act (AMA, Article 20, para.1). The main subcontracting entrepreneur can make a request for a hearing for rescission or modification of the order and the JFTC shall commence hearing procedures regarding the order (AMA, Article 52, paras 1 and 3).

The Subcontract Act prevents conduct such as delay in payment of subcontract proceeds, etc. The purpose is to ensure that transactions between main subcontracting entrepreneurs and subcontractors are fair and, at the same time, to protect the interests of the subcontractors, thereby contributing to the sound development of the national economy.[14] This applies to

---

[14] About the necessity of applying the Subcontract Act to information-based product creation contracts and service contracts, *see* JFTC, *Kigyo Torihiki Kenkyukai Hokokusho (Report of the Research Group on Corporation Transaction)* (2002).

(1) manufacturing contracts (machine parts manufacturing, metal mold production etc.); (2) repair contracts; (3) information-based product creation contracts (software development, broadcasting program production, commercial messages for TV production, etc.); and (4) service contracts (transportation services, building maintenance services etc.).

The most important point of this Act is that a main subcontracting entrepreneur has to immediately deliver to the subcontractor a written statement setting forth (1) the contents of work of the contract; (2) the amount of subcontract proceeds; (3) the date of payment; and (4) the method of payment (Article 3). A main subcontracting entrepreneur is also obliged to prepare and preserve documents or electromagnetic records, to fix the date of payment of subcontract proceeds within sixty days, to pay the interest for the delay of payment after the sixty days (Articles 5, 2-2 and 4-2).

The Subcontract Act prohibits the following conduct by main subcontracting entrepreneurs, who without valid reasons related to the subcontractor, (1) refuses to accept the work from a subcontractor; (2) fails to make payment of subcontract proceeds after the due date of payment; (3) reduces the amount of subcontract proceeds; (4) forces a subcontractor to take back the goods after receiving them from the said subcontractor; (5) unjustly fixes a conspicuously lower amount of subcontract proceeds than the price ordinarily paid for the same or similar contents of wor; (6) coerces the subcontractor to purchase designated goods or to use designated services; (7) causes a subcontractor to provide cash, services or other economic gains for oneself; and (8) causes a subcontractor to effect changes to the work, or to re-work after the receipt of the work, etc. (Articles 4, para 1, 2).[15]

These issues also arise in relation to information-based product creation contracts. Relevant are the actual conditions of the broadcasting program production. TV stations, who are also producers, contract out two thirds of that production to subcontractors. This is a multilayered transaction structure like a pyramid with main subcontracting entrepreneurs and subcontractors. In forty percent of cases there is a written contract between the TV stations and subcontractors. 60 per cent of subcontracted production is by way of an oral contract. In some cases, subcontractors' payments are reduced by more than ten percent because of poor management by the main subcontractors. Delays in payment can be of the order of 20

[15] About the actual conditions of transaction in car manufacturing industry, *see* Takahashi, Iwakazu (1994), *Seisan ni kakawaru Trohiki-kankou to Dokkinhou (Business Practices in Production and Antimonopoly Law)* Nippon Keizaihogakkai Nenpou (Annual Report of Japan Academy of Economic Law) No.15, pp. 17–36.

per cent with about 60 per cent of subcontractors being required to redo work after delivery of the work. In about 10 per cent of cases the subcontractor is forced to cover additional cost.[16]

4 COMPETITION LAW AFTER THE 1990s – PROGRESS OR SETBACK?

The AMA provides in Article 1 that it aims to promote the democratic and 'wholesome development' of the national economy as well as to assure 'the interests of consumers in general'. Therefore, the AMA as a whole can be said to be a law for 'the ensuring of the interests of consumers in general.' In fact, the AMA is closely related to (1) the consumers' right to choose, or the right to take part in the decision of prices and other conditions of transaction (AMA Art.3 second part); (2) the right to access information (AMA Article 19 concerning unjust representation etc.); and (3) the right to be compensated for injury (AMA Articles 25 and 26 concerning the damages suit).

As to the consumers' right to choose, there has been a strict enforcement on cartel prohibition, especially on bid-rigging in the construction industry after the 1990s, to which the leniency program introduced in 2005[17] has contributed much. However, the cartel regulation is still powerless to prevent 'parallel price increases' in an oligopolistic market, which is due to the limitations of the provisions on cartels in the AMA, and basically mirrors the situation found worldwide.

The right to access information is governed by the Act against Unjustifiable Premiums and Misleading Representation 1956 (hereinafter referred to as the Premiums and Representation Act). This Act is a complementary act of the AMA and has also been positively applied in the 1990s and after. The Premiums and Representation Act prohibits the following representations as misleading: (1) any representation by which the quality, standard or any other matter relating to the substance of a commodity or

---

[16] JFTC, *Terebi-bangumi Seisaku-gyo ni okeru Shitauke-torihiki no Jittai (Report on the Situation of Subcontract Transaction in Broadcasting Program Production Industry)* (2004).

[17] As to the introduction of leniency program in Japan, EU competition law and German competition law were mainly referred. See Takahashi, Iwakazu (2003), *EU Kyousou-hou ni-okeru Seisai-kin oyobi Doitsu GWB ni-okeru Karyo no Gen-men Seido no Mokuteki to Kinou (The Purpose and Function of Leniency Program in EU Competition Law and GWB of Germany)* Kosei Torihiki (Fair Trade) No 629, pp. 42–49.

service will be misunderstood to be much better (Better Misunderstood Representation) (Article 4, para 1); (2) any representation by which price or any other terms of transaction of a commodity or service will be misunderstood to be much more favourable (More Favourably Misunderstood Representation) (Article 4, para 2); and (3) any representation by which any matter relating to transactions as to a commodity or service is likely to be misunderstood, and which is designated by the JFTC (Likely to be Misunderstood Representation) (Article 4, para 3). JFTC has so far designated the following representations: (1) Representation concerning drinks containing no fruit juice (FTC Notification No. 4, 1973; (2) Misleading representation concerning product's country of origin (FTC Notification No. 34, 1973); (3) Representation concerning the finance charge for consumer credit (FTC Notification No. 13, 1980); (4) Representation concerning bait advertisement of real estate (FTC Notification No. 14, 1980); and (5) Representation concerning bait advertisement (FTC Notification No. 17, 1993).

However, these regulations of misleading representation by the AMA and the Premiums and Representation Act are only targeted at deceptive representation (including deception by non-representation) and extravagant advertisement; regulations that enable consumers' voluntary and rational choice of goods are limited to those by the fair competition codes authorised by JFTC (Article 10). It is necessary, therefore, to provide obligations to positively represent important information as to particular commodities through the designation by JFTC of unfair trade practices (AMA Article 2, para 9) of the AMA and of misleading representations (Article 4 of the Premiums and Representation Act) along with the enhancement of the authorised fair competition codes.

As to the right to compensation, the AMA, Articles 25 and 26 deal with damages suits. The most important point is the scope of the person injured. Although the provision merely stipulates that the entrepreneur shall be liable to indemnify 'the person injured' and does not define its scope, the 'person injured' is interpreted to include not only (1) competitors and those who are engaged in direct transactions with the entrepreneur, but also (2) those who are engaged in indirect transactions including consumers in general. Precedents have qualified consumers as plaintiffs as seen in the following judgments. The consumer who has bought a commodity whose retail price was maintained at an unreasonably high level by means of unfair trade practices is the person who has suffered injury regarding the difference with the appropriate price that might have been determined by free and fair competition. Therefore, the 'person injured', in relation to whom the entrepreneur has exercised unfair trade practice and whom the entrepreneur is liable to indemnify by AMA, Article 25, should be interpreted to include such a consumer.[18] JFTC under Article 25 is actively involved in the process of a damages suit. First, the final decision of JFTC must be made before filing a lawsuit. The active involvement of JFTC in damages suits seeks to reduce the injured person's burden of proof. Secondly, the court has to request JFTC's opinion. The AMA, Article 84 stipulates, 'When a suit for indemnification of damages under the provisions of Article 25 has been filed, the court shall, without delay, request the opinion of the Fair Trade Commission with respect to the amount of damages caused by such violations as provided for in the said section.' This is for the purpose of having JFTC state its opinions as a specialist agency as to 'amount of damages' (opinions on the relevancy of the acts in violation to the injuries and on the amount of damages) concerning the case on which JFTC has made a decision, thereby reducing the plaintiff's (injured person's) burden of proof. The aim of such active involvement of JFTC in lawsuits is obvious. The active involvement by JFTC is defined as described above because acts in violation of the Anti-Monopoly Act harm not only individual persons but also the entire economy, distorting market functions and making resource allocation inefficient.

In damages suit the plaintiffs were unable to win in spite of the active involvement of JFTC, because the amounts of damages were extremely difficult to identify because of the lack of a clear standard for calculating damages.[19] In the process of the identification of the amount of damages,

---

[18] The Case of *Resale Price Maintenance by Matsushita Electric Industry Co (1977)* Judgment of the Tokyo High Court, 19 September. It said as follows:

> As there is no reason that the 'person injured' should be interpreted restrictively, if there are persons who have suffered injuries with reasonable and probable causation as a result of such unreasonable restraint of trade as price agreement on the part of the oil wholesalers as the plaintiffs have contended, then such persons should be deemed to be the 'persons injured' as stipulated in the first subsection of this chapter even if such persons are not direct trading partners of the said oil wholesalers (*The Case of Tokyo Oil Suit* (1981) Judgment of the Tokyo High Court, 17 July).

[19] In the Case of *Tokyo Oil Suit*, consumers sued under s. 25 of the Anti-Monopoly Act oil wholesalers for damages they suffered from the unjustly high retail prices maintained by the price cartel of the wholesalers, after the final decision of the Fair Trade Commission. The Supreme Court decided that the price cartel among wholesalers did exist, that the cartel raised the retail price of kerosene, and that there was a causal relationship between the cartel and the damages consumers suffered. But, the court judged against the plaintiffs because the amount of damages was not identified. The court decided that in order to identify the amount of damages the plaintiffs should explain by specific proofs the factors that contributed to the change of the kerosene prices between the start of the cartel and

consumers are required to calculate the amount of damages as the difference between the actual purchase price and the assumed purchase price after estimating the assumed purchase price taking into account all the factors of price change. This demands the impossible from a customer. It is no wonder that consumers or consumer associations can never win a damages suit under the AMA. In order to change this state of affairs, it is necessary to reform the system of the damages suit under Article 25. To be more specific, when JFTC has submitted its opinion with respect to the amount of damages, the court should assume that the amount of damages has been established by the opinion and thus lighten consumers' burden of proof (AMA, Article 84).

In relation to mergers and acquisitions (M&A), the regulation of M&A is, from the interest of consumers in general, also very important to prevent the establishment of oligopolistic markets in which cartel behavior will become easier. In the 1990s, under the influence of the Chicago School, the purpose for regulating M&A changed from the maintenance of a competitive market structure in a market to the achievement of efficiency in a market. Consequently, mergers were often approved by the competition authority that created large corporations. As a result of M&A, which brought highly concentrated oligopolistic or duopolistic market structures into many markets, there was little opportunity for small- and medium-sized business to compete with large corporations on quality and price.

The AMA prohibits mergers and stockholdings that constitute 'a substantial restriction of competition in a particular field of trade'. This means that the issue becomes one of how to determine precisely what constitutes 'a substantial restriction of competition'. According to the guidelines of

---

the consumers' purchase of kerosene. The judgment states as follows: As the retail price that might have been formed if the price cartel had not been implemented (the assumed purchase price) is a price that was actually non-existent, it will be generally appropriate to presume the price immediately before the conclusion of the price agreement to be equal to the said assumed purchase price, insofar as there is no change, before and after the conclusion of the price agreement, in the economic factors such as economic conditions, market structure and so on that determine the price of the commodity in question. However, when during the period between the conclusion of the price agreement and the purchase by the consumers of the commodity there is a noticeable change in the economic factors that may influence the retail price, it is unacceptable to estimate the assumed purchase price merely from the retail price immediately before the conclusion of the agreement. It is necessary [for the consumers] to estimate it considering, in addition to the said retail price, the factors that determine the price including the price-forming characteristics of the commodity and the nature and degree of the economic change. The Case of *Tokyo Oil Suit* (1986) Judgment of the First Petty Bench of the Supreme Court, 2 July.

the JFTC, these standards include the following: (1) the market share, ranking, and past competitive practices of the company in question; (2) characteristics of the market such as the number of competing companies and their degree of concentration, prospects for new entrants, import pressures, and whether business relationships are closed or exclusionary in nature; and (3) efficiency in terms of overall business capabilities, competitive pressure from related markets, economies of scale, and research and development efficiency.

In recent years, there are increasing numbers of cases in which mergers between companies with very large market shares over 50 per cent in a domestic market are approved. These cases have been allowed due to a greater consideration being given to import pressures or efforts to improve efficiency. But stricter examination for future merger applications will be necessary in order to prevent companies from gaining control of specific markets and thereby restricting competition.[20]

5 CONCLUSION

Competition law has been introduced in many developing and transitional economies in the past 25 years. Competition law has become a fundamental rule of both domestic and international transactions in those economies. The competition law model for those economies is in many cases EC competition law, which has provisions prohibiting cartel agreements and concerted action, abuse of dominant market position, and restricting M&A. American antitrust law, which has a different structure of provisions from the EC competition law, has a similar function in its application.

In developing countries, there are often economies in which 90 per cent of entrepreneurial businesses are small- and medium-sized and the rest are state-owned enterprises, which are usually monopolies. Because of this, multinational corporations from developed countries might be able to achieve a market dominance easily in many industrial sectors. For example, in some developing economies, the abuse of economic power in transactions between big department stores and small suppliers, or between the manufacturer of finished products and the subcontractor of

---

[20] About the problems of the application of AMA regarding M&A, *see* Takahashi, Iwakazu (2007), *Kigyo-baishu Soshiki-saihen to Dokkin-hou (Acquisition and Re-organization of Corporations and Anti-Monopoly Act)*, Horitsu-Jihou, No 982, pp. 39–45.

the parts are very common. This is because small suppliers or subcontractors cannot bring a suit to the court for breach of contract or breach of a contractual duty of good faith, knowing that the consequence of suing a large corporation is most likely that the small business would not be able to continue to do business with the corporation in the future. If the disputes are not settled properly by the application of provisions in the Civil Code, which provide 'No abuse of rights is permitted' or 'A juristic act with any purpose which is against public policy is void', it might be necessary to solve the problems by the Anti-Monopoly Act. But, it is very difficult to apply the Anti-Monopoly Act to conduct which amounts to an abuse, because the law only applies to the entrepreneur with a market-dominant position.

Reflecting upon the economic structure and the stage of economic development of developing economies, it may be necessary to consider whether there should be several different kinds of competition laws based on the differences of economic structure etc., which cover the needs of each particular economy. In this sense, it might be possible to consider a type of competition law having a provision that regulates the conduct in vertical transactions mentioned above as the abuse of a dominant bargaining position. Looking around the competition laws of the world from this viewpoint, there are several types of competition laws existing, and among them there is a type of competition law regulating the abuse of dominant bargaining position, of which Japan's AMA is one.[21]

If no uniform single competition law is suitable for every economy, it is possible to consider that there are several different kinds of competition laws which cover the needs of each particular economy according to the economic structure and the stage of economic development of each economy. A distinction might be drawn between 'a competition law for small and medium entrepreneurs' and 'the competition law for big corporations in developed economies.' The former should be a competition law bringing the best benefit to promote a sound and democratic economy for the small- and medium-sized enterprises. In this sense, the purpose of this type of competition law might be mainly the achievement of 'fair competition' or the achievement of 'fairness in the process of competition' or 'competition with fair method' rather than the achievement of 'free

---

[21] *See* International Competition Network (ICN) *Report on Abuse of Superior Bargaining Position* (7th Annual Conference in Kyoto Japan, 14–16 April 2008). The competition law of Germany (the Act Against Restraints of Competition 1958, ARC) has possibility to regulate 'abuse conducts in transaction'. Article 20, para 2 of ARC prohibits discrimination and unfair hindrance by 'undertaking with superior market power in relation to small- and medium-sized competitors'.

competition'. The latter should be a competition law aiming at mainly the achievement of 'economic efficiency'.

Although this distinction is a theoretical one, and the competition law in reality might have both aspects, there should be scope for 'a competition law for small and medium-sized entrepreneurs' in the concept of competition law. This view attempts to apply the brakes to the tendency to create a uniform single competition law to promote only free competition. It will make it possible to move to the idea of competition law to promote 'fair and free competition' in the era of globalisation of the economy.

5. Metamorphosis of Indian Competition Law

Srinivasan Chakravarthy*

1 INTRODUCTION

This chapter addresses the evolution of competition policy and law in India, tracing the economic scenario in India before and after the 1991 reforms; a description of the extant competition law (Monopolies and Restrictive Trade Practices Act 1969, briefly referred to as the MRTP Act) in the country; and a description of the metamorphosis of the MRTP Act into a new law (Competition Act 2002, as amended in 2007, hereinafter referred to as the Act) and its features.

Since attaining independence in 1947, India, for the better part of half a century thereafter, adopted and followed policies comprising what are known as 'command and control' laws, rules, regulations and executive orders. The competition law of India, namely, the MRTP Act was one such policy. In 1991 widespread economic reforms were undertaken and consequently the march from 'command and control' economy to an economy based more on free market principles commenced its stride. As is true of many countries, economic liberalisation has taken root in India and the need for an effective competition regime has also been recognised.

2 HISTORICAL DEVELOPMENTS LEADING TO THE ENACTMENT OF THE MRTP ACT

2.1 Constitutional Provisions

The Constitution of India, in its essay in building up a just society has mandated the State to direct its policy towards securing that end. Articles 38 and 39 of the Constitution of India, which are part of the Directive

* Dr. S. Chakravarthy is a civil servant in India. He was a Member of the Monopolies and Restrictive Trade Practices Commission and also a Member

Principles of State Policy, mandate, *inter alia*, that the State shall strive to promote the welfare of the people by securing and protecting as effectively as it may, a social order in which justice – social, economic and political – shall inform all the institutions of the national life, and the State shall, in particular, direct its policy towards securing:

(1) that the ownership and control of material resources of the community are so distributed as best to subserve the common good; and
(2) that the operation of the economic system does not result in the concentration of wealth and means of production to the common detriment.

The MRTP Act was in consequence of the aforesaid mandate in the Directive Principles in the Constitution of India, namely, prevention of concentration of economic power. In what follows, the circumstances that led to the need and enactment of the MRTP Act have been highlighted.

2.2 Development Strategy after Independence and its Impact

India has adopted a strategy of planned economic development since the early 1950s. An important watershed in this strategy was the Industrial Policy of 1956, which emphasised growth, social justice and self-reliance; defined the parameters of the Government's regulatory mechanism; and made industrialisation subject to Government intervention and regulation. In particular, the private sector was allowed limited licensed capacity in the core sector and the public sector was given the mantle to achieve the 'commanding heights' of the economy by being made responsible for the major share of production.

Government intervention and control pervaded almost all areas of economic activity in the country. For instance, there was no contestable market. This meant there was neither an easy entry nor an easy exit for enterprises. Government determined the plant sizes; location of the plants; prices of goods in a number of important sectors; and allocation of scarce financial resources.

The licensing policy of the Government favoured big business houses for they were in a better position to raise large amounts of capital and had the managerial skill to run the industry. The business houses also had the advantage in securing financial assistance from the banks and financial

of the High Level Committee on Competition Policy and Law appointed by the Government of India. He was also a Member of the Competition Law Drafting Committee and Advisor to Government on Competition Policy and Law. Presently, he is an advisor/consultant on competition. He is a consultant to World Bank, ADB etc.

institutions. With no proper system of allocating licences in place, licensing authorities were naturally inclined to prefer those who had proved their ability by success in big industrial ventures in the past to those who had still to establish their ability. This also led to pre-empting of licences by a few business houses.

2.3 Trigger Cause

In 1964, the Government appointed a committee called the Monopolies Inquiry Commission (MIC) to enquire into the extent and effects of concentration of economic power in private hands and the prevalence of monopolistic and restrictive trade practices in important sectors of economic activity.

The Monopolies Inquiry Commission presented its report[1] in October 1965 noting therein that there was a concentration of economic power in the form of product-wise and industry-wise concentration. The Commission also noted that a few industrial houses were controlling a large number of companies and that there existed in the country large-scale restrictive and monopolistic trade practices. As a corollary to its findings, the MIC drafted a Bill to provide for the operation of the economic system so as not to result in the concentration of the economic power to the common detriment. The Bill provided for the control of monopolies and prohibition of monopolistic and restrictive trade practices, when prejudicial to public interest.

3 ENACTMENT OF THE MRTP ACT 1969

3.1 MRTP Act 1969

The Bill drafted by the MIC as amended by a Committee of the Parliament became the MRTP Act 1969 and was enforced from 1 June 1970. The Preamble to the Act says that the statute is enacted to provide that the operation of the economic system does not result in the concentration of economic power to the common detriment, for the control of monopolies, for the prohibition of monopolistic and restrictive trade practices and for matters connected therewith or incidental thereto. Thus, one of the products of the planned and controlled economy was the Monopolies and Restrictive Trade Practices Act 1969 (MRTP Act).

---

1 *Monopolies Inquiry Commission Report* (1965), New Delhi: Government of India.

3.2 Thrust Areas

The thrust of the MRTP Act is directed towards:

(1) the prevention of concentration of economic power to the common detriment;
(2) the control of monopolies;
(3) the prohibition of monopolistic trade practices (MTP);
(4) the prohibition of restrictive trade practices (RTP); and
(5) the prohibition of unfair trade practices (UTP) (introduced in 1984)[2]

In terms of competition law and consumer protection, the objective of the MRTP Act is to curb monopolistic, restrictive and unfair trade practices. The regulatory provisions in the MRTP Act apply to almost every area of business – production, distribution, pricing, investment, purchasing, packaging, advertising, sales promotion, mergers, amalgamations and takeover of undertakings (provisions relating to mergers, amalgamations and takeovers were deleted in the MRTP Act by the 1991 amendments to it). Under the MRTP Act, a Regulatory Authority called the MRTP Commission (briefly, Commission) has been set up to deal with offences falling under the statute.

4 REFORMS OF 1991 AND METAMORPHOSIS

4.1 Reforms

The present decade looks to be one of significant change. The changes are nothing but a continuum from the last decade or two, when changes in the political and economic fields had taken place on a tempestuous note. All over the world, one of the dominant economic themes in the last decade and a half has been the process of globalisation and a progressive international economic integration of the world economy. The movement is towards the widening of international flows of trade, finance and information in a single integrated global market.

Globalisation has the fundamental attributes of relying significantly

[2] Unfair Trade Practices were brought into the MRTP Act through an amendment to it in 1984, following the recommendations of the High Powered Committee. *See Report of the High-Powered Expert Committee on Companies and MRTP Acts* (1978), Ministry of Law, Justice and Company Affairs, New Delhi: Government of India.

on market forces, ensuring competition and keeping market functioning efficient. Measures adopted by many countries are essentially designed to open competition in strategic sectors such as telecommunications, airlines, electricity generation and distribution etc. Such measures are a part of a tripod architecture with the three vertices, one may christen as liberalisation, privatisation, and globalisation (LPG). A veneer running across the LPG measures is the element of competition. The LPG paradigm seeks to make competition a driving force in the economic and commercial activities of the world. As observed by Professor Wolfgang Kartte[3], the Chairman of the German Federal Cartel Office, 'Competition is the engine of market economy'.

It was in 1991, that India took the initiative in favour of economic reforms consisting essentially of liberalisation and de-regulation. In a manner of speaking, India embarked on the LPG regime and has been, and is, undergoing the process of transition into a market economy. While planned economic development had been the strategy adopted by India since the 1950s, since 1991 the strategy has undergone significant metamorphoses. Since 1991, the economic reforms and the evolution of the new strategy have been well documented.[4]

In this chapter, the reforms since 1991 are not listed for want of space and as they may not be directly relevant. Suffice it to say that the industrial policy, trade and commercial policy, foreign and investment policy and financial sector policy were all deregulated and liberalised to embrace the LPG process. For instance, licensing has been abolished in all but six industries. Major industries, including iron and steel, heavy electrical equipment, aircraft, air transport, shipbuilding, telecommunication equipment and electric power are now open for private sector investments. The monopoly of the public sector industries was abolished in 1991 except for those where security and strategic concerns still dominated. The system of price preference for public sectors has been discontinued. Reservation of certain goods for production in the small-scale sector is gradually being phased out. Tariffs are being reduced in a phased manner. As a result of liberalisation

---

3 Professor Wolfgang Kartte in Brusick, Philippe, *The 1990s: The Decade of Global Competition, Without Restrictive Business Practices?* (1992), Occasional Paper, International Coalition for Development Action, Brussels, November 1992.

4 *See* Ahluwalia, I..J. (1991), *Productivity and Growth in Indian Manufacturing*, New Delhi: Oxford University Press; Bhagwati, J.N. and Desai, P. (1970), *Planning for Industrialisation and Trade Policies since 1951*, New Delhi: Oxford University Press; and Bhagwati, J.N. and Srinivasan, T.N. (1975), *Foreign Trade Regimes and Economic Development: India*, Special Conference Series on Foreign Trade Regimes and Economic Development, New York: NBER.

of regulatory controls, rationalisation and mergers, there is more effective competition in the banking sector. The main objective has been and still is to make the market driven by competitive forces, so that there could be incentives for raising productivity, improving efficiency and reducing costs.

The MRTP Act conceived and legislated nearly four decades ago, was a consequence of the 'command and control' policy approach of the Government. The so-called MRTP firms with assets more than Rs. 100 crores (about US $22 million) were prohibited from entering and expanding in any sector (except a few listed). Even, in respect of such listed sectors, the MRTP firms were required to obtain MRTP clearances in addition to the usual industrial licenses. In other words, the MRTP firms, generally considered big in size, were allowed to grow only under Government supervision. Size, therefore, was a pejorative factor in the thinking of the Government, the premise being 'big becoming bigger is ugly'.

It is after the 1991 reforms that the said premise 'big becoming bigger is ugly' yielded to a metamorphosed approach, namely, 'big becoming bigger may not be handsome but certainly is not ugly'. In other words, size has not been a pejorative factor since 1991.

Another dimension is the dynamic context of international trade and markets as well as the domestic trade and markets. When the MRTP Act was drafted in 1969, the economic and trade milieu prevalent at that time constituted the premise for its various provisions. Subsequently, there has been a sea change in the milieu with considerable movement towards LPG. The law has to yield to the changed and changing scenario on the economic and trade front. The Expert Group[5] observed that competition law and policy were an essential complement to investment liberalisation. It advised that a sound competition policy and law would contribute to securing an attractive environment for foreign investment, particularly foreign direct investment by providing a stable and transparent legal framework and signaling a commitment to market institutions and mechanisms. The competition law should be capable of providing safeguards against possible abuses of market power by foreign investors.

4.2 Mergers and Amalgamations

Concentration of economic power may result from merger, amalgamation or takeover. Prior to the 1991 amendments, the MRTP Act did not

---

[5] *Report of the Expert Group on Interaction between Trade and Competition Policy* (1999), Ministry of Commerce, Government of India. The author was the Chairman of the Group.

prohibit merger, amalgamation or takeover, but sought to ensure that the arrangement subserved public interest and was not anti-competitive. After the 1991 amendments, the MRTP Act has been restructured and pre-entry restrictions with regard to prior approval of the Government for amalgamation, merger or takeover have been removed.

4.3 Metamorphosis from MRTP Act 1969 to Competition Act 2002

A perusal of the MRTP Act will show that there is neither definition nor even a mention of certain offending trade practices, which are restrictive in character. Some illustrations of these are:

- Cartels, collusion and price-fixing
- Bid-rigging
- Boycotts and refusal to deal
- Predatory pricing

In the absence of specific definitions and mention in the MRTP Act of some of the anti-competition practices like cartels, predatory pricing, bid-rigging etc., the MRTP Commission, over the years, has attempted to fit such offences under one or more of its sections by way of interpretation of the language used therein.

During the administration of the MRTP Act over the last three decades and more, there have been a large number of rulings of the Supreme Court of India (binding on everyone in India) and also Bench decisions of the MRTP Commission. These decisions have interpreted the various provisions of the MRTP Act from time to time often not in consonance with each other and have constituted precedents for the future. Thus, where the wording of the existing law has been considered inadequate by judicial pronouncements, redrafting the law to inhere the spirit of the law and the intention of the lawmakers became inevitable and hence the new law, namely, the Competition Act 2002.

4.4 High Level Committee on Competition Policy and Law

In October 1999, the Government of India appointed a High Level Committee[6] on Competition Policy and Competition Law to advise on a modern competition law for the country in line with international developments and to suggest a legislative framework.

---

[6] *Report of The High Level Committee on Competition Policy and Law* (2000), Department of Company Affairs, New Delhi: Government of India.

The Committee was chaired by Mr. S.V.S. Raghavan, a senior retired official of the Central Government. Among others on the Committee were the Chairman of Hindustan Lever Limited, a large company manufacturing fast moving consumer goods, a consumer activist, an economic journalist, a chartered accountant and an advocate, besides the Joint Secretary in the Department of Company Affairs (now Department of Corporate Affairs) dealing with competition law and an expert in the field (the author was a Member of the Committee). The Committee took evidence from the representatives of different Chambers of industries and commerce, professional institutes, consumer organisations (NGOs), experts, academics and Government officials.

At the time of the High Level Committee's deliberations, there were available about 80 competition laws of different countries. No competition law of any one country was adopted as a model, but features of different competition laws considered relevant for India and its prevalent milieu were reckoned in giving a shape to the report.

In terms of the evidence received by the Committee, there was almost unanimity among those who gave their depositions that the MRTP Act had outlived its utility and that a new competition law was required for the country in tune with the post-1991 LPG paradigm. Anterior to the constitution of the Committee, this was well reflected in the announcement of the Finance Minister in his budget speech[7] in February 1999. He observed that,

> The MRTP Act has become obsolete in certain areas in the light of international economic developments relating to competition laws. We need to shift our focus from curbing monopolies to promoting competition. The Government has decided to appoint a committee to examine this range of issues and propose a modern competition law suitable for our conditions.

The Committee presented its Competition Policy report to the Government in May 2000. On the basis of the recommendations of the Committee, a draft competition law was prepared and presented in November 2000 to the Government, which thereupon held wide consultations with stakeholders, like Chambers of Industry and Commerce, consumer organisations etc. A bill on the new competition law was introduced in the Parliament outlining the objects and reasons for its enactment. After effecting some refinements, the Parliament passed in December 2002 the new law, namely, the Competition Act, 2002. This was further amended in 2007.

---

7 *Proceedings of the Parliament* (1999), New Delhi: Indian Parliament.

5 THE NEW INDIAN COMPETITION LAW (COMPETITION ACT 2002)

5.1 New Law

In the context of the new economic policy paradigm, India has chosen to enact a new competition law. In this process, the MRTP Act has metamorphosed into the new law, Competition Act 2002, since amended in 2007 (Act, for brief). The new law is designed to repeal the extant MRTP Act. As of now, only a few provisions of the new law have been brought into force and the process of constituting the regulatory authority, namely, the Competition Commission of India under the new Act, is on. The remaining provisions of the new law will be brought into force shortly. For the present, the outgoing law, MRTP Act 1969 and the new law are concurrently in force, though as mentioned above, only some provisions of the new law have been brought into force.

The narrative that follows[8] addresses the contours and scope of the new law, the Act and contrasts it with the outgoing law, MRTP Act.

The new competition law of India, namely the Act, in its Preamble[9] highlights its major objectives. It seeks *inter alia*, 'to prevent practices having adverse effect on competition, to promote and sustain competition in markets, to protect the interests of consumers and to ensure freedom of trade carried on by other participants in markets in India'.

Singh[10] has argued that competition policy in developing economies should support their overall development path. The Preamble of the Act in line with this approach also mandates that the economic development of the country needs to be kept in view in implementing the Act's objectives.

5.2 Rubric of the New Law, Competition Act 2002 (Act)

The rubric of the Act, as in most competition laws in the world, has essentially four compartments:

---

[8] The narrative that follows is a description of India's new 'Competition Act 2002', as amended in 2007.

[9] Competition Act 2002, *available at:* http://www.cci.gov.in/images/media/competition_act/act2002.pdf (accessed 18 June 2009).

[10] Singh A. (2002), *Competition and Competition Policy in Emerging Markets: International and Development Dimensions*, G-24 discussion paper series, Paper No 18, New York: United Nations.

1 Competition advocacy
2 Anti-competitive agreements
3 Abuse of dominance
4 Combinations regulation

The Competition Commission of India (CCI, for brief) will be responsible for the administration, implementation and enforcement of the Act. The four compartments listed above are described below. Case laws have been cited in support of descriptions of offences under the competition law.[11]

6 COMPETITION ADVOCACY

The Act extends the mandate of the CCI beyond merely enforcing the law. Competition advocacy creates a culture of competition. There are many possible valuable roles for competition advocacy, depending on a country's legal and economic circumstances.

The CCI, in terms of the advocacy provisions in the Act, is enabled to participate in the formulation of the country's economic policies and to participate in the reviewing of laws related to competition at the instance of the Central/State Government. The Government can make a reference to the Commission for its opinion on the possible effect on competition of a policy under formulation or of an existing law related to competition. The CCI is mandated to proffer its opinion to the Government within 60 days of receiving the reference and will therefore be assuming the role of competition advocate, acting pro-actively to bring about Government policies that promote competition in the market place. The opinion, however, will not be binding upon the Government. One of the main objectives of competition advocacy is to foster conditions that lead to a more competitive market structure and business behavior without the direct penalty-loaded intervention of the CCI. Under the scheme of the Act, the CCI's opinion will constitute an important input for the Government to finalise its law or policy, in so far as it impacts on competition.

In order to promote competition advocacy and create awareness about competition issues and also to accord training to all concerned (including the Chairperson and Members of the Commission and its officials), the

[11] As the new Indian Competition Act is yet to be enforced, case laws cited are under the outgoing MRTP Act or under competition regimes outside India. As of now, there is no case law under the new Indian Law.

Act enjoins the establishment of a fund christened the *Competition Fund*. The Fund will be credited with the fees received for filing complaints and applications under the law, grants from the Government, and the interest accrued thereon.

At first glance, the advocacy role of the Commission might seem somewhat of a luxury, especially for a developing country such as India, which faces numerous competing priorities in implementing competition disciplines. However it cannot be gainsaid that competition policy advocacy has the potential for a significant impact upon general economic development. Investment in competition advocacy is bound to bear fruit in the long term by reducing the challenges to competition. Recognising this, the Act provides for statutory grounding of the advocacy role of the CCI, while at the same time providing for adequate resource support.

7 ANTI-COMPETITIVE AGREEMENTS

The Act is designed to allow scrutiny by the CCI of any agreement between enterprises that has an appreciable adverse effect on competition. This standard is similar to the 'substantial lessening of competition' standard used in the United States and Australia, for example. Although expressed in somewhat different words, it is also similar to the new European Commission standard which governs practices/activities/mergers that 'significantly impede effective competition'.

7.1 Horizontal Agreements

Following the general view of most other competition regimes, the Act lists horizontal agreements among competitors and vertical agreements between enterprises at different levels of manufacturing or distribution processes. The Act generally adopts what is usually described as the 'rule of reason' which requires proof of an anti-competitive effect, but also adopts '*per se*' illegal rule for a category of offences which are regarded to have no useful or pro-competitive effect. The Act presumes (*per se* rule) that the following four types of agreements have an appreciable adverse effect on competition if entered into between enterprises involved in the same or similar manufacturing or trading of goods or provision of services:

1. Agreement that directly or indirectly determines purchase or sale prices (for example, cartels);

2. Agreement that limits or controls production, supply, markets, technical development, investment or provision of services;
3. Agreement that directly or indirectly results in bid-rigging or collusive bidding;
4. Agreement that shares the market or source of production or provision of services by way of allocation of geographical area of market or type of goods or services or number of customers in the market or any other similar way.

All other horizontal agreements will be subject to the 'rule of reason' test in the Act. Case laws describing some of the *per se* offences listed above merit inclusion here.

Under the outgoing Indian Competition Law, the MRTP Act, 1969, a soda ash export cartel of the US was challenged and the charge of cartelisation was tested by domestic producers. Box 5.1 below provides a summary of the case.

BOX 5.1 SODA ASH EXPORT CARTEL

In September 1996, American Natural Soda Ash Corporation (ANSAC), an export trading company comprising six American producers of soda ash and registered under the Webb-Pomerene Act in the US attempted to ship a consignment of soda ash to India. ANSAC, for its export activities stood exempted from the operation of competition law in US. The Alkali Manufacturers Association of India (AMAI), whose members included the major Indian producers of soda ash, filed a complaint against ANSAC before the MRTP Commission alleging, *inter alia*, cartelisation. The Commission[12] imposed an interim injunction on ANSAC restraining it from exporting soda ash to India as a cartel. Quoting from the ANSAC membership agreement, the Commission held that ANSAC was *prima facie* a cartel, which was carrying out part of its trade practices in India, giving the Commission extra-territorial jurisdiction under the MRTP Act. The Commission clarified that the American firms could export to India individually.

---

12 *Alkali Manufacturers Association of India v American Natural Soda Ash Corporation (ANSAC) and others* (1997)–1997 (5) CTJ, 288, MRTP Commission. *See* also n 26.

The now famous (or infamous) case of the Vitamins cartel is illustrative of the manifest adverse effect on consumers particularly in the developing countries. See Box 5.2 below.

Enterprises may combine to limit supply of goods to the market and to impose conditions restricting dissemination of technology and thus prejudice competition. Box 5.3 below bears testimony to such prejudice.

Bid-rigging is often resorted to in public procurement tenders. The possibility of bid-rigging will be particularly relevant to public sector purchasers, given their legal obligations to award contracts by competitive tender. The rigging parties perceive the Government to be blind to collusive practices and consequently indulge in bid-rigging while responding to tenders. This imposes heavy costs on the public treasury and therefore on taxpayers. This also undermines confidence in the Government. Consumers are visited with high prices and with prejudice to their interests. See Box 5.4 below.

BOX 5.2 INTERNATIONAL VITAMINS CARTEL

Vitamins constitute an important ingredient/product supplied to the food processing industry and the animal feed industry. Food companies blend raw vitamins into bread, rice and juice. An example of animal feed industry would be huge chicken farms. Producers of vitamins formed a cartel dividing up the world market for different types of vitamins during the 1990s. The conspiracy appears to have begun in 1989, when executives at Roche AG and BASF began holding talks about price-fixing. They decided to carve up the vitamin market. Many other vitamin producers joined the cartel. The cartel operated for over ten years in a fairly stable manner. The cartel was prosecuted.[13] Roche paid fines of US $500 million and the total fines collected exceeded US $1 billion in the US alone.

The overcharges paid by 90 countries importing vitamins were estimated at US $2700 million. Damage-wise, India incurred overcharges of more than US $25 million (if PPP ratio is reckoned, US $220 million).

---

[13] Clarke, J.L. and S.J. Evenett (2003), 'The Deterrent Effects of National Anti-Cartel Laws: Evidence from the International Vitamins Cartel', *Antitrust Bulletin*.

BOX 5.3 LIMITING PRODUCTION AND RESTRICTING TECHNICAL KNOW-HOW

Sarabhai M. Chemicals Private Limited entered into a technological know-how agreement with its overseas collaborator, E. Merck A.G., providing for the provision of know-how by the latter to the former to enable Sarabhai to manufacture pharmaceutical chemicals, vitamins, insecticides etc. in India. The agreement stipulated that Merck's licensees (like Sarabhai) should not directly or indirectly manufacture certain items (about 520 out of 600 items) in India and that Merck would be free to import into India such items and sell the same. Sarabhai's request for technological know-how for the manufacture of certain pharmaceuticals and Vitamins was turned down by Merck. The MRTP Commission[14] held that the agreement had an adverse effect on competition because of the denial of access to the technological know-how and was also a barrier to entry to other intending manufacturers.

BOX 5.4 MEDICAL OXYGEN SUPPLY – BID-RIGGING CARTEL

Four foreign companies, namely, Air Liquide (France), Praxair (US), AGA (Germany) and Indura (Chile) were the suppliers of medical oxygen to both public and private hospitals in Argentina. These companies formed a cartel and entered into an agreement to indulge in bid-rigging and to distribute and divide customers among themselves. The Competition Authority in Argentina conducted four raids, in which it found certain documents showing exchange of information about the customers, bids, prices etc. As a result of bid-rigging and collusion, hospitals and consumers were forced to pay high prices. And the cartel members enjoyed illegally high profits. The Competition Authority succeeded in

[14] *In re Sarabhai Chemicals Private Limited* (1978), RTPE No 45/75, 49 Comp Cases 145, MRTP Commission.

getting the four companies prosecuted and levied with fines amounting to US $24 million. The successful prosecution of the bid-rigging and price-fixing cartel was welcomed by the consumers in Argentina.[15]

7.2 Vertical Agreements

By and large, in most competition regimes, vertical agreements are not subjected to the rigours of competition law. However, where a vertical agreement has the character of distorting or preventing competition, it is placed under the surveillance of the law, subject to the 'rule of reason' test. The Act does not mention any such approach but has listed *inter alia*, the following types of agreements, to be treated under the 'rule of reason' test.

- Tie-in arrangements;
- Exclusive supply agreements;
- Exclusive distribution agreements;
- Refusals to deal; and
- Resale price maintenance.

Some simple examples of tie-ins are requiring the buyers of cars to pay towards the servicing of cars with the sale price; insistence by the gas distributor on the buyer of a gas connection to buy a gas stove as a condition; and prescribing a condition by banks on a customer to take a fixed deposit for allocation of a locker etc. Box 5.5 below is an illustration of a tie-in arrangement undermining the interest of consumers.

7.3 Factors to be Reckoned in Adjudicating Appreciable Adverse Effect

The Act lists the following factors to be taken into account for determining whether an agreement or a practice has an appreciable adverse effect on competition, namely,

- creation of barriers to new entrants in the market;
- driving existing competitors out of the market;
- foreclosure of competition by hindering entry into the market;
- accrual of benefits to consumers;

15 *Recent Important Cases* (2005), Report by UNCTAD Secretariat, Geneva.

BOX 5.5 *FEDERAL TRADE COMMISSION V BROWN SHOE COMPANY* – A TIE-IN ARRANGEMENT

One of the largest shoe manufacturers in the US is the Brown Shoe Company. It owned some retail shoe stores. In addition, there were about 650 retail stores, franchisees of Brown. Only about 250 of the said 650 retail franchisees had executed franchise agreements. The franchise agreements stipulated that the franchisee should concentrate on Brown's shoes in return for Brown's provision of architectural plans, merchandising records and group insurance at lower rates than what the franchisee could individually obtain and so on. Brown admitted that it did not grant such benefits to retailers who did not participate in the franchise programme. The Federal Trade Commission held the franchise programme violative of the Federal Trade Commission Act 1914 and the Clayton Act 1914, both competition laws of the US.

The matter went up to the Supreme Court of the US. In its ruling, the Supreme Court observed that the franchise programme conflicted with the policy of the Sherman Act and the Clayton Act against anti-competitive contracts and that it infringed on the freedom of purchasers to buy in an open market. In other words, the Brown franchise programme was unfair and was undermining competition in the market.[16]

- improvements in production or distribution of goods or provision of services; and
- promotion of technical, scientific and economic development by means of distribution of goods or provision of services.

8 ABUSE OF DOMINANCE

8.1 Dominant Position

The phrase 'Dominant Position' has been appropriately defined in the Act in terms of the 'position of strength, enjoyed by an enterprise, in the

[16] *See* 384 US 316 (1966).

relevant market, in India, which enables it to (i) operate independently of competitive forces prevailing in the relevant market; or (ii) affect its competitors or consumers or the relevant market, in its favour'.

This definition may perhaps appear to be somewhat ambiguous and to be capable of different interpretations by different judicial authorities. But then, this ambiguity has a justification having regard to the fact that even a firm with a low market share of just 20 per cent with the remaining 80 per cent diffusedly held by a large number of competitors may be in a position to abuse its dominance, while a firm with say 60 per cent market share with the remaining 40 per cent held by a competitor may not be in a position to abuse its dominance because of the key rivalry in the market. Specifying a threshold or an arithmetical figure for defining dominance may defy objectivity and may either allow real offenders to escape (as in the first example above) or result in unnecessary litigation (as in the second example above). With this suggested broad definition, the regulatory authority will have the freedom to correct errant firms and encourage competitive market practices, even if there is a large player around.

Abuse of dominance is key for the Act, in so far as dominant enterprises are concerned. As already stated, there is no single objective market share criterion that can be blindly used as a test of dominance. The Act seeks to ensure that only when dominance is clearly established can abuse of dominance be alleged. Any ambiguity on this count could endanger large, efficient firms.

8.2 'Relevant Market' Definition

Before assessing whether an undertaking is dominant, it is important to determine what the relevant market is. There are two dimensions to this – the product market and the geographical market. On the demand side, the relevant product market includes all such substitutes that the consumer would switch to, if the price of the product relevant to the investigation were to increase. From the supply side, this would include all producers who could, with their existing facilities, switch to the production of such substitute goods. The geographical boundaries of the relevant market can be similarly defined. Geographic dimension involves identification of the geographical area within which competition takes place. Relevant geographic markets could be local, national, international or occasionally even global, depending upon the facts in each case. Some factors relevant to geographic dimension are consumption and shipment patterns, transportation costs, perishability and existence of barriers to the shipment of products between adjoining geographic areas. For example, in view of the high transportation costs in cement, the relevant geographical market may be the region close to the manufacturing facility. The Act defines 'Relevant Market'.

The Act posits the factors that would have to be considered by the adjudicating Authority (namely, the CCI) in determining the 'Relevant Product Market' and the 'Relevant Geographic Market'. The determination of 'Relevant Market' by the adjudicating Authority CCI is to be done, having due regard to the 'Relevant Product Market' and the 'Relevant Geographic Market'.

8.3 Abuse of Dominance is the Evil Prohibited

In general, actions that are considered anti-competitive and illegal in the context of agreements are also illegal, if undertaken by a dominant firm. These would include charging or paying unfair prices, restriction of quantities, markets and technical development. Discriminatory behavior and any other exercise of market power leading to the prevention, restriction or distortion of competition would obviously be included. Dominance and its abuse are defined in the Act.

8.4 Factors Governing Dominance and Abuse of Dominance

The Act lists factors constituting 'dominance' and 'abuse of dominance'. Dominance is determined by taking into account one or more of the following factors:

- size and resources of the enterprise;
- size and importance of the competitors;
- economic power of the enterprise including commercial advantages over competitors;
- vertical integration of the enterprise, or sale or service network of such enterprise;
- dependence of consumers on the enterprise;
- monopoly or dominant position whether acquired as a result of any statute or by virtue of being a Government company or a public sector undertaking or otherwise;
- entry barriers including barriers such as regulatory barriers, financial risk, high capital cost of entry, marketing entry barriers, technical entry barriers, economies of scale, high cost of substitutable goods or service for consumers;
- countervailing buying power;
- market structure and size of market;
- social obligations and social costs;

- relative advantage, by way of the contribution to the economic development, by the enterprise enjoying a dominant position having or likely to have an appreciable adverse effect on competition; and
- any other factor which the Commission may consider relevant for the inquiry.

Abuse of dominance having an appreciable adverse effect on competition occurs if an enterprise:

- directly or indirectly, imposes unfair or discriminatory –
  (i) condition in purchase or sale of goods or service; or
  (ii) price in purchase or sale (including predatory price) of goods or service,
- limits or restricts –
  (i) production of goods or provision of services or market therefor; or
  (ii) technical or scientific development relating to goods or services to the prejudice of consumers; or
- indulges in practice or practices resulting in denial of market access; or
- makes conclusion of contracts subject to acceptance by other parties of supplementary obligations which, by their nature or according to commercial usage, have no connection with the subject of such contracts, or
- uses its dominant position in one relevant market to enter into, or protect, other relevant market.

An explanation in the Act declares that an unfair or discriminatory condition in purchase or sale of goods or service and an unfair or discriminatory price in purchase or sale of goods or service will not include such discriminatory condition or price *which may be adopted to meet the competition.*

A great threat to competition arises from actions of dominant firms that are inimical to future competition. Predatory pricing is one such.

8.5 Predatory Pricing

One of the most pernicious forms of abuse of dominance is the practice of predatory pricing. Predatory pricing occurs where a dominant enterprise charges low prices over a long enough period of time so as to drive a competitor from the market or deter others from entering the market and then

BOX 5.6 PREDATORY PRICING – MODERN FOOD INDUSTRIES

In a case[17] that came up before the MRTP Commission involving a complaint of predatory pricing against Modern Food Industries, the Commission observed that the essence of predatory pricing is pricing below cost with a view to eliminating a rival. Further, the Commission made it clear that the 'mere offer of a price lower than the cost of production cannot automatically lead to an indictment of predatory pricing' and that evidence of 'malafide intent to drive competitors out of business or to eliminate competition' is required. Price-cutting has therefore to be coupled with the *mens rea* of eliminating a competitor or competition to become an offence under competition law.

raises prices to recoup its losses. Predatory pricing as specifically explained in the Act, must have the *mens rea* of reducing competition or eliminating competitors. See Box 5.6.

Distinguishing predatory behavior from legitimate competition is difficult. The distinction between low prices which result from predatory behavior and low prices which result from legitimate competitive behavior is often very thin and not easily ascertainable. Predatory pricing can be benign to consumers in some circumstances, but can be malignant to them, if the predator's intent is to eliminate competition or competitors. Indeed, it is sometimes argued[18] that predatory behavior is a necessary concomitant of competition. An 'unreasonably low price' is determined according to the relationship of the price to the underlying cost of production. The Act has left it to the CCI to deal with the determination of the cost of production. Framing an economic test is necessary to adjudicate as to when a price is predatory.

It may therefore be seen that the Act does not frown upon dominance as such but frowns upon *abuse* of dominance.

---

17 *In Re Modern Food Industries Ltd* (1996) 3 Comp LJ 154, MRTP Commission.

18 Bhagwati Jagdish (1999), *A Stream of Windows – Unsettling Reflections on Trade, Immigration and Democracy*, New Delhi: Oxford University Press.

9 COMBINATIONS REGULATION

9.1 Combinations

Combinations, in terms of the meaning given to them in the Act, include mergers, amalgamations, acquisitions and acquisitions of control.

The compartment dealing with combinations was one of the most debated ones among the four compartments in the Act, when it was in its draft form (which was placed on the website inviting comments and suggestions). Even though the expression 'Combinations', is wide in its purport as noted above, for the purposes of the discussion that follows, mergers regulation alone has been reckoned.

9.2 The Act on Combinations Regulation

The Act makes it compulsory for the parties to notify their proposed agreement or combinations to the CCI, if the aggregate assets of the combining parties have a value in excess of Rs. 1000 crores (US $220 million) or turnover in excess of Rs. 3000 crores (US $660 million). In the event either of the combining parties is outside India or both are outside, the threshold limits are US $500 million for assets including at least Rs. 500 crores in India, or US $1500 million for turnover, including at least Rs. 1500 crores in India.

If one of the merging parties belongs to a group, which controls it, the threshold limits are Rs. 4000 crores (US $880 million) in terms of assets and Rs. 12000 crores (US $2640 million) in terms of turnover. If the group has assets or turnover outside India also, the threshold limits are US $2 billion for assets including at least Rs. 500 crores in India, and US $6 billion for turnover including at least Rs. 1500 crores in India.

For this purpose, 'group' and 'control' are defined in the Act. The threshold limits of assets and of turnover would be revised every two years on the basis of the Wholesale Price Index or fluctuations in exchange rate of rupee or foreign currencies.

In terms of the Act only big combinations are placed under its regulatory provisions. In other words, small and medium combinations would be outside the pale of the Act.

9.3 Adjudication on Combinations

The Act has prescribed a number of factors (not listed here for want of space) to be taken into account for the purpose of determining whether the combination would have the effect of or be likely to have an appreciable adverse effect on competition.

The Regulatory Authority, namely, the CCI is mandated to adjudicate on combinations by weighing potential efficiency losses against potential gains. An example of weighing the benefits of a combination against its adverse impact on competition is at Box 5.7. In order that the CCI should not delay its adjudication on whether a combination may pass through or may be stopped because of its anti-competitive nature, the Act admonishes the Regulatory Authority to hand in its adjudicatory decision within 210 days from the date of notice given to the CCI by the parties, lest the combination be deemed to have been approved.

The Act also provides for limiting the regulatory Authority's power to ask for information from the merging parties within a time frame of 15 working days with a corresponding obligation on the merging parties to furnish the information within a further 15 days. Thus by law, the sequencing of the adjudicatory exercise has been set within specific time frames, so that possible delays are avoided.

BOX 5.7 GOOGLE WRAPS UP DOUBLECLICK ACQUISITION

Google Inc, owner of the world's most popular search engine, won European Union approval to buy DoubleClick Inc, clearing the way for the completion of the biggest acquisition in its nine-year history. Google announced the proposed purchase of DoubleClick in April 2008 to bolster its sales of Internet advertisements that include pictures and videos. DoubleClick is a significant player in the $40 billion online advertising business. Google accounted for 58.5 per cent of all searches in the US in January 2008, according to ComScore[19]. In some European countries, it has 80–90 per cent. Google also accounted for 28 per cent of the $21.4 billion online advertising market in the US in 2007, according to eMarketer (see footnote 19).

Google's competitors including Yahoo! Inc and Microsoft Corp, expressed concerns that the combination would allow Google to extend its Internet dominance and hurt competition in the global online advertising market. Microsoft complained to US and EU officials that it may be shut out of the combined company's advertisement network. They also apprehended that the combination

[19] *See* Deccan Chronicle, Hyderabad, 13 March 2008.

(acquisition) could help create a digital colossus by allowing Google to strengthen its position in other kinds of online advertising including display advertisements like banners and television-like video spots.

The European Commission, the 27-Nation EU's anti-trust authority in Brussels accorded approval to the acquisition and said in a statement on 11 March 2008 that the $3.1 billion deal can proceed without conditions.[20]

The Commission said in the statement: 'The Commission's in-depth market investigation found that Google and DoubleClick were not exerting major competitive constraints on each other's activities and could, therefore, not be considered as competitors,' implying thereby that the benefits of the combination would outweigh the adverse impact on competition.

10 EXCEPTIONS AND EXEMPTIONS

10.1 Exceptions of IPR Statutes

The Act has some exceptions on its applicability. For instance, provisions relating to anti-competition agreements will not restrict the right of any person to restrain any infringement of intellectual property rights or to impose such reasonable conditions as may be necessary for the purposes of protecting any of his rights which have been or may be conferred upon him under the following intellectual property right statutes:

- the Copyright Act 1957;
- the Patents Act 1970;
- the Trade and Merchandise Marks Act 1958 or the Trade Marks Act 1999;
- the Geographical Indications of Goods (Registration and Protection) Act 1999;
- the Designs Act 2000; and
- the Semi-conductor Integrated Circuits Layout-Design Act 2000.

The rationale for this exception is that the bundle of rights that are subsumed in intellectual property rights should not be disturbed in the

20 *See* Business Line, Chennai, 12 March 2008.

interests of creativity and intellectual/innovative power of the human mind. No doubt, this bundle of rights essays an anti-competition character, even bordering on monopoly power. But without protecting such rights, there will be no incentive for innovation, new technology and enhancement in the quality of products and services. For example, a licensing arrangement may include restraints that adversely affect competition in goods markets by dividing the markets among firms that would have competed using different technologies. Similarly, an arrangement that effectively merges the research and development activities of two of only a few entities that could plausibly engage in research and development in the relevant field might harm competition for development of new goods and services. Exclusive licensing is another category of possible unreasonable condition. Examples of arrangements involving exclusive licensing that may give rise to anti-competition concerns include cross licensing by parties collectively possessing market power, grantbacks and acquisitions of intellectual property rights.

The conflict between IPRs and the competition law came up before the Monopolies and Restrictive Trade Practices Commission (MRTPC) in India in *Vallal Peruman and another v Godfrey Phillips (India) Ltd.* Box 5.8 narrates the Commission's ruling.

10.2 Another Exception – Export Cartels

Yet another exception in the Act to the applicability of the provisions relating to anti-competition agreements is the right of any person to export goods from India, to the extent to which an agreement relates exclusively to the production, supply, distribution or control of goods or provision of services for such export.

While cartels are generally outlawed in many competition statutes, export cartels are generally exempted. Competition laws implicitly or explicitly exempt export cartels, perhaps on the consideration of 'beggar thy neighbour'. A justification for this exemption is that most countries do not desire any shackles on their export effort in the interest of balance of trade and/or balance of payments. Holistically, such a consideration may not be ethically justified, but yet most, if not all, countries are bothered about their domestic markets rather than the global. Exemption of export cartels is against the concept of free competition. There are however proponents of export cartels, which reasonably relate to the lawful realisation of cost-reducing or output-enhancing efficiencies.[21] Many countries regard

---

21 *Hard Core Cartels: Recent Progress and Challenges Ahead* (2003), Paris: OECD.

BOX 5.8 *VALLAL PERUMAN AND ANOTHER V GODFREY PHILLIPS*

The MRTP Commission[22] in *Vallal Peruman v Godfrey Phillips* observed as follows:

> 'Applying the above principles to the controversy at hand, it seems . . . that a certificate of registration held by an individual or an undertaking invests in him/it, an undoubted right to use trade mark/name etc. so long as the certificate of registration is in operation and more importantly, so long as the trade mark is used strictly in conformity with the terms and conditions subject to which it was granted. If however, while presenting the goods and merchandise for sale in the market or for promotion thereof, the holder of the certificate misuses the same by manipulation, distortion, contrivances and embellishments etc. so as to mislead or confuse the consumers, he would be exposing himself to an action . . . of indulging in unfair trade practices. It will, thus, be seen that the provisions of the Monopolies and Restrictive Trade Practices Act would be attracted only when there is an abuse in exercise of the right protected . . .' This principle was reiterated in *Manju Bhardwaj's* case[23] by the same Commission.

export cartels as competition-restricting in character, but still exempt them from their competition laws and some others regard them as having competition-enhancing efficiencies. Evenett et al[24] and OECD[25] between them have listed 15 countries whose competition laws explicitly or implicitly exclude export cartels.

10.3 Exemptions Granted by the Central Government to a Class of Enterprises, Any Practice, or Any Agreement

The Central Government has power under the Act to exempt from the application of the Act, or any provision thereof, a class of enterprises in the interest of security of the State or public interest, any practice or agreement arising out of any obligation assumed by India under any treaty,

---

22 *Vallal Peruman and Dileep Singh Bhuria v Godfrey Phillips (India) Ltd*, (1994) IA 91/92 in UTPE 180/92, MRTP Commission.

23 *Manju Bhardwaj v Zee Telefilms Ltd and Others* (1996) UTPE 148/95, MRTP Commission.

24 Evenett, S.J., M.C. Levenstein and V.Y. Suslow (2001), 'International Cartel Enforcement: Lessons from the 1990s', *The World Economy*, **24**, 1221–1245.

25 *Coverage of Competition Law: Illustrative Examples of Exclusions* (2003), Document CNM/GF/COMP/TR(2003) 17, Paris: OECD.

agreement or convention with other countries and any enterprise which performs a sovereign function on behalf of the Central Government or any State Government.

11 EXTRA-TERRITORIAL REACH

The Act has extra-territorial reach. Its arm extends beyond the geographical contours of India to deal with practices and actions outside India which have an appreciable adverse affect on competition in the relevant market in India. The Commission has the power to inquire into an agreement, abuse of dominant position or combination, if it has or is likely to have an *appreciable adverse affect on competition in the relevant market in India,* notwithstanding that:

- an agreement has been entered into outside India;
- any party to such agreement is outside India;
- any enterprise abusing the dominant position is outside India;
- a combination has taken place outside India;
- any party to combination is outside India; or
- any other matter or practice or action arising out of such agreement or dominant position or combination is outside India.

The above provisions are based on what is known as the 'effects doctrine'. This doctrine implies that even if an action or practice is outside the shores of India but has an impact or effect on competition in the relevant market in India; it can be brought within the ambit of the Act, provided the effect is appreciably adverse on competition. Box 5.9 below describes a case law on extra-territorial jurisdiction of the outgoing MRTP Act 1969.

In September 1998 the All India Float Glass Manufacturers' Association filed a complaint in the MRTP Commission against three Indonesian companies manufacturing float glass alleging that the latter in association with Indian importers were resorting to restrictive and unfair trade practices and in particular selling float glass at predatory prices in India. They further alleged that the sale of float glass by the Indonesian manufacturers at predatory prices would restrict, distort and prevent competition by pricing out Indian producers from the market. The MRTP Commission issued an injunction against the Indonesian companies from exporting float glass to India. However, this was carried in appeal to the Supreme Court,[26] which

[26] *Haridas Exports v All India Float Glass Manufacturers Association* (2002), Supreme Court 6 SCC 600.

BOX 5.9 EXTRA-TERRITORIAL JURISDICTION – *FLOAT GLASS* CASE

Extra-territorial jurisdiction is based on the concept of 'effects doctrine'. Both the MRTP Act 1969 and the Competition Act 2002 have provisions empowering the Competition Authority to have extra-territorial jurisdiction. If enterprises outside India indulge in trade practices, not necessarily restricted to the effectuation of prices within India, which have the effect of preventing, distorting or restricting competition in India or give rise to restrictive trade practices in India, then in respect of those restrictive trade practices, the Competition Authority will have jurisdiction.

ruled that the MRTP Commission had no extra-territorial jurisdiction in the float glass case and that it cannot pass an order determining the export price of an exporter to India or prohibiting him to export to India at a low or predatory price. This decision of the Supreme Court led to arming the Competition Commission of India under the Competition Act 2002 (as amended in 2007) with the power to temporarily restrain any party from carrying on an act which constitutes an anti-competitive practice or abuse of dominance until the conclusion of its inquiry. How the Competition Commission of India would be dealing with such cases in future will be eagerly awaited.

12 SECTORAL REGULATORS

Over the years, especially after economic reforms were initiated in India in the early nineties, a number of sectoral regulatory authorities have been formed. For telecoms, there is the Telecommunications Regulatory Authority of India (TRAI). For electricity, there is Central Electricity Regulatory Commission (CERC) at the federal level and State Electricity Regulatory Commission (SERC) in most States. Securities and Exchange Board of India (SEBI) looks after the operation of the capital market while the banking and the financial sectors are regulated by the Reserve Bank of India, the Central Bank. Insurance Regulatory and Development Authority (IRDA) has been created to regulate the newly opened insurance sector. There are other statutory bodies for regulating some other sectors and some more are in the offing.

Regulatory authorities have been set up in several sectors to produce competitive outcomes, that is, foster greater efficiency in resource allocation and consumer welfare through maintaining and promoting competition. The question of overlapping jurisdictions between the competition authority and sectoral regulators is a challenge and the Act has evolved a mechanism to resolve the same.

The Act empowers any Statutory Authority regulating any utility or service to make a reference (discretionary, not mandatory) to the CCI, if an issue is raised by a party that any decision of that Authority is or would be contrary to its provisions. The Statutory Authority has the right to decide on the raised issue without making a reference to the Commission. Even if the issue is not raised by a party, the Act gives the Statutory Authority the power *suo motu* to make a reference to the CCI. Section 21 further requires the Statutory Authority to consider the opinion of the CCI and thereafter give its findings recording reasons therefor on the issues referred to in the said opinion. Though not explicit, this would imply that the opinion of the CCI is not binding on the Statutory Authority.

13 LENIENCY PROVISIONS

A unique feature in the Act is the presence of what are known as 'Leniency Provisions'. These provisions allow for the imposition of a reduced penalty on a participant in a cartel, who makes full, true and vital disclosures of having violated the Act. The logic behind these provisions is that cartels are a hard nut to crack. More often than not, cartels will not have formal or written agreements. Essentially, they operate on oral understandings. Consequently, proving a cartel or cartelisation is beset with practical difficulties and in particular, absence of evidence. But, if a participant in a cartel is prepared to blow the whistle, the CCI should be able to secure evidence through him/it and in return offer amnesty or reduction in penalty to the whistle blower. Aditya Bhattacharjea[27] commenting on this provision, suggests that leniency should be available to more than one participant and at various stages of the proceedings in exchange for evidence that could be used to prosecute co-conspirators. He has cited the US and EU schemes in support. The Act reckons this.

[27] Aditya Bhattacharjea (2003), 'India's Competition Policy: An Assessment', *Economic and Political Weekly*, XXXVIII, **34**, 23 August.

14 INVESTIGATION, PROSECUTION, ADJUDICATION AND SELECTION PROCEDURE

14.1 Investigation and Prosecution

The adjudicative wing is distinct and separate from the investigative wing in the Act. At the apex level of the investigative wing, there is an official who has been designated as Director General (DG). The Director General does not have *suo motu* powers of investigation. He will only look into the complaints received from the CCI and submit his findings to it. Investigators will be solely responsible for making enquiries, for examining documents, for making investigations into complaints and for effecting interface with other investigative agencies of the Government including Ministries and Departments. The DG will be the prosecuting authority.

14.2 Adjudication

A two-tier arrangement is provided in the Act to consider and dispose of competition cases and make adjudications thereon. The first tier is the Competition Commission of India (CCI) and the other is the Competition Appellate Tribunal (CAT).

14.2.1 Competition Commission of India

The Competition Commission of India is the adjudicating body under the Act with autonomy and administrative powers.

The Act will be administered by the CCI, which will be composed of a Chairperson and not less than two and not more than six other members appointed by the Central Government, and assisted by a staff led by a Director General. Initially, the Commission consisting of only one Member has been addressing just the *competition advocacy function* with the other functions to be brought into force when the Central Government decides.

CCI will be a multi-member body with its Chairperson and Members chosen for their special knowledge and experience (of not less than 15 years) in International Trade, Economics, Business, Commerce, Law, Finance, Accountancy, Management, Industry, Public Affairs or Competition Matters including Competition Law and Policy. Besides, they need to be persons of ability, integrity and standing.

The Act has provided for a 'Collegium Selection Process', in the form of a Selection Committee which will recommend a panel of names to the Government. The Committee will be chaired by the Chief Justice of India or his nominee and will include the Secretary in the Ministry of Corporate Affairs, Secretary in the Ministry of Law and Justice and two experts of repute with special knowledge of and professional experience in the areas listed for the Chairperson and Members of the CCI. This collegium selection approach is expected to ensure minimisation of politicisation of appointments and rational selection of suitable persons to man the CCI.

14.2.2 Competition Appellate Tribunal (CAT)

CAT is the second tier and constitutes the appellate body to hear and dispose of appeals against any direction issued or decision made or order passed by the CCI under various provisions of the Act. The appellate body is also empowered to adjudicate on claims for compensation that may arise from the findings of the CCI or the orders of CAT in an appeal against any finding of the CCI.

The composition of CAT consists of a Chairperson and not more than two other Members to be appointed by the Central Government. The Chairperson is required to be a person, who is, or has been a Judge of the Supreme Court or the Chief Justice of a High Court. A Member of CAT is required to be a person of ability, integrity and standing having special knowledge of, and professional experience of not less than 25 years in, competition matters including competition law and policy, international trade, economics, business, commerce, law, finance, accountancy, management, industry, public affairs, administration or in any other matter which in the opinion of the Central Government, may be useful to the Appellate Tribunal.

Like in the case of CCI, the Chairperson and Members of CAT will be appointed by the Central Government from a panel of names recommended by a Collegium (Selection Committee). The Selection Committee for CAT consists of:

(a) the Chief Justice of India or his nominee – Chairperson;
(b) the Secretary in the Ministry of Corporate Affairs – Member;
(c) the Secretary in the Ministry of Law and Justice – Member.

The Chairperson or a Member of CAT will hold office for a term of five years from the date on which he enters upon his office, and shall be eligible for re-appointment; provided that no Chairperson or other Member of the Appellate Tribunal shall hold office as such after he has attained:

(a) in the case of the Chairperson, the age of 68 years;
(b) in the case of any other Member of CAT, the age of 65 years.

14.3 Powers of CCI and CAT

Where after inquiry the CCI finds that any anti-competitive agreement or action of an enterprise in a dominant position is in contravention of the relevant provisions of the Act, it may pass all or any of the following orders, namely:

(a) direct any enterprise or association of enterprises or person or association of persons, as the case may be, involved in such agreement, or abuse of dominant position, to discontinue and not to re-enter such agreement or discontinue such abuse of dominant position, as the case may be;
(b) impose such penalty, as it may deem fit which shall be not more than ten per cent of the average of the turnover for the last three preceding financial years, upon each of such person or enterprises which are parties to such agreements or abuse; provided that in case any agreement has been entered into by a cartel, the CCI may impose upon each producer, seller, distributor, trader or service provider included in that cartel, a penalty of up to three times of its profit or ten per cent of its turnover for each year of the continuance of such agreement, whichever is higher;
(c) direct that the agreements shall stand modified to the extent and in the manner as may be specified in the order by the CCI;
(d) direct the enterprises concerned to abide by such other orders as the CCI may pass and comply with the directions, including payment of costs, if any;
(e) pass such other order or issue such directions as it may deem fit.

The CCI has the power to direct division of an enterprise enjoying dominant position to ensure that such enterprise does not abuse its dominant position. The CCI also has the power to approve a combination, to direct that a combination shall not take effect or approve a combination with suitable modifications.

14.4 Independence and Autonomy of CCI

Independence and autonomy of the CCI are to a great extent protected in the Act. Firstly, the selection of Chairperson and Members of the CCI is through the collegium selection process, minimising politicisation of appointments. Secondly, removal by the Central Government of the Chairperson and Members is conditioned by prior enquiry and concurrence of the Supreme Court (concurrence is required in respect of specific grounds listed in the Act). Thus there cannot be arbitrary removal of the Chairperson and Members. This facilitates independence of the CCI.

15 APPEAL PROVISIONS

Appeals against decisions and orders of the CCI lie to CAT as noted above. The appeal has to be filed within 60 days of receipt of the CCI's order or direction. A further appeal lies to the Supreme Court within the limitation period of 60 days from the date of communication of the decision or order of CAT to the party. Thus, the status given to CAT is very high with only the Supreme Court having the power to overturn its orders.

16 NEW WINE IN A NEW BOTTLE

The Act is therefore a new wine in a new bottle. Wine gets better as it ages. The extant MRTP Act, 1969 has aged for more than three decades and has given birth to the new law, Competition Act 2002 (amended in Sept 2007) in line with the current economic thinking comprising the post-1991 liberalisation paradigm. The Act covers all of the 29 States (and six Union Territories) of India, except for the State of Jammu and Kashmir. The differences between the MRTP Act and the Competition Act are captured in Table 5.1.

17 EFFECTIVE ENFORCEMENT

The gains sought through competition law can only be realised with effective enforcement. Weak enforcement of competition law is perhaps worse than the absence of competition law. Weak enforcement often reflects a number of factors such as inadequate funding of the enforcement authority. The Government should provide the required infrastructure and funds to make the CCI an effective Tribunal to prevent, if not eliminate anti-competition practices and also to play its role of competition advocacy.

18 FINALE

In the context of the new economic policy paradigm, India has chosen to enact a new competition law called the Competition Act 2002 (Act). The MRTP Act has metamorphosed into the new law. The new law is designed

Table 5.1 Differences between the MRTP Act and the Competition Act

	MRTP Act 1969	Competition Act 2002 (amended in 2007)
1	Based on the pre-reforms scenario	Based on the post-reforms scenario
2	Based on size as a factor	Based on structure as a factor
3	Competition offences implicit or not defined	Competition offences explicit and defined
4	Complex in arrangement and language	Simple in arrangement and language
5	14 *per se* offences negating the principles of natural justice	Four *per se* offences and all the rest subjected to rule of reason.
6	Frowns upon dominance	Frowns upon abuse of dominance
7	Registration of agreements compulsory	No requirement of registration of agreements
8	No combinations regulation (after 1991 amendments to the Act)	Combinations regulated beyond a high threshold limit.
9	CCI appointed by the Government	CCI and CAT selected by a Collegium (search committee)
10	Very little administrative and financial autonomy for the CCI	Relatively more autonomy for the CCI
11	No competition advocacy role for the CCI	CCI has competition advocacy role
12	No penalties for offences	Penalties for offences
13	Reactive and rigid	Proactive and flexible
14	Unfair trade practices covered	Unfair trade practices omitted (consumer fora will deal with them)

to repeal the extant MRTP Act. As of now, only a few provisions of the new law have been brought into force and the process of constituting the regulatory authority, namely, the Competition Commission of India under the new Act, is on. Everything depends on who would be at the steering wheel to implement the Act.

No law is better than a poorly administered law. 'Singer not the Song'[28] is the title of the lyrics of a song by the Rolling Stones. That title sums up the future for India.

[28] Available at: www.mp3lyrics.org (accessed 18 June 2009). There is a novel by Audrey Erskine-Lindop published in 1954 with the same title, on the basis of which a movie was made in 1961 by Rank Organisation.

6. Thirty Years of PRC Anti-monopoly Law under 'State-Market' Yardstick: From Retrospective and Prospective Viewpoints

Yong Huang* and Shan Jiang**

1 INTRODUCTION

The reform and opening-up of China has had a 30-year-long history since 1978 and the formation of the substantive anti-monopoly law in China has also gone through about thirty years from 1980, when the Temporary Regulation of the State Council on Expansion and Protection of the Socialist Competition was enacted, to 2007 and 2008, when the formal Anti-monopoly Law was enacted and became effective.[1] Anti-monopoly law is deemed the 'Magna Carta of free enterprise'[2] in major developed countries in the western world, while the transplant of the law in China is a tortuous process, during which the top-down state will was the main power to push the enacting of laws and regulations.[3] With the in-depth

* Professor of Law, Director of the Economic Law Department, University of International Business and Economics, Beijing, P.R. China.

** Economic Law Department, University of International Business and Economics, Beijing, P.R. China.

1 The term 'anti-monopoly law' is used in this chapter to refer to all the laws and regulations policing monopoly, while the short name AML is used to refer to the Law of Anti-Monopoly, the formal antitrust code, i.e. the Anti-Monopoly Law of the People's Republic of China enacted on 30 August 2007.

2 'Antitrust laws in general and the Sherman Act in particular, are the Magna Carta of free enterprise. They are as important to the preservation of economic freedom and our free-enterprise system as the Bill of Rights is to the protection of our fundamental personal freedoms.' *See*, *United States v Topco Associates, Inc* 405 US 596 (1972).

3 For more complete exposition, see Huang Yong (2008), 'Pursuing The Second Best: The History, Momentum, And Remaining Issues Of China's Anti-Monopoly Law', *Anti-monopoly Law Journal*, **75**, 1, pp. 118–124.

development of the reform and opening-up as well as the penetration of the marketisation logic, the market has gradually imposed more and more influence on the development and the shaping of the anti-monopoly law. Based on such a comprehension, we will analyse the 30 years' development of the anti-monopoly law from a 'state-market' yardstick point of view, and put forward a forecast under the concepts of 'law of suppression', 'autonomous law' and 'responsive law', which is originated by the 'Berkeley Perspective'[4].

2 THE CHANGE OF THE 'STATE-MARKET' YARDSTICK AND THE FORMATION OF THE 'ANTI-MONOPOLY LAW'

Philippe Nonet and Philip Selznick noted that 'a legal order has many dimensions and that inquiry is best served when we treat those dimensions as variables. Instead of talking about necessary connections between law and coercion, law and the state, law and rules, or law and moral aspiration, we should consider to what extent and under what conditions those connections occur.'[5] In China, we believe, the change of the 'state-market' yardstick has always been an important reflection of the development of the market legal systems in China. According to the literatures on Chinese ancient economic history relating to market issues, no matter when it comes to the market for living articles during the Spring and Autumn and Warring States period or the state financial market after unification, the change of the 'state-market' yardstick was an issue in both.[6] During the entire Chinese feudal history, before the unification, the state power was decentralised and the market for living articles was rather developed, while after the unification, the market for living articles was occupied by the state financial market piece by piece. The more 'flourishing' and 'developed' the 'commodity economy' of the financial market was, the more stagnant and depressed the commodity economy of the market for living articles of the countryside would be.[7] The 'decentralisation and centralisation' of the feudal history of China has always been accompanied by

---

4 Nonet prudently referred to the common research field of the scholars of the 'Research Center of Law and Society' of Berkeley as the 'Berkeley Perspective'.

5 Philippe Nonet and Philip Selznick (2001), *Law & Society: Toward Responsive Law*, New Jersey: Transaction Publishers, p. 9.

6 Nianqi, Cheng (2006), *The Historical Variance of State Power and Chinese Economy*, Beijing: New Star Press, pp. 164–200.

7 *Ibid.*, p 199.

the development and underdevelopment of the market for living articles and the state financial market. This problem continued to exist after the establishment of the People's Republic of China, especially during the thirty years of growth of the market system and the relevant system under the reform and opening-up policy, as represented by the development and underdevelopment of the state monopoly and state planning as opposed to the market competition and market regulation.

With the development history of the People's Republic of China being reviewed, it is very important to analyse the documents of policy passed in each National Representative Conference of the Communist Party of China (hereinafter referred to as 'CPC') and each Central Conference of the CPC, among which there were important documents on orientation passed in all the third sessions with regard to the economic sector. This has become a node of the thirty years under the reform and opening-up policy. The documents of policy passed separately in the third sessions of 1978, 1993 and 2003 actually reflected the three phases of the 'state-market' relationship, and the formation of the 'anti-monopoly law' was perfectly embedded in such a process.

2.1 The 'Anti-monopoly Law' during the period of Market Gestation: 1978–1993

In 1978, the Communique of the Third Plenary Session of the 11th Central Commission of the CPC was passed in the Third Plenary Session of the 11th Central Committee of the CPC[8], in which it was stated that, 'it is unanimously consented that . . . the focus of the Party's work and the attention of the people all over the country should be turned to the construction of socialism modernization.' It has been generally accepted that the fundamental change of the socialist China was the historical determination made in the Third Plenary Session of the 11th Central Committee of the CPC to turn the focus the Party and the State's work to the construction of economy and the reform and opening-up by completely denying the wrong theory and practice of 'class struggle creed'. [9]

---

[8] The Communique of the Third Plenary Session of the 11th Central Commission of the CPC (passed on 22 December 1978), available at: http://www.people.com.cn/GB/shizheng/252/5089/5103/5205/20010428/454803.html (accessed 18 June 2009).

[9] Xinhua News Agency: The Third Plenary Session of the 11th Central Committee of the CPC Started a New Phase for the Reform and Opening-up in History, available at: http://news.xinhuanet.com/newscenter/2007-10/31/content_6980737.htm (accessed 18 June 2009).

In 1982, the report entitled 'Create Fresh Phase for the Construction of the Socialism Modernization Entirely'[10] was put forward at the 12th National Representative Conference of the CPC, the theory of 'planning economy as the main body, market regulation as the subsidiary' was formally re-worded as '[t]he planning economy should be carried out on the basis of state ownership system in China. The planned production and circulation should be the main body of the national economy of China. Meanwhile, the production and circulation of some products are permitted not to be planned, and should be regulated by the market. That is to say, according to the specific situation of different periods, the state would give a certain scope, which should be regulated by the law of value spontaneously.'

In 1984, the Third Plenary Session of the 12th Central Commission of the CPC issued the Decision on the Reform of the Economic System[11], definitely pointing out that the socialism economy of China should refer to the planned commodity economy based on the state ownership system and bringing forward the basic issues of the planning system of China. [12] It was stated that, 'In order to reform the current planning system according to the above-mentioned issues, the scope for mandatory planning should be narrowed down step by step appropriately, and the scope for guidance planning should be expanded properly. The mandatory planning should be

---

[10] Hu Yaobang: Create Fresh Phase for the Construction of the Socialism Modernization Entirely – Report at the 12th National Representative Conference of the CPC (passed on 1 September 1982), available at:http://www.people.com.cn/GB/shizheng/252/5089/5104/5276/20010429/455569.html (accessed 18 June 2009).

[11] The Central Commission of the CPC: Decision on the Reform of the Economic System (passed at the Third Plenary Session of the 12th Central Commission of the CPC on 20 October 1984), available at:http://news.xinhuanet.com/ziliao/2005-02/07/content_2558000.htm (accessed 18 June 2009).

[12] 'According to historical experience and the practices after the Third Plenary Session of the 11th Central Commission of the CPC, the basic concept of the planning system of China should be summarised as follows: firstly, as a whole, China is carrying out the planning economy, i.e. a planned commodity economy, not the sort of market economy completely regulated by the market. Secondly, the free production and trade completely regulated by the market mainly apply to some agricultural products and by products, daily used articles and services provided in the service and repair industries, which should exert a subsidiary but indispensable function in the national economy. Thirdly, to carry out planning economy does not mean the mandatory planning should prevail, the mandatory planning and guidance planning are both detailed forms of the planning economy. Fourthly, the guidance planning is realised mainly through economic leverage, and the mandatory planning must be obeyed, but with the rule of value being adopted.' For detailed information please refer to the Central Commission of the CPC: the Decision on the Reform of the Economic System, *ibid.*

applied to the part of the products essential to the national economy and the people's livelihood that needs to be distributed by the state and important economic activities of nationwide significance; while other products or economic activities, which should be of a great amount, should be regulated under the guidance planning or completely by the market.'

In 1987, the 13th National Representative Conference of the CPC published a report entitled 'Move Forward along the Socialist Road with Chinese Characteristics'[13], stating that, 'the socialist planned commodity economy system should be the result of the inherent consolidation of planning and market.' It is also stated in the report that 'the basis of planning should be the exchange of commodity and law of value,' and 'the function of the planning and the market should cover the whole society'. On the whole, the new economy operating system should be a system, in which 'the market is regulated by the state, and the enterprises are guided by the market.' Besides, the report pointed out that the establishment and cultivation of the socialist market system should be speeded up, and that 'the socialist market system should also be competitive and open; monopolised or separated market will never encourage the producers of commodity to improve efficiency, and closed market will go against the development of reasonable division of work internally and the improvement of international trade.'

In 1988, the Third Plenary Session of the 13th Central Commission of the CPC approved the guideline, policy and measures to change the economic environment, rectifying the economic order and advancing the reform all-around submitted by the Central Political Bureau. In 1989, the Fifth Plenary Session of the 13th Central Commission of the CPC passed the Decisions of the Central Committee of CPC on Further Governance, Rectification and Advancement of Reform[14], bringing forward that 'the socialism direction of the reform should be preserved, and the emphasis of the advancement of the reform should be defined,' and pointing out that 'The socialist economy of China should be a planned commodity economy based on the state-owned system . . . The key issue of the reform should be

[13] Zhao Ziyang, Zhao (1987), 'Moving Forward along the Socialist Road with Chinese Characteristics' Report at the 13th National Representative Conference of the CPC (25 October), available at: http://news.xinhuanet.com/ziliao/2003-01/20/content_697061.htm (accessed 18 June 2009).

[14] The Central Commission of the CPC (1989), 'Decision of the Central Committee of CPC on Further Governance Rectification and Advancement of Reform' (abstract) (passed by the Fifth Plenary Session of the 13th Central Commission of the CPC on 9 November), available at: http://www.people.com.cn/GB/shizheng/252/5089/5105/5188/20010429/455917.html (accessed 18 June 2009).

to establish an economic operating system, in which the planning economy and the market regulation should be consolidated. The degree, manner and scope of such consolidation should be adjusted and improved according to the actual situation regularly . . . During the current period for governance and rectification, the key issues to advance and consummate the reform are firstly to stabilise, enrich, adjust and improve the reform measures of the previous years according to the principle of consolidation of the planning economy and market regulation; and secondly to properly strengthen the centralization according to the requirement that there should be more planning during the governance and rectification period.'

The period from 1978 to 1993 was the period when the market was seeded under the reform and opening-up policy of China. The state firstly denied the class struggle in the top grade documents on political line, and came back to the route of economy construction, which unsealed the possibility of state and market interaction. During the initial stage of the reform, the 'state-market' relationship was defined as 'the main body being the planning economy and the subsidiary being the market regulation.' Under the precondition of state planning, the market was permitted to regulate the economy to a certain extent. The market regulation in this period may be deemed as an exception to state planning. With the improvement of the reform, the concept of 'planned commodity economy' was brought up, and the keynote that 'state-market' should interact was confirmed. The 'mandatory planning-guidance and planning-market regulation' constituted a mixed form of economic regulation. Thereafter, the 'planned commodity economy' was interpreted into the 'result of the inherent consolidation of planning and market', and it was further brought forward that 'the function of the planning and the market should cover the whole society'. Finally, during the latter part of this period of governance and rectification, it was still emphasised that '[t]he key issue of the reform should be to establish an economic operating system, in which the planning economy and the market regulation should be consolidated', just stating that such 'consolidation' could be adjusted according to the actual situation. It turned out that the keynote of the economic reform was still a planned commodity economy. As a whole, the dominant power in the 'state-market' relationship was the state, the possible space for the market could only be explored as encouraged by the top-down policy. During the period of market gestation, 'the principal responsibility for creating and extending the market's role while defining and delimiting that of government rests with the government itself.'[15]

---

[15] Wolf, Charles (1993), *Markets or Governments: Choosing Between Imperfect Alternatives, Massachusetts:* MIT Press, p. 176.

The above policies and guidelines were reflected in legislation as well, the Temporary Regulation of the State Council on Expansion and Protection of the Socialist Competition (the Ten Stipulations on Competition)[16] enacted in 1980, the Notification on the Settlement of Tie-in Problems enacted in 1986, the Regulations on Price Governance enacted in 1987, by the State council and the Temporary Measures on Enterprise Acquisition issued in 1989 and the Notification on Breaking the Regional Market Blockade and Further Freeing the Commodity Circulation enacted in 1990 jointly issued by the State Commission for Economic Restructuring, the State Planning Commission, the Ministry of Finance and the State-owned Assets Administration Bureau, separately stipulated the framework to handle monopoly related issues. Furthermore, the former Legal Affairs Bureau of the State Council delivered the Temporary Regulation on Anti-Monopoly and Unfair Competition (Draft).

2.2 The 'Anti-monopoly Law' during the Period of Market Establishment: 1993–2003

At the end of 1992, the 14th National Representative Conference of the CPC published a report entitled 'Speed Up the Reform, Opening-up and the Modernization Construction, Achieve Greater Success for the Socialist Career with Chinese Characteristics', in which it was pointed out that '[i]n order to establish a socialist market economic system, the market should play a fundamental role in resource allocation under the macro-control of the socialist state, so that the economic activities could be in accordance with the law of value and the change of the supply-demand relationship.' It was also declared in the report that 'a nationwide, unified and open market system should be formed as soon as possible. The market system and construction of legal system . . . should be strengthened and the separation, blockade and monopoly should be broken with a firm hand so as to improve and protect fair competition.'[17]

---

[16] The State Council (1980), 'Temporary Regulation of the State Council on Expansion and Protection of the Socialist Competition' (17 October), since the Regulations were composed of ten articles, it was also referred to as the 'Ten Articles on Competition', the shortened form should be used below, available at: http://law1.chinalawinfo.com/newlaw2002/slc/slc.asp?db=chl&gid=816 (accessed 18 June 2009).

[17] Zemin, Jiang (1992), 'Speed up the Reform, Opening-up and the Modernization Construction, Achieve Greater Success for the Socialist Career with Chinese Characteristics' (12 October), available at: http://cpc.people.com.cn/GB/64162/64168/64567/65446/4526311.html (accessed 18 June 2009).

At the beginning of 1993, in the Proposals of the Central Commission of the CPC for the Amendment of Part of the Content of the Constitution Law, the Central Commission of the CPC provided suggestions for the amendment of Article 15 of the Constitution Law, in which it was stipulated that 'The state should carry out planning economy based on the socialist state own system. The state should ensure the proportionate and harmonised development of the state economy by comprehensively balancing the economy according to the economic plan and realising the subsidiary function of the market regulation', should be replaced by 'The state should carry out a socialist market economy.' [18] In Annex 2 entitled 'Explanation on the Proposals for the Amendment of Part of the Content of the Constitution Law of the Supplementary Proposals of the Central Commission of the CPC for the Amendment of Part of the Content of the Constitution Law', it was suggested that 'The first section of Article 15 of the Constitution Law should be amended as 'the state should carry out a socialist market economy,' and explained why the 'socialist market economy' was not defined.[19] As a result, the First session of the 8th National People's Congress held on 29 March 1993 passed the Amendments to the Constitution Law for the first time, in which Article 15 was amended as, '[t]he state should carry out a socialist

[18] The Central Commission of the CPC (1993), 'Proposals of the Central Commission of the CPC for the Amendment of Part of the Content of the Constitution Law' (14 February 1993), available at: http://www.npc.gov.cn/npc/oldarchives/dbdh/dbdh/common/zw.jsp@label=wxzlk&id=2888.htm (accessed 18 June 2009).

[19] 'It has been proved according to the practice of reform and opening-up that the socialist market economy is a economic system that continuously improve the abundance of the material products. The liberation and development of productivity will be benefited. It was put forward in the 14th National Representative Conference of the CPC that the aim of the economic system reform of China is to establish the socialist market economic system. This amendment of the Article 15 of the Constitution Law will certainly and extremely promote the development of the economy of China. Among the proposals, some colleagues suggested that the concept of the socialist market economy should be defined in details. Given the fact that the socialist market economy is still in the process of developing, a detailed definition would hardly be given with legal language. Jiang Zemin interpreted the socialist market economy in the report for the 14th National Representative Conference of the CPC. As long as it's necessary, a constitutional explanation of the socialist market economy could be given according to the Report.' The Central Commission of the CPC (1993), 'Supplementary Proposals of the Central Commission of the CPC for the Amendment of Part of the Content of the Constitution Law' (14 March 1993), available at: http://www.npc.gov.cn/npc/oldarchives/dbdh/dbdh/common/zw.jsp@label=wxzlk&id=2889.htm (accessed 18 June 2009).

market economy. The state should strengthen the economic legislation and consummate the macro-control. The state should forbid any organization or person from disturbing the social economic order.' Till then, the constitution basis for the socialist market economy was radicated in a definite way.

At the end of 1993, the Third Plenary Session of the 14th Central Commission of the CPC passed the Decision of the Central Commission of the CPC on Several Issues as to the Establishment of a Socialist Market Economic System[20], in which it was pointed out that 'The 14th National People's Congress clearly stated that a socialist market economic system should be established, and this is an essential part of the theory for building socialism with Chinese characteristics . . .', furthermore, '. . . the socialist market economic system should be combined with the basic socialist system. To establish a socialist market economic system, the market should play a fundamental role in resource allocation under the macro-control of the state . . . A nationwide unified and open market economic system should be established, the markets of the cities and countryside should be integrated closely, and the domestic and international markets should be linked so as to improve the optimization of the resources . . .' Meanwhile, as to the cultivation and development of the market system, it was also emphasised in the Decision that 'In order to exert the fundamental function of the market in resource allocation, the market system must be cultivated and developed. For the time being, emphasis should be given to the development of the market for production factors, regulation of market behavior, breaking of the regional and sectoral separation and blockade, anti-unfair competition, creation of an environment for fair competition, formation of a unified, open, competitive and orderly great market . . . the establishment of normal access of the market, market competition and market trade order, the assurance of fair trade, fair competition and the protection of the lawful rights and interests of the market players and the consumers . . .' As it can be seen, after the Constitution Law confirmed the key note of 'socialist market economy', the Decision has drawn the curtain for 'the period of market establishment' as a programmatic document. Thereby, when it comes to the establishment of the market, it would be unavoidable to set up a legal framework for the

---

20 The Central Commission of the CPC (1993), 'Decision of the Central Commission of the CPC on Several Issues as to the Establishment of a Socialist Market Economic System' (passed by the Third Plenary Session of the 14th Central Commission of the CPC on 14 November 1993), available at: http://www.people.com.cn/GB/shizheng/252/5089/5106/5179/20010430/456592.html (accessed 18 June 2009).

market system, which pushed the enacting of a series of competition laws and regulations afterwards.

In 1997, the 15th National Representative Conference of the CPC published a report entitled 'Hold High the Great Banner of Deng Xiaoping's Theory High, Push the Construction of the Socialist Careers with the Chinese Characteristics Entirely into the 21st Century', in which it was stated that, 'The maketization of the national economy should speed up. . . . The circulation system should be reformed, the market rules should be consummated, the governance of the market should be strengthened, the obstacles in the market should be cleared, the regional blockade and sectoral monopoly should be broken, the unified, competitive and orderly market system should be established as soon as possible, and the fundamental function of the market for resource allocation should be further exerted.'[21] This report provided a consecutive policy support for the marketization of the economy of China.

In 1992, Article 4 of the Memorandum of Understanding between the Government of the People's Republic of China and the Government of the United States of America on the Protection of Intellectual Property as entered into by China and US negotiation on intellectual property required that the Chinese government should protect trade secrets according to the Paris Convention, so as to prevent unfair competition effectively.[22] Correspondingly, the Anti-unfair Competition Law of the People's Republic of China was promulgated on 2 September 1993, and became effective on 1 December 1993, and the protection of trade secrets was

---

[21] Jiang Zemin, Jiang (1997), 'Hold the Great Flag of Deng Xiaoping's Theory High, Push the Construction of the Socialist Careers with the Chinese Characteristics Entirely into the 21st Century', (September), available at: http://cpc.people.com.cn/GB/64162/64168/64568/65445/4526288.html (accessed 18 June 2009).

[22] Article 4: '1. For the purpose of ensuring effective protection against unfair competition as provided for in Article 10bis of the Paris Convention for the Protection of Industrial Property, the Chinese Government will prevent trade secrets from being disclosed to, acquired by, or used by others without the consent of the trade secret owner in a manner contrary to honest commercial practices including the acquisition, use or disclosure of trade secrets by third parties who knew, or had reasonable grounds to know, that such practices were involved in their acquisition of such information. 2. The term of protection for trade secrets shall continue so long as the conditions for protection are met. 3. The competent authorities of the Chinese Government will submit the bill necessary to provide the levels of protection specified in this Article to its legislative body by July 1, 1993 and will exert its best efforts to enact and implement this bill before 1 January 1994.'

stipulated in Article 10 thereby. [23] Such a link of causality seemed to have been pushed by outside power, but in fact it should be the consequence of the market logic itself. It was inevitable according to the market logic that among the three proposals as to the legislation of the anti-monopoly law, the one claiming that 'some classic monopolistic behaviors should be included in the Anti-unfair Competition Law as unfair competition behaviors, and the other monopolistic behaviors should be included in the future Anti-monopoly Law' prevailed.[24]

The period from 1993 to 2003 was the period of market establishment under the reform and opening-up policy of China. After a long time of reform for the marketisation of circulation, 'substantive material, institutional and conceptual basis has been founded for the cultivation and development of the market system.'[25] At the beginning of this period, the 'state-market' relationship was clearly defined as 'the state should carry out socialist market economy.' This indicates that the traditional dispute about planning and market with regard to the 'state-market' relationship should not be an underlying issue any more. In the new period of reform, it has become a precondition to carry out the socialist market economy. During this phase, the emphasis was given to how to 'establish

---

[23] It is stipulated in Article 10 of the Anti-unfair Competition Law that 'Operators shall not use the following methods to infringe upon business secrecy: 1. To steal, coerce, or use any other unfair method to obtain the other's business secrets; 2. To disclose, use or permit others to use the business secrets mentioned in Section 1 of this Article; 3. To violate the contract or the requirement to publish, use or permit others to use the business secrets, which were maintained as secrets by the legal owner of the business secrecy. The third party who knows or should know the illegal activities as first mentioned, and who gains, uses or publishes the business secrecy shall be looked as activities of infringing upon the others' business secrecy. "Business secrecy", in this Article, means the utilized technical information and business information which is unknown by the public, which may create business interests or profit for its legal owners, and also is maintained secrecy by its legal owners.'

[24] The other two concepts are: firstly, the issues under anti-monopoly laws should be included in the Anti-Unfair Competition Law, thereby the Anti-monopoly Law should not be enacted in the future. Secondly, the Anti-Unfair Competition Law should only include unfair competition behavior, and should not involve any issues under the anti-monopoly law, therefore anti-monopoly law should be enacted in the future. Qiong, Zhang (2007), *Research on Anti-monopoly Theory*, China: Legal Publishing House, p. 74.

[25] Yongjun, Chen, Xiaojun, Zhang, Shangwen, Zhuang (2008), *Thirty Years of Construction of the Modern Market System in Our Country, Report on the Development of Economy and Reform of System of China, No 1: Thirty Years of Reform and Opening-up of China (1978–2008)*, Beijing: Social Sciences Academic Press, p. 135.

a nationwide, united and open market system', and how to 'regulate the market behaviors, break the regional and sectorial separation and blockade, anti-unfair competition, create an environment for fair competition, and form a unified, open, competitive and orderly great market' when policy was discussed. Meanwhile, this phase was accompanied with two issues all along. Firstly, the reform of the state-owned enterprises was the core topic for discussions on national policy for most of the time. The definition of the relationship between planning and market brought the reform of the state-own enterprises from the phase of policy adjustment to the phase of institutional innovation;[26] and the market players emerging thanks to such reform furthered the exertion of the market function. Secondly, the price system was going through a transition period from double-track to single-track mechanism. By the mid-term of the 90s, the price reform was mostly completed, and only the price of the monopolistic industries that were still controlled by the State was not fully deregulated. Actually, the process of liberalisation and rationalisation of price would be the process of the perpetual marketisation of the Chinese economy. However, during the period of market establishment, the dominant power influencing the change of the 'state-market' yardstick was still the state. But with the improvement of the reform, besides the top-down push, the power of self-realisation of the market that became more and more mature was also shown.

The evolution of policy was deeply reflected in the legal documents. Except for the Anti-unfair Competition Law, there are other competition laws, regulations and rules promulgated during this period, *inter alia*: Several Rules on Prohibition of Restrictive Competition Behavior by Public Utilities issued by the State Administration for Industry and Commerce in 1993, the Temporary Rules on Preventing the Seeking of Exorbitant Profits issued by the State Planning Commission in 1995, the Rules on Administrative Punishment for Illegal Price Behaviors and the Rules on Prevention of Under-price Dumping issued in 1999, the Procedural Rules on Price-related Administrative Punishment issued in 2001, the Price Law issued by the National People's Congress in 1997; the Rules on Preventing Unfair Competition Behaviors in the Civil Aviation Transportation Market issued by the Civil Aviation Administration of China in 1996, the Regulations on Prohibiting Regional Blockade in

[26] Tianyong, Zhou, Xuqian, Xia (2008), *Thirty Years of Reform and Development of the State-owned Enterprises in Our Country, Report on the Development of Economy and Reform of System of China, No 1: Thirty Years of Reform and Opening-up of China (1978–2008)*, Beijing: Social Sciences Academic Press, p. 349.

Market Economic Activities and the Decision of the State Council on Rectification and Regulation of the Market Economic Order issued by the State Council in 2001; and the PRC Telecommunication Regulations issued by the State Council in 2002.

2.3 The 'Anti-monopoly Law' during the Period of Market Consummation: from 2003 till now

As early as in November 2002, the 16th National Representative Conference of the CPC published a report entitled 'Build a Well-off Society in an All-round Way, Create a Fresh Phase for the Socialist career with Chinese Characteristics',[27] in which it was stated that 'The modern market system should be consummated, the macro-control should be strengthened and consummated . . . The fundamental function of the market for resource allocation should be exerted to a greater extent, the unified, open, competitive and orderly modern market system should be consummated . . . The market economic order should be rectified and regulated, the social credit system of the modern market economy should be consummated, the industrial monopoly and regional blockade should be broken and the free circulation of the commodity and production factors should be improved.'

In 2003, the Third Plenary Session of the 16th Central Commission of the CPC passed the Decision of the Central Commission of the CPC on Several Issues for the Consummation of the Socialist Market Economic System[28], in which it was provided that 'the aim for consummating the socialist market economic system' was 'exerting the fundamental function of the market for resource allocation to a greater extent, enhancing the macro-control of the state, consummating the function of the government to administrate the society and provide public service . . .', and that 'the construction of the unified, open, competitive and orderly modern market system' should be one of the 'tasks to consummate the socialist market economic system'. Besides, as to the 'consummation of the market system and regulation of the market order', it was emphasised in the Decision that, 'The construction of a nationwide unified market should speed up.

---

[27] Zemin, Jiang (2002), 'Build a Well-off Society in an All-round Way, Create a Fresh Phase for the Socialist career with Chinese Characteristics', (November), available at:http://cpc.people.com.cn/GB/64162/64168/64569/65444/4429120.html (accessed 18 June 2009).

[28] Passed by the Third Plenary Session of the 16th Central Commission of the CPC on 14 October 2003, available at: http://www.people.com.cn/GB/shizheng/1024/2145119.html (accessed 18 June 2009).

It is an essential task for the construction of the modern market system to strengthen the unification of the market. The market should be further opened both domestically and internationally. The mercerization of the factor price should speed up . . . the free movement and full competition of the commodity and all kinds of factors nationwide should be improved. The rules that separate the market by preventing fair competition, setting up administrative barriers or excluding products and services from other places should be abolished. . ..' Ten years after the issuance of the Decision of the Central Commission of the CPC on Several Issues for the Establishment of the Socialist Market Economic System, the Decision again drew the curtain for the 'period of market consummation' as a programmatic document. Moreover, the requirements to consummate the market and solve the problems left by the 'period of market establishment' both pointed to the enacting of the Anti-monopoly Law more directly.

On the other side, the entrance of China into the World Trade Organization (WTO) was the main external power to push the draft of the Anti-monopoly Law. China became the 143rd member state of WTO officially, and the transition period nearly ended by 11 December 2006. Five years after the 'entrance into WTO', the concept of marketisation and globalisation has penetrated into the economic and social life in China.[29] As to the competition policy, after the first Ministerial Conference was held in Singapore in December of 1996, the WTO Trade and Competition Policy Relationship Working Group was set up.[30] The major task of the working group was to study and demonstrate the necessity and feasibility of international harmonisation of the competition law within the WTO framework. Ever since 1997, the working group would form a working plan every year for the research and study of issues involving the agreements on multinational competition policy within the WTO framework. The working group would integrate and analyse the comments of the members, and submit annual reports to the WTO General Council. By June 2004 when the WTO General Council ended the work, the working group had been submitting annual reports for seven years. China entered into WTO in 2001, when the competition policy topic was under furious discussion, therefore China was affected on a policy level.[31]

---

[29] Editor in Chief Li Xiaoxi (2008), *Thirty Years of Reform of the Chinese Economy, Volume on Marketization Process*, Chongqing: University Press, p. 217.

[30] WTO (1997), 'Working Group on the Interaction between Trade and Competition Policy Report to the General Council', WT/WGTCP/W/1.

[31] At the Doha Ministerial Conference, 'recognizing the case for a multilateral framework to enhance the contribution of competition policy to international

Furthermore, we hold the opinion that the more direct reason why the enacting of the Anti-monopoly Law was accelerated was the dispute about China's market economy status in 2004. According to Article 15 of the Protocol on the Accession of the People's Republic of China, China was defined as a non-market economy country with conditions for as long as 15 years.[32] The influences of the 'non-market economy position' were manifold: firstly, as a result, the exporting enterprises of China encountered extremely unfavourable situations in the anti-dumping lawsuits, and became the main reason for their failure. Secondly, the fact that Chinese enterprises could hardly win any lawsuit stimulated certain WTO members to bring lawsuits against the products from China, adding that the Chinese enterprises were discouraged to respond to the claims, a vicious circle was formed. Thirdly, such a position will affect the international image of China in a negative way.[33] There were a series of indicators deciding whether the 'market economy position' would be admitted, and these indicators themselves are in dispute too. However, it was generally consented that as the fundamental legal framework of market economy, the anti-monopoly law was indispensable to the market economy. As a result, we finally saw the draft of the anti-monopoly being submitted by the Ministry of Commerce to the State Council in 2004. In 2005, the State Council organised the first expert discussion, and the legislation of the Anti-monopoly Law was driven to the fast lane.

---

trade and development, and the need for enhanced technical assistance and capacity-building' was agreed on by the ministers. The conference also required that before the Cancun Ministerial Conference, the working group should focus on core principles (including transparency, non-discrimination and procedural fairness), and provisions on hard-core cartels; modalities for voluntary co-operation; and support for progressive reinforcement of competition institutions in developing countries through capacity building. Doha Ministerial Conference, paras 23–25, available at: http://www.wto.org/english/thewto_e/minist_e/min01_e/mindecl_e.htm#interaction (accessed 18 June 2009).

[32] It is stipulated in Article 15 of the Protocol on the Accession of the People's Republic of China that, '(d). Once China has established, under the national law of the importing WTO Member, that it is a market economy, the provisions of subparagraph (a) shall be terminated provided that the importing Member's national law contains market economy criteria as of the date of accession. In any event, the provisions of subparagraph (a)(ii) shall expire 15 years after the date of accession. In addition, should China establish, pursuant to the national law of the importing WTO Member, that market economy conditions prevail in a particular industry or sector, the non-market economy provisions of subparagraph (a) shall no longer apply to that industry or sector.'

[33] As to why China fights for the market economy position, please refer to: http://www.people.com.cn/GB/jingji/1045/2545943.html (accessed 18 June 2009).

In 2007, the 16th National Representative Conference of the CPC published a report entitled 'Hold High the Great Banner of the Socialism with Chinese Characteristics, Fight for the New Success for the Construction of a Well-off Society'[34] in which it was stated that 'the fundamental economic system should be consummated, and the modern market system should be perfected', and in which it was pointed out that '. . . a new pattern should be formed, in which all kinds of economies with different ownership could compete fairly and get promoted mutually . . . The reform of the monopolized industries should be furthered, and the competition mechanism should be imported . . . fair entrance should be encouraged, financing conditions should be improved, systematic barriers should be exploded and the development of individual and private economy as well as the medium and small sized enterprises should be improved. . . . A unified, open, competitive and orderly modern market system should be formed as soon as possible, the market for all kinds of production factors should be developed, the price formation mechanism for production factors and resources reflecting the supply and demand relationship, resource scarcity and the cost of environment damage should be perfected, the industrial association and intermediary organization on the market should be regulated and developed, and the social credit system should be perfected.' The report continued the policy orientation of the 16th Conference, and stated the main challenge that may appear during the future implementation of the Anti-monopoly Law.

The period from 2003 till now should be the period of market consummation under the reform and opening-up policy of China. After the aim of the reforms such as the reforms of price and state-owned enterprises was gradually achieved or some initial effects were shown, and after the socialist market economic legal system was framed primarily, the underlying work to establish the market has been mostly accomplished. The 'state-market' relationship was further solidified on the original basis, the focus of discussion changed from 'formation' to 'the consummation of' the 'unified, open, competitive and orderly modern market system'. In order to perfect and consummate the socialist market economy, it is important to solve the problems left by the 'period of market establishment' as well as the new ones bought by the entrance into WTO. On one side, some problems that the Government strived to resolve during the period of market

---

[34] Hu Jintao, Hu (2007), 'Hold the Great Flag of the Socialism with Chinese Characteristics, Fight for the New Success for the Construction of a Well-off Society', (October), available at: http://news.xinhuanet.com/newscenter/2007-10/24/content_6938568_4.htm (accessed 18 June 2009).

establishment still exist, including industrial monopoly, regional blockade and other problems relating to fair competition. On the other side, there are still problems because the 'market economy position' of China failed to be admitted. Those problems could all come down to the establishment of competition mechanism. Without the support of the 'Anti-monopoly' as the 'Economic Constitution', the dispersive regulations in the Anti-unfair Competition Law and the relevant laws and regulations obviously cannot establish the competition mechanism, which should be the principal mission of the period for market consummation. During the period for market consummation, the national policies tend to be stable and consecutive; and the market demand, especially the requirement of market integration and marketisation under the background of globalisation, the 'state-market' relationship has become more and more mature.

As a whole, after the issuance of the Decision of the Central Commission of the CPC on Several Issues for the Consummation of the Socialist Market Economic System, there were more competition laws, regulations and rules on board, *inter alia*: the Temporary Regulations on Acquisition of Domestic Enterprises by Foreign Investors issued by the Ministry of Commerce in 2003, the Temporary Regulations for Preventing Price Monopolistic Behaviors and the Notification on Guidance and Regulation of Market Price Behaviors issued by the National Development and Reform Commission in 2003, the Regulations on Acquisition of the Domestic Enterprises by Foreign Investors issued by the Ministry of Commerce in 2006. On 31 August 2007, after 13 years drafting and disputing, the PRC Anti-monopoly Law was finally promulgated. The promulgation of the law should be the result of promotion by all the above-mentioned powers jointly together with the change of the 'state-market' yardstick.

3 THE FOCUS AND BOTTLENECK IN IMPLEMENTING THE SUBSTANTIVE AML

As discussed above, the development of the substantive AML experienced three phases under the yardstick of 'State-Market'. The three periods constituted the overall background for the generation of the substantive AML. However, the systemic analysis of the substantive AML in different periods dated before the enactment of the AML can roughly be divided into two phases, namely, the 'Temporary Stipulation of the State Council on the Promotion and Protection of Socialist Competition' (known as 'Ten Stipulations on Competition') phase and the Anti-unfair Competition Law phase. The similarities between the two phases can be used as an integrated sample for analysing the pre-AML phase.

3.1 The Substantive AML during the 'Ten Stipulations on Competition' Phase

The 'Temporary Stipulation of the State Council on the Promotion and Protection of Socialist Competition' enacted by the State Council in 1980 should not be understood as simply a legal document regulating the 'competition process', its substantive stipulations rather incorporated competition right, competition incentives, competition environment and other content, including the stipulation concerning activating the main bodies of other economic elements, encouraging enterprises of non-public economic element 'to bring into full play of their advantages and carry out competition' (article 3); concerning the expanding of the enterprises' 'decision-making right' by the market, respecting the enterprises' 'relatively independent status as commodity producers' (article 4); concerning the prices, pointing out 'the prices of some commodities fixed by the state are allowed to float within the designated range' (Article 5). Among which, the stipulation on the AML problems was mainly found in Article 6. During the 'Ten Stipulations on Competition' phase, the laws, regulations and normative legal documents concerning anti-monopoly were mainly made based on the 'Ten Stipulations', while their implementation mainly concerned regional blockade; tying arrangements; and concentrations of undertakings.

3.1.1 Regional blockade

Article 6 of the 'Ten Stipulations on Competition' promulgated by the State Council provides:

> No districts and departments concerned are allowed to blockade the market, to forbid the commodities from other districts to be sold in the local district and departments. The materials produced in the local district should be maneuvered in line with the state's plan without being blockaded. The industrial department, transportation department, financial department and trade department should revise the content in their existing bylaws, modifying the part hindering competition and facilitating the launching of competition. It is illegal and rescindable to protect the backwardness, repress the forwardness and hinder the normal circulation of commodities by way of administrative methods.

The 'Notice on Breaking the Regional blockade and Further Livening Commodity Circulation' promulgated by the State Council in 1990 provides, 'It is a must to break district blockage and department division when carrying out competition', 'the circulation of commodities should be remained unblocked. No districts and departments are allowed to presume to set up the checkpoints on roads, at stations, docks, and the boundaries between provinces and districts, which may hinder the normal transportation of commodities . . . Industrial and commercial administrative management department, quality supervision and inspection department, as well as sanitation inspection department are not allowed to raise the inspection standard for ecdemic commodities and blockade the sales of ecdemic commodities in the local places in disguised form, e.g. in the name of investigating the counterfeit and low-quality products.'

3.1.2 Monopolistic behavior

On tying arrangement. In respect of the situation such as 'tying arrangement is being practiced in many districts, i.e. the name-brand, high quality and salable commodities are sold tying with less-known and inferior brands, low quality and unmarketable commodities', the 'Notice on Solving the Problem of Tying Arrangement with regard to Commodity' promulgated by the State Council in 1986 tried to deal with the situation by 'strictly supervise the production and commerce activities', 'draft the concrete solutions in time', and 'pay great attention to the work on inspection and supervision'.

On pricing. The 'Price Management Regulation' promulgated by the State Council in 1987 provides, 'the State adopts a principle combining the direct management and the indirect management in controlling prices. Implementing three forms of pricing: the State fixes the price, the State guides the pricing, and the market regulates the pricing acts.' Of the 12 kinds of illegal pricing activities listed under Article 29 of the Regulation, 'price being fixed between undertakings or negotiated between guilds' was also one of the forbidden activities.

3.2 Concentrations of Undertakings

In 1989, the State System Restructuring and Reform Commission, the State Planning Commission, the Ministry of Finance and the State-owned Assets Supervision and Administration Commission of the State Council jointly issued the 'Temporary Method on Undertakings Annexation'. The 'Principle of Undertakings Annexation' provides, '(ii) undertakings annexation should follow the principle of voluntary, mutual-beneficial and non-gratuitous, and realise survival of the fittest in the course of competition. It is not allowed to force the superior undertakings to annex inferior undertakings by administrative orders.' '(iv) except for special ordain by the State, undertakings annexation is not restricted by factors like district, ownership, trade and affiliation.' '(v) undertakings should both promote scale economy and prevent anti-monopoly, so as to create a favourable environment for undertakings to compete with each other.'

3.3 The Substantive AML during the 'Anti-unfair Competition Law' phase

The 'Anti-unfair Competition Law' of 1993 has four substantive AML articles, including the forbiddance of restricting competition by public utilities, administrative monopoly, predatory pricing, and tying arrangement. During the 'Anti-unfair Competition Law' phase, the laws, regulations and normative legal documents concerning anti-monopoly were mostly based upon the 'Anti-unfair Competition Law', and the implementation of those laws, regulations and legal documents mainly concerned pricing, regional blockade, public utilities and concentrations of undertaking.

3.3.1 Monopolistic behavior

On predatory pricing. Article 11 of the 'Anti-unfair Competition Law' provides: 'An operator shall not sell its or his goods at a price that is below the cost for the purpose of excluding its or his competitors'. This article forbids predatory pricing activities. Article 14 of the 'Pricing Law' (1997) provides the abnormal pricing behavior which the operators must not act, including the forbiddance of cartel agreement, predatory pricing, and discrimination treatment.[35] The 'Regulation on Forbidding Dumping Sales at Low Prices' promulgated by the State Planning Commission in 1999, clearly forbids dumping sales at very low prices: 'dumping sales at low prices', as stipulated in this regulation, refers to 'the operators, other than sales of merchandises at discount, engaging in dumping sales at below-cost prices in order to attain an upper hand over rivals or dominate the market and disrupt the normal production and operation order to great detriments to the interests of the State or the lawful rights and interests of other business operators.'

On monopolistic pricing, the State Planning Commission promulgated

[35] Article 14 of the 'Pricing Law' provides: '. . . (i) to work collaboratively with others to control market prices to great detriments to the lawful rights and interests of other business operators or consumers; (ii) to engage in dumping sales (except the cases of sales of fresh and live merchandises, seasonal merchandises and stockpiled merchandises at discount) at below-cost prices in order to attain an upper hand over rivals or dominate the market and disrupt the normal production and operation order to great detriments to the interests of the State or the lawful rights and interests of other business operators; and (v) to discriminate in terms of prices same kinds of merchandises or services offered by certain business operators under same trading conditions.'

the 'Temporary Regulation on the Prevention of Seeking Extravagant Profits' in 1995, which provided that the standard of a commodity's price and the charge on services shall not be higher than 'the reasonable scope of the market average price'.[36] It also listed the illegal profit-seeking methods which the operators are not allowed to employ, including conducts such as monopolistic pricing and price-fixing acts, which were similar to the stipulations in the existing AML.[37] In 2003, the State Development and Reform Commission promulgated the 'Temporary Regulation on Repressing Price Monopolistic Behavior', which defines the 'price monopolistic behavior' as, 'the behavior carried out by operators to manipulate the market regulative price, disrupt the normal production and operation order, damage the legal interests of other operators and consumers, or imperil the social and public interests by colluding with each other or abusing their dominant market position.' Article 4 provides that operators are not allowed to launch three kinds of price monopolistic behaviors by working collaboratively among themselves, namely, concluding agreements, making decisions, or coordinating with each other;[38] Article 5 to Article 6 stipulate on

---

[36] Article 5 of the 'Temporary Regulation on the Prevention of Seeking Extravagant Profits' provides: 'the standard of commodity's price and the charge on services (hereafter referred as price) , shall comply with the following requirements: (i) the price level of a commodity or service shall not exceed the reasonable scope of the market average price of the same kind of commodity or service in the same district, the same period, and of the same grade; (ii) the rate of price differences of a commodity or service shall not exceed the reasonable scope of the market average price of the same kind of commodity or service in the same district, the same period, and of the same grade. However, the profit margin obtained by the operator through improving business management, applying new technology, lowering the cost, and enhancing the efficiency is excluded.'

[37] Article 8 of the 'Temporary Regulation on the Prevention of Seeking Extravagant Profits' provides: 'business operators shall not violate the regulation and seek illegal profits by means listed as follow: (i) don't mark the prices clearly or ask for higher prices beyond the marked prices; (ii) implementing fraudulent prices by lying about the price cutting, or by giving fictitious preferential prices, discount prices, reduced prices, the lowest prices, and other false information on prices; (iii) business operators and trade organizations collude and force up prices between themselves; (iv) force the opposite side to accept high prices by violating the fair and voluntary principle; (v) employ other fraudulent price methods.'

[38] Article 4 of the 'Temporary Regulation on Repressing Price Monopolistic Behavior' provides: '(i) to fix, maintain and change prices unitedly; (ii) to manipulate the price by restricting the output or supply; (iii) to manipulate the prices in the course of tendering and bidding or the auctioning activities; (iv) other price manipulating activities. '

the forbiddance of resale price maintenance, monopolistic prices, predatory prices, and discriminating treatment.[39]

On the tying arrangement, Article 12 of the 'Anti-unfair Competition Law' provides, 'In selling goods, an operator shall not make a tie-in sale against the wish of the buyer or attach other unreasonable conditions.' This Article forbids the tying arrangement.

Besides, the State Planning Commission also promulgated the 'Regulations on the Administrative Punishment of Illegal Price Behavior' and the 'Regulation on the Administrative Punishment Procedure concerning Price Behavior' in 1999 and 2001 respectively, which stipulate on the substantive and procedural problems of the punishment concerning price behavior. While the 'Notice on Guiding and Standardizing Market Pricing Behavior' promulgated by the State Development and Reform Commission in 2003 made the stipulation in principle on how to guide and regulate the market pricing behavior.[40]

3.3.2 Regional blockade

Article 7 of the 'Anti-unfair Competition Law' provides, 'A local government and its subordinate departments shall not abuse their administrative power to force others to buy the goods of the operators designated by them so as to restrict the lawful business activities of other operators. A local government and its subordinate departments shall not abuse their administrative power to restrict the entry of goods from other parts of the country into the local market or the flow of local goods to markets in

---

[39] Article 5 of the 'Temporary Regulation on Repressing Price Monopolistic Behavior' provides: 'operators shall not use their dominant market position to forcibly restrict distributors' resale prices when supply commodities to them.' Article 6 provides: 'operators shall not violate the stipulations of the laws and regulations to seek extravagant profits relying on their dominant market position;' Article 7 provides: 'operators shall not sell their goods at a price that is below the cost for the purpose of excluding or harming their competitors relying on their dominant market position; or lowering the price in disguised form by discounting, subsidizing, and giving as present, for the purpose of making the actual prices of commodities lower than their cost.' Article 8 provides: 'operators shall not apply discriminating treatment on trade prices to relative trading parties with equal standing when supplying the same commodities or services, relying on their dominant market positions.'

[40] The 'Notice on Guiding and Standardizing Market Pricing Behavior' provides: 'to guide and standardize the market pricing behavior on the premise of bring into full play of the basic function of allocating resources by the market is very important to constantly deepen the reform, break the trade monopoly and regional blockade, improve a fair and competitive market environment and price order, and perfect the market economic system.'

other parts of the country.' The 'Law of the People's Republic of China on Tenders and Bids' promulgated in 1999 also provided that the tender and bid activities shall not be restricted by the districts or departments.[41]

Article 3 of the 'Regulation on Prohibiting the Regional blockade in Market Economic Activities' promulgated by the State Council in 2001 synoptically prohibits the regional blockade.[42] Article 4 provides that local governments at different levels and their subordinate departments (including organisations authorised or entrusted with the administrative rights) shall not violate the laws, regulations and the stipulations by the State Council to launch seven kinds of regional blockade activities.[43]

---

[41] Article 6 of the 'Law of the People's Republic of China on Tenders and Bids' provides: 'Tender and bid activities for a project subject to tender according to law shall not be restricted by areas or departments. No units or person may illegally restrict or exclude legal persons or other organizations from other areas or systems to take part in bidding or interfere in tender and bid activities in any form.'

[42] 'Regulation on Prohibiting the Regional blockade in Market Economic Activities' provides: 'No units or person may violate the laws, regulations and stipulations of the State Council, obstructing and interfering with the entry into the local market of products and construction services (hereafter referred to as "services") from other parts of the country in any form, or conniving and covering up the behaviors obstructing and interfering with the entry into the local market of products and services from other parts of the country, restricting fair competition.'

[43] 'Regulation on Prohibiting the Regional blockade in Market Economic Activities' provides: '(i) restricting in any form and restricting in disguised form that units and person can only operate, purchase, and use the products produced in the local places, or can only accept services provided by local undertakings, designated undertakings, and other economic organizations or person; (ii) setting up checkpoints on roads, stations, docks, airports or the boundaries of the local administrative district to block the entry of the non-local products or the exit of local products; (iii) setting discriminatory charging items, fixing discriminatory prices, or implementing discriminatory charging standard; (iv) imposing technical requirements or inspection standards on non-local commodities and services which are different from those on local comparable commodities, or taking discriminatory technical measures such as repeated inspection or certification on non-local commodities, so as to restrict the entry of non-local commodities and services into the local market; (v) implementing discriminatory treatment and creating special requirements such as monopoly of operation, monopoly of sales, examination and approval, and licensing on non-local products and services, so as to restrict those non-local products and services into the local market; (vi) by setting up discriminatory qualification requirement, assessment standard, or not publishing information concerned according to laws so as to restrict or exclude non-local undertakings, other economic organizations and person from taking part in the local bidding activities; (vii) using of discriminatory treatment to reject or restrict either investment or establishment of branches by non-local undertakings in local area, or implementing discriminatory treatment on non-local undertakings, other

Article 5 provides that local administrative districts shall not make stipulations implementing regional blockades or containing regional blockade-concerned stipulations, which may impede the establishment and improvement of a united, fair and competitive, normative and orderly market system throughout the country, and which may harm the fair competition environment.[44]

3.3.3 Public utilities

Article 6 of the 'Anti-unfair Competition Law' (1993) provides, 'Public utility enterprises or other operators having monopolistic status according to law shall not force others to buy the goods of the operators designated by them so as to exclude other operators from competing fairly.'

Article 3 of the 'Regulation on Prohibiting the Behaviors of Public Utility Enterprise in Restricting Competition' (1993) provides, 'Public utility enterprises should abide by the laws and not to use its own advantageous status to hinder the fair competition between other operators, and not to infringe consumers' legal interests.' Article 4 requires that the public utility enterprise shall not practice seven kinds of restrictive competition activities in marketing.[45]

---

economic organizations and person who have investment or branches in the local area, infringing their legal interests; (viii) other district blocking activities.'

[44] Whereafter, the State Council promulgated the 'Decision on Consolidating and Standardizing the Market Economic Order' in the same year, which pointed out that the 'the main job and focus of consolidating and standardizing market economic order' include 'breaking the regional blockade as well as department and trade monopoly, investigating and dealing with the behaviors of administrative authorities, institutions, monopolistic industries, and public utilities in impeding fair competition and restricting the non-local products and services from entering into the local market, together with other practices restricting the undertakings to compete with each otter.' The Decision also required 'breaking the regional blockade and trade monopoly. Sorting out and repealing the regulations made by different districts and departments, which contain the stipulations on regional blockade and trade monopoly. Prohibiting any unit or person to violate the laws and regulations to impede and interfere with the entry into the local market of non-local products and services, or to connive and cover up the behaviors of impeding and interfering with the entry into the local market of on-local products and services, thereby restricting fair competition.'

[45] Article 4 of the 'Regulation on Prohibiting the Behaviors of Public Utility Enterprise in Restricting Competition' provides: '(i) restricting that users and consumers can only purchase and use the related supplementary merchandises provided by them, while not to purchase and use the same kind of merchandises provided by other operators, which also meet the requirement of the technical standards; (ii) restricting that users and consumers can only purchase and use the merchandises produced or operated by the operators designated by them, while

3.3.4 Regulated industries

Article 17 of the 'Regulations on Telecommunications of the People's Republic of China' (2002) provides, 'Interconnection between telecommunications networks shall be carried out according to the principles of technological feasibility, economy, fairness and co-ordination. Principal public telecommunications business providers shall not reject the requests for link-up of other telecommunication business providers and private networks operators.' Article 41 provides that while providing telecommunications services, a telecommunications business operator shall not carry out six kinds of acts.[46] Article 42 stipulates that during the course of telecommunications business operations, telecommunications business operators shall not carry out three kinds of acts.[47]

Article 6 of the 'Regulation on Repressing the Unfair Competition in the Civil Aviation Transportation Market' (1996) provides, 'Aviation

---

not to purchase and use the same kind of merchandises provided by other operators, where also meet the requirement of the technical standards; (iii) forcing users and consumers to purchase unnecessary commodities and accessories provided by them; (iv) forcing users and consumers to purchase unnecessary commodities and accessories provided by the operators designated by them; (v) in the name of inspecting the quality and performance of commodities, impeding users and consumers to purchase and use other commodities provided by other operators, which also meet the requirement of technical standard; (vi) refusing, stopping or cutting down the supply of commodities concerned to users and consumers who don't accept their unreasonable terms, or overcharging the fees; (vii) other restrictive competition activities.'

[46] Article 41 of the 'Telecommunications Regulation' provides: '(i) limiting, by any means whatsoever, telecommunications subscribers to use telecommunications services designated by it; (ii) limiting telecommunications subscribers to use telecommunications terminal equipment designated by it, or refusing telecommunications subscribers to use self-supplied telecommunications terminal equipment which has obtained the permission to connect to the network; (iii) violating the State regulations, presumably modifying or modifying in disguised form the charging rates, presumably increasing or increasing in disguised form the items for which it charges fees; (iv) refusing, delaying or terminating the provision of telecommunications services to telecommunications subscribers without legitimate reasons; (v) not performing the undertakings it publicly made to telecommunications subscribers or making false publicity that is likely to cause confusion; (vi) making use of improper means to harass telecommunications subscribers or retaliating against telecommunications subscribers who have filed a complaint.'

[47] Article 42 of the 'Telecommunications Regulation' provides: '(i) using any method whatsoever to limit a telecommunications subscriber from selecting telecommunications services legally provided by other telecommunications business operators; (ii) unreasonably cross-subsidizing other business that it operates; (iii) engaging in unfair competition by providing telecommunications business or services below cost, in order to squeeze out competitors.'

transportation undertakings shall not engage in the following unfair practices in their business operation: (i) violating the regulations on domestic aviation transportation fees management stipulated by the state and the Civil Aviation Administration of China (CAAC) to presumably raise or lower the aviation transportation prices; and (iv) restricting the passengers and cargo owner to select the carriers by themselves, so as to repel other aviation transportation undertakings. Otherwise stipulations made by the State shall be abide by.'

3.3.5 Concentrations of undertakings

The 'Interim Provisions on the Takeover of Domestic Enterprises by Foreign Investors' (7 March 2003), altogether 26 articles, establishes a basic framework with regard to the following situations, 'foreign investors purchasing equities of the shareholders of domestic companies or subscribing to the increased capital of domestic companies; or a foreign investor establishing a foreign-funded enterprise, and through which it purchases by agreement the assets of a domestic enterprise and operates its assets; or a foreign investor purchasing by agreement the assets of a domestic enterprise, and then invest such assets to establish a foreign-funded enterprise and operate the assets.' In 2006, the 'Regulations on the Takeover of Domestic Enterprises by Foreign Investors' made even detailed stipulations on the procedural matters about the notification with six chapters and 61 articles altogether.

4 THE CHARACTERISTICS AND BOTTLENECK OF THE IMPLEMENTATION IN THE PRE-AML PHASE

4.1 Deficiencies of Systems during the 'Ten Stipulations on Competition' Phase

The substantive AML in this phase had not been able to form a primary system, and were mostly enacted in the form of 'interim regulation' or 'notice' with relatively low binding effect. The major purpose of these regulations and notices was to give an immediate response to the specific problems emerging during the evolution process from the planned economy to the socialist market economy.

As far as the 'Ten Stipulations' are concerned, we have an impression that the law-makers at the time were only vaguely aware of the 'importance of competition', whereby the concept 'market competition' was not clearly mentioned in those legal documents. In terms of the overall situation at the time, first, speaking of the institutional system, it was quite impossible to generate an integrated substantive AML system, according to the development level of the market economy in this phase; second, speaking of the regulative mode, the stipulations concerning monopolistic behaviors in this phase, taking 'tie-in commodities' as an example, were not instituted based on the standard AML analytical method, they were rather expedient measures trying to make checks at all levels by inspecting and supervising specific problems, and the fact that no 'concrete solutions' had ever been stipulated at the time reflects the serious deficiency of a formal AML system. Last, speaking of the legal liability, the only monopolistic behavior which shall bear legal liability was 'monopolistic agreement'.[48] As to the matter of regional blockade, the method adopted by the 'Ten Stipulations on Competition' is to revise the relevant regulations and systems as well as rescind the illegal regulations.[49] While the 'Notice on Breaking the Market Blockade between Districts and further Livening Commodities Circulation' requests departments concerned to dismiss relevant checkpoints, rescind relevant regulations and take action against relevant leaders.[50] In fact, due to the deficiency of the specific legal liabilities, the investigation of the actions mentioned above often turned out to be fruitless.

---

[48] The ways of punishment provided in the 'Regulation of the People's Republic of China on Price Control' (article 30) includes: '(i) Issuing a notice of criticism; (ii) ordering the violators to return the illicit gains to the buyers or users; (iii) confiscating any illicit gains that can not be returned; (iv) imposing a fine; (v) requesting the administration of industry and commerce to suspend the license of the offender; (vi) issuing a fine to the person held directly responsible and the person in charge if the offender is an enterprise or a public institution; and recommend to the relevant department that certain administrative action is taken.'

[49] The 'Ten Stipulations on Competition' provide: 'the departments of industry, transportation, finance and trade should revise the content impeding competition in their respective existing regulations and systems so as to facilitate competition. It is illegal to protect the backwardness and repress forwardness by administrative methods.'

[50] The 'Notice on Breaking the Market Blockade between Districts and further Livening Commodities Circulation' provides: 'to clean up and rectify the existing checkpoints thoroughly and dismiss all kinds of checkpoints impeding the normal circulation of commodities . . . relevant regulations issued by various districts and departments should be rescinded if they fail to meet the requirement of the notice, immediately dismiss all the approving authorities restricting the purchasing of commodities from non-local markets and all the checkpoints blocking the entry into the local market of non-local commodities. . . . should the regional blockade persist after the issuance of the notice, relevant leaders should be held responsible.'

4.2 Deficiencies of Enforcement Power during the 'Anti-unfair Competition' Phase

During this period, the substantive AML had gradually formed a primary competition law system with the 'Anti-unfair Competition Law' as the centre. Within the legal system, the legislative level of the substantive AML was quite elevated, and the number of relevant legal documents was also increased. However, due to the inferior legislative techniques, the loosely constructed AML legal system consists of the Anti-unfair Competition Law and other relevant laws, regulations and normative legal documents features a lacking of enforcement power.[51] According to the statistics provided by the industry and commerce administrative authorities of Guangdong Province (1993–2003), of the 17 categories of unfair competition behaviors, 'the restrictive competition cases caused by the public utilities enterprises or other operators enjoying monopolistic status according to laws' account for 1.65 per cent of the total cases; 'restrictive competition cases incurred by abusing administrative power' account for 0.08 per cent of the total; 'cases of regional blockade' account of 0 per cent; 'cases concerning tie-in arrangements or other unreasonable terms' account for 0.22 per cent; 'cases of dumping sales at low prices' account for 0.04 per cent; 'cases concerning the manipulation of market and impediment of fair competition' account for 0.18 per cent; 'cases concerning collusively division of market and restriction of commodities' prices and sales by way of contracts, agreements, or other methods between operators' account for 0.20 per cent.[52] The enforcement of the regulations relating to the substantive AML appears feeble as a whole.

However, it should be noted that the phenomenon mentioned above cannot be fully attributed to the poor awareness of the law enforcement officials or the lacking of the competition restriction stipulations mentioned above in the existing market system. Because, according to the statistics of the same period, of the seven kinds of 'unfair competition behaviors on which the law enforcement officials think should carry out key investigation', the number of 'restrictive competition' acts account for 13.71 per cent; the 'four major reasons resulting in the unfair competition in the market as concluded by the operators' are all restrictive competition acts, of which, 'regional blockade implemented by governments' account

---

[51] Haibin, Peng (2006), *The Choice of Fair Competition System*, Hong Kong: The Commercial Press, p. 319.

[52] Haibin, Peng (2006), *The Choice of Fair Competition System*, Hong Kong: The Commercial Press, p. 315.

for 12.52 per cent; 'large enterprises monopolizing the market with their economic advantages' account for 27 per cent; 'public utility institutions and undertakings implementing monopolistic operation' account for 43.3 per cent; and 'departments subordinating to governments implementing discriminatory treatment on enterprises of different ownership' account for 17.83 per cent.[53]

4.3 The Bottleneck of the Implementation in the Pre-AML Phase

We believe that the deficiency of the system and the feebleness in the enforcement is due to the legal system being designed too sketchily, while the more profound reason is that the whole system reform is still in the course of transformation. Different from the 'shock treatment' adopted by the Soviet Union and other Eastern European countries, China's transformation is a gradual process, rather than changing from the planned economy into the market economy on a whole basis within a very short time. In the course of gradual transformation, the inertia being left from the old system is the main factor impeding the implementation of the substantive AML. It is the market economy that nourishes the existence of the AML, in other words, there is the room and necessity for the AML to exist only under the market economy. However, in the course of China's system transformation, it takes time both for the government to form the ideas about market and for the consumers and enterprises to elevate their awareness about market; besides, it also takes time for the old planned economy system to link up with the new market economy system and for two systems to co-ordinate systemically.

It was impossible for the enactment of AML under the planned economy system before the socialist market economy was formally written in the Constitution in the 1990s. All the problems raised in the above mentioned phase give us an impression that the entire competition law system during the primary stage of the substantive AML development featured a sense of mixture, vividly displayed the chaotic state at the initial stage of the State's economic management mode transiting from the planned economy to the market economy. The subsequent normative legal documents concerned also expressed nothing but the recognition, to some extent, of the harmful impact to the economy caused by some specific acts, while the responses to those harmful impacts were mainly some roughly made prohibitive stipulations targeting at the mixed problems generated from the linking up of the planned economy and the

53 *Ibid.*, pp. 315–317.

market economy, which were practically irrelevant to the institutional and technical aspects of the AML, let alone referring to the existence of the idea of the AML.

At the beginning of the 1990s, when China was taking great initiative in transforming from the planned economy to the market economy, the State's thoughts, ideas, systems, and government's functions as a whole were still fettered by the planned economy. The 'obstruction', to be exact, the 'inertia' generated from the planned economy had a direct impact on the competition policy's situation in the course of economic reform in the transformation period: the political system reform lagged behind, the key function of price control in the market economy, the difficulty in the reform of the State-owned enterprise, and the leading role of the industrial policy have all determined the inferior position and the fate of the competition policy, especially the status of the AML. It will take a relatively long period to eliminate this kind of 'inertia' in constructing our market economy.

Based on the above analysis, if we take the pre-AML phase as whole for inspection, we can draw the conclusion that the ultimate bottleneck that runs through the '30 years of AML' should be the system disorder. The system disorder had originated both from the disordering linking up between various systems inside the existing loose system, always lacking of a united purpose to command the whole system of the AML laws, regulations, and normative legal documents; and from the lacking of lively interaction between the above mentioned systems and the outside systems, always unable to establish a favourable communication with other policy systems represented by the industrial policy. Being beset with troubles internally and externally, how can the AML win out?

5 THE PERSPECTIVE OF THE IMPLEMENTATION OF THE AML IN THE FRAMEWORK OF THE 'AUTONOMOUS-RESPONSIVE' LAW

In terms of the system construction, the promulgation of the AML not only helps to form a relatively integrated system; the law also makes stipulations, in the form of separate chapters, on the problems concerning the following occasions: monopolistic agreement, the abuse of dominant market place, concentrations of undertakings, and administrative monopoly. Meanwhile, the AML has made great progress in coordinating the legal liabilities and the enforcement measures, forming a dual enforcement system consisting of the government enforcement and the private litigation, and endowing the AML enforcement authorities with great powers. However, the implementation of the AML still has a long way to go.

5.1 Establish the 'Autonomous-Responsive' AML in the Market Economy Perfection Period

Nonet and Selznick clarify the 'law-in-society' into three modalities or three basic 'states'.[54] First, law as the servant of the repressive power, i.e. the 'Repressive Law';[55] second, law as a differentiated institution capable of taming repression and protecting its own integrity, i.e. the 'Autonomous Law';[56] and third, law as a facilitator of response to social needs and aspirations, i.e. the 'Responsive Law'.[57]

On the whole, legal institutions passively and opportunistically adapting

---

[54] Nonet, Philippe and Philip Selznick (2001), *Law and Society in Transition: Toward Responsive Law*, New Jersey: Transaction Publishers, p. 14.

[55] Main characteristics of the Repressive Law include: (i) Legal institutions are directly accessible to political power; law is identified with the state and subordinated to raison d'etat. (ii) The conservation of authority is an overriding preoccupation of legal officialdom; (iii) Specialized agency of control become independent centers of power; they are isolated from moderating social contexts and capable of resisting political authority; (iv) A regime of 'dual law' institutionalises class justice by consolidating and legitimating patterns of social subordination; (v) The criminal code mirrors the dominant mores; legal moralism prevails. Nonet, Philippe and Philip Selznick, *Ibid.*, p. 33.

[56] The chief attributes of the Autonomous Law include: (i) Law is separated from politics. Characteristically, the system proclaims the independence of the judiciary and draws a sharp line between legislative and judicial functions; (ii) The legal order espouses the 'model of rules'. A focus on rules helps enforce a measure of official accountability; at the same time, it limits both the creativity of legal institutions and the risk of their intrusion iinto the political domain; (iii) 'Procedure is the heart of law'. Regularity and fairness, not substantive justice, are the first ends and the main competence of the legal order; (iv) 'Fidelity to law' is understood as strict obedience to the rules of positive law. Criticism of existing laws must be channeled through the political process. Nonet, Philippe and Philip Selznick, *Ibid.*, p. 54.

[57] The main characteristics of the Responsive Law include: (i) The dynamics of legal development increases the authority of purpose in legal reasoning; (ii) Purpose makes legal obligation more problematic, thereby relaxing law's claim to obedience and opening the possibility of a less rigid and more civil conception of public order; (iii) As law gains openness and flexibility, legal advocacy takes on a political dimension, generating forces that help correct and change legal institutions but threaten to undermine institutional integrity; (iv) Finally, in an environment of pressure the continuing authority of legal purpose and the integrity of the legal order depend on the design of more competent legal institutions. Nonet, Philippe and Philip Selznick, *Ibid.*, p. 87.

to the social political environment is the marked indication of the repressive law. The autonomous law focuses on the maintenance of legal institutions' integrity, thereby isolating itself and narrowly defining its own responsibility. While the responsive law will relax the tension between the two legal modalities mentioned above, and it tries every means to make the integrity and openness to support mutually when conflict breaks out between them. Most importantly, the responsive law 'interprets the social pressure as the source of knowledge and the opportunity for self-correction'.[58]

We think that the deficiency of systems, the feebleness in enforcement, and the overall system disorder exposed in the course of institution and implementation of the substantive AML over the 30 years before the promulgation of the AML has altogether not been able to meet the criteria of the 'autonomous law', if observed with the 'Berkeley Perspective', let alone generating the self-knowledge of the 'responsive law'. This kind of situation is related to the gradualness of China's reform and the pursuit of multiple and mixed goals during the transforming period, and it is more closely related to the reality that China's economic regime reform has started off before its political regime reform. We noticed that Nonet and Selzick also realised 'no complex legal order, or sector of it, ever forms a fully coherent system; any given legal order or legal institution is likely to have a "mixed" character.'[59] Considering, on an overall basis, the theory model under the 'Berkeley Perspective', the reality of China's transformation, and the conclusion of the AML's practices, we think that the orientation of the AML's implementation should take the 'autonomous-responsive' law as the goal; and while advocating the 'responsive law' orientation, great importance should be given to the capability construction of the factors in the framework of the 'autonomous law', whereby to carry out the

---

[58] They also treat the classification of the law into three modalities as a kind of development model. They believe that, to some extent, the repressive law 'takes the leading place', and the fundamental problem to be solved by it is to establish the political order or define a kind of state. If conditions are insufficient, the repressive law will not be able to look up to a 'higher' pursuit. The autonomous law is based on the achievement of the repressive law. Likewise, the cornerstone of the responsive law is the Constitution, which is more limited but more fundamental during the period ruling by law. The author also points out that they have placed their focus on the autonomous law, as the autonomous law makes it possible for laws to acquire more responsivity. *See*, Nonet, Philippe and Philip Selznick, *Ibid.*, pp. 76–77.

[59] *Ibid.*, Nonet, Philippe and Philip Selznick, p. 17.

self-realisation of the AML in the course of the transformation of the society's legal institutions.

5.2 Objective Positioning of the AML in the Framework of the Genre of 'Autonomous-Responsive' Law

5.2.1 The objective of the responsive law

The responsive law is mainly characterised by advocating and attaching great importance to the objective. Unlike the autonomous law, the latter mainly distinguishes itself by caring a lot about the rules. Important as they are, rules are mainly used for protecting its feasibility and vitality. The institution and transformation of any rules should be adaptable to the historical conditions, the social environment, and the universal needs of human beings, to make themselves meaningful. Therefore, in the mode of 'responsive law', 'It is necessary for the institution to be led by the purpose. Purpose can set the benchmark for criticizing the extant regulations and institutions, and whereby opening up a path for reform. Meanwhile, if the purpose is sincerely implemented, it naturally can restrict the administrative discretion, and whereby relaxing the risk of institutional submission.' According to Nonet and Selznick, 'In the transition from autonomy to responsiveness, the critical step is the generalization of law's objectives. Particular rules, policies, and procedures come to be regarded as instrumental and expendable. They may be respected as funded experience, but they cease to define the commitments of the legal order.'[60] Based on this kind of awareness, the effective implementation of the AML should be based on reasonable legal objectives. The objectives of the AML include: 'safeguarding the market fair competition', 'improving economic efficiency', 'protecting consumer and public interests', 'promoting the healthy development of the socialist market economy'. Of the legislative objectives of AMLs in developed jurisdictions, the following three objectives prevail: protecting competition rather than competitors, improving the economic efficiency, and maximizing the consumers' benefits. The objectives of China's AML can also be reduced to the three objectives. However, here comes the problem: does the AML have its core objective of value? How to make the choice among many objectives? It is difficult to solve the problem thoroughly. We believe that the key job for the time being is to establish the objective for the implementation of the AML.

---

60 *Ibid.*, Nonet, Philippe and Philip Selznick, pp. 78–79.

5.2.2 The objective orientation of the AML's implementation

We think that the AML, by its nature, is highly abstract and professional, with its impact far-reaching. Therefore, it is regarded as the most important issue to grasp, implement and apply the extant AML in the economic life and legal practices on an overall basis after the promulgation of the AML. The premise of effective implementation of the AML is to define the orientation of the implementing objective pursued by the AML. 'What the AML protects is the competition structure, rather than the competitors' is an established judgment rule of most developed jurisdictions, namely, to realise the maximum economic efficiency, technology innovation, and protection of consumers by protecting the competition structure. The starting point in designing the rules of AML is the maintenance of competition order rather than the protection of some individual operator's interests under the normal competition order. In the course of the AML legislation, such an idea prevailed among the legislators, while its implementation will be the core objective in future work. The establishment of the objective has both indicated the objective pursued by the AML and the functional orientation of the AML enforcement authorities defined by the AML: protecting competition rather than getting involved, and correcting nonstandard competition rather than intervening. The AML, on one hand, should sort out and tries to shape the government power that maintains the market competition order, on the other hand, should make sure the power being applied only when necessary. We believe that as the objective of the AML's implementation, the idea of 'protecting competition structure rather than competitors' helps to establish a sound support for the profound and effective implementation of the AML.

5.2.3 The institutional construction of AML in the framework of the 'autonomous-responsive' law

Except for establishing the objective orientation of the implementation, the AML should also absorb the reasonable elements of the 'autonomous-responsive' law in respect of institutional construction.

5.2.3.1 The uniting and co-ordinating of enforcement authorities The AML is a new kind of legal institution and is highly professional, cross-disciplinary, and highly influential. It should first of all stress the unity, independence, specialty and authoritativeness of its enforcement institutions, so as to guarantee the stateliness of the law. As yet, the AML has not clearly defined the institutional set up and the allocation of the enforcement power; it is very likely to be jointly enforced by several enforcement authorities. Therefore, the co-ordination and co-operation between the enforcement authorities should be given special attention, which will decide on the efficiency of the AML's implementation. At the same time, the co-ordination between the AML enforcement authorities and other legal enforcement authorities, especially with the authoritative industrial administering institutions will also be taken into consideration.

5.2.3.2 The stipulation of procedural rules Whilst the AML is highly professional and complex, its system of rules is very abstract. Therefore, the market correction mechanism and the individual relief rules provided by the enforcement authorities should also be timely stipulated or modified according to the subsequent market situation and different social periods. Therefore, corresponding effective legal documents should also be stipulated for these procedural rules. While in terms of the substantive criterion used to judge the specific cases, it would be proper for the AML enforcement authorities to issue more detailed 'guidelines' based on the reasonable judgment rule, which does not have the abstract binding effect, but is applicable to individual cases.

5.2.3.3 Judicial review and litigation No matter as an administrative institution or as a quasi-judicial organ, the AML enforcement authorities' actions and decisions will ultimately be placed under the review of judicial organs. Besides, individual operators or consumers should also be allowed to seek private relief directly by way of judicial means against the monopolistic behaviors disrupting the market competition order, whereby bringing into full play the function of judicial supervision. To this end, it is only necessary for the judicial organs to obtain a relatively independent status and judicial officials to elevate their levels.

5.2.3.4 The deficiency of and cultivation of competition culture The deficiency of competition culture in China's market environment can be a serious problem for the future implementation of the AML. The cultivation and formation of competition culture is the result of multiple factors: consumers' ideas; industry behaviors; the orientation of government function; the ways of exchanging ideas between the main bodies of market; the understanding and application of commercial transaction rules; and promulgation and implementation of economic laws. It can be said that every detail in economic operations is silently helping the formation of the competition culture. In the course of function transformation, the government should stick to its function orientation and remain an impartial and neutral umpire. As the important participants of market competition, operators shall voluntarily bear the pressure and consequences resulting from competition in a free market, avoid seeking help and shelter from the competent authorities at every turn. While the mass of consumers, who play an important role in maintaining the market, should try their best to strive for the benefits yielding from the market competition, and constantly enhance their yearning for market competition.[61]

5.2.4 The overall co-ordination surrounding the AML

Nonet and Selznick point out, 'We call it responsive, rather than open or adaptive, to suggest a capacity for responsible, and hence discriminate and selective, adaptation. A responsive institution retains a grasp on what is essential to its integrity while taking account of new forces in its setting. To do so, it builds upon the ways integrity and openness sustain each other as they conflict.'[62] Based on this kind of reality and China's realistic condition, we think that it is very important to harmonise the various legal relationships in implementing the AML in the future.

5.2.4.1 Co-ordination with industrial policy AML is actually the legalisation of the State's competition policy. The coordination of the AML with the industrial policy is essentially the coordination between the competition policy and the industrial policy. In terms of the value orientation, competition policy means the task of promoting economic efficiency and social welfare being handed over to the law of the market by the government, while the government is only responsible for constructing a framework to control the restrictive competition acts. Industrial policy stresses the management of specific industries, the promotion of specific industries' development, and the optimisation of the State's industrial structure by the government, rather than maintaining an efficient competitive market structure and market order. The nature of the relationships between the government and the market is nothing but who takes precedence in the course of promoting economic efficiency. This question has actually already been answered since China began to reform the market economy system, namely, market has always been the basic measure to allocate resources in the market economy. It is therefore reasonable to conclude that competition policy takes the core place in a fully developed market

---

[61] For more complete exposition, see Yong, Huang and Jiang Shan (2008), 'An Outline of the Cultural Dimension of AML's Implementation: Competition Culture, Litigation Culture and Rights Culture', *Jiangxi Social Sciences*, **7**.

[62] Nonet, Philippe and Philip Selznick (2001), *Law and Society in Transition: Toward Responsive Law*, New Jersey: Transaction Publishers, p. 77.

economy structure, while the industrial policy can only be implemented in the premise of sticking to the basic function of competition policy. When the two factors conflict with each other, the competition policy enjoys the priority. However, it should be noted that there is a premise for competition policy to enjoy priority. In developing countries like China, the government takes a leading role in the development, the economic regime is still in the phase of transformation, the economic development still lags far behind that of the developed countries, the industrial structure is neither sound nor healthy, the market economy system has not fully been established, the importance of the industrial policy is therefore not negligible. The rational choices are: on one hand, make sure that competition policy enjoys the priority; the industrial policy can only be applicable when it complies with the competition policy, and the institution and implementation of the industrial policy should generate the least harm to competition. On the other hand, channels should be provided to help with the bridging of the industrial policy and competition policy by taking into consideration the economic efficiency factors.

5.2.4.2 Co-ordination with trade policy Seen from the AML's point of view, the conflicts between trade policy and the AML are mainly reflected in the trade relief measures, like anti-dumping measures, anti-subsidiary measures, and safeguarding measures, which obviously conflict with the value and the objective of the AML.[63] However, in the face of economic globalisation and competition between countries, trade policy is of unusual importance to China who have recently joined the WTO. Therefore, it is necessary for the AML to coordinate well with the trade policy. Considering China's actual situation, we think that the framework construction for coordinating trade policy and the AML should stick to the following principles. First, give priority to competition policy in the course of legislation and policy stipulation, and make sure the Chinese trade policy and competition policy remain consistent. Second, make sure the institutions and systems established give priority to competition policy in implementing policy and laws, for example, establishing a unitary, independent and authoritative AML competent authority as well as a co-ordinating mechanism responsible

---

[63] For example, due to the low price of products exported from China, other countries may levy anti-dumping tax on these products, and when the Chinese guild concerned asks all its members to raise the prices, enterprises or institutions concerned in foreign countries would then lodge a complaint against the Chinese guild and its members for collusion in monopolistic pricing, which may incur the criminal law sanction.

for co-ordinating the relationship with trade policy making department. Third, introduce the competition policy into the implementation of trade relief measures, for example, while investigating and judging on the anti-dumping, anti-subsidiary, and safeguarding actions, competition should be taken into consideration as part of the public social welfare; when the adoption of these trade relief measures may seriously harm the Chinese domestic market competition order, the department concerned shall not make decisions to carry out these trade relief measures. Last, China should pay close attention to the restrictive competition acts in international trade, and effectively maintain China's competitive interests as well economic and trade benefits. The AML should implement the extraterritorial application doctrine against the extraterritorial restrictive competition acts harmful to China's competition order; meanwhile, China should also carry out international co-operation on competition law enforcement with other countries.

5.2.4.3 Co-ordination with intellectual property law Intellectual property (IP) rights are exclusive rights on intellectual achievements and trade marks confirmed by laws, whose basic value lies in encouraging innovation; while the AML takes it as its own obligation to restrict or break monopolistic behaviors or restrictive competition behaviors. The profound objectives of both IP law and the AML are identical, i.e. increasing social welfare and protecting public interests. The proper exercise of IP rights will not be concerned by the AML, while the abuse of IP rights will certainly be challenged by the AML. Excessive interference with the exercise of IP rights will restrain people's initiative in innovation, and hinder the development of social economy; while being over indulgent to the exercises of IP rights will unavoidably harm the free competition order and ultimately harm economic development. Therefore, it is necessary to keep a balance between IP law and the AML in the age of knowledge economy. As far as China's real situation is concerned, the AML enforcement authority, as well as People's Court's enforcement experiences and enforcement level, are very important factors to consider. In our opinion, IP-abusing actions should be regulated using the reasonable doctrine in a prospective framework, guided by the proper and highly definite legal documents. The application of AML in the field of IP should remain cautious, as the innovation acts encouraged by IP rights should be fully protected. The IP-abusing actions should also be prevented by further improving the internal controlling mechanism within the IP law framework.

6 CONCLUSION

Raymond Aron said: 'analysis of present facts, or prognostications about facts to come, alter with the unfolding of history and the knowledge we acquire of it.'[64] Standing on this node of history and looking into the future, we can say that no matter what will become of the analyses and prediction, the AML will never cease to shape itself in its implementation.

[64] Aron, Raymond (1977), *The Opium of the Intellectuals, translated by Terence Kilmartin*, Santa Barbara, CA: Greenwood Press, p. 236.

7. Transition Countries Facing Transitory Competition Rules: 'Moving Shooter' Taking Aim at a 'Moving Target'

Josef Bejček*

1 GENERAL INTRODUCTORY REMARKS

It is a somewhat strange feeling to talk about the issue of development of competition law from the perspective of a new member state of the EU. It resembles the situation of proverbial 'talking about rope in hangman's house'. The reason why is as follows: new member states are to blame (at least indirectly) because of the pressure on modernisation of the EU competition law. This law and its enforcement were difficult enough even before the accession of new joining states. The shock of accession of ten new states partially without sufficient antitrust legislation and antitrust culture might have been fatal and deadly. It is, of course, too early to assess the 'modernisation package' of the EU competition law and its direct impact on the legal systems of particular member states. Anyway, it is a strategic attempt to remove internal faults of the system and to secure its workability under changed circumstances by the means of 'residual decentralization and selective recentralization'.[1]

Some argue that the word 'modernisation' usually only disguises the fact that there is not enough money or other resources for anything and that it should be therefore changed. I think it was (at least partially) the case in so-called modernisation of European competition law though its reasons were obviously more complex. Nevertheless we might admit

* Professor of Law; Director of the Department of Commercial Law, Masaryk University Brno; Member of the Appellate Committee of the Czech antitrust authority in Brno, Czech Republic.

[1] Rodríguez, T (2004), 'Decentralized Application of EU Competition Law: A Strategic Approach', Working Paper No 05, CLASF Workshop 22.4, p. 12, available at www.clasf.org (accessed 18 June 2009).

they were not complex enough and they were not sufficiently reasoned in theoretical terms and their prevalent motive was a pragmatic one.[2]

On the other hand, a cynical argument may be that no theory of competition was ever more persuasive than legal norms based and grounded thereon, so that just the norms count. Economic theory does not offer irrefutable scientific evidence (both generally and in competition affairs) so that sufficiently massive political support of the new approach is decisive. That modernisation approach is based on more- or less-acceptable theoretical foundations but it was mainly enforced by the vigour of the reality of competition policy and of the feed-back indicating the low functionality of the former system.

The pendulum of views on the competition law in transition countries quite naturally has had great amplitude and a neo-liberal attitude was a natural reaction to former overregulation of the society and economics. So, it was argued with reference to academic authorities, that it is precisely competition legislation that is seen[3] as one of the main obstacles to effective competition as it does not restrict monopolies but rather persistently and erratically bothers efficiently working businesses. The monopolisation tendency was not recognised as an objective economic phenomenon of an economy left to its own self-development but only as the result of anti-liberal economic policy.[4]

Activities associated with the combating of monopolies are deemed to be – perhaps well meant but still clumsy – interference with the mechanics of the market that hinders competition. The idea that the government is able to propose a policy that would create or guarantee competition, and that competition would degenerate into a complete or partial monopoly in the absence of such policy, is considered dubious, and no special legislation or its enforcement is purported to be required on the market (save for completely extraordinary situations when someone owns a unique and indispensable source for the production of important consumer goods) to ensure dynamic competition in the market; the government's sole activity towards securing dynamic competition is to be precisely the removal of all such obstacles to competition created by the government.[5]

Anti-monopoly laws were viewed as a form of regulation that lessens the

---

2 The reactions on the White book in 1999 especially from the proponents of 'ordoliberal school' were reluctant, if not outright repudiating.

3 *See* Rothbard, M.N. (2001), *Ekonomie státních zásahů*, Liberální institut, Praha, at p. 146 *et seq.*

4 Mises, L. (1998), *Liberalismus*, Liberální institut, Praha, at p. 81.

5 Cf. Kirzner, I. (1998), *Jak fungují trhy*, Praha: Liberální institut, at pp. 71–72.

efficiency of economics, and a form of faith,[6] which in effect entrenches in the law special interests of selected entities at the expense of all the other players; it is natural for the advantaged groups to oppose the abrogation of such legislation, and citizens and consumers are insufficiently motivated to joint their forces against the anti-monopoly monster. Anti-monopoly policy is viewed as a type of sector policy and a form of state planning,[7] and not even the Chicago School followers will be willing to abolish it because they too are held in captivity of the error of the 'daring illusion of knowledge'.[8]

2 GENERAL INTRODUCTORY DOUBTS

Talking about competition policy and competition law developments in transition countries means inter alia to be aware of fundamental axiological and terminological difficulties.

Does (and should) a democratic state in a newly shaped would-be market economy have any other objectives than ensuring that the market mechanism is not disturbed by anyone (including the state itself) because the optimum situation is achieved through a decentralised market mechanism?

Even if the state did consistently declare certain society-wide objectives, would such objectives not pertain to interest groups whose interests are merely declared and enforced by bodies of the state while they may jeopardise the competition? A government that formulates the objectives of its government policy is not a homogeneous monolith, voting takes place and the result is declared to constitute an interest of the state which, however, is not identical with the spectrum of views and positions within a specific and temporary government. After all, there are system interests transcending the terms of office of many governments and parliaments.

We do not even know what precisely the interests of the society or state are.[9] What if the interests or objectives of the state merely serve to disguise the formulated group interests of strong players, capable of ensuring that politicians who promote their own interests and the interests of those

6 *See* Armentano, D.T. (2000), *Proč odstranit protimonopolní zákonodárství*, Praha: Liberální institut, at 37 and 39.

7 *Ibid.*, at p. 43.

8 *Ibid.*, at p. 115.

9 Stiglitz, J.E.(1997), *Ekonomie veřejného sektoru*, Praha: Grada Publishing, at p. 207.

pulling the strings backstage in accordance with the 'public choice' theory remain in power?

Should the state interventions be limited to cases of compensations of market failures[10] (failure of competition, public goods existence, externalities, incomplete markets, inadequate information, unemployment), or can they pursue specific sector goals?

Should a democratic state be allowed to correct decisions taken by individuals, who decide contrary to their interests despite possessing perfect information, and perhaps to restrict harmful consumption and encourage the consumption of useful goods (thus inevitably distorting competition on both markets, and perhaps also related markets)?

Despite the urgency of these questions, I do not dare to answer them. There is probably no right or wrong answer – there are only answers that do or do not conform to this or that particular value basis.[11] The value basis correlates with the political trend in power at the time which may impose its version of 'state interests' even on that part of the society that did not support it in the elections.

Non-existence of sufficiently developed self-regulating market mechanism in transition countries calls for direct state interventions into the economics. For example, the process of privatisation is not transferable to the market itself. The question of where is the borderline of 'artificial' privatisation behind which only the market should be active, whether first to demonopolise and then to privatise, or first to privatise the incumbent monopolies and then to try to split up them, or whether just to keep an eye on their behavior . . . those and similar questions are exclusively of political nature. Of course, privatised monopolies or dominant firms will be better off after the state will loose its substantial managing influence – it is more urgent for the would-be owners of those firms and their political proponents than some care about competitive economics of the future.

Although values are entrenched in legal regulations, their fluctuations are manifested in their interpretation, sometimes comparable to legislative amendments in terms of function. Even independent state officials and independent judges carry value ideas, professional opinions and prejudices, and may shift the factual meaning of legal norms. According to a sarcastic piece of wisdom, a conservative person is a liberal who was

---

[10] *Ibid.*, at p. 102.

[11] I once overheard a comment that antitrust is a matter of mentality. While in the USA, they are worried about making a mistake in the process of intervention, in Europe they worry about the mistake of not intervening.

mugged the day before.[12] This is particularly pronounced in the case of competition regulations characterised by indefinite notions not defined in the law (and usually impossible to be defined in the written law), allowing for both a substantial restriction and expansion under administrative and judicial discretionary powers.

A kind of highly virulent interpretation 'infection' rages within the EU. Even in cases lacking in community significance, domestic antimonopoly authorities and courts derive inspiration from interpretations of notions, and accept judicial definitions and doctrines and introduce them into their decision-making. Court decisions obviously do not constitute and cannot substitute for competition policy, but may have a significant impact on the decision making of antimonopoly authorities and even indirectly lead to changes in both competition policy and competition law in both directions: judicial interpretation and doctrines may become a part of written law[13]; however, this does not rule out attempts on the part of the coalition of competition opponents to put forward exceptional provisions of law that would narrow or completely eliminate room for perfection of the law by courts.

3 FORMAL AND INFORMAL COOPERATION IN ENFORCEMENT OF THE COMPETITION LAW

Decentralised enforcement of competition law is possible only with a decentralised system of decision making bodies. For the first period of European integration, the ECJ alone was enough. The Court of First Instance (CFI) with more competences was created as the result of permanently increasing ECJ's workload. The enlargement of the EU and putting through federalist elements led to an idea of founding a third level of communitary courts under the CFI[14]. Recently only national courts and national competition authorities are available – their diversity may bring about fruits as from

---

[12] Cf. the marked difference in the approach to competition policy (in particular merger control) in the USA during president Reagan's term of office, as opposed to the term of his successor, president Clinton. 'Reaganomics' meant a shift to the view that 'if size is efficient, it will prevail'; during Clinton's term, the influence of the 'Chicago school' diminished somewhat. Cf. Samuelson, P.A. and W.D. Nordhaus (1991), *Ekonomie*, Praha: Svoboda, at pp. 623–624.

[13] For instance, the 'European infection' of ECJ case law affecting our legislation, whereby the concept of 'essential facilities' or statutory definition of 'market power', which arose out of ECJ case law, was incorporated into our legislation.

[14] Compare McCurdy, G. (2004), 'The Impact of Modernisation of the EU Competition Law System on the Courts and Private Enforcement of the Competition Laws: A Comparative Perspective', *ECLR*, **8**, at p. 510.

an 'intellectual incubator'[15] but sometimes at the expense of consistent decision making. The system of coordination between Commission and national antitrust authorities on one hand is assessed to be better than that between communitary and national courts on the other hand. Introduction of some kind of European guidelines affecting decisions of national courts and addressing cases interfering into different jurisdictions is mere illusion incoherent with traditional European values of independent judicial decision making.[16]

3.1 Decentralised Enforcement

Enhanced level of legal uncertainty connected with decentralised enforcement of competition law may lead to an effort to make use of potential incoherence of decision making of national antitrust authorities. Nevertheless there are some measures available now to prevent tactically proceeding and picking and choosing the body competent to solving the case (forum shopping). First of all the ban in Article 3/2 Regulation 1/2003 is to be interpreted in sense[17] that Competition Acts (CA) of member states cannot be applied in a manner differing from a result according to application of European competition law unless positive decision of the Commission exists or is being prepared. Article 16 of Regulation 1/2003 supports this approach further.

'Extraordinary safeguard' of Article 10 Regulation 1/2003 is somewhat unclear. It stipulates that Commission may declare from its own initiative that Article 81 or 82 are not applicable because of the 'public interest of the Community'. Despite its declaratory meaning[18], this decision will be ultimately (according to Article 16 of the Regulation) binding both for the national competition authorities and for the national courts[19]. This measure can be interpreted (as to the final result) as an extraordinary exception from the principle of legal exception of legal ban of cartel agreements, decisions of undertakings and concerted practices; under extraordinary circumstances a return to individual exception is therefore possible,

---

15 *Ibid.*

16 *Ibid.*, at p. 516 and p. 514.

17 Canenbley, C. and M. Rosenthal (2005), 'Co-operation Between Antitrust Authorities In and Outside the EU: What does it Mean for Multinational Corporations? Part 1', *ECLR*, **2**, at p. 108.

18 *See* point 14 (recital) to Regulation 1/2003.

19 Canenbley, C. and M. Rosenthal, *ibid.* Article 16 is talking about the formal decisions of Commission without discerning between declaratory decisions and constitutive ones.

even if from the Commission's initiative and in the public interest of the community only.

Homogeneity and consistency of approach of different official bodies from different member states is also fostered by the entitlement of the Commission to offer informal consultations and recommendations.[20]

The duty of direct application of community law by national bodies according to Article 3 Regulation 1/2003 has a controversial and non-traditional consequence, namely a mirror-duty of these bodies (with no possibility of their discretion) not to apply national law that is incompatible with Community rules of competition.[21] Even if the principle of supremacy of European law is not explicitly stipulated in the European Treaty (obviously due to diplomatic reasons), the goals of the EU could not have been reached without its validity (that was later confirmed by the decisions of the ECJ). The only exception may be made if the non-appliance of national law would deprive the individual of making use of rights laid down in European law. European competition law prohibits violation of Community competition rules even if the violation would be assisted or motivated by the member state itself. Such legal rules must not be applied by national courts nor by national administrative bodies (effect *erga omnes*, though it is hardly to be guaranteed in organisational terms especially in the independent courts). The possibility of imposing a fine for anticompetitive behavior against the community rules depends (according to the ECJ) on the fact, whether the behavior laid down by the national legal rule took place before this rule was declared incompatible with community law, or thereafter. In case of follow-on behavior so called state defence action may be applied against the liability of the undertaking (if there was no space available for its free behavior; if it is not the case, the undertaking itself is liable for the infringement). Requirements of priority of European law and of proportionality of its use are properly taken into consideration since the existence of national rules incompatible with Community law is assessed as a mitigating circumstance.[22]

3.2 Competitive Culture and Path-Dependence

It is still too early to assess the breakthrough into the concept of European competition law with direct impact into the national law orders of member

---

20 *See* 38. Recital to Regulation 1/2003.

21 *See* Kaczorowska, A. (2004), 'The Power of a National Competition Authority to Display National Law Incompatible with EC Law – and its Practical Consequences', *ECLR*, **9**, at p. 591 *et seq.*

22 *Ibid.*, at pp. 598–599.

states. We can hardly observe some decline of competition discipline in our country that might be put down to the change from notification system to the system of legal exception.

A country with an ever-changing legal framework (even nearly 20 years after the 'velvet revolution') and that is accustomed to some kind of a permanent transition is obviously ready to accept and 'digest' these changes, even if it happens at the cost of legal security. The lowering of legal security is evident but only if compared with former situation.

Use of similar uncertain terms like in competition law in other fields of law and the necessity of self-assessment without previous administrative authorisation connected therewith has been always quite common. Decline of the former legal certainty may be outweighed by increase of efficiency that was declining in the former notification model.

The speculative question is whether higher administrative efficiency of relevant bodies will not lead to higher latency of cartels and worsening of the competitive environment. The question of latency is, of course similarly to the measurement of the level of 'competitiveness', methodologically very dubious and depends inter alia on the condition of 'ceteris paribus' that is not to be achieved in the reality due to a dynamic development of social, economic, legal and other conditions. As a rule in similar situations, majority conviction of the relevant European politicians and respective specialists will have a decisive role.

The reform of European competition law may be named as a de facto raising the threshold or enlarging the use of de facto '*de minimis* rule'. Lowering of the enforcement of less important violations of competition law is an inevitable consequence of the orientation on the more serious infringements. The possibility of higher latency of anticompetitive behavior and of a destroying impact of a cumulative effect of untouched 'hotbed' of smaller cartels is quite legitimate.

Expectations about how the new system will work in practice seem to prevail until now. Even very convinced articles supporting and accenting its advantages and playing down its risks occurred.[23] Following advantages are emphasised: good co-ordination within this system (compared to the less-consistent US system), actual impact of soft law and of decision making practice, the proportionality protecting to impose more duties than it is necessary for the sake of attaining the goals of common market. National competition authorities have been partially transformed into de facto national branch offices of the Commission – even if it might have not

---

[23] *See e.g.* Pijetlovic, K. (2004), 'Reform of Antitrust Enforcement: Criticism of the New System is Highly Exaggerated', *ECLR*, **6**, at pp. 356–369.

been intended so,[24] it may be assessed as one of the effects of the reform, similarly as the level of co-operation among not so fully independent national antitrust authorities within the European Competition Network.[25]

Such a fundamental change as the modernisation of EU competition law was naturally subject to mistrust and concerns that were motivated by very different sources, among others by lacking competition culture and tradition. Nowadays it is sufficiently mirrored and transferred into the national legal system. Troubles and misusable possibilities immediately connected with the introduction of the change have passed already. The approach to the introduction of antitrust law and to its modernisation was affected by some peculiarities having created some kind of path-dependence.

4 SOME SPECIFIC CZECH STARTING POINTS AND CONDITIONS

The Velvet Revolution in Czechoslovakia in 1989 produced great changes in every aspect of the Czechoslovakian legal and political systems. Political differences between the Czech and Slovak parts of the country led to the splitting of Czechoslovakia into two republics on 1 January 1993.

The Czech Republic, first as a part of Czechoslovakia and then as an independent republic, has fared well in developing a stable and growing economy. However, the changes have built upon the legal and economic systems of the past. The Czech Republic has continued to build upon that economic base. Indeed, the history of the free market economy of the Czech Republic has its roots in its pre-1989 industrial status.

With the necessary changes in the economic and political system have come equally significant developments in the drafting of a myriad of rules and laws to regulate the new business climate. In addition, there have been significant developments in the revision of domestic and foreign business laws and practices of the Czech Republic. The need for creating new commercial law became apparent after the 'velvet revolution'. The amendments to the Economic Code could not meet the requirements of the newly born market economy. One of the most important changes in business law in the Czech Republic has been the promulgation of the Commercial Code in 1991. The new Commercial Code has effectively launched the Czech business community into a free market economy protected and supported by law.

---

24 Schaub, A., point of view referred to by Pijetlovic, at p. 364.
25 *Ibid.*

However, it is quite natural that contemporary business practices in the Czech Republic have been resting for a long time, at least in part, on the legacy of interpreting legal norms or concepts applicable in earlier times.

4.1 The Civil Code

Before World War II, the Austrian Commercial Code of 1863 governed business and economic relations in the territory of today's Czech Republic. This old Austrian regulation was in force until 1950, when it was amended by the Act No. 141/1950 Coll. In 1948 the existing Commercial Code was abrogated as incompatible with the new centrally planned economy. This was an inevitable part of the road to the nationalisation of property and to the practical end of private enterprise in Czechoslovakia. The socialist regime divided the laws regulating property relations in Czechoslovakia into three codes: the Civil Code[26]; the Economic Code[27]; and the Code of International Trade[28].

The Civil Code, as far as the law of property was concerned, applied only to relations between citizens and 'socialist organisations'. The determination of an organisation as a 'socialist organisation' was an ideological and often arbitrary determination. Yet, the determination of status as a 'socialist organisation' was very important because it affected the organisation's relations with others. Thus, if an organisation was not a 'socialist organisation', the Civil Code did not apply to it, even in the unusual case when socialist organisations had an urgent need to deal with either the few private entrepreneurs or with domestic 'non-socialist organisations'. In those cases, legal relationships were, at best, ambiguous[29].

4.2 The Economic Code

The Economic Code regulated the management and operation of socialist organisations. The Economic Code preferred the 'vertical' regulation

---

[26] Act No 40/1964 Coll.
[27] Act No 109/1964 Coll.
[28] Act No 101/1963 Coll.
[29] *E.g.* the purchase contract concerning the same goods was governed by different rules depending on the fact, if both parties are 'socialist organisations' or not. The consequence was among others other guarantee terms, other jurisdiction of disputes between those organisations (arbitrating by special state bodies in accordance with 'principles of state economic policy' standing outside the law, and not judging by independent courts).

or public law over-regulation reached as a result of the parties' contractual freedom. Indeed, the Economic Code actually suppressed contractual freedom and distorted the relative equality of bargaining power in exchange for attempts to promote economic growth and fulfilment of the central plan. The Economic Code effectuated this intent by implementing a contractual duty. In addition, the Economic Code instituted obligatory and closed contracts if it coincided with the needs of the national economy's desire for proportional development. Under the Economic Code, socialist organisations enjoyed many advantages over other entities, including entrepreneurs and 'non-socialist organisations'. Socialist organisations enjoyed better access to resources and finances, in addition to more favourable tax rates. Socialist organisations also enjoyed a superior legal status. This system created many anomalies. Many nominally 'socialist' organisations actually harmed the economy, while 'non-socialist organisations' were often socially useful and successful despite their inferior status.

In effect, the Economic Code was a tool of the 'dirigistic', or state-controlled, philosophy of the government. It rejected a market approach and had no understanding for competition that was excluded in practice as incompatible with the planned economics and with the stated goal of business 'to promote socialist relations'; that was often the name given to disguise the redistribution of goods and capital. In turn, this redistribution was often a substitute for wealth creation.

Both the Economic Code and the Civil Code blurred the long-standing distinctions between public law and private law. The Economic Code allowed both the State and the 'supervising bodies of the socialist organisations' to intervene in the internal corporate management of socialist organisations. There was no adequate legal redress for the mistakes dictated by this intervention because the State never acknowledged any harm to the economy brought about by its attempts at supervision. Ultimately, the Economic Code did not regulate any forms of private business and it ensured the 'socialist organisations' a relatively privileged status. The Czechoslovakian Economic Code enabled the destruction of the unitary property system. The Economic Code, with the support of the allegedly consumer-oriented aspects of the Civil Code, deepened the theoretical and actual differences among the several forms of property ownership. This destroyed an element perceived to be an essential element of a market economy in pre-war Czechoslovakia: a unitary system of property ownership formally subjecting everyone to the same economic conditions and legal regulation.

The destruction of a unitary system of property ownership had several important results, all of which affected the prosperity of the Czech economy. One result was the curbing of the freedom to contract. Another result was that the relative positions of those entering into contracts were no longer equal and independent. The third result was the abandonment of many traditional legal principles in favour of a narrowing of the scope of many legal regulations governing corporations, forms of security, many special contracts, anti-monopoly measures, unfair trading practices and bankruptcy.

4.3 The Code of International Trade

Because the Czechoslovakian Economic Code was designed for a centrally-planned economy in which the state could often intervene, foreign business partners did not have the assurance that they would be able to contract freely with Czech businesses. Furthermore, the structure of the Economic Code prevented foreign parties from determining their legal rights and obligations with any degree of certainty. In market economies, such assurances would be regarded as 'givens' and considered necessary to the conduct of a successful business transaction.

To foreign investors, this lack of certainty was a risk inherent in any business dealing in any socialist country. In light of this environment, Czechoslovakia adopted a Code of International Trade. Specifically, the Code of International Trade was to increase the legal certainty for foreign business partners, regulate relations with foreign business partners, and finally, to develop international economic cooperation. Since the presence of a socialist regime was an inherent deterrent when foreign businesses faced dealings with their Czech counterparts, the Code of International Trade sought to remedy this obstacle despite the still apparent socialist structure.

Even though the Code of International Trade was thus a departure from the domestic laws regulating commerce, it could not adequately accommodate foreign investment, joint ventures, or other forms of non-socialist economic cooperation.

After 1989, laws such as the Civil Code, the Economic Code and the Code of International Trade were clearly inadequate to govern the regulation of business and trade in the emerging Czech market economy.

5 ANTITRUST POLICY NOT LONG AGO

So, the non-existence of antitrust legislation before 1990 is to be seen in this broader economic and legal frame and stemmed from a value-based fundamental approach – the socialist organisations were supposed to co-operate in order to achieve a common goal and not to compete with each other. Officially supported term of so-called 'socialist competition' among them was a very soft ideological tool of raising motivation (and substituting non-existing real economic incentives of competition). In fact, 'socialist competition' was a kind of co-operation rather than competition as a veil of the 'creative destruction'. Real competition was only supported with (or even against) capitalist undertakings.

Thus in a society known as 'real socialism', the meanings of some traditional terms became empty or illusory. For example, 'economic competition' was often a meaningless term in the dirigistic and monopolistic economics. Terms like 'economic contracts' disguised inadequate contractual subject matter in that the contracts did not really cover the subject matter intended. In short, the meaning of 'economic competition' and 'economic contracts' was very different from the meaning those terms would have had in a private law system.

Socialist law limited free and fair competition, which is a key factor in any economic reform. In order to create a functional and operating environment for participants in a free market, it was necessary to remove the socialist legal system and restore the dual system of public and private law. This required both the destruction of the monolithic vertical control that facilitated state intervention in the economy and the creation of a plurality of mutually independent and autonomous subjects of business ownership. The creation of a law protecting the competition was an inevitable part of this move.

After a long intermission in the development of antitrust law and a difficult development worldwide of this field of law, this specialised instrument of economic policy started from zero and began to operate in gradually rising market conditions in the Czech Republic. Apart from the advantage of awareness of antitrust law from the short historical period of pre-war experience and of the 'real-socialistic' mutation of competition law, we could seek guidance in theoretical conclusions reached abroad and in usable foreign judicial decisions; however, it is evident that antimonopoly and antitrust law are in the first place determined by the state of a particular economics and the resultant order of economic policy priorities. That is why the criterion of a standard and stabilised market economics (including the antitrust decisions) was used only to a limited extent in the Czech economics in transformation.

The requirement of harmonisation of the Czech competition law with the EU law, resulting from the Association Agreement, created a pressure on legislative changes, while providing a basis for interpretation. However, harmonisation was not able to change the economic conditions in which our law operated. These conditions include, among others, a particular system of institutions, capacity limitations, and various interests of economic subjects.

5.1 Antitrust and Economic Transformation

The main priorities of Czech economic policy seemed to be currency stability, privatisation, gaining the amount of capital absorbable by our economics and maintaining high employment and social stability. Creating and protecting an environment for competition as a presumption of a functional market economy did not seem to be a priority, at least not in the practical economic policy.

Apparently, the most important thing for environment of competition is not antitrust law but rather the contestability (competitiveness) of markets – liberalised foreign trade, open frontiers, minimum of special branch policies, minimal to the market access, etc. Antitrust law is a technical means for achieving these desirable elements of a thriving market.

A vital condition to developing market economy was a development of a strict definition of business ownership. Private ownership implied the ability to control the business entity and to respond to the market forces. Czech privatisation during the early 1990s was not only a 'success story' as it was usually being pronounced in the past. The most negative of carrying out this process was lacking legal frame of privatisation. It enabled enrichment of many shady 'entrepreneurs', who deprived small shareholders, in an unfair way, of their shares gained during the privatisation[30].

---

[30] By the way, one of the undisputable contributions of Czech privatisation is the world-known term 'tunnelling' as a kind of destroying the economic substance of a company at the expense of small shareholders under conditions of poor protection of small shareholders or even of lacking this regulation at all. Some similarities to the Miloš Forman movie 'Hoří má panenko' (translated as 'Fire, My Dear! ' or 'The Firemen's Ball') come to mind. The situation is as follows: there is a pile of things in front of the stage in a village hall, where a firemen's ball is being held. The items are to be distributed among the happy winners of the ball raffle. Just before the raffle tickets are drawn, the organisers of the ball find out that one of the prizes, a piece of sausage, has been stolen. They want to give the unknown thief a chance to put the sausage back honestly without being identified, so they agree to switch off the light in the hall hoping that the thief will acct honestly and return the prize. But what a surprise! After switching on the light in the hall again, they find out that more prizes have disappeared. Another attempt to restore morality in the same way fails as well, and the pile of prizes to be drawn diminishes again and moreover an old honest fireman, who finds out that the thief was his wife and wants to put the sausage back on the pile on behalf of his cowardly wife, does not make it on time because the light is switched on surprisingly soon. As a presumed

Frequently responsible firms have not been shaped or created, but rather 'easy riders' who acted in the terms of 'hit and run'. In some cases functionally indivisible units were split up under the parole of demonopolisation (and with hidden incentive just to privatise an important and profitable deal of the enterprise).[31]

Nevertheless, many things had been done well. So, for example the same entrepreneurs conditions for business people (regardless if domestic or foreign ones) had been shaped. It was necessary to reorganise the applicable laws for the benefit of both national business organisations and potential foreign business partners and investors. In this way a legal framework had been gradually introduced to promote competition.

The priority of privatisation often led, paradoxically, to confirming the prior monopolisation, with the difference being that a private monopoly is not so closely connected with the state by different interests as is a state monopoly. The sense of privatisation in general is certainly not to replace the state enterprises with a monopoly or dominant position by enterprises with the same market power, only executed by private owners.[32]

A prospective buyer was willing to pay more for a monopoly enterprise, and thus a future pro-competition structure was often sacrificed on the altar of privatisation, which conserved the present monopolisation of economics. The buyers of privatised enterprises frequently gained an unlimited position on the market, the access to which can be made impossible for other competitors for decades. In this context, there is an unflattering opinion that 'the Czechs achieved their goals to a great extent by privatizing the state monopoly.'[33]

---

thief, he dies of a heart attack in undeserved shame. There is an analogy to our privatisation. Its often-used method was to switch off the light, privatise in the dark and then either not switch the light on at all or only a little bit (and by no means prematurely) while protecting the new owners because 'private ownership is inviolable'.

[31] An illustrative example might be splitting-off the plant producing raw iron, and following technological stages (foundry and rolling mill). An artificial monopolistic position on the supply side has been created in this way that might be misused (which, naturally, was the case some years later).

[32] Hayek, F.A. (1990), *Cesta do otroctví*, Praha: Academia, at p. 152; Hansen, K. (1994), 'Wettbewerbsschutz in Mitteleuropa', *Wirtsschaft und Wettbewerb*, **12**, at p. 1000.

[33] *See* Hospodářské noviny (1993), referred to *Wall Street Journal* from 12 October 1993.

5.2 'Schizophrenic' State

The difficult balancing between short-term advantages from selling the monopoly enterprises to a domestic or a foreign buyer (who often required a monopoly) and long-term interests in the existence of a competitive environment just confirms the universal rule that frequently the immediate interest is preferred, even on the state level.

Apart from that, the government had to be circumspect and critical to numerous opinions and primarily well-intentioned advice from abroad about the unconditional necessity of splitting up the great industrial complexes in the process of privatisation. Such a radical act could weaken the national economics by confronting fragmented domestic enterprises, which were not really able to compete, with concentrated foreign and multinational enterprises, which operate legally supported export trusts.

Even admitting the foreign capital to joint enterprises with a monopoly position on the domestic market can be two-edged. It can block a natural change of the market structure.

Privatisation is only an operative aim which should create the conditions for the functioning of a market economy. Along with other aims, it should provide for the existence of competition once privatisation is over. Privatisation, at the same time, was a unique and unrepeatable chance (unfortunately often not very well used) to form new pro-competition structures such as those already in existence for decades or that, due to rapid monopolisation, never existed and probably never will exist.

The state could artificially split up the economic, technical, commercial and other structures and connections and, thus, put an end to monopolies. However, it could also support the rise of a real competition by privatising deliberately with pro-competition intentions, thus supporting the rise of new entrepreneurial subjects, the restructuring of which is stimulated by the market. The endeavour to split up monopolies naturally cannot be a call for the last and final intervention of state power in the economy, after which everything should be all right.[34]

Another controversial problematic point was (and still partly is) the maintenance of state or privatised monopolies in network branches, for-

---

[34] *See* Estrin, S. and L. Takla (1993), 'Competition Policy in the Czech and Slovak Republic', *Seminar on Competition Policy in the Transforming Economies*, Třešť: The World Bank Economic Institute, 27.6.–2.7; Fassman, M. and J. Rusnok (1995), 'Konkurenční způsobilost české ekonomiky zaostává', Hospodářské noviny z 12.12., at p. 11.

merly regarded as so-called 'natural monopolies' (electricity suppliers, transport, gas, water and heat industries, postal services and others). A far-reaching influence of their monopolistic behavior on living standard, if a consistent antimonopoly policy does not strive to eliminate it, can endanger the priority of social and currency stability.

Theoretically, the process of deetatization and privatisation can bring about an 'inverse adjustment' of a negative market structure (replacing the state monopoly with a private one) or a negative development of the market structure (a new private monopoly or private oligopolies can originate from a lot of formerly independent enterprises). Legal rules should eliminate such a negative development as efficiently as possible.

The decision-making practice of the Antitrust Authority (AA) used to take place in the difficult conditions of transformation and uncertainty connected with it. In this situation, it would not have been advisable to apply law that would prohibit or go as far as criminalising anticompetitive activities. Legal certainty (which prefers explicit prohibitions with a few explicit exceptions, in the context of economic policy), was not a first-rate value that should be asserted at all costs. An economic mind necessarily compares it with possible loss of certain economic advantages, which is connected with its unconditional preference.

The decision-making practice of the AA could not be (and in my view it was not) narrow-minded and it could not be guided by the paranoid idea that everyone wants to endanger the competition. The competitors frequently find themselves without any bad intention in the initial state of starting to adopt decent market manners and they often respected the recommendation of the AA. The authority then did not have to undertake frequent administrative action against would-be monopolists. All the potential enemies of the competition (not including the monopolists and the dominants) are in the first place the movers of the competition. Any potential danger to competition can come only through those capable of initiating and perpetuating it.

A certain amount of tolerance towards a monopolising behavior of smaller competitors was necessary, if only for reasons of size, and it is common even in standard market economies. Such an approach was based on tolerating certain structures up to the limit of dominance and on taking steps against the abuse of market power only after this limit was exceeded. This approach takes into account that with regard to deformation of the market structure, evidence becomes more difficult to collect by the time abuse of market power occurs.

6 DEVELOPMENTS IN CZECH ANTITRUST LAW[35]

6.1 The Period 1991–2000

The Act on Protection of Competition[36] introduced some measures particularly appropriate for transition settings, such as a strict test for dominance and merger control (simply and mechanistically deducible from exceeding the 30 per cent market share) that have been revised later on to conform to EU norms.

The independent Office for the Protection of Economic Competition was reshaped into a Ministry for the Protection of Economic Competition in 1992[37] which enabled it to be more directly involved in decision making on the governmental level during a critical period of the economic transformation. The approval of AA was a regular part of any privatisation project being dealt with by the government. When the project was disapproved by the AA, it would be solved politically by the government. The Ministry succeeded to prevent creation (privatisation) of some monopolies at that time. Even local authorities were required by the law to ensure that assets were not spun off to firms that would have dominant position in local markets[38].

The competition regulation toolkit contained all traditional items, including the possibility of individual exemption of prohibited restrictive agreements (no block exemptions[39], but three types of exempted agreements – rationalisation, specialisation, '*de minimis*').

The abuse of dominant position was connected with the exceeding the 30 per cent market share, which was a conclusive irrefutable presumption. The achieving of the threshold had to be notified by the respective firm.

Merger control was based on a simple dominance test and the burden of proof was on the party to demonstrate that any distortion of competition is outweighed by economic benefits. No other body or sector regulator had the power to (dis)approve mergers or acquisitions. Only some per mile

---

[35] Generally based on OECD report (*Competition law and policy in the Czech Republic*) from 2001 and the draft for 2008 (internal documents of the Czech Office for Protection of Economic Competition).

[36] Act No 63/1991 Coll.

[37] The change back to an independent 'Office' took place in 1996 again.

[38] This regulation was abolished later and nowadays the AA cannot intervene when governmental or local authority takes action restricting or eliminating competition.

[39] The only one block exemption on franchise agreement was introduced only in 2000.

mergers were not approved in practice. Industrial policy was not a factor in mergers decisions and the decisions were based only on net competitive effects. Several decisions approving mergers have promoted restructuring in traditionally monopolised industries.

There were no specific exemptions for sectors or types of enterprises which provided a sound framework for broad-based regulatory reform. Efforts to create special exemptions from general competition policy have been resisted successfully. Even small- and medium-sized business did not receive special treatment or consideration.

6.2 The Period 2001 to Present

The reconstruction of the pre-1990s institutional system, economic as well as political, culminated with membership of the European Union in 2004. Privatisation is essentially complete, except for holdings in network sectors.

The Competition Act (CA) has been substantially revised twice since the 2001 Review. The first revision, in 2001, updated the transition-era framework statute that had been adopted in 1991. That earlier law had drawn on European models and substantive concepts, but it also included features designed to address particular national problems, notably the historically monopolised structure of most markets at that time. The Czech law adopted the system of block exemption regulations and individual exemptions from the general prohibition against restrictive agreements, as well as the *de minimis* thresholds for applying it. The definition of 'dominance' incorporated terms from European jurisprudence, superseding a definition that had presumed dominance at a market share of 30 per cent. The law added provisions about merger control. It also replaced a rule targeting anti-competitive actions by government-related entities with provisions that parallel the EC Treaty in applying competition law to holders of exclusive rights and providers of public services. The only general provision that implies an exclusion from the CA is for firms providing general public services. The terms of the CA parallel Article 86 of the EC Treaty. The CA does not apply to 'undertakings which provide, on the basis of a special act or on the basis of a decision issued pursuant to a special act, services of general economic interest' if its application would obstruct the provision of these services.[40]

[40] The postal service, the central bank, broadcasting and telecoms are listed, in a footnote, as examples of laws that authorise such services of general economic interest. Determining whether a service qualifies for this treatment depends on

The second major revision of the basic law accompanied the Czech Republic's accession to membership in the EU in 2004. This revision adapted Czech law to the modernised EU system of enforcement. Now, under Czech law as under EU law, exemption criteria as well as prohibitions apply directly. Block exemption regulations under EU law are incorporated into Czech law automatically. Conforming enforcement practice to the new EU methods, the Office no longer deals with applications for individual exemption. The standard for mergers is now the same in Czech law and the EU merger regulation, and the Czech merger notification rules have also been revised. The law empowers the Office to apply EU law as well as national law. The first case under the EC treaty, about abuse of dominance in telecoms, was opened in 2004. As the Office has embraced EU enforcement methods, in 2007 it replaced its original 2001 leniency program, which had not produced many results, with a revised program that follows the European Competition Network model. The overall theme of the improvements in Czech legislation is clearly to align with EU institutions and practices.[41]

Czech competition law is now based on familiar European concepts, prohibiting restrictive agreements and abuse of dominance and requiring approval for major mergers. Features of the original 1991 law that were tailored for dealing with transition problems have been removed or revised. As a result, the substantive law is essentially identical to EU norms. Enforcement practice is also now fully integrated into the EU system. Czech competition law is likely to become increasingly derivative of EU law, in substance and practice, as the circumstances that called for special national rules have passed.[42]

---

general principles of European law, developed in the interpretation and application of Article 86. The Czech Supreme Administrative Court has confirmed that Czech law is to be interpreted consistently with European case law under Article 86. Notably, the service must be provided continuously over the entire area at uniform price and quality. Czech law does not include the phrase from Article 86 that extends this treatment to services having the character of a revenue-producing monopoly.

41 Proposals to legislate special treatment for particular sectors have created some controversy. The Parliament excluded the telecoms sector from the jurisdiction of the Czech competition law in 2005. That exclusion only lasted for two years before being repealed in 2007. Another, continuing controversy is over whether to add the concept of 'economic dependence' to the competition law, in order to regulate disparities of bargaining power in distribution relationships. Parliament approved such an amendment, but the President vetoed it. The Office supports the goal but would prefer a more narrowly targeted measure.

42 The most prominent and important recent case, announced in April 2007, was the Czech contribution to the multi-jurisdiction enforcement against the

Sanctions against individuals may be strengthened. The AA has proposed to hold individuals criminally liable for cartel conduct. The government has agreed to include this proposal in the new criminal code that is being submitted to Parliament.

The Czech law about abuse of a dominant position adds some detail to the EC treaty model. One addition is a competitive-effects test: abuse is prohibited if it harms other businesses or consumers. The list of abuses in the CA is longer. Competition law enforcement reinforces sector regulation. Fines in cases about abuse of dominance are often substantial.

Only the AA has merger control power with respect to competition. There is no provision for involving ministries or other bodies or for invoking the public interest or other policies[43]. The merger policy continues to be very liberal.[44]

An amendment to the CA about merger review is now in preparation.

A new leniency policy was adopted in 2007. Compared to the previous program from 2001, it promises greater legal certainty to applicants who

---

international bid-rigging cartel for gas-insulated switchgear. The EU had issued its decision in the matter in January 2007, and some national Competition Offices were also taking action against this cartel. There has been a controversy because the appellate court cancelled the decision of the AA because of alleged infringement of the principle '*ne bis in idem*', despite only the conduct of the participants to the cartel agreement prior to accession of the Czech Republic to the EU being considered. Only the impact on the Czech national market was taken into consideration. The court assessed this approach as an artificial splitting 'on purpose' and for the sake of punishment. The case is now being assessed by the Supreme Administrative Court. Older cases typically involved exchanges of information, common prices or simultaneous price increases. Sometimes the pattern was condemned as a concerted practice, and sometimes it was the basis for inferring that the parties had reached a prohibited agreement. One well-known 'concerted practice' case, from 2001, resulted in a very large fine against petroleum distributors who had communicated about price levels at a time when prices were increasing. (This case is still on appeal, to correct a curious judicial ruling denying that a firm could be held liable for a violation by its pre-merger corporate antecedent.)

43 Concentrations in the financial sector also require approval from the Czech National Bank, but that review does not assess effects on competition. The Office's merger decisions do not show explicit consideration of other policies or a balancing between restraints on competition and improvements in efficiency.

44 Out of 687 merger decisions from 2001–2007, the Office only rejected three transactions. In 22 decisions imposing conditions, those most frequently imposed were divesting shares or assets (13), prohibiting discrimination (9), maintaining supply arrangements (9), prohibiting price increases (6) and transferring intellectual property rights (4).

qualify. Unlike the previous program, the current leniency policy applies only to horizontal agreements.[45]

The functions of sector regulators in telecoms and energy are carefully defined to be distinct from the AA's enforcement role. In Czech jurisprudence it is particularly important to define jurisdictions clearly and avoid overlapping competences. Regulators act ex ante, to promote competition where it does not yet exist and to prevent harm to the public where competition is not possible. The AA acts *ex post*, to protect competition by correcting and deterring conduct that undermines or restrains it.[46]

The electric power industry has been substantially open for competition since 2006, when all customers were allowed to choose their supplier. Transmission is a publicly held monopoly, and transmission and distribution are still regulated. Generation was structurally separated from distribution in the 1990s. But then, in the course of partial privatisation, the industry was substantially re-integrated through acquisitions.[47] Further privatisation is not foreseen, at least not soon.

Restructuring and regulation in electric power and gas involved consultation with AA, but the result was not satisfactory enough. The Czech Republic passed up an opportunity, made possible by its welcome early

---

[45] The program generally follows the standard model of the European Competition Network, with one exception. The Czech program does not authorise the parties to continue the conduct in order not to tip-off other conspirators before the investigation can be launched. Czech jurisprudence would not accept such a commitment by the enforcer not to pursue illegal conduct (or such a declaration of tolerance for it), at least formally.

[46] Court rulings in all of these sectors have confirmed this division of responsibilities, preserving the Office's role of *ex post* law enforcement against restraints on competition in regulated sectors. Competition law enforcement has supplemented regulation to promote liberalisation, sometimes through simultaneous action against the same abuse.

[47] A project to privatise separately ČEZ and the eight regional distribution companies was abandoned in 2002. ČEZ remains publicly controlled, with two-thirds of its shares held by the government. Instead, the government took ownership of the transmission grid, and ČEZ acquired control over five of the distributors. The AA decision approving this combination, which would have had a national market share of about 65 per cent, required ČEZ to divest one of the five distributors. This was not done immediately. The Parliament then amended the Competition Act to permit parties that were subject to an order to ask that it be reconsidered on the basis of changed conditions. The amendment was clearly intended to permit reopening this divestiture order. In 2005, AA revised the order, eliminating the divestiture requirement and substituting a 'virtual power plant'.

structural separation of operating levels, to create quickly conditions for strong competition in the liberalising European market.[48]

The telecoms sector was largely excluded from the CA between May 2005 and May 2007. The AA objected to this limitation on the CA and pointed out that EU competition law would still apply in the sector, even if the national competition law did not. The European Commission also objected to the exclusion and began an infringement proceeding over it against the Czech Republic. Facing that opposition, Parliament repealed this exclusion in 2007.

7 BOTH GENERAL AND 'NEW MEMBER' – SPECIFIC CONCLUDING DOUBTS

7.1 National 'Backyard' Preferred

'The unity in variety' prevailing in the world says that private restrictions, exclusions and distortions of competition by means of cartels, in principle are harmful for the very essence of market economy and, in a way, to the freedom of citizens. It is, therefore, necessary to face them unless the restriction of competition in a value consideration would be less important than the economic, social and other advantages connected with impairing the competitive environment. Quite naturally, there is no such unity in the easing of restrictions and the endangerment or exclusions of competition which the state itself initiates, supports, or carries out.

Due to the preference of a state's own economic interests (or the national egoism), this attitude is strengthened on the level of international economic competition. It is difficult even for the European Community member with compatible economies and values to find common grounds, for example on an approach to mergers, because of the diverse political ideas about competition and different ways of assessing concentration. However, particular economic interests and advantages are even stronger than doctrinal ideas and are very hard to abandon for the sake of general principles.

It is clear that only extensive deregulations and liberal policies can enable firms to take part in international competition. The opinion that

48 The 2001 OECD Review specifically called for requiring Transgas to divest enough storage capacity to support a competitive market, or failing that, for setting up an effective regulatory regime to assure access. Neither has been done, and the predictable consequences are hindering effective competition.

a free competition should be encouraged only among the countries of the same economic and cultural standard denies the existence of comparative advantages and runs counter to the interests of both the developed and the less developed countries.[49]

Artificial advantages (not earned by a competitive performance) for domestic enterprises and artificial barriers for foreign enterprises, in fact, are being created. The vicious circle of justifying certain steps as responses to the steps of another state is hard to break. However, globalisation and internalisation of economy leads inevitably to globalisation of competition.

Internal regulations (including Czech) generally focus only on the competition environment in their own national economy and have no extraterritorial effects. Export cartels (outside the European Economic Area), for example, are commonly exempted from the prohibition of cartel agreements, which can create artificial advantages for domestic enterprises and disadvantages for their foreign competitors doing business in commerce with a country with no such exemption.

The restrictions of competition which reach beyond country borders generate a struggle among different competition policies of individual countries, while the states suffer and overlook if an enterprise with a domestic seat acts in an anticompetitive way abroad. However, strict recourse would be taken against such an enterprise in its home country. At other times, the states hope at times to gain economic advantages from such behavior of their enterprises.[50]

If states want their competition policies to better reflect the rules of international competition, they also must consider the effect of their national antitrust laws on the international level. That means that an inland regulation of competition must be applied to the restriction of competition caused abroad. The Czech law does not make this possible.

7.2 Competition Policy is a Mere Policy

Competition policy is not only about law. Economic competition as a covert conflict of interests takes place in a broad moral, social and governmental context in which the legal regulation is assigned only a certain limited role. The political power of the competitors, direct or indirect, is

---

[49] Sutherland, P. (1995), 'Protekcionismus versus politika volného obchodu', *Ekonom*, **45**, at p. 20.

[50] Duijm, B. and H. Winter (1993), 'Internationale Wettbewerbsordnung – Alternativen und ihre Probleme', *Wirtschaft und Wettbewerb*, **6**, at p. 466.

a more effective instrument for influencing the competition environment than their market power, because it precedes the creation of a legal frame for development and protection of competition.[51]

However precise a legal regulation protecting competition may be, the anticompetitive pressures may prevail by means of politics. The government is not a mere 'organiser of industry' but also the main instrument used by corporations for forming and maintaining the concentration of economy and for creating oligopolies and monopolies.[52] Thanks to the use of political means, economic subjects can achieve various effects traditionally ascribed to the concentration of economic power. Political power of intervention, in turn, often is the source of economic power, and these two powers can be correlated but do not necessarily have to correlate.

Governmental competition policy in a broader sense means not only improving antitrust laws but also taking actions against attempts of economic entities to gain political power by, *inter alia* financing political parties, enacting laws about conflict of interests, and introducing a system of control in the society including the information right of the mass media.

Any measures which potentially or factually limit the attainment of political power by economic subjects, at least, can be comparable to the normative instruments of antitrust law. Otherwise, political power might well be used for diverting the neutrality of self-regulating and self-controlling economic competition for the benefit of one or more participants against others, for example, by supporting big enterprises against the small ones or vice versa.

The practice of political intervention in the competition environment by other than normative (legal) means cannot be considered to be out of the question. The mere fact that small- and medium-sized enterprises would be excluded from the possibility of defensively asserting their interests for structural reasons can morally legitimate their political lobbyism. This is likely because big industry usually co-operates with the state in ways that influence the competition environment. Nationally self-serving reasons for political influence, particularly in the process of economic concentration, are probably traditional as well.

Hardly any government will be capable of preferring a general pro-competitive structural policy – one not encouraging anyone in particular but the competition – to a particularly- and directly-aimed industrial

---

[51] Etzioni, A. (1995), *Morální dimenze ekonomiky*, Praha: Victoria Publishing, at p. 185 et *seq.*

[52] *Ibid.*

policy. A fatal consequence of one-sided industrial policy can be to permanently subsidise certain industrial sectors, which means that the ability to compete then can be increased only artificially. In accordance with the ordoliberal theory, the state should first split up or at least limit the power and interest groupings and create forms of economic order, or institutions, rather than concentrate on directing particular economic processes.[53]

If a decision about concrete support and interventionism is made on the basis of political power, extensive help should be directed, at least partly, toward a sector or a sub-sector, not toward selected individual enterprises. Supporting the weakest production units leads to the artificial survival of the subjects least able to compete. This policy, apart from direct economic costs, brings about deteriorated parameters of the competition environment.[54]

In a number of cases, however, support is addressed to particular competitors, and it does not result from political lobbying but from an effort to get on an equal footing with concentrated foreign competitors at a national level standard. A typical target conflict took place, for example, in Czech banks: despite considerable concentration and interrelations within the domestic banking sector, another process of merging and mega-merging, seeking strategic partners and increasing capital banks took place in view of the fact that capital of all our banks together was equal to that of any one major German bank. At the same time, German banks were seeking foreign partners to be able to stand up to the giant competition of the unified market.

7.3 Legal Rules, Traditional, Political and Modern Economic Approaches

Antagonistic trends in competition policy and in competition law (due to a number of vague concepts, exemptions and rules of reason) and the controversial character of target conflicts often are confusing. The application of competition law increasingly resembles a quasi-judge-made law which, apart from the subsuming of a case under very generally worded legal norms, is based particularly on value judgments.

The political approach to competition, 'restricted' only by a general legal regulation, makes it possible to react more flexibly to inevitable value

---

53 Klusoň, V. (1995), 'Ordoliberalismus a transformace ekonomiky', *Ekonom*, **31**, at pp. 14–15.

54 Czesaný, S. (1995), 'Cíle i nástroje průmyslové politiky se mění', *Hospodářské noviny*, **12**, p. 9.

conflicts than an approach limited by rigorously compulsory and apodictic regulation. Decision making in these questions will always be a kind of extrapolation – an endless seeking of indefinite and ever-changing limits – which should be characterised by readiness to experiment, to go back and by cognitive humility.[55]

As to the cognitive humility – the problem is that the politicians and reformers usually do not belong to those people who are blessed with this virtue. Our economic transformation is an example of putting through a far-reaching change without having sufficient institutional frame.[56] The importance of the institutional framework of the economic transition has been underestimated and neglected. It is said half jokingly in our country, that 'the economists took to flight and the lawyers had no real chance to catch them'.

Nevertheless, we have already established a standard legal environment of a market economy, which is, naturally, a never-ending story. At this time, all 'new' member countries are facing jointly with the 'old' EU countries a new challenge. The problem of 'more economic approach' may show some resemblances to the Czech flight of economists and to the lawyers trying to catch them. The traditional institutional frame of competition law is endangered by opportunist and case-by-case and short-term economic assessments. It may deprive the law of its genuine substance of setting transparent and predictable rules of conduct. I just wonder whether simply another round of a fight is taking place; the fight of prejudices, biases and faith – and let's face it: sometimes insufficiently justified on both sides. The result will decide, whether the law will remain

---

[55] Etzioni, A., *ibid.*, at p. 205.

[56] One example is illuminating enough: we had to solve the leftovers of so-called 'banking socialism', the legacy of pseudo privatisation from the early 1990s. Many Czech banks gained shares in industrial companies in that time and they gave these companies much insufficiently secured credit to help them overcome their bad economic results. This resulted in frequent failures to pay off credits, and in the instability of the entire banking system. Many banks have lost their banking licences and thousands of common people and entrepreneurs have suffered substantial financial damage. In addition, the loss of the small savers' money deposited in commercial banks has led to a general loss of trust in the banks and to an increased dissatisfaction with the economic system as such. No exact figures are available, but one can learn in Czech newspapers that over 100 billion CZK, approximately 1/5 of the Czech state budget, were granted from the state budget in order to stabilise the endangered banking system and keep it in operation.

Due to the substantial shares of the banks in the property of debtor companies, of course, the banks often were not prepared to initiate the bankruptcy proceeding. The potential possibility to re-order the structure of the national economy through bankruptcy thus was reduced or eliminated.

a set of rules or just a sort of postmodernist 'mash' composed of case-by-case economic decisions, that primarily follow the benefit of strong market players.[57]

The question only is which of the groups will run out of breath sooner.

The impact of this obstinate economic relativeness (under the parole 'everything depends', or 'just short-term consumer benefit counts') may be devastating especially in the 'new' member states with a newly established fragile institutional frame and would-be competition culture.

---

[57] Both short-term (rule of reason in each particular case, e.g. RPM) and long-term (particular 'efficiencies' as a counterbalance in merger control).

8. Cartel Deterrence and Settlements: the Brazilian Experience

Paulo Furquim de Azevedo* and Alexandre Lauri Henriksen**

1 INTRODUCTION

There is not much controversy that settlements are an important part of a policy of cartel deterrence (Hammond, 2006a; Connor, 2007). Some authors emphasise the win–win feature of negotiated procedures to abbreviate the administrative and judicial disputes related to cartel prosecution as opposed to fully adversarial procedures (Landes, 1971; Scott and Stuntz, 1992; Wils, 2008). This almost consensus[1] in the literature is absolutely expected, provided that parties are rational and do not have significant cognition problems. In as much as litigation costs may be avoided and the fully adversarial procedure is always an alternative to the settlement, parties must be at least better off if they opt to settle a case.

More relevant and with important policy implications is the discussion about the appropriate design of this type of contract, particularly because it is not a trivial solution given the information asymmetry between the competition authority and defendants, and the complex interaction among settlements and other investigative mechanisms, such as leniency agreements. This chapter addresses this issue both theoretically, by means of a simple game theoretical model, and empirically, by means of the Brazilian experience.

A quite straightforward model explores the relationship among three alternatives available to cartel participants: pursuing the trial, engaging in a leniency agreement, or settling the case. The model leaves out the

* Commissioner at CADE-Brazil and Professor of Economics at Getúlio Vargas Foundation - FGV-EESP.

** From CADE-Brazil.

[1] Although the literature is quite convergent about the potential benefits of settlements, there is a dissent regarding some actual results, mainly related to the punishment of innocent defendants. About these critics, *see* Schulhofer (1992) and Bar-Gill and Gazal-Ayal (2006).

well-known problem of asymmetric information about risk preferences (Grossman and Katz, 1983; Reinganum, 1988), focusing on the private information, unknown to the competition authority, about the costs of the admission of guilt and of pursuing the trial (i.e. the benefits of finality). As a traditional result in the contract theory with asymmetric information, a menu of contracts that separates the various types of defendants is the recommended solution. When it is difficult to design a mechanism that is able to separate the various types, the competition authority may opt to ration the access to the settlement (Stiglitz and Weiss, 1981).

The Brazilian experience with settlements, although very recent, is particularly interesting because the amendment in the Brazilian Competition Law allowing settlements in cartel cases delegated to the Competition Authority (CADE) great discretion in the design of such agreements. As a consequence, the Brazilian experience allows analysis of different models of settlements and the complex interaction between settlements and leniency agreements.

This chapter is organised as follows. First, it describes the historical and institutional background in order to provide the foundations for understanding the Brazilian case. Next, based on the international experience, it provides the basic principles for the design of settlements in cartel cases. As a core section, we then theoretically discuss two polar models for settlements (second Leniency agreement and pre-judicial settlements) and the controversial issues of pleading guilty and the amount to be paid by applicants for settlement. Lastly, we draw some lessons from the recent Brazilian experience with settlements. As a main finding, we claim that there is leeway for the complementary models of settlements, the first oriented mainly to increasing the likelihood of detection, and the second oriented to saving social costs of litigation.

2 CARTEL DETERRENCE IN BRAZIL

The Brazilian program for cartel deterrence experienced a substantial change in the first decade of 2000. This change has strict connections with the discussion regarding the convenience of the use of settlement agreements in cartel cases. Up to the 1990s, the vast majority of successful conduct cases prosecuted by the Brazilian Competition Policy System (SBDC[2]) were trivial to detect.[3] Cartel cases were rare and generally resulted from complaints

---

[2] Sistema Brasileiro de Defesa da Concorrência.

[3] According to information compiled by CADE, 73 per cent of CADE's convictions were imposed on medical cooperatives. Although such kind of cases are

or evidence brought from outside the SBDC usually by independent public prosecutors. These cases have the common characteristic of not requiring substantial investigative effort of the SBDC, because the complaints were often accompanied by evidence or the required evidence could be obtained from public sources such as public registrars or notaries. In short, the ability of the SBDC to investigate cartels was still to be developed.

The change began with the amendment of the Competition Law in 2000 by means of Law No. 10.149/2000, which allowed the SBDC to enter into lenience agreement with whistleblowers. The same amendment prevented the mechanism of settlements in cartel cases, aiming at providing more powerful incentives for cartel participants to engage in the lenience program, which was the single instrument of agreement between the SBDC and a member of a cartel. This was important to introduce the new institute as a concrete and attractive alternative for possible cartel's whistleblowers and, more importantly, to grant to the competition authority a fundamental instrument for detecting and punishing cartels (Brenner, 2005).

The legal change was not yet sufficient to induce the use of this type of investigative instrument for cartel deterrence. Competition Law was not yet a self-enforcing institution,[4] as there was not yet the general belief about punishment for cartel participants. Without expectations regarding the likelihood and the severity of the punishment, cartel participants did not have incentives to ask for full immunity as beneficiaries of a leniency agreement. This is probably the main reason why the first lenience agreement was concluded only in 2003, three years after its legal provision in the Brazilian Competition Law.

Equally or more importantly than the change in the legal framework, has been the fostering of expertise and adoption of more appropriate mechanisms for the detection of cartels, such as wiretapping and, in

still common in the first decade of 2000, there was a clear diversification of the profile of convictions, particularly the increase of cartel cases.

4 The concept of self-enforcing institution is drawn from Greif (2006), who defines institutions as 'a system of rules, beliefs, norms, and organizations that together generate a regularity of (social) behavior'. The Competition Policy is an institution that has rules (Competition Law), beliefs (expectations that the unlawful behavior will be punished), norms (e.g. procedures to apply for a leniency agreement) and organisations (e.g. the competition authority). An institution is self-enforcing if 'each individual, taking the structure as given, finds it best to follow the institutionalized behavior that, in turn, reproduces the institution in the sense that the implied behavior confirms the associated beliefs and regenerates the associated norms', that is to say, that the institution is 'effective in generating a particular behavior'.

particular, dawn raids. This change started at the beginning of the first decade of 2000, but has been intensified considerably in its second half. According to the Secretary of Economic Law (SDE), between 2003 and 2005, only 11 search warrants had been granted. In 2006, 19 warrants were granted. In 2007, once again the number of warrants exceeded the number accumulated throughout SBDC's history, reaching 84 warrants granted and accomplished[5].

Concomitantly, with the purpose of preservation of evidence, two orders of temporary arrest were granted between 2003 and 2005. This instrument was used with stronger intensity in 2007, when SDE, in partnership with the Public Attorney's Office, obtained, just in this year, 30 warrants of temporary arrest.[6]

The use of new investigative mechanisms, such as dawn raids and wiretapping, increased the likelihood of cartel detection, and, as a consequence, the demand for leniency agreements, which also had an additional effect on the probability of the disclosure of a cartel. Within the next four years as of 2003 approximately ten agreements were signed, including several which revealed antitrust violations yet unknown by the SBDC.

With the use of such investigative instruments, a more intense action against cartels was possible, including the selection of cases of greater economic relevance and which have higher probability of conviction, allowing a more efficient use of investigation resources. As SDE summarises in its annual report, 'the investigative operations took place in sectors of great relevance to the economy, including alleged domestic cartels, such as the ones involving cement and gasoline stations, as well as alleged international cartels investigated simultaneously within several jurisdictions, such as the ones involving marine hoses and air freight.'[7]

Lenience agreements and the new investigative mechanisms caused a significant change not only in the profile of cases brought to administrative trial at CADE but also in the strength of evidence supporting the cases. Until 2003, cartels cases were based on indirect evidence and price parallelism. The discussion within the administrative proceedings focused on whether there was or was not a violation to the law. The denial of the existence of the conduct used to be the main content of the defendants' defense before CADE as well as of the appeals filed before the judiciary.

---

5 In 2008, from January to September, the number of search warrants was 54, close to the figures of 2007 for the same nine months.

6 In 2008, from January to September, the number of temporary arrests increased to 32, denoting a more intense use of this type of instrument to allow collecting evidence on collusive behavior.

7 DPDE/SDE/MJ annual report, 2007, p. 21.

In such cases, the role of the judiciary focused on reviewing the CADE's decision after the conclusion of the administrative proceedings and as of the issuance of a conviction decision. The judiciary used to review mainly aspects related to due processes and defendants' rights.

In contrast, in a context of direct evidence, which grows in relevance due to the lenience agreement and the new investigative instruments, the defense focuses on the legality or validity of each piece of direct evidence, reserving a secondary role to the question of whether a violation to the law existed. In this new stage of the Brazilian program of combating cartels, defendants access the judiciary predominantly while the administrative proceeding is still in progress, increasing the costs of litigation. Such resources, in the event of termination of the dispute, could be more efficiently used in new investigations and, thus, in the deterrence of violations to antitrust law.

The increasing costs of litigation with defendants fostered the demand for a negotiated procedure to end cartel cases. Settlements are pareto-efficient if they eliminate the costs of litigation while maintaining or enhancing the dissuasive effect of the enforcement of the competition law. As a consequence, settlements are an important mechanism in a program of cartel deterrence, particularly when the success in detection is sufficient to generate relevant cartel cases and, hence, the effort of defendants to fully contest the entire administrative procedure. The next section discusses the main aspects of settlement in cartel cases, exploring its features as a contract between the competition authority and defendants.

3 SETTLEMENT AS A CONTRACT

The settlement is a contract between the authority and individuals and companies accused of antitrust offenses, for instance engaging in a cartel. The main items of this contract are the waiver of rights or the waiver of the exercise of such rights. The ability to practice such act of disposal has been granted by the competition law in the case of the authority and, regarding the defendant, belongs to his/her sphere of waiver powers.

As to the defendant, the waiver of rights may take various forms. It essentially takes the form of obligations of not acting which are usually accompanied by other types of obligations such as collateral ones. Brazilian law provides for some mandatory content in cartel settlements. Obligations other than those depend upon mutual agreement between the parties. The mandatory provisions of a cartel settlement are: (i) obligation to cease the unlawful conduct; (ii) setting a fine in cases of breach of the agreement; and (iii) the obligation to pay a pecuniary sanction.[8] Examples of provisions which depend upon the negotiation between the parties are: (i) implementation of a compliance program by means of which the defendant is obliged to adopt internal procedures to prevent further violations to the antitrust law; (ii) the obligation to co-operate with the investigation in progress within the SBDC by means of the production of additional evidence[9]; (iii) admission of guilt, which has relevant implications to the credibility of the commitment to cease the dispute[10]; and (iv) waiver of procedural rights, such as to continue litigating, both within the administrative proceeding and the judiciary.[11]

The competition authority, in its turn, interrupts the administrative proceeding and, once the obligations therein are duly accomplished, closes the case. Furthermore, depending on the terms of the agreement, the amount that would be due upon conviction for violation of the competition law may be reduced.

4 INTERNATIONAL EXPERIENCE

Settlements in Brazil[12] share several features with other negotiated mechanisms to finish litigation, which are applied in other jurisdictions; the

---

[8] The amount paid as a fine is granted to the Federal Fund of Diffuse Rights (FDD), which is then allocated to projects oriented to the benefit of general diffuse rights, such as environment conservation, cultural and history preservation, and consumer protection.

[9] This obligation may be split into sub-items, which allows setting various formats thereto. These sub-items may be the obligation to grant access to information and documents to the antitrust authority, or obligations such as instructing employees to provide information or documents.

[10] By pleading guilty, the defendant shall incur higher costs to restart the litigation, because his/her chances of success become lower once his/her involvement in the offense is admitted. Therefore, this fosters a credible commitment as to the end of the dispute with the antitrust authority, either in the administrative proceeding or within the judiciary.

[11] Specifically, this obligation may take the form of recognition of the legality and withdraw of contests of the search performed by the authority within defendant's facilities in order to gather evidence of the offense. The contests against searches performed by the authority usually block the use of such evidence within both the administrative and criminal spheres. Because all cartel members are usually prosecuted in a single administrative proceeding, such contests may block the progress of the proceeding as well as the overall prosecution of the members of such cartel.

[12] The settlement in Brazil is denominated *Termo de Compromisso de Cessação*, as disposed in the article 53 of the Brazilian Competition Law (Lei 8.884/94).

US plea bargaining is one of the most prominent. There is considerable international experience regarding these mechanisms to terminate judicial or administrative disputes. In order to provide some empirical foundations for the design of settlements, this section summarises the main aspects of the international experience in using these types of agreement between the competition authority and participants of alleged cartels.

First, it is necessary to acknowledge that the legal framework providing for settlement agreements is embedded in the institutional environment of each jurisdiction, which varies significantly among countries (North, 1990; 2005). The institutional environments may vary in many aspects such as the functioning of the judiciary, the costs and benefits to litigate, and the possibility of negotiating administrative and criminal penalties in a single settlement. Thus, other jurisdiction experiences should always be examined taking into account these differences, which, generally, prevent the mere emulation of international practices to a particular country.

Two recent studies prepared, respectively, by the OECD and the ICN,[13] compiled the practice and opinions of various antitrust authorities with regard to the form and desirability of settlements in cartel cases. These studies show that legal boundaries and usage of these agreements are quite different among jurisdictions. According to ICN, within 20 surveyed jurisdictions, the legal statutes of only nine of them allow antitrust agencies to enter into settlements in cartel cases.[14] The authorities who have more experience in the use of the instrument are the United States, Germany, France and Canada. The main differences are the following:

(i) Requirements to enter into the agreement.
Some jurisdictions require a plea of guilty and the commitment to active co-operate in the prosecution of others cartel members, such as the United States and Canada.[15] Others, like South Africa and France, do not make such requirements. Those countries allow the

---

13 OECD, 2008; ICN, 2008.

14 The antitrust authorities in South Korea, Hungary and Sweden are studying the adoption of settlement instruments in cartel cases. The antitrust division of the European Commission have just introduced this mechanism but as yet without any concluded settlement.

15 The regulations of the European Commission go in this same direction, restricting the bargaining possibilities of the defendants. In this sense, the European Commission clarifies that the regulations shall not allow negotiation regarding the existence of the violation or the sanction to be applied.

conclusion of agreements without explicit admission of participation in the offense, but the party shall not contest charged violations.[16]

(ii) Evaluation of the cooperation offered by the defendant.
The evaluation of the cooperation obviously varies according to the circumstances of the case. The difference fundamentally regards the degree of predictability that each jurisdiction provides for the mechanism.[17] In general, greater predictability as to the adopted criteria implies a smaller range of cooperation valuing.[18] In this regard, the

---

[16] The study published by the OECD (2008) discusses the possible strategies that may be adopted by antitrust authorities, and their consequences when the admission of guilt is required at the discretion of the authority. In their words, 'while in certain jurisdictions such as the United States a negotiated settlement will always include a defendant's admission of guilt that could be used as evidence in private follow-on litigation, in certain other jurisdictions the competition authority or prosecutor might not invariably insist on a guilty plea. In these jurisdictions, where the guilty plea is "on the negotiating table", defendants are likely to resist a demand to plead guilty if they are concerned about the effects of a plea in follow-up civil litigation. Presumably, where the competition authority agrees to settle without a guilty plea, it can extract a higher fine. But that case might be the worst outcome for private litigants because they will end up without a formal decision finding liability and without a settlement admitting liability. That outcome might deprive at least some private litigants of the only realistic opportunity to bring an action against cartel members at reasonable costs. Without the evidence from a competition authority decision based on a settlement with guilty plea, they might find it too burdensome and risky to establish a full case in civil litigation. Conversely, if the competition authority insists on a guilty plea, it may have to lower the fine it can obtain in a settlement. Which solution a competition authority prefers should ideally be determined by the goal of maximizing overall deterrence. A lower fine in a plea agreement as a price to "buy" a guilty plea might be justified if the guilty plea makes civil litigation more likely and litigation can lead to fines that exceed the discount granted in the plea agreement.'

[17] In order to provide greater predictability regarding the expected value of the cooperation with the authorities, the US Department of Justice, through speeches of its Deputy Assistant Attorney General, Mr. Scott D. Hammond, reports that the following factors largely determine the value of that co-operation, taking in consideration the experience in the previous cases: (i) the cooperation must be provided at a time when investigation is benefited, (ii) the importance of the cooperation and its value to significantly advance the investigation, and (iii) whether the company is able to bring additional evidence of collusive behavior in other markets, thus qualifying for the 'Amnesty Plus' program. Regarding the importance of the last factor, Mr. Hammond emphasises that a large number of investigations were initiated because of evidence brought under the 'Amnesty Plus' program.

[18] Generally, the jurisdictions have adopted more flexible criteria, which involve greater discretion in setting the conditions of the agreement. Regarding a possible trade-off between transparency and predictability about the terms of

most notable difference is in the models used in the US and in the European Union (EU). While in the former the agreement is essentially a mechanism for obtaining evidence and reducing the costs of identifying perpetrators, in the EU, the agreements can only be executed after the completion of the investigation, and, therefore, their key role is to reduce the costs of defense of the antitrust authority decisions in the judiciary. Issues such as the valuation of the contribution to the investigations (Hammond, 2006b) are, therefore, irrelevant according to the method used by the EU. In part, such distinction may stem from the admissibility of lenience agreements with more than one defendant in the EU, in opposition to the US, where, like in Brazil, only the first-in applicant may qualify for the agreement.

(iii) Assessment of the relationship between settlement and the leniency program.
Some authorities – notably in Common Law countries where negotiated procedures are more usual – believe that settlement and lenience agreements are integrated policies. Nevertheless, both surveys of ICN and OECD note that settlements may undermine the demand for lenience agreements; therefore, they might be conflicting policies.[19] This complex interaction between lenience agreements and settlements are the main subject of the theoretical analysis presented in the next section.

(iv) Differences concerning the tradable rights.
According to each legal system, some rights may not be waived or granted, which reduces the scope of the agreement and prevents some arrangements that could be of mutual interest for the parties. For instance, the legal literature regarding plea bargaining sometimes expresses concern about the fact that such agreements might undermine the right to defense or subvert the justice within punitive

---

the plea bargaining, Hammond (2006b) states that 'if the Division [DOJ] were to establish an absolute, fixed discount for second-ins without consideration of these types of variables [cooperation, etc.], then the need for proportionality would be sacrificed for increased transparency. Proportional treatment also often requires consideration of factors shared only with the sentencing court and not the public, factors such as the state of the investigation at the time of the cooperation, the nature and extent to which the cooperation advanced the investigation, and whether the cooperation earned Amnesty Plus credit for disclosing undetected cartel offenses. The Division carefully weighs all of these variables in measuring the value of a company's cooperation to ensure proportional treatment of cooperating parties across all Division matters.'

[19] The OECD emphasises that if the antitrust authorities can obtain substantial punishment by means of a negotiated instrument, in theory, negative effects upon the demand for leniency should not exist. (OECD, 2008: 9).

system. This would happen if an innocent pleads guilt in order to avoid a more severe penalty (Schulhofer, 1992; Bjerk, 2007).

There seems to be some consensus points, which are briefly summarised as follows:

1. Settlements may be an efficient way to successfully terminate cartels cases, promoting a better allocation of investigative and processing resources and increasing the detection and punishment of offenses to antitrust law.[20] Such agreements may also provide certain benefits to defendants which are socially desirable, such as saving litigation costs and reducing the uncertainty about the punishment. The reduction of uncertainty is beneficial both for the defendant since it reduces his/her degree of exposure to an unknown penalty – as well as to society – because spending substantial resources and extensive prosecution do not always result in an appropriate punishment.
2. A reputation of consistency and fair negotiation may be important for effectiveness of a settlement. Uncertainty and asymmetric information about the negotiation process may be undesirable for both parties.[21] Similarly, there seems to be consensus that an antitrust authority may only conclude an agreement if it has sufficient information about the relevant facts of the case.
3. A concern of most jurisdictions regards possible effects that negotiated agreements may have in reducing punishment and thus undermine the enforcement of antitrust law. In this regard, a history of credible threats based on substantial punishment imposed in previous cases may decrease or even eliminate the negative effect such agreements may have on general deterrence of antitrust violations.[22]

---

[20] Such agreements may maximise the deterrence effect by promoting better use of existing resources. Thus, even if the agreement involves a slight reduction in punishment of the defendant, the saving of public resources could be used to detect and process new offenders, thereby enhancing overall punishment and deterrence.

[21] In this sense, the OECD recommends that 'Negotiated settlements will work best if the competition authority can establish a public record of its settlement practice and a reputation of being transparent, consistent and fair in settlement negotiations. Publishing negotiated settlements, guidelines, and public speeches can contribute to these goals.' (OECD, 2008: 9).

[22] The OECD recommends that negotiated instruments for termination of cartel cases should be used with caution in jurisdictions in which the program of combat to cartels is still developing and the threat of future sanctions has some degree of uncertainty due to the lack of confirmation of sanctions imposed in previous cases by the judiciary.

5 PRINCIPLES THAT SHOULD GOVERN SETTLEMENT DESIGN

5.1 Introduction

Roughly speaking, actual or potential defendants in a cartel case have three options: (i) application for a lenience agreement; (ii) application for a settlement; and (iii) pursuing the trial, being subject to possible conviction for violation of competition law. As a consequence, the design of a settlement has possible effects not only on the continuity of litigation, but also on the demand for lenience agreements, one of the main instruments for detecting cartels.

The interaction between these instruments has important implications on the controversial issues of admission of guilt and the amount to be paid as a pecuniary sanction. In this section, these and other issues are explored in more detail in order to ground the analysis of the Brazilian experience.

The analysis of defendants' decisions comprehends the identification of costs and benefits in each possible option. Such options may have great variability and complexity. They may be affected by characteristics of the defendants themselves, the businesses affected by the unlawful conduct, and the cartel's modus operandi. For sake of clarity, this section will present a simple model of defendants' choice, which points out the main principles relevant to the design of a settlement. Therefore, we begin with a discussion of the goals pursued by the antitrust authority. Such goals shall be the basis for the evaluation of the most appropriate design of a settlement. Then, the choice model is presented, emphasising items such as the need of admission of guilt, commitment to co-operate with the investigation, and the level of the pecuniary sanction.

5.2 Authority's and Defendants' Goals in a Settlement

In order to assess the convenience of a settlement, it is necessary to consider the goals each party pursues within such contract. As usual in economics, it is reasonable to assume that a defendant chooses the alternative (e.g. entering into a settlement vis-à-vis pursuing the trial) which offers the greatest return, taking into account the expected fine at the end of the trial, pecuniary sanction in the settlement, collateral obligations, litigation costs and his/her degree of risk aversion.

In its turn, the goal of the antitrust authority is the enforcement of competition law as provided for in most of the jurisdiction's legal statutes. What is generally understood as enforcement of the competition law is the ability of the authority to prevent and guide individuals' and companies' behavior, more specifically, to prevent anticompetitive behavior and mergers which may harm the consumer or social welfare by means of anticompetitive actions (Farrel and Katz, 2006). Therefore, agreements between defendants and the authority must be signed if, and only if, they enhance the deterrence of anticompetitive behavior.

Negotiated mechanisms between the competition authority and defendants, the lenience agreement included, affect the effectiveness of the competition policy in two ways. First, the agreement may exchange punishment for co-operation with the authorities. On the one hand, the punishment of a cartel member who co-operates with the authority is reduced. Ceteris paribus, this under-punishment mitigates the deterrence effect of the policy. On the other hand, the cooperation with the authorities offered in exchange will raise the likelihood of detection of illegal conducts, which is especially relevant in cartel cases since this practice is undoubtedly known to be unlawful, and, as a consequence, the offenders often try to hide any evidence of such behavior, making it more difficult for the authority to build the case.

The second way whereby a contract between the competition authority and defendants may affect the enforcement of the competition policy is reducing litigation costs. Eliminating costs regarding investigation, advocacy and legal representation saves time, as well as financial and human resources, which ceteris paribus leads to greater efficiency of the competition policy. The enforcement of competition policy being more efficient, the authority may, with the same budget, increase the deterrence of anticompetitive behavior. The economic literature also defines as additional benefits derived from settlements (i) the reduction in risks, since it was not possible to precisely anticipate the authority's decision, only to be known as of the administrative trial, and (ii) the screening mechanism which may help to distinguish guilty from innocent defendants (Grossman and Katz, 1983).

The analysis of the appropriate design of a settlement shall consider the increased effect in the deterrence of anticompetitive behavior and possible undesirable effects related to inadequate punishment of the agreement applicants, whether punishing innocents or under-punishing perpetrators. The interaction between these effects is detailed below, using a simple model of the defendants' choice.

5.3 A Simple Model for Defendant Choice

The defendant faces the three basic alternatives already mentioned: leniency agreement, settlement and trial. The timing of this decision is variable and its outcome may depend on actions of other defendants in a cartel case (Baker and Mezzetti, 2001; Perloff et al., 1996). For example, if a defendant engages in a lenience agreement, this alternative will not be available to any other defendant. In addition, the applicant for a lenience agreement is eligible for full immunity only if the competition authority has not yet opened investigations against that particular cartel. Similar incentives for early application are provided for in CADE's Resolution No. 46/2007 regarding settlements. Such resolution explicitly determines that the timing of the settlement proposal be taken into account for evaluation of the amount of the discount that the applicant is eligible for. The presentation that follows aims to isolate in a simple model the alternatives available to the defendants. Therefore, it deliberately ignores two aspects of defendants' decision process: the timing of the decision and the strategic interaction among defendants.

Cartel deterrence is based on three main instruments: (i) administrative sanctions, especially the imposition of fines and collateral obligations; (ii) criminal sanctions; and (iii) compensatory private suits by those who were directly damaged by the cartel. These instruments may be set by a single judicial body, as is the case of the US, or by different bodies, as is the case of Brazil and France. In the latter, the decision about an administrative sanction or settlement, taken by an administrative tribunal, may have unknown consequences on the likelihood of the decisions in other areas, inasmuch as the information about the conviction in the administrative tribunal may affect the decision in the other judicial bodies. In our model, we allow for these indirect effects and take the single judicial body as a special case.

In addition to these burdens related to cartel deterrence, the administrative proceeding results in costs related to defense, representation, and loss of reputation, which does not distinguish guilty from innocent defendants. As a consequence, those costs do not play the role of inhibiting the unlawful behavior, as they do not provide different pay-offs related to different conducts. These costs incurred by both guilty and innocent are net social costs, even if privately incurred.[23]

In our model, these privately incurred costs related to the development of the administrative proceedings are separated into two groups: dissuasive punishment, which gathers the administrative sanctions and possible changes in the likelihood of conviction in criminal and civil areas, and other costs of pursuing litigation up to the administrative trial. These costs

[23] In addition to these social costs incurred privately by guilty and innocent defendants, the dispute between the authority and defendants involves direct costs to the authority itself and the judiciary, the latter used in the arbitration of the dispute.

are respectively represented herein by X_T and C_T, where the subscript 't' is mnemonic for 'trial'.[24] The lenience agreement, in turn, may or may not involve costs of cash disbursement, according to the timing of its application, and provides for criminal immunity. In contrast, there are costs related to the admission of guilt and the effective cooperation with the investigation, which may vary significantly among defendants of a cartel case. Such costs may result both from changes in the likelihood of success of claims for civil damages as well as from retaliation by cartel members. For the sake of comparison between the lenience agreement and the settlement, these costs are divided into two: X_L, which corresponds to pecuniary sanction and other obligations included in the agreement, and Y_L, which corresponds to the costs of pleading guilty and the effective co-operation with the authorities, where the subscript 'L' is mnemonic for 'leniency'.

Finally, the settlement implies costs of cash disbursement and collateral obligations, represented herein by X_S, and, as the lenience agreement, costs related to pleading guilty and effective co-operation with the authorities, represented herein by Y_S, where the subscript 'S' stands for 'settlement'. Y_S can be zero if the settlement does not include the admission of guilt and obligations of effective co-operation with the authorities. Some relevant aspects to the decision of the parties, such as if the transaction encompasses both criminal and administrative spheres, are ignored at present, but they will be taken into consideration later when the details regarding the principles that should govern the design of settlements are explored.

The defendant's decision problem may be represented in Figure 8.1, which links each alternative to its costs.

The competition authority has all the bargaining power to define the administrative sanctions, including the cash disbursement and collateral obligations, as well as to determine the need of admission of guilt and cooperation with the investigation. On the other hand, the competition authority does not know the magnitude of the costs related to the admission of guilt and co-operation with investigation (Y_S and Y_L), and the costs of carrying on with the trial (C_T). In addition, the authority does not know if defendants are guilty or innocent. Even in possession of sufficient evidence to file administrative proceedings against the defendants and of additional evidence gathered during the investigation of a case, it is not possible to conclude at the time of the settlement (i.e. before the

24 These values correspond to the certainty equivalent of the yet unknown trial outcome, taking into account the defendant's risk aversion and the discount rate. The certainty equivalent is the value whose utility is equivalent to the expected utility associated to an uncertain outcome (e.g. a lottery).

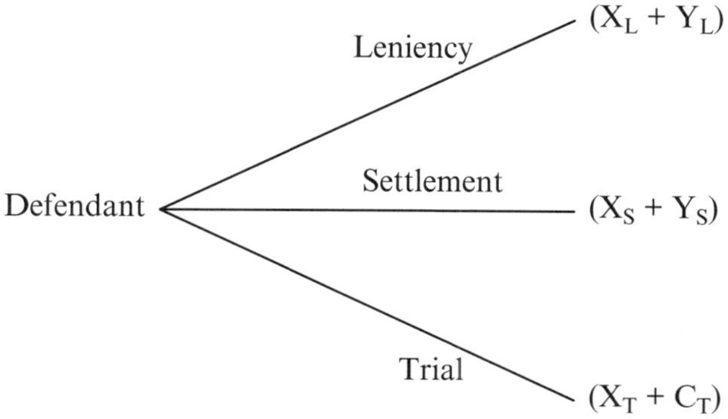

Figure 8.1 A simple model of defendant's choice

administrative trial and closing of the case in the administrative sphere) if defendants are guilty.

Since the authority does not have complete information regarding such variables, there is the risk that the design of the agreement may under-punish perpetrators (i.e. $X_S + Y_S < X_T$) or punish the innocent (i.e. $X_S + Y_S < C_T$), which are both undesirable from a social perspective. As it is relatively consensual in economic and legal literature, agreements such as the settlement should be designed to avoid the under-punishment of guilty defendants as well as the punishment of innocent ones. This can be done, even if imperfectly, by raising the cash disbursement (X_S) to an amount sufficiently high to dispel the interest of innocent defendants in seeking a settlement.[25]

The information asymmetry regarding the costs of admission of guilt and co-operation with the investigation may also limit the ability of the authority to design agreements which might reduce administrative costs, and, therefore, increase the enforcement of the competition policy. On the one hand, the requirement of admission of guilt is desirable in order to potentially increase the deterrence effect of the administrative sanction, in particular because it undermines trust among cartel members, which is an important component of the enforcement of informal contracts (Lazaric and Lorenz, 1998). On the other hand, costs of pleading guilty usually vary among defendants, especially in hard-core cartels, whose mechanisms of punishing defection often go beyond purely economic retaliation. Such costs may be higher than those of a conviction, as suggested by the fact

25 This is the main conclusion reached by Grossman and Katz (1983) and further by Bjerk (2007).

that there is no lenience agreement in several hard-core cartels. In other words, in such cases, even the greatest of prizes – i.e. full immunity to criminal and administrative sanctions – is not enough to attract potential applicants for lenience agreements. When this occurs, any agreement between the authority and defendants that requires admission of guilt, either settlement or lenience agreements, is, in the defendant's perspective, worse than carrying on with the trial, and, therefore, unfeasible.

The differences in costs of pleading guilty define two groups among those who participate in a cartel. A first group gathers the potential applicants to a lenience agreement and is characterised by costs of pleading guilty and co-operating with the investigations that are not too high so that $(X_L + Y_L) < (X_T + C_T)$. In other words, the lenience agreement is preferable to the risk of prosecution by means of an administrative proceeding and possible conviction. The second group includes those whose costs of pleading guilty and co-operating with the investigations (Y_L) is sufficiently high so that $(X_L + Y_L) > (X_T + C_T)$. In as much as there are several cartel cases that go to administrative trial without lenience agreements, this second group is probably fairly large.

As to the request for a settlement, there are two possible scenarios. If the proceeding has already a lenience agreement, then the costs of pleading guilty and collaborating with investigations is not so high [i.e. $(X_L + Y_L) < (X_T + C_T)$], which means that this case fits in the first group. Thus, even assuming that the costs of pleading guilty and co-operating with the investigation is different among the members of a same cartel, it is reasonable to assume, as a general rule, that requiring a plea of guilty in those cases will not dissuade potential applicants for settlement.[26] Moreover, there is no need to discuss possible negative effects on the leniency program since the lenience agreement was already executed. In this case, the settlement shall require admission of guilt and the obligation to co-operate with the investigation, as CADE's Resolution No. 46 appropriately provides for.

If the administrative proceeding has not benefited from a lenience agreement, there are two cases. First, the costs of pleading guilty and collaborating with investigation are comparatively lower [i.e. $(X_L + Y_L) < (X_T + C_T)$], which means that there are potential applicants to a lenience agreement. Second, those costs are sufficiently high [i.e. $(X_L + Y_L) > (X_T + C_T)$] so that a lenience agreement will not be reached, even if a settlement is not available. The abundant evidence about cartel prosecutions without

[26] This conclusion does not necessarily apply to cases where individuals are parties in lenience agreement due to their limited liability, which reduces the costs of civil damages they may be obliged to pay.

leniency agreements before settlements were allowed, in mid-2007, suggests that this second case is empirically relevant, perhaps more likely than the first. Furthermore, there are relatively few cases of lenience agreements executed after the beginning of an administrative proceeding, even at the time settlements in cartel cases were prevented, suggesting that the likelihood of potential applicants for lenience agreement is much lower in cases in which the administrative proceeding is already in progress.

In such cases, offering a single contract schema to the defendants[27] – e.g. requiring the admission of guilt and collaboration with investigation in all cases – would clearly under-use settlements, and, thus, prevent saving litigation costs. As part of the defendants may present high costs of pleading guilty [i.e. $(X_L + Y_L) > (X_T + C_T)$], such requirement would eliminate the possibility of settlement by members of that group.

This single contract schema for settlements, in which only the value of the collaboration with investigation is variable, is, in essence, the practice in the US, the jurisdiction that most intensely uses negotiated proceedings to finish cartel cases. This practice implies that settlements in situations where $(X_L + Y_L) > (X_T + C_T)$ – i.e. when no lenience agreement would be feasible regardless of the possibility of settlement – would be discarded prima facie. Additionally, since the lenience agreement provides for the maximum punishment reduction (i.e. $X_L < X_S$), a settlement with admission of guilt would never be signed in cases in which no lenience agreement is reached. As a result, this practice reduces the settlement to a second lenience agreement, which is exactly the role of plea bargaining in US jurisdiction.

There are three plausible explanations for why the US model of settlements is widely used, despite the obligation of pleading guilty. First, the costs of admission of guilt are probably much lower in the US due to the fact that all possible sanctions to cartel participants are decided by a single judicial body. As a consequence, a settlement does not generate spillovers or unintended consequences to other areas, such as criminal prosecution. Second, the litigation costs for the authority are probably lower in the US since the conviction is not subjected to judicial review as it is in the case of ordinary administrative decisions. Inasmuch as litigation costs are lower, the benefits resulting from abbreviating the trial and giving finality are relatively lower. Third, as suggested by Scott and Stuntz (1992), the pecuniary discounts may be so attractive that some innocent defendants opt to plead guilty.

For the general case, requiring admission of guilt for all cartel proceedings

[27] This strategy is also known in the Economics of Contracts as 'pooling'.

implies underutilization of the settlement. The question that remains to be answered is whether one can design different contracts for the group that has potential interest to negotiate the admission of guilt and collaboration with investigation [i.e. $(X_L + Y_L < X_T + C_T)$] and for the group whose costs of pleading guilty are high enough to exclude them as potential applicants to the lenience agreement [i.e. $(X_L + Y_L > X_T + C_T)$].

For those who are in the first group – i.e. who want to negotiate a plea of guilty and the co-operation with the investigation – just offering a slightly less favourable agreement than the leniency agreement would make the defendants prefer the latter. Since the demand for leniency agreements remains unaltered, there is no adverse effect on the likelihood of cartel detection. Moreover, all the potential applicants for settlements that have a low cost of pleading guilty will probably be willing to settle as a second leniency, thereby decreasing litigation costs and bringing about new evidence about the same or other antitrust offences.

For those who do not intend to negotiate the admission of guilt and collaboration with investigations, the authority can offer a contract in which the pecuniary sanction is equivalent to the present value of the punishment that the defendant would receive by the time of the conviction in the administrative trial, discounted by an amount just enough to induce the defendant to settle [i.e. $X_S = (X_T + C_T - \varepsilon)$]. In this case, the settlement is featured as a pre-judicial agreement, since the reference for the agreement is the administrative decision, which could, in turn, be reviewed in the judiciary.

It is important to note that the authority does not know who the potential applicants for the lenience agreement are. Therefore, these potential applicants may apply for a settlement without a plea of guilty, which, if accepted, would reduce the ability to identify new cartels, and, hence, decrease deterrence. Therefore, the settlements without a plea of guilty should be sufficiently unattractive to the group who has relatively lower costs of admitting guilt.

Due to this interaction between the settlements and the demand for lenience agreements, the size of the discounts offered to induce the defendants to sign the agreement (ε)[28] should be carefully analysed for an optimal

28 If the authority had complete knowledge of all variables and there was common knowledge about their values, a discount equivalent to one monetary unit would be sufficient to motivate the execution of a settlement without any loss of demand for the lenience agreement. As the authority does not know the defendants' reservation value, it is reasonable to assume that the probability of concluding a settlement (and thus achieving the benefits of interruption of the dispute) will grow as the discount increases, i.e. $\frac{\partial p(Settlement)}{\partial \varepsilon} > 0$. However, it is expected that this effect is mitigated as the discount grows, i.e. $\frac{\partial^2 p(Settlement)}{\partial^2 \varepsilon} < 0$.

design of a settlement without pleading guilty. The greater the discount, the greater the likelihood of the execution of a settlement, and the greater the benefits from the interruption of the dispute in terms of resource saving. This saving of resources allows deepening the investigation, both in the cartel case in which the settlement was executed as well as in other cartel cases, and enhances the enforcement of the antitrust policy as a whole. On the other hand, if the discount is excessive, it may happen that potential applicants for the lenience agreement will prefer the settlement without admitting guilt, which would occur if $\varepsilon > (X_T + C_T)(X_L + Y_L)$. As a result, the ideal size of discount (ε) is defined by this trade-off, in which rising (ε) increases deterrence by reducing inefficiency due to litigation (finality of the proceedings) and reduces deterrence directly by decreasing the punishment and, indirectly, by reducing the demand for the lenience agreement.

It is worth mentioning that the requirement of admission of guilt for all settlements only maximises the enforcement of the antitrust law if the benefits arising from the interruption of the administrative proceedings are negligible in comparison to the costs arising from the possible reduction in the demand for lenience agreements. As mentioned in section 2 of this chapter, the costs of litigation are particularly relevant at this stage of the Brazilian program of cartel deterrence, so that the benefits of a negotiated mechanism are significant.

In addition to saving litigation costs, even with no admission of guilt, the settlement brings finality and as a consequence mitigates the risks associated to the final outcome. Given that defendants are likely risk averse, they are better off paying the expected value of their probable fines for certain (Grossman and Katz, 1983). It is expected that the defendants that are most likely to apply for a settlement, with or without admission of guilt and full collaboration with investigation, are those with a higher cost of carrying on with the trial, or, alternatively, those for whom finality is more valuable [i.e. C_T is significantly high].

In short, the flexibility of the settlement allows the negotiation of two models of agreements that may enhance the deterrence of anticompetitive behavior: (1) an agreement requiring the admission of guilt and full collaboration with investigation, taking the form of a second lenience agreement; and (2) an agreement which, although it does not require the admission of guilt, involves the payment of the expected value of the punishment on the part of the applicant, taking the form of a pre-judicial settlement.

6 THE BRAZILIAN EXPERIENCE WITH SETTLEMENTS: SOME PRELIMINARY CONCLUSIONS

Within the first year since the amendment in the Brazilian Competition Law allowing settlements in cartel cases, several companies and a few individuals applied to settle their cases. The variety of proposals by defendants in different industries and cartel cases permit us to draw some lessons from the Brazilian experience.

The number of applicants was substantial for the first year, particularly taking into account the experience with the introduction of the leniency program in Brazil, which took three years to conclude the first agreement. Although substantial, the number of proposals is still much lower than the number of potential applicants. Within the first year, sixteen companies, three trade associations and ten individuals (all managers) applied for a settlement, whereas the number of defendants currently being prosecuted in cartel cases, considering only cases of hard-core cartels with direct evidence obtained by dawn raids or communication interception, exceeds 200.[29]

More remarkable is the rate of rejection of settlement proposals by CADE. The competition authority has approved four out of sixteen settlement proposals presented by companies in cartel cases so far: JBS/SA (slaughterhouse soft cartel), Lafarge Brasil SA (alleged cement cartel), Alcan Embalagens do Brasil (alleged aluminum bags cartel) and Bridgestone Corporation (alleged marine hoses cartel). Three individuals that applied for settlements, all of whom were managers of those companies, also had their proposal accepted: two from JBS/SA and one from Alcan.

Five of the rejected proposals are related to cases that have at least one proposal accepted – the alleged cartel of the cement industry and that of aluminum bags – which is evidence that there is, indeed, significant variability in the costs and benefits of settling a case within the same industry. In those cases, not only did the applicants offer a settlement sum considered insufficient to deter collusion, but also they did not offer any effective collaboration with the investigations. The remaining rejected proposals, all from the security guard services cartel, were set forth on the day of

[29] These are cases with a very high probability of conviction as a trial outcome. The number of defendants in all cartel cases probably exceeds one thousand. Among the actual applicants for settlements, the majority is from those cases with direct evidence, but there are also some proposals from soft cartels.

CADE's final decision, in that they were rejected for not meeting some requirements of CADE's Resolution No. 46/2007 and for being requested too late.

Regarding the model of settlement, as described in the theoretical discussion, three out of four settlements with companies did not require the admission of guilt and full collaboration with investigation (pre-judicial model), whereas just one proposal, in a case that had benefited from a leniency agreement, followed the second leniency model. It is noteworthy that no settlement with individuals included the admission of guilt, which may be due to the higher cost of pleading guilty when criminal prosecution is investigated by a different judicial body, as is the case of Brazil.

Table 8.1 below shows the timing, requirements, amounts paid and existence of leniency agreement.

The comparison between accepted and rejected proposals shows a remarkable regularity. In all accepted proposals the applicant valued significantly finality [i.e. C_T was significantly high]. JBS, for instance, was planning an IPO that could be adversely affected by its antitrust uncertainty. A similar situation led Alcan to apply for a settlement, as it was about to sell the business unit that was under investigation, and was willing to clear it for sale. Finally, Lafarge and Bridgestone applied for settlements in Brazil as a result of the company transnational policy, probably related to their application for settlements in other jurisdictions. Pleading guilty or committing to collateral obligations in one jurisdiction may have adverse spillovers on the prosecution of a cartel in other jurisdictions, particularly in the case of international cartels. That is probably why part of the demand for settlements in Brazil, similar to the experience with leniency agreements, is from multinational companies that are settling simultaneously in several countries.

Finally, there is no evidence that the current settlement policy has any adverse effect on the demand for leniency agreements. On the contrary, as stated in the Brazilian submission to OECD, Working Party No 3, 2008, 'there is a growing number of candidates to the [leniency] program, including members of international cartels'. This positive result may be due to the rationing of settlements, which are actually designed for guilty defendants with a higher reservation value for finality. Expanding the settlements for a larger group of applicants, by means of a higher discount on the expected fine, may have the adverse effect of attracting innocent defendants with a higher value for finality and/or those who would be otherwise candidates for leniency agreements. In short, although the Brazilian experience with direct settlements in cartel cases is still incipient, it shows that the leniency and settlement agreements, when properly designed, are complementary mechanisms in a program of cartel deterrence.

Table 8.1 Settlements concluded in Brazil

Company	Alleged Conduct	Affected market	Timing	Requirements	Contribution	Leniency Agreement
Bridgestone Corporation	Hard-core cartel	Marine hose	After dawn raid, during investigation (08/2008)	Admission of guilt; Brazilian market only; effective and full co-operation	R$1,594, 000.00 (Approx 13% equivalent to the present value of a fine of roughly 20%)	Yes
Lafarge Brasil S/A	Hard-core cartel	Cement	After dawn-raids, during investigation (11/2007)	No admission of guilt; compliance program	R$43,000,000.00 (Approx 10% of the annual gross turnover; equivalent to the present value of a fine of roughly 15%)	No
JBS/SA	Soft cartel	Slaughter-house	By the time of the judgment (11/2008)	No admission of guilt; compliance program	R$13,761, 944.40 (Approx 2.5% of total gross turnover in the relevant market)	No
Two individuals (manager and employee)					10% of the company's contribution (manager) and approx. US$3,600.00 for the other one (employee)	
Alcan Embalagens do Brasil	Hard-core cartel	Aluminum bags	During investigation	No admission of guilt; compliance program	R$24,218,550.57 (Approx 10% equivalent to the present value of a fine of roughly 15%)	No
One individual (manager)					10% of the company's contribution (manager)	

7 CONCLUDING REMARKS

Settlements are an important part of a program of cartel deterrence, particularly when the likelihood of conviction and the litigation costs are higher. This type of negotiated procedure to reach finality is in essence complementary to the fully adversarial procedures associated to the trial by the administrative or judicial courts, and to other investigative instruments, such as the leniency agreement.

The Brazilian experience provides some insights about the different models of direct settlement in cartel cases and the complex interaction among settlements, leniency agreements, and trial outcome. Brazil has experienced a substantial change in cartel prosecution since 2000. The use of new investigative instruments, such as dawn raids, communication interception, and the leniency program, caused a significant increase in the likelihood of cartel detection, bringing about cases of major economic relevance, in sectors such as the cement industry, chemicals, among others. As an unintended consequence, the costs of litigation increased substantially, fostering the demand for a mechanism of settlement, launched in 2007.

Within the first year of the settlement program several proposals from different industries and cartel cases were submitted, allowing the identification of some patterns of the current policy. First, there is leeway for the complementary models of settlements, the first oriented mainly to increasing the likelihood of detection, and the second oriented to saving social costs of litigation. The two models are designed to separate those defendants that have lower costs of admitting guilt and collaborating with investigations from those with higher costs, particularly managers that may still be subjected to criminal prosecution by a different judicial body. Second, the concern with the preservation of the demand for leniency agreements led the competition authority to restrict the use of settlements, which are effectively designed for the defendants that are likely guilty and give higher value to finality. The recent experience illustrates that the current settlement policy has not caused any adverse effect on leniency agreements, while reducing litigation costs and granting finality in some cases. The more intense use of this type of negotiated procedure shall be made with caution. On the one hand, greater discounts for settlements increase efficiency but, on the other hand, decrease the dissuasive effect of direct sanctions, and the likelihood of detection of new cartel cases by means of leniency agreements. This fine tuning adjustment is a major challenge for competition authorities.

REFERENCES

Baker, S. and C. Mezzetti (2001), 'Prosecutorial Resources, Plea Bargaining and the Decision to go to Trial', *Journal of Law, Economics and Organization*, **7** (1), 149–167.

Bar-Gill, O., and Gazal-Ayal, O. (2006), 'Plea Bargains Only for the Guilty', *Journal of Law and Economics,* **49**, 353–364.

Bjerk, D. (2007), 'Guilt Shall Not Escape or Innocence Suffer? The Limits of Plea Bargaining When Defendant Guilt is Uncertain', *American Law and Economics Review*, **9** (1), 1–25.

Brenner, S. (2005), *An Empirical Study of the European Corporate Leniency Program*, Humboldt-University Berlin.

Connor. J. (2007), *Global Antitrust Prosecutions Of International Cartels: Focus on Asia*, Purdue University.

Farrel, J. and M. Katz (2006), 'The Economics of Welfare Standards in Antitrust', *Competition Policy International*, October 2006.

Greif, Avner (2006), *Institutions and the Path to the Modern Economy: Lessons from Medieval Trade*, Cambridge University Press.

Grossman, G. and M. Katz (1983), 'Plea Bargaining and Social Welfare', *The American Economic Review*, **73** (4), 749–757.

Hammond, S. (2006a), 'The U.S. Model of Negotiated Plea Agreements: A Good Deal With Benefits For All', U.S. Department of Justice.

Hammond, S. (2006b), 'Measuring the Value of Second-In Cooperation in Corporate Plea Negotiations', U.S. Department of Justice.

ICN (2008), 'Cartel Settlements'.

Landes, W.M. (1971), 'An Economic Analysis of the Courts', *Journal of Law and Economics*, **14**, 61–107.

Lazaric, N. and E. Lorenz (1998), 'The Learning Dynamics of Trust, Reputation and Confidence', in N. Lazaric and E. Lorenz, *Trust and Economic Learning*, Edward Elgar Publishing.

North, Douglass (1990), *Institutions, Institutional Change and Economic Performance,* Cambridge University Press.

North, Douglass (2005), *Understanding the Process of Economic Change*, Princeton University Press.

OECD (2008), 'Plea Bargaining/Settlement of Cartel Cases', in *OECD Series Roundtables on Competition Policy n. 69*, (DAF/COMP(2007)38).

Perloff, J., D. Rubinfeld and P. Ruud (1996), 'Antitrust Settlements and Trial Outcomes', *The Review of Economics and Statistics*, **78** (3), 401–409.

Reinganum, J. (1988), 'Plea Bargaining and Prosecutorial Discretion', *The American Economic Review*, **78** (4), 713–728.

Schulhofer (1992), 'Plea Bargaining as Disaster', *The Yale Law Journal*, **101** (8), Symposium: Punishment (June, 1992), 1979–2009.

Scott, R. and W. Stuntz (1992), 'Plea Bargaining as Contract', *The Yale Law Journal*, **101** (8), Symposium: Punishment (June, 1992), 1909–1968.

Stiglitz, J.E. and A. Weiss (1981), 'Credit Rationing in Markets with Imperfect Information', *American Economic Review*, June 1981, 393–410.

Wils, W.P.J. (2008), 'The Use of Settlements in Public Antitrust Enforcement: Objectives and Principles', *World Competition*, **31** (3), 335–352.

PART III

Perspectives

9. The Development of the World Economy and Competition Law

Rainer Geiger*

1 INTRODUCTION

It is the purpose of this chapter to discuss the role of competition in a changing world economy. This analysis will reflect market globalisation, the emergence of new players, the challenges of sustainable development and the recent financial and economic crisis. Against this background, key features of competition law and policy will be highlighted. The chapter will conclude by offering some perspectives for the future. Can competition serve as a tool for recovery from recession? What role will it play in any necessary reshaping of economic policies and institutions? What will be the impact of large rescue plans being put in place to restore stability and growth? What will be the relationship to other policy instruments? Is there still scope for greater harmony of national policies? Should new initiatives for multilateral rules on competition be launched to strengthen the international trading system? What would be the interest of developing countries to support such initiatives?

After decades of continuous growth in trade and investment, 2009 will be a year of recession, the most serious economic downturn since the end of the Second World War[1]. Real economic growth rates will be negative for many countries including some of the major economies. International trade and foreign direct investment are expected to decline significantly. Food and energy prices will remain volatile and unemployment is about to rise. It is not sure when economic stimulus packages will show their effects and whether new problems are not looming on the horizon. Government intervention is bound to increase as a result of capital injections into the

* Professor of International Economic Law; Senior regional advisor, OECD, Paris, France.

[1] Economic Outlook N.84, OECD December 2008; Furceri, D. and A. Mourougane (2009), 'Financial Crises: Past Lessons and Policy Implications', *ECO Working Paper*, 23 January.

private sector and a strengthening of the regulatory system is inevitable for the management of systemic risk in the market economy system.

Over the last few years emerging market economies have gained considerable weight in the world economy in terms of inward and outward investment. In 2007, Brazil, Russia, India and China had accumulated an FDI inward stock of respectively 214.3; 93.9; 67.7 and 699.5 billion USD. Even more remarkably the same countries accounted for an FDI outward stock of billion USD of 107.5 for Brazil, 75.2 for Russia, 21.1 for India and 82.3 for China.[2] The period where OECD countries could set the rules is gone and new forms of co-operation will have to be developed.

With the Washington summit of 15 November 2008, the G20 has become a key institution for discussing the remedies to the world crisis. Even before, at the G8 Summit held in 2007 in Heiligendamm/Germany, the seven Western industrialised countries and Russia have engaged in a structured dialogue with emerging market economies. Joint working groups have been set up to address issues of energy, development, investment and innovation and a report on the outcome of this work and proposed future directions is due for this year's summit to be held in Italy.[3]

Thus far, competition has not been at the heart of these debates. Does it still have a role to play as one of the pillars of our market economy? And what should be its impact on the ongoing debate on rules of the game for the world economy? What does it mean for economic development, competitiveness of national economies, trade and investment? Will there be any voice for competition advocacy in the necessary update and strengthening of regulatory systems? The short answer is that competition policy instruments are as important as ever but tools and objectives may need to be redefined to maintain relevance. And there is a need to have a fresh look at international co-operation on trade, competition and development.

When competition experts of OECD countries started to meet in 1961 in the context of a committee 'on restrictive business practices' a mere 25 countries in the world had adopted and were implementing competition laws and not all laws in force at the time had merger control provisions.[4] Today there are more than 100 countries which apply competition laws among which are quite a number of relatively small economies. Competition provisions can be found in international trade agreements

---

2 EIU, *World Investment Prospects to 2011: Foreign Direct Investment and the Challenge of Political Risk*, September 2007.

3 For the conclusions of the Heiligendamm G8 Summit *see* http://www.g-8.de (accessed 18 June 2009).

4 *See* Proceedings of the 100th Competition Committee meeting, Background note DAF/COMP(2008)4, p. 163 et seq.

– bilateral, regional and multilateral – and the importance of competition as an underlying principle of the multilateral trading system is increasingly recognised.[5]

In many countries the autonomy of competition authorities for law enforcement has been strengthened and some of these authorities play an important advocacy role in regulatory processes.

Yet the role of competition remains fragile in the political context and in public opinion. Governments over time have adopted trade and regulatory policies in open contradiction with competition principles. The interaction between competition authorities and centres of Government has remained limited. As witnessed by a number of spectacular cartel cases company performance is uneven and we are still far from a competition culture permeating individual and collective behavior. Public information campaigns, where they took place, did not show a strong impact on public opinion.

On the only major occasion where competition was at the centre of a political debate, the outcome was negative: the discussions surrounding the European Constitution: Elevated by the proposed Treaty texts to a constitutional principle, the concept of 'free and unfettered competition' did not meet the understanding of voters in those countries where the ratification of the Constitutional Treaty was to be subject to referendum. In France for instance it was successfully used by the opponents of the Treaty as a red flag to frighten voters. In the current debate on how to master the economic crisis there is a lot of talk about 'strategic industries' and 'national champions' but hardly any mention of competition. If competition is to prevail as it should as one of the pillars of our market system its role in economic development and a democratic society should be highlighted, realistically designed and better explained.

2 COMPETITION AND ECONOMIC DEVELOPMENT

Market economies are about competitiveness, performance and efficiency and cannot function without competitive conduct of market operators. It is true that markets are shaped by a multitude of other factors including government policies but without a minimum amount of economic freedom and a culture of competition we are back to a managed economy dominated by rent seeking of operators and a predominance of regulators.

---

[5] *See* Trade and Competition Policies: Options for a Greater Coherence, OECD 2001.

This is why the famous Washington consensus according to which development will result from trade liberalisation, privatisation and deregulation cannot produce efficient results. Liberalisation can be circumvented by private restraints and the privatisation of public monopolies is missing its target if substituted by private market dominance and collusive practices.

Competition is thus essential to achieving the benefits of market liberalisation and competitiveness. This has been recognised by the Monterrey consensus of 2002, which stressed the importance of private sector development but also the need for good governance in both the public and private sectors.[6] The idea of competition is fundamental to modern economic thinking and there is a well-developed body of theory to explain how the pursuit of economic self-interest, within an appropriate framework, has beneficial effect for economic efficiency, consumers and society as a whole.[7] Economic reforms that disregard market functioning and fail to promote competitive behavior are bound to fail in their very objectives.

But, competition will never be perfect in any society. Its successful functioning may lead to market power and economic concentration which in itself needs to be monitored to prevent abuse. Competition principles will always have to co-exist with other government policies designed to correct market failure, to respond to externalities and to deal with the issue of asymmetric information in the market place. Competition authorities will always need to engage in an intellectual contest with regulators and they need to be convincing to avoid that regulations overshoot their stated targets and create inefficiencies.

In the past for various reasons – sometimes due to the influence of powerful lobbies – whole sectors of the economy have been exempted from the application of competition laws: agriculture, banking, transport being the most prominent examples for a number of countries. There is an increasing consensus today that there is no case for wholesale exemption. The results of a productivist and narrowly controlled agricultural policy are well known and reforms are pursued in the sector to introduce a higher degree of flexibility. The harmful effects to consumers arising from collusion in the banking sector are amply documented and lack of competition in that sector may be one of the reasons for the lack of accountability which has amplified the current financial crisis. Restrictive trade policies have led to enormous losses to consumers and economic efficiency, in

[6] Financing for Development-Building on Monterrey, United Nations, 2002.

[7] A Framework for the Design and Implementation of Competition Law and Policy, World Bank and OECD, 1998, chapter 6.

particular in the area of services where productivity has suffered from lack of modernisation and high costs.

Have competition authorities been in a position to play a useful role in the design of economic policies? Are they equipped to intervene efficiently? Are procedures for interagency consultations in place? Can decisions taken on the basis of sound competition analysis be overridden by political authorities? The answers to these questions depend on individual country situations and institutional frameworks.

The most shining example here is provided by Australia. In 1995, the Australian Government set up a program of reviewing and revising legislation that limited competition and was not justified by an overriding public interest. This reform was applied at both federal and state levels with ample resources allocated to it at all levels. It resulted in the review of 1700 laws, with most reviews being completed by 2001. Since the implementation of the program, Australia's economic performance has been among the strongest in the OECD area.[8]

In other countries competition advocacy has been less successful. There is not much evidence that competition considerations ever prevailed in antidumping proceedings and in the European Union the agricultural sector has been most resilient to increasing competition on internal markets. But the tide is turning: the Work of the OECD Committee on Competition, through its Working Group on Competition and Regulation has provided powerful arguments for precompetitive modernisation of rules in numerous sectors. It was a strong party in country regulatory review conducted within OECD and contributed to the elaboration of checklists for regulatory reform[9]. It has elaborated a Competition Assessment Toolkit, which is already widely used for the review of regulatory policies and in the context of regulatory impact assessments.[10]

Economic efficiency both in domestic and export markets depends on competitiveness and competitiveness in turn is the result of a conjunction of natural comparative advantages, public policies and entrepreneurial initiatives. For this reason there is a need to develop an integrated approach to development which is based on a variety of policies and patterns of business conduct in order to build confidence in business activities and the general investment climate. Competition is important but only one of several factors in this equation and it depends on overall policy coherence whether stated targets for reform can be reached. Investment is not just a

---

8 Competition Assessment Toolkit, OECD 2007, p. 21.
9 The OECD Report on Regulatory Reform, Synthesis, OECD 1997.
10 Competition Checklist, Competition Assessment Toolkit, op cit p. 9.

function of cross-border liberalisation and protection of foreign investors. It will only prosper within an overall framework of measures and practices which lifts unnecessary constraints but also ensures a fair distribution of benefits. Seen from this angle, competition policy forms part of good governance and responsible corporate behavior.

Based on that philosophy, the OECD has adopted in 2006 a Policy Framework for Investment (PFI) as a guide for the improvement and evaluation of national policies.[11] It covers the following ten policy areas which are considered relevant for a favourable investment climate: Investment Policy, Investment Promotion and Facilitation, Trade Policy, Competition Policy, Corporate Governance, Policies for Promoting Responsible Business Conduct, Human Resource Development, Infrastructure and Financial Sector Development, Public Governance.

Under the heading 'competition' the PFI sets out a relatively simple checklist of criteria for successful policies, together with commentaries. This includes transparency of rules; non-discriminatory application; guidance for compliance; status and resources of competition agencies; degree of law enforcement; competition advocacy role in regulatory policies and privatisation; arrangements for notification; exchange of information; and consultations with competition agencies of other countries.

Several features of the framework are unique:

- It provides a comprehensive and interdisciplinary approach to investment and development;
- It is evolutionary and can be adjusted in light of experience;
- It covers both domestic and international investment;
- It has been developed through a participatory approach bringing together 30 OECD and 30 non-OECD countries in a joint Task Force co-chaired by Japan and Chile;
- It relies on stake-holder participation: i.e. the Business Community, the international trade union movement and NGOs were fully involved in the drafting process; and
- It is not prescriptive, does not set rules but provides criteria which can serve as guidance for the development and reform of national policies; a toolkit for implementation is being elaborated by the OECD Investment Committee.

Going one step further the OECD, in the context of regional investment co-operation with non Member countries, has elaborated a process

---

11 Policy Framework for Investment, OECD 2006.

for assessment of national policies which is comprehensive, based on performance indicators and action orientated. And what is essential, it is participatory. The process that has been initiated aims to increase competitiveness and boost private sector development. It starts with the OECD Secretariat and the participating country conducting an analysis of the state of reform which highlights strong and weak points in the policy framework, to provide a basis for setting of time bound targets for reform; guidance is then provided for the implementation of the measures aimed at reaching these targets. The participating country remains in the driving seat throughout the process and this creates a strong motivation for the Government to implement the reforms that are recommended. The input of the private sector and civil society of the country concerned is solicited throughout the process.

This process was successfully tested and applied within the Investment Compact for South East Europe in 2006. The publication which results provides a comparative overview of the achievements by each country within the region and allows cross-country comparisons of experience[12]. A new publication is envisaged for 2009 on the basis of a set of performance indicators which have been expanded and refined in light of the experience with the 2006 version. In this respect the assessment can draw on the experience of the Competition Resource Centre in Budapest which provides workshops and training events for participants from the region as well as the competition assessment toolkit mentioned above.

The Business Climate Development Strategy for Middle East and North Africa (MENA) is another important step forward which can serve as a model for other regions as well. This strategy is part of the MENA-OECD Investment Program, a regional initiative aimed at improving the environment for both domestic and international investment through a series of interrelated policy reforms.[13] From the beginning, the World Bank acted as a partner in this exercise providing advice and staff resources for the development of indicators which are then checked and finalised with the partner countries. The program starts with the constitution of a country team bringing together the representatives of Ministries and the agency which is involved in the various policy areas that are covered. Leadership is in general exercised by Ministries in charge of economic development (e.g. Economy, Industry, Finance, and Economic Planning). The program

---

12 Progress in Policy Reforms to Improve the Investment Climate in South East Europe: The Investment Reform Index 2006, OECD 2006.

13 Making Reforms Succeed: Moving forward with the MENA Investment Policy Agenda, OECD 2008.

also includes the assessment of competitiveness strategies for specific sectors selected by the Government. The assessment of SME policies is part of a separate but related exercise conducted jointly by the OECD and the EU Commission.[14]

Within these frameworks, competition policies and law enforcement in the MENA region need to be given more emphasis in the future. In some countries like Morocco laws are on the books but have never been applied. In others, like Egypt and Jordan, new competition authorities have started their work and can still benefit from outside support and advice. Others like Lebanon have drafted laws which have not yet been enacted and legislative procedures may be lengthy and unpredictable. Finally the countries members of the Gulf Co-operation Council (GCC) are committed to the introduction of competition laws as part of market integration but work towards a model competition law is proceeding at a very slow pace.

3 THE TRADE/COMPETITION INTERFACE

As pointed out in numerous studies and articles, trade and competition policies are supposed to pursue similar objectives. 'Competition policy is aimed at ensuring the efficient functioning of markets by the removal or control of restrictive business practice. Trade liberalisation policies focus upon the removal of barriers to international trade both through action to reduce tariff levels and through agreement to limit the effects of non-tariff measures'.[15]

But, there is not always harmony between the two policy areas and in the beginning of the 1980s there was a rather sharp conflict. As a result of a recession, trade liberalisation was perceived to lose momentum and trade restrictions like voluntary export restraints were proliferating in a number of sectors. Protectionism in agriculture through border measures and internal subsidies was reaching its peak and trade in services was subject to numerous constraints through restrictions to both foreign and domestic competition.

In 1982, the OECD Council issued a mandate to the Competition Committee 'to study possible longer-term approaches to an improved international framework for dealing with problems arising at the frontier of competition and trade policies'. The result of these efforts was a path

---

14 2008 Enterprise Policy Assessment: Report on the Implementation of the Euro-Mediterranean Charter for Enterprise, OECD 2008.

15 Competition and Trade Policies: Their Interaction, OECD, 1984, p. 11; Trade And Competition Policies: Comparing Objectives and Methods, OECD 1994.

breaking report on the interaction between trade and competition policies which sharply criticised a number of trade protection measures and highlighted the harmful economic effects of these restrictions.[16] This was followed by a major study on the anticompetitive effects of formal and informal import restraints in the automobile sector which were in place at that time in some OECD Member countries.[17] Following the Committee's proposals, the OECD Council adopted in 1986 a recommendation calling for a comprehensive assessment of trade restrictions on the basis of a list of indicators (the so-called checklist).[18]

Some of these points were subsequently picked up in the international trade policy context. First, the GATT engaged in a comprehensive set of trade policy reviews.

The Marrakesh Agreement instituting the World Trade Organization after the conclusion of the Uruguay Round of Multilateral Trade Negotiations outlawed the practices of 'voluntary export restraints' and included competition provisions in the General Agreement on Trade in Services (GATS). On the other hand, little was achieved to prevent the abuse of anti-dumping procedures, another area of concern that had been highlighted by the Competition Committee's report. It is in this particular area that clashes between competition and trade law approaches are most likely to occur.

'While competition policy is designed to preserve competitive domestic market structures and the efficient allocation of resources, laws dealing with unfair trade practices aim to protect domestic industry from unfair import pressures causing injury to domestic competitors. Accordingly, in the enforcement of anti-dumping and countervail laws, different standards are applied to import pricing practices than if such practices were examined under competition statutes. As a result, some actions brought under the unfair trade laws can reduce competition in domestic markets, particularly where high levels of concentration already exist, through the foreclosure of foreign firms.'[19]

This statement contained in the 1984 report of the Competition Committee was further underpinned by a subsequent study which could unfortunately not be published over the politically motivated resistance of one influential Member state.

---

[16] Competition and Trade Policies: Their Interaction, op cit.

[17] Competition and International Trade: Import Restrictions in the Automobile Sector, OECD 1987.

[18] C (86) 65(Final), Competition Policy and International Trade: OECD Instruments of Co-operation, OECD 1986, p. 24.

[19] Competition and Trade Policies: Their Interaction, op cit, p. 19.

The study realised for the Committee by Professor Robert Willig (Princeton University) conserves its pertinence today and for this reason its main conclusions should be mentioned here.

First, Willig distinguishes between different situations where dumping as defined by national statutes and the Anti-Dumping Code of WTO may occur. In most of these situations no anti-competitive effects arise, the behavior of the foreign firms appears completely rational and it is difficult to detect an element of unfairness.

Possible concerns do arise when the exporting company benefits from import restrictions in place in its home market to cross-subsidise its export operations with the effect of charging lower prices for exports than those practiced in the protected domestic market ('strategic dumping'). The second category where dumping can raise competition concerns would be situations where an exporting firm in a position of market power charges below cost prices with the intent of destroying domestic competition ('predatory dumping'). The analysis of anti-dumping cases in major OECD countries showed that such instances were hard to detect.[20]

As a result, the author concluded, 'that in the overwhelming majority of cases where anti-dumping procedures were applied, there was no plausible threat to competition in the domestic market. The application of anti-dumping procedures, however, has led to a variety of competition-reducing outcomes, including the application of duties, undertakings to rise prices or reduce quantities, voluntary export restraint agreements and the perhaps unintended facilitation of collusion.'[21]

In the following years, the discussion within OECD and other international bodies shifted to the trade distorting effects which may result from the absence of competition law enforcement in import markets. The concern was that trade liberalisation could be frustrated by private restraints such as selective distribution arrangements restricting entry of foreign firm into domestic distribution channels.[22] In 1996, at its Singapore Ministerial the WTO agreed to consider competition for inclusion into future trade negotiations and established a Working Group on Trade and Competition to look at the issues and come forward with

---

[20] Competition Policy and Antidumping, Chapter 1: The Economic Effects of Anti-Dumping Policy, OECD 1994, DAFFE/CLP/WP1 (94) 11 (unpublished).

[21] Competition Policy and Antidumping, Chapter 9, Summary and Conclusions, OECD 1995, DAFFE/CLP/WP1 (95) 3 (unpublished).

[22] As an illustrative example see *US v Japan Measures* affecting consumer photographic film and paper, WTO Panel Report of 5 December 1997, WT/DS44/R ('Kodak/Fuji').

recommendations.[23] To support this process an OECD joint Working Group of the Trade and Competition Committees engaged in conceptual discussions. Unfortunately, after the failure of the Cancun Ministerial Meeting in 2003, competition along with investment was eliminated from the Doha Round of Multilateral Trade Negotiations which is still unfinished business today.

Is there a chance in the aftermath of the Doha Round to reintegrate competition as a building block into the international trading system? In which way? Under which conditions? The following section examines the merits and the conditions for success of a new initiative.

4 MULTILATERAL RULES ON COMPETITION – WHERE AND WHEN?

There is widespread agreement on the value of international co-operation to deal with issues of competition within a globalised economy but views still differ on the level and intensity of such co-operation. It is also admitted today that competition rules need to reach beyond national borders in order to capture the behavior of multinational enterprises and other operators in worldwide markets. The acrimonious disputes of the 1970s on the so-called extraterritorial application of competition laws seem to have dissipated today. Moving beyond comity considerations in cases of concurring or conflicting jurisdiction, bilateral and regional arrangements for bilateral consultations among competition authorities have been developed and thanks to the work of the OECD considerable progress has been achieved in this area.

Even where fundamental differences on law enforcement measures remained, these instruments serve to diffuse tensions and today the principle of co-operation is widely accepted as a tool to make enforcement more effective. For the OECD the main reference is the 1986 Revised Council Recommendation on co-operation among Member countries on restrictive business practices affecting international trade with guiding principles for notifications, exchanges of information, consultations and conciliation.[24] Experience with this instrument has been broadly satisfac-

---

23 WT/MIN (01)/DEC/1, N.20 Ministerial Declaration of 13 December 1996; Jenny, F. (2002), *Globalization, Competition and Trade Policy: Convergence, Divergence and Co-operation*, in C.A. Jones and M. Matsushita (eds), *Competition Policy in the Global Trading System*, p. 295.

24 C (86)44 (Final), in Competition Policy and International Trade: OECD Instruments for Co-operation, op cit, p. 16.

tory although its provisions about exchange of confidential information are weak and tentative.

Further progress was achieved on merger control procedures. In the early 1990s, cross-border mergers were reshaping the corporate landscape. In a path-breaking report the OECD Committee studied nine cases of cross-border mergers and offered procedural recommendations.[25] Frequent formal and informal contacts developed among competition authorities through concurrent case reviews and meetings. The consensus that developed was then codified in the 2005 OECD Recommendation on Merger Review.[26] As a result, there are now regular notifications and contacts among review agencies, notification rules are handled flexibly to facilitate simultaneous filings. In some case the competition authorities concerned engaged in joint investigations and contacts are taking place during the remedies phase to reduce risk of conflicting outcomes.

Convergence of substantive rules has also increased. Hard-core cartels, i.e. anticompetitive practices without any redeeming value such as horizontal price-fixing and market sharing arrangements, are universally condemned. According to a 1998 Council Recommendation, 'Member countries should ensure that their competition laws effectively halt and deter hard-core cartels'.[27] As a result co-operation in discovering, investigating and prosecuting international cartels has reached unprecedented levels. Best practices for leniency programs have been developed and companies now apply simultaneously for leniency in several jurisdictions if they are willing to waive confidentiality rights. The European Commission, US, Canada and Japan have practiced co-ordinated inspections and the level of fines has been increasing. In 2005 the Committee agreed on a set of best practices for the formal exchange of information between competition authorities in hard-core cartel cases.[28]

In the area of merger controls in most cases similar substantive standards are applied by different competition authorities but there is a need for further work and more uniform approaches to prevent different outcomes where criteria still diverge.

Is there a need to go further? Even if there is no immediate strong

---

[25] Merger Cases in the Real World – A Study of Merger Control Procedures, OECD, 1994.

[26] Proceedings of the 100th Meeting of the OECD Competition Committee, op cit.

[27] Recommendation of the Council Concerning Effective Action Against Hard Core Cartels of 25 March 1998, in Fighting Hard-Core Cartels: Harm, Effective Sanctions and Leniency Programs, OECD, 2002.

[28] *See Journal of Competition Law and Policy*, **7**, 3, OECD, 2005.

pressure for multilateral rules, this question should remain on the agenda. A multilateral approach would be a useful tool to resist protectionist pressure that will inevitably surface as a result of the current crisis. Undeniably the multilateral trading system will remain imperfect if trade concessions can be circumvented through anti-competitive practices of private operators and markets can be compartmentalized by exclusive dealing arrangements excluding foreign parties.

Much has been written about the merits and drawbacks of multilateral approaches.[29] While political positions still diverge it is possible today to define elements for a set of minimum rules. It is clear that the setting up of an international competition agency with adjudicatory powers is not a viable option. It is also widely accepted that WTO dispute settlement should not extend to the review of decisions taken by national competition authorities and courts.

Whilst recognising these limitations, there is still scope for a meaningful multilateral system of rules based on the areas where strong consensus has developed within the international community.[30] The first principle would be the desirability of having a national competition system. This does not mean that each participating country would be expected to have a state-of-the art legislation commensurate to that in force in most industrialised countries. Smaller economies may start on a modest scale depending on the size of their markets and their available resources. Some may rely on regional schemes rather than building up a sophisticated system of their own. Regional models may be particularly appropriate for countries seeking market integration such as the Gulf Co-operation Council or the creation of free trade areas in Africa and the Caribbean.

The second important element would be consensus on fundamental principles such as transparency, non-discrimination and procedural fairness. There could also be agreement on the establishment of a competition agency having a certain degree of autonomy within the Government and the necessary resources to carry out its activities.

Action against hard-core cartels with effective and dissuasive sanctions should be a common factor in all jurisdictions. Finally, the agreement could contain principles of co-operation among competition authorities codifying best practices that have emerged from bilateral and regional

---

[29] *See* Drexl, Josef (2004), *International Competition Policy after Cancun: Placing Singapore Issue on the WTO Development Agenda, World Competition*, Kluwer, pp. 419–457.

[30] Trade and Competition: From Doha to Cancun – Background Documentation, OECD, 2003.

agreements. Technical assistance for developing countries would be desirable to make the multilateral approach effective.

Is there scope for reaching an agreement on this rather modest set of rules? It is clear that the system proposed does not compete with sophisticated national competition rules and this could attenuate the scepticism voiced by the US against seemingly more ambitious proposals. Developing countries would have much to gain from the proposed system. It would not only strengthen the movement for economic reform and modernisation but would also provide them with tools to defend their interest against powerful multinational corporations. The problem they had perceived within the WTO process was less related to the substance of the proposals but rather to the fear that competition rules could turn into yet another protectionist device used by industrialised countries to deny market access and promote the interests of their own corporations operating abroad.

A sensible reaction to these concerns would be to deal with competition rules on their own merits outside the bargaining process of a major trade round. It will therefore be necessary to wait for the Doha Round to be concluded. If there is the political will to move forward, the WTO Working Group on Trade and Competition (which has never been disbanded) could be easily revived, with a new mandate.

5 THE WAY FORWARD

The current crisis, with its emerging stimulus programs, may be perceived as a potential threat by the purists of competition policy. Will government intervention displace market mechanisms? Will efficiency suffer? Will the old industrial policies raise their 'ugly face'? In my view, this crisis can provide an opportunity for reconsidering some key aspects of competition policy; containing inconsiderate Government action; and devising a realistic set of multilateral rules.

Fundamental questions have been raised about the future for the world economic system. Whatever the outcome of the systemic discussion, it is likely that the market economic system will remain within a different frame of rules, and the legitimacy of competition policy as one of the pillars of that system cannot be contested.

However, competition advocates should become somewhat more modest than they used to be in the past. They do not have the monopoly of wisdom on economic efficiency or on 'consumer welfare'. Competition is not a constitutional principle – not an end in itself. It is a process which helps create efficient outcomes and is an emanation of economic freedom indispensable to any democratic system. This process should be defended against accumulation of economic power ('anti-trust' in the original sense of the word), against restrictive practices – by Governments and market operators – which raise barriers to market entry and limit the possibilities of innovation.

Competition should become an integral part of government policy to manage the crisis, to revive investment and to promote competitiveness and business development. As a policy device, competition should move back to the centres of government while independence in law enforcement should be preserved.

Governments should not forget about competition when dealing with the crisis. In a number of instances governments will get more involved in economic management through ownership rights in enterprises which benefit from rescue packages. In such cases the government does not need to remain a passive owner, but the exercise of management oversight should be strictly separated from regulatory functions. Financial aid should not distort market competition and the EU State Aid Rules and the WTO obligations should be complied with.

Where governments are moving back to the economic stage they should respect international rules for governance in the exercise of their ownership policies and through the operation of state-owned enterprises.[31] Industrial policies that provide support to certain sectors and categories of enterprises to help them weather the storm and preserve employment, should be strictly limited in time and these companies should not be allowed to engage in collusive practices.

There seems to be a good prospect for reviving the dialogue on multilateral rules of competition – within the WTO, but outside the constraints of global rounds of negotiations. Such rules are in the interest of all and should not become a bargaining chip for exchanging concessions. The rule-making process will have to reflect the new power relations in the world economy, with the OECD remaining as a centre of excellence.

Finally, communications efforts should be stepped up to provide a better understanding of the merits of competition policy – what it can realistically achieve and where it can contribute to efficient outcomes. If policy makers and entrepreneurs together create a culture of competition and innovation, together with better governance, there will be a solid basis for recovery and a promising future.

---

[31] Guidelines on Corporate Governance of State-Owned Enterprises, OECD 2005.

10. Is Criminalisation of EU Competition Law the Answer?

Wouter P.J. Wils*

1 WHAT DO WE MEAN BY 'CRIMINALISATION'?

1.1 No Definition of 'Criminal' in EC or EU law

Article 23(5) of Regulation No 1/2003,[1] the main regulation governing the enforcement of Articles 81 and 82 EC, provides that decisions by which the European Commission imposes fines on undertakings for violations of Articles 81 and 82 EC, or for obstruction of investigations into possible violations, 'shall not be of a criminal law nature'.[2] The last sentence of Recital 8 of the same Regulation says that 'this Regulation does not apply to national laws which impose criminal sanctions on natural persons except to the extent that such sanctions are the means whereby competition rules applicable to undertakings are enforced'.[3]

The EU Treaty has a Title VI concerning 'Provisions on police and judicial co-operation in criminal matters'. Article 30(a) EU provides that common action in the field of police co-operation shall include operational co-operation in relation to the prevention, detection and investigation of 'criminal offences'. Article 31 EU provides for common action on judicial

* Member of the Legal Service of the European Commission, Brussels, Belgium, Visiting Professor at King's College London.

1 Council Regulation (EC) No 1/2003 of 16 December 2002 on the implementation of the rules of competition laid down in Articles 81 and 82 of the Treaty [2003] OJ L1/1. This regulation has replaced, as of 1 May 2004, Council Regulation No 17 [1962] OJ 13/204 (Special English Edition 1959–62, p. 87).

2 On the interpretation of this provision, *see* text accompanying notes 18 to 21 and 46 to 48 below, and further Wils W.P.J. (2005), *Principles of European Antitrust Enforcement*, Oxford: Hart Publishing, section 1.1.4.3.3 (footnote 88).

3 On the meaning of this sentence, *see* further *Principles of European Antitrust Enforcement*, as note 2 above, paragraphs 153–157; Wils, W.P.J. (2008), *Efficiency and Justice in European Antitrust Enforcement*, Oxford: Hart Publishing, paragraphs 532; and text accompanying notes 57 and 58 below.

co-operation 'in criminal matters'. EC or EU law does not, however, contain any definition of what is criminal.

1.2 Distinguishing Characteristics of Criminal Law

Looking across legal systems (of the EU Member States, and of third countries, in particular English-speaking third countries), criminal law, as opposed to public law enforcement of a civil or administrative nature, appears to have the following six distinguishing characteristics.[4]

1.2.1 Criminal penalties

First, it appears that criminal law has a monopoly on the use of imprisonment. Whereas fines can be criminal, civil or administrative, imprisonment appears to be essentially a criminal sanction. The possibility of a prison sanction does not seem to be a necessary condition for a prohibited act or for an enforcement procedure to be criminal, but it is certainly a sufficient condition.

Compared with civil or administrative enforcement, criminal enforcement tends to make relatively more use of penalties imposed on individuals (natural persons), and relatively less of penalties imposed on corporate entities or legal persons. However, individual penalties are neither a necessary nor a sufficient condition for enforcement to be criminal. In Denmark, for instance, violations of Articles 81 and 82 EC and of the parallel prohibitions under national competition law are punishable with fines, which are of a criminal law nature, but which are in practice only imposed on undertakings, not on natural persons. In Germany, on the other hand, leaving aside the specific criminal law provisions on bid-rigging, violations of Articles 81 and 82 EC and of the parallel national prohibitions are punishable through fines, which are imposed on natural persons, and only derivatively also on undertakings, but which are of an administrative law nature.[5]

---

[4] *See* Wils, W.P.J. (2002), *The Optimal Enforcement of EC Antitrust Law*, Oxford: Kluwer Law International, section 8.7.2.1.

[5] For an overview of antitrust enforcement in the 25 Member States, *see* Cahill, D. and J. Cooke (eds) (2004), *The Modernisation of EU Competition Law Enforcement – FIDE National Reports*, Cambridge: Cambridge University Press; Koeck, H.F. and M.M. Karollus (eds) (2008), *The Modernisation of European Competition Law; Initial Experiences with Regulation 1/2003 – FIDE 2008 National Reports*, Nomos; and Holmes, M. and L. Davey (eds) (2004), *A Practical Guide to National Competition Rules Across Europe*, Kluwer Law International.

1.2.2 Criminal intent

Second, the commission of a criminal offence usually requires that the prohibited act be committed with a guilty state of mind (criminal intent), not by mere negligence.

1.2.3 Moral condemnation

Third, the imposition of criminal sanctions carries, and is designed to carry, a stigma effect. Criminal enforcement has a stronger message-sending role or expressive function than civil or administrative enforcement.[6]

1.2.4 Less strict relationship between penalty and harm

Fourth, in criminal law there appears to be a less strict relationship, if any, between the size of the penalty and the size of the harm caused than in the setting of civil sanctions. This appears to reflect the idea that criminal law does not seek to price certain behavior (by making the actor bear the external costs of his behavior) but rather to prohibit it (unconditionally, i.e. irrespective of the actual size of the external costs).[7]

1.2.5 Criminal powers of investigation

Fifth, under criminal law, enforcement authorities tend to have stronger investigative powers.[8]

---

[6] *See* Andenaes, J. (1971), 'The Moral or Educative Influence of Criminal Law', *Journal of Social Issues*, **27**, 17; Andenaes, J. (1975), 'General Prevention Revisited: Research and Policy Implications', *Journal of Criminal Law & Criminology*, **66**, 338, at 341–343; Dau-Schmidt, K.G. (1990), 'An Economic Analysis of the Criminal Law as a Preference-Shaping Policy', *Duke Law Journal* **1**; Sunstein, C.R. (1996), 'On the Expressive Function of the Law', *University of Pennsylvania Law Review*, **144**, 2021; Kahan, D.M. (1997), 'Social Influence, Social Meaning, and Deterrence', *Virginia Law Review*, **83**, 349; Katyal, N.K. (1997), 'Deterrence's Difficulty', *Michigan Law Review*, **95**, 2385; Lynch, G.E. (1997), 'The Role of Criminal Law in Policing Corporate Misconduct', *Law and Contemporary Problems*, **60**, 23; Kahan, D.M. (1998), 'Social Meaning and the Economic Analysis of Crime', *Journal of Legal Studies*, **27**, 609; and Dau-Schmidt, K.G. (1998), *Preference Shaping by the Law*, in P. Newman (ed.), *The New Palgrave Dictionary of Economics and the Law*, Hampshire, UK: Palgrave Macmillan, p. 84.

[7] *See* Cooter, R. (1984), 'Prices and Sanctions', *Columbia Law Review*, **84**, 1523 and Coffee, J.C. (1992), 'Paradigms Lost: the Blurring of the Criminal and Civil Law Models – and What Can be Done About It', *The Yale Law Journal*, **101**, 1875.

[8] For an overview of the law and economics of the collection of intelligence and evidence by the competition authorities from antitrust offenders, *see* Wils, W.P.J. (2003), 'Self-incrimination in EC Antitrust Enforcement: A Legal and Economic Analysis', *World Competition*, **26**, 567, and chapter 5 of *Principles of European Antitrust Enforcement*, as note 2 above; *see also* Wils, W.P.J. (2006),

1.2.6 Criminal rights of defence

Finally, criminal procedures tend to have stronger procedural protections, designed to avoid false convictions. In particular, in criminal enforcement systems the adjudicative or decision-making function is always separated from the investigative and prosecutorial function or functions.[9] Whereas it appears to be a necessary condition of criminal enforcement that the body which imposes the criminal penalties is separate and independent from the investigator and prosecutor, it is however not a sufficient condition. In Finland, for instance, violations of Articles 81 and 82 EC and of the parallel national prohibitions are punished with fines on undertakings, which are of an administrative law nature, but which are imposed by the Market Court, a specialised court which is entirely separate and independent from the Competition Authority, which acts as investigator and prosecutor. In criminal enforcement systems, the standard of proof for establishing violations also tends to be higher. In the English-speaking countries, criminal convictions normally require proof 'beyond reasonable doubt', whereas civil or administrative findings can normally be made 'by a preponderance of the evidence' or a 'balance of probabilities'.

1.2.7 Links between the six characteristics

The six characteristics listed above are clearly interrelated. The use of imprisonment and the stigma effect create a stronger need for procedural protections to avoid false convictions. These stronger procedural protections create, in their turn, the need for stronger investigative powers so as to avoid enforcement becoming ineffective. On the other hand, the message-sending role of criminal enforcement explains the requirement of a guilty state of mind (as this shows the need for wrong valuations to be repudiated) as well as the absence of a strict relationship between punishment and actual harm, reflecting the desire to deter the criminal behavior unconditionally rather than merely to price it.

'Powers of Investigation and Procedural Rights and Guarantees in EU Antitrust Enforcement: The Interplay between European and National Legislation and Case-law', *World Competition*, **29**, 3, and Wils, W.P.J. (2007), 'Leniency in Antitrust Enforcement: Theory and Practice', *World Competition*, **30**, 25, and chapters 1 and 5 of *Efficiency and Justice in European Antitrust Enforcement*, as note 3 above.

[9] *See The Optimal Enforcement of EC Antitrust Law*, as note 4 above, section 8.7.4.5; Wils, W.P.J. (2004), 'The Combination of the Investigative and Prosecutorial Function and the Adjudicative Function in EC Antitrust Enforcement: A Legal and Economic Analysis', *World Competition*, **27**, 201, and chapter 6 of *Principles of European Antitrust Enforcement*, as note 2 above.

1.3 The Wider Notion of 'Criminal' in the European Convention on Human Rights

The notion of 'criminal' enforcement as described above and as used throughout most of this chapter should be distinguished from the wider notion of 'criminal' as conceived under Article 6 of the European Convention on Human Rights.[10]

The European Court of Human Rights has developed, within the framework of Article 6 ECHR, an autonomous notion of 'criminal', which covers proceedings of an administrative law nature that fulfill the following conditions:[11]

- the offences are defined by a general rule, applicable to all citizens;
- the rule is linked to penalties in the event of non-compliance;
- the sanctions are intended not as a pecuniary compensation for damage but essentially as a punishment to deter reoffending;
- and – the sanctions are severe.[12]

The European Court of Human Rights has never had occasion to rule on an antitrust enforcement procedure at the level of the EU institutions.[13]

---

[10] *See* Dekeyser, K. and C. Gauer (2004), 'The New Enforcement System for Articles 81 and 82 EC and the Rights of Defence', paper presented at the 31st Annual Fordham Corporate Law Institute Conference on International Antitrust Law and Policy (New York, 8 October), in B.E. Hawk (ed.) *2004 Annual Proceedings of the Fordham Corporate Law Institute – International Antitrust Law and Policy*, New York: Juris Publishing, pp. 537–573, at pp. 540–542; *The Optimal Enforcement of EC Antitrust Law*, as note 4 above, section 8.7.2.3; and *Principles of European Antitrust Enforcement*, as note 2 above, sections 1.1.4.3.3 (footnote 88) and 6.1.4.1.

[11] Restated in the words of Dekeyser, K. and C. Gauer, as note 10 above, at 541.

[12] *Engel and Others v the Netherlands*, judgement of the 8 June 1976, Series A No 22, paragraph 82; *Özturk v Germany*, judgement of the 21 February 1984, Series A No 73, paragraph 50; *Bendenoun v France*, judgement of the 24 February 1994, Series A No 284, paragraph 47.

[13] In the case of *Senator Lines GmbH v the 15 Member States of the European Union* (Application No 56672/00), the question was raised. The European Commission had imposed a fine of € 273 million on Senator Lines. The EC Courts rejected the request of the company to suspend the payment of the fine. Senator Lines GmbH alleged a violation of Article 6 ECHR (right of access to court), in that it was required to pay the fine before a decision was taken in the substantive proceedings before the EC Courts. It claimed that this would have resulted in the insolvency and liquidation of the company before the substantive issues were determined. The application was declared inadmissible by the European Court of

In 1989, the European Commission of Human Rights (a body which has since been abolished) decided on a case involving competition proceedings before the French competition authority.[14] It decided that the sanctions imposed by that authority were of a criminal nature within the meaning of Article 6 ECHR. The case was not brought before the European Court of Human Rights. In one case concerning a Finnish competition law enforcement procedure, the European Court of Human Rights found a violation of Article 6 ECHR, but the question of the criminal nature of the procedure was not discussed, because the Finnish Government did not contest the applicability of Article 6 ECHR.[15]

In 2004, the European Court of Human Rights decided on a case concerning proceedings under the Russian Law on Competition and the Restriction of Monopolies in the Commodity Markets, which had led to the confiscation of profits obtained by a number of companies in violation of that law. The European Court of Human Rights declared the application brought by the companies concerned for alleged violation of Article 6 ECHR inadmissible on the ground that the proceedings at issue were not criminal within the meaning of Article 6 ECHR.[16]

The EC Court of Justice appears to have acknowledged since its *Hüls* judgment of 1999 that the fines imposed by the European Commission under then Regulation No 17 and now Regulation No 1/2003 may be qualified as 'criminal' within the meaning of Article 6 ECHR.[17]

Antitrust proceedings at the level of the EU institutions or in the EU Member States which are, according to EU law or to the applicable national law, of an administrative or civil nature, may thus fall under the wider notion of 'criminal' within the meaning of Article 6 ECHR.

However, it should be pointed out that, in its case law on the compatibility of specific proceedings with the substantive requirements of Article 6 ECHR, the European Court of Human Rights appears to distinguish

---

Human Rights after the EC Court of First Instance decided to set aside the fine imposed by the European Commission; see Grand Chamber Decision of 10 March 2004, available at http://www.echr.coe.int/Eng/Judgments.htm (accessed 19 June 2009).

[14] European Commission of Human Rights, *Stenuit v France*, decision of 11 July 1989, A/232-A. Stenuit withdrew its application in 1991.

[15] Judgment of 15 July 2003, *Fortum Corporation v Finland* (Application No 32559/96), paragraph 36.

[16] Decision of 3 June 2004 as to the admissibility of applications by *OOO Neste St. Petersburg and Others v Russia*, available at http://www.echr.coe.int/Eng/Judgments.htm (accessed 19 June 2009).

[17] Case C-199/92P, *Hüls v European Commission* [1999] ECR 4287, paragraph 150.

between enforcement proceedings which are criminal within a more traditional, narrower sense, or which are considered as criminal under the applicable domestic law, and proceedings which are only criminal within the wider meaning of Article 6 ECHR.[18]

This distinction appears most clearly in the case law of the European Court of Human Rights on the separation of the decision-making function from the investigative and prosecutorial function or functions. Indeed, the European Court of Human Rights has ruled that, for reasons of efficiency, the determination of civil rights and obligations or the prosecution and punishment of offences which are 'criminal' within the wider meaning of Article 6 ECHR can be entrusted to administrative authorities, provided that the persons concerned are able to challenge any decision thus made before a judicial body that has full jurisdiction and that provides the full guarantees of Article 6(1) ECHR.[19] This means that antitrust proceedings such as those at the level of the EU institutions are not incompatible with Article 6 ECHR, even if the European Commission combines the investigative and prosecutorial function with the decision-making function, given that the addressees of European Commission decisions imposing fines can bring an action for annulment before the EC Court of First Instance, which manifestly provides the full guarantees of Article 6(1) ECHR and which undertakes a comprehensive review of the Commission's decisions.[20] This alternative means of satisfying the requirements of Article 6(1) ECHR does however not appear to be available in more traditional

---

[18] *See* also points 62 to 67 of the Opinion of Advocate General Geelhoed of 19 January 2006 and paragraphs 39 to 49 of the Judgment of the EC Court of Justice of 29 June 2006 in Case C-301/04 P *Commission v SGL Carbon* [2006] ECR I-5915, points 54 to 60 of the Opinion of Advocate General Geelhoed of 12 September 2006 and paragraphs 31 to 49 of the Judgment of the EC Court of Justice of 25 January 2007 in Case C-411/04 P *Salzgitter Mannesmann v Commission* [2007] ECR I-959, and paragraph 113 of the Judgment of the EC Court of First Instance of 8 July 2008 in Case T-99/04 *Treuhand v Commission*, not yet reported in ECR.

[19] Judgments of 23 June 1981, *Le Compte, Van Leuven and De Meyere v Belgium*, A/43 paragraph 51, of 1 February 1983, *Albert and Le Compte v Belgium*, A/58 paragraph 29, of 21 February 1984, *Öztürk v Germany*, A/73 paragraph 56, and of 24 February 1994, *Bendenoun v France*, A/284, paragraph 46.

[20] *See* Judgment of the EC Court of First Instance of 15 March 2000 in Joined Cases T-25/95 a.o. *Cimenteries CBR and Others v Commission* [2000] ECR II-700, paragraph 719 ('When the Court of First Instance reviews the legality of a decision finding an infringement of [Article 81(1) and/or Article 82 EC], the applicants may call upon it to undertake an exhaustive review of both the Commission's substantive findings of fact and its legal appraisal of those facts'), and Judgment of the EC Court of First Instance of 8 July 2008 in Case T-54/03 *Lafarge v Commission*, not yet reported in ECR, paragraphs 44 to 46.

areas of criminal law or in areas considered criminal under domestic law. In those areas the case law of the European Court of Human Rights appears to require separation of the adjudicative function from the investigative and prosecutorial function already at first instance.[21]

2 IS THERE A TENDENCY TO CRIMINALISE ANTITRUST ENFORCEMENT IN THE EU MEMBER STATES?

2.1 US Antitrust Enforcement

To the extent that there currently is a tendency in the EU Member States to criminalise antitrust enforcement,[22] this is undoubtedly inspired by US antitrust enforcement, even if criminal antitrust legislation in the US may historically in turn have been inspired by older European precedents.[23]

Since the original 1890 version of the Sherman Act, violations of Sections 1 and 2 of the Sherman Act have been punishable under US federal law with criminal fines for both enterprises and individuals and with imprisonment for individuals.[24] Initially the maximum jail term was one year.[25] In 1974, Congress raised the maximum jail term to three years[26] and in 2004 to ten years.[27] The maximum criminal fines for enterprises were similarly

---

[21] *See* Judgments of 26 October 1984, *De Cubber v Belgium*, A/86 paragraphs 31-32, and of 25 February 1997, *Findlay v United Kingdom*, Reports 1997-I paragraph 79.

[22] *See* text accompanying notes 76 to 89 below.

[23] In particular English 16th century legislation, which had however fallen into disuse by the 19th century; see Green, N. (2004), 'The Road to Conviction – The Criminalisation of Cartel Law', in B.E. Hawk (ed.) *Annual Proceedings of the Fordham Corporate Law Institute International Antitrust Law & Policy*, New York: Juris Publishing, p. 13, at pp. 13–22. In France, following the Loi Le Chapelier of 2–17 March 1791, a criminal cartel prohibition was also contained in Article 419 of the Napoleonic Penal Code.

[24] For an overview of the history of US criminal antitrust enforcement from 1890 to 2001, *see* Baker, D.I. (2001), 'The Use of Criminal Law Remedies to Deter and Punish Cartels and Bid-Rigging', *George Washington Law Review*, **69**, 693 at 694–696.

[25] Sherman Act, ch. 647, 26 Stat. 209 (1890).

[26] Antitrust Procedures and Penalties Act, Pub. L. No 93–528, § 3, 88 Stat. 1706, 1708 (1974).

[27] Antitrust Criminal Penalty Enhancement and Reform Act of 2004, H.R. 1086.

increased to $1 million in 1974,[28] to $10 million in 1990,[29] and to $100 million in 2004.[30]

More than half of the US states also have criminal antitrust statutes that provide for jail sentences, and many of these statutes predate the federal Sherman Act.[31]

It was not until 1959, however, that prison sentences were imposed against businessmen for price-fixing without acts or threats of violence.[32] Since then, enforcement has increased very strongly. During the 1990s, the US Department of Justice successfully prosecuted an average of more than 35 individuals each year.[33] Since 2000, more than 150 individuals have served or are currently serving prison sentences, of an average length of 19 months, in cases prosecuted by the US Department of Justice. Among them are around 30 foreign nationals from France, Germany, Japan, Korea, Norway, the Netherlands, Sweden, Switzerland and the United Kingdom.[34]

Although the text of the criminal provisions in the Sherman Act covers all types of restrictive agreements as well as unilateral monopolistic behavior, by long tradition the US Department of Justice limits criminal prosecution to hard-core violations of Section 1 of the Sherman Act such as price-fixing, bid-rigging, market division, or customer allocation schemes among horizontal competitors.[35]

---

[28] As note 26 above.

[29] Antitrust Amendments Act of 1990, Pub. L. No 101-588, § 4, 104 Stat. 2879, 2880 (1990).

[30] As note 27 above.

[31] Dau-Schmidt, K.G. (1983), 'Sentencing Antitrust Offenders: Reconciling Economic Theory with Legal Theory', *William Mitchell Law Review*, **9**, 75 at 75–76.

[32] Gallo, J.C., K.G. Dau-Schmidt, J.L. Craycraft and C.J. Parker (1994), 'Criminal Penalties Under the Sherman Act: A Study of Law and Economics', *Research in Law and Economics*, **16**, 25 at 40.

[33] 'Antitrust Deterrence in the United States and Japan', remarks by Chemtob, S.M. at a Conference on Competition Policy in the Global Trading System (Washington DC, 23 June 2000), available at http://www.usdoj.gov/atr/public/speeches/5076.pdf, at 7–8 (accessed 19 June 2009); for more statistics, see Gallo, J.C., K. Dau-Schmidt, J.L. Craycraft and C.J. Parker (2000), 'Department of Justice Antitrust Enforcement, 1955–1997: An Empirical Study', *Review of Industrial Organization*, **17**, 75.

[34] Hammond, S.D. (2008), 'Recent Developments, Trends, and Milestones in the Antitrust Division's Criminal Enforcement Program', paper presented at the 56th Annual Spring Meeting of the ABA Section of Antitrust Law (Washington DC, 26 March), available at http://www.usdoj.gov/atr/public/speeches/232716.htm (accessed 19 June 2009).

[35] Waller, S.W. (2003), 'The Incoherence of Punishment in Antitrust', *Chicago-Kent Law Review*, **78**, 207, at 216, and *Antitrust Modernization Commission, Report and Recommendations* (April 2007), at 296–297 and 303.

As the US Department of Justice has no powers to impose or to seek the imposition of civil or administrative fines, it only seeks prospective, injunctive relief against other violations of Section 1 and all violations of Section 2 of the Sherman Act. The Federal Trade Commission has relatively recently applied in competition cases its power, which it had traditionally used in consumer protection cases, to seek disgorgement of unlawful profits.[36] Otherwise deterrence and punishment are left to private treble-damage suits.[37]

The imposition of criminal penalties for violation of Section 1 of the Sherman Act requires a finding of criminal intent. It also carries a rather strong moral condemnation. Indeed in the US, antitrust values enjoy a very wide consensus,[38] and price-fixing is considered to be immoral, like theft.[39]

To investigate suspected criminal antitrust violations, the US Department of Justice can make use of a full arsenal of criminal investigatory powers.[40] Defendants in turn benefit from a full range of criminal rights of defence – less extensive however for corporations than for individuals,[41] and violations have to be proven 'beyond reasonable doubt'.

---

36 Section 13 (G) of the FTC Act; see *FTC v Mylan Laboratories Inc*, 62 F. Supp. 2d 25, 36 (DDC 1999); Waller, S.W., as note 33 above, at 218; and *Antitrust Modernization Commission*, as note 35, at 286–287.

37 *See* Waller, S.W., as note 35 above, at 210 and 230–232; Calkins, S. (1997), 'Corporate Compliance and the Antitrust Angencies' Bi-Modal Penalties', *Law and Contemporary Problems*, **60**, 127, at 136–139 and 150; letter dated 5 January 2005 from R.H. Pate, Assistant Attorney General, Department of Justice Antitrust Division, to D.A. Garza, Chair, Antitrust Modernization Commission, 'Suggested Topics for Antitrust Modernization Commission Study', available at http://www.usdoj.gov/atr/public/comments/207122.pdf, at 2 (accessed 19 June 2009); and *Antitrust Modernization Commission*, as note 35, at 287–288.

38 In the words of Robert Reich, 'antitrust is popular with the public' and 'has a compelling ideologic attraction', 'the ideal of competition continuing to receive broad support from a wide spectrum of American public opinion'; Reich, R.B. (1980), 'The Antitrust Industry', *Georgetown Law Journal*, 68**,** 1035 at 1054 and footnote 1.

39 *See The Optimal Enforcement of EC Antitrust Law*, as note 4 above, section 8.6.7, and D.I. Baker, as note 24 above, at 714.

40 *See* text accompanying notes 151 to 156 below.

41 Corporations can in particular not invoke the privilege against self-incrimination enshrined in the 5th Amendment to the US Constitution; see *White v US*, 322 U.S. 694 (1911).

2.2 Antitrust Enforcement at the Level of the EU Institutions

As to the enforcement of Articles 81 and 82 EC at the level of the EU institutions, Article 23(2) of Regulation No 1/2003 only empowers the European Commission to impose fines for violations of Articles 81 and 82 EC on 'undertakings'. Neither the Treaty nor Regulation No 1/2003 contains any definition of the term 'undertaking'. The EC Court of Justice has held that 'in competition law, the term "undertaking" must be understood as designating an economic unit [. . .] even if in law that economic unit consists of several persons, natural or legal'.[42]

In practice the Commission does not simply impose fines on undertakings thus defined as economic units. For reasons of enforceability, it rather addresses its fining decisions to entities possessing legal personality, typically companies, to which the violation committed by the undertaking is imputed.[43] As to the choice of the person or persons to whom a violation is to be imputed, the general rule formulated by the Community Courts is that 'when [. . .] a violation is found to have been committed, it is necessary to identify the natural or legal person who was responsible for the operation of the undertaking at the time when the violation was committed, so that it can answer for it'.[44]

If the undertaking found to have committed a violation were found to consist of an unincorporated business (a single trader, with or without employees, who has not incorporated his or her business, or a professional exercising his or her profession alone and unincorporated, or several natural persons operating a single business without any employment relationship between them and without any form of legal person), the Commission would necessarily have to address its fining decision to the natural person or persons operating the business. However, in the

---

42 Judgment of 12 July 1985 in Case 170/83 *Hydrotherm v Compact* [1985] ECR 3016 paragraph 11. For a detailed analysis of the notion of undertaking and the relationship between undertaking and legal or natural person, see *The Optimal Enforcement of EC Antitrust Law*, as note 4 above, chapter 7.

43 *See* Opinion of Judge Vesterdorf, acting as Advocate-General, in Case T-1/89 *Rhône-Poulenc v Commission* [1991] ECR II-869 at 916, Judgment of the Court of First Instance of 20 April 1999 in Joined Cases T-305/94, T-306/94, T-307/94, T-313/94, T-314/94, T-315/94, T-316/94, T-318/94, T-325/94, T-328/94, T-329/94 and T-335/94 *Limburgse Vinyl Maatschappij and Others. v Commission* [1999] ECR II-945 paragraph 978.

44 Judgment of the Court of First Instance of 17 December 1991 in Case T-6/89 *Enichem Anic v Commission* [1991] ECR II-1695 paragraph 236, and Judgment of the Court of Justice of 16 November 2000 in Case C-279/98 P *Cascades v Commission* [2000] ECR I-9709 paragraph 78.

more than one hundred decisions in which the Commission has imposed fines under Regulation No 17 and Regulation No 1/2003 up to now, this situation has never occurred: up to now, all fines have been imposed on companies or other legal persons. Indeed, the undertakings found to have committed violations of Article 81 or 82 EC invariably either coincided with a single company or other legal person, which was the obvious addressee of the fining decision, or consisted of a group of companies, in which case fines were imposed on one or more of the companies in the group.[45]

According to Article 23(2) of Regulation No 1/2003, fines can be imposed on undertakings where they infringe Article 81 or 82 EC 'either intentionally or negligently'. Criminal intent is thus clearly not required.

Article 23(5) of Regulation No 1/2003 expressly provides that the decisions by which the European Commission imposes fines 'shall not be of a criminal law nature'. As explained above,[46] this provision appears to have some relevance not for the question whether Article 6 ECHR is applicable to the antitrust enforcement proceedings at the level of the EU institutions, but rather for the question of the compatibility of those proceedings with the substantive requirements of Article 6 ECHR. The EU Council, when it adopted Regulation No 1/2003, may also have considered that this provision had some relevance as to the necessary legal basis under the EC Treaty.[47] It may also have some importance as to the status of such fines under national law, for instance whether they are tax deductible.[48]

The affirmation that fining decisions 'shall not be of criminal nature' could also be read as reflecting the absence of moral condemnation of violations of Articles 81 and 82 EC. On the other hand, there appears to

---

45 In *Pre-Insulated Pipes*, one of the undertakings was controlled and managed by a natural person, Dr. W. Henss, but the Commission appears to have made an effort (for reasons unexplained) to avoid imposing the fine on him, identifying instead a collection of companies which it held jointly and severally liable for the fine; see recitals 157–160 and Article 3(d) of the Decision of 21 October 1998, *Pre-Insulated Pipe Cartel*, [1999] OJ L24/1, and paragraph 105 of the judgment of the EC Court of First Instance of 20 March 2002 in Case T-9/99 *HFB and Others v Commission* [2002] ECR II-1530, in which the Court found that the European Commission had 'intentionally' not established Dr. Henss's liability.

46 Text accompanying notes 17 to 21.

47 *See* further *Efficiency and Justice in European Antitrust Enforcement*, as note 3 above, paragraphs 618–624 and note 176 below.

48 *See Principles of European Antitrust Enforcement*, as note 2 above, section 1.1.4.3.3, footnote 88, and Kerse, C.S. and N. Khan (2005), *EC Antitrust Procedure* (5th edition, Thomson, Sweet & Maxwell), at paragraph 7-090.

have been in the last years from the side of the European Commission an increase in the rhetoric of condemnation of cartels in particular. For instance, in a speech in 2000, Mario Monti, the then Member of the European Commission in charge of competition, declared that 'cartels are cancers on the open market economy, which forms the very basis of our [European] Community'.[49] It may also be noticed that the European Commission has in the last years started using the term 'antitrust' alongside the official term 'competition law'.[50] As Christopher Harding has pointed out, the North American term 'antitrust' reflects the proscriptive and negative character of US antitrust law, as opposed to the historically more tolerant European approach.[51]

As to the European Commission's powers of investigation, Regulation No 17 already gave the European Commission significant powers, in particular the power to conduct inspections at business premises, including the possibility to overcome opposition with the assistance of the police or other authorities of the Member State where the inspection takes place. But these powers are clearly much more limited than those of the US Department of Justice or those which are common for criminal investigations in the EU Member States.

Regulation No 1/2003 has strengthened the European Commission's powers of investigation in two respects.[52] First, Article 21(1) of Regulation No 1/2003 empowers the Commission to conduct investigations in other premises than business premises, including the homes of directors and employees of the undertakings concerned, 'if a reasonable suspicion exists that books or other records related to the business and to the subject-matter of the inspection, which may be relevant to prove a serious violation of [Articles 81 or 82 EC], are being kept in [those] premises'. Article 21(3) adds that a decision to conduct such inspection can only be executed

---

49 'Fighting Cartels Why and How? Why should we be concerned with cartels and collusive behaviour?', speech at the 3rd Nordic Competition Policy Conference (Stockholm, 11–12 September 2000), available at http://europa.eu.int/comm/competition/speeches (accessed 19 June 2009).

50 *See* for instance the European Commision's Report on Competition Policy 2007, COM(2008)368 of 16 June 2008, available at http://ec.europa.eu/comm/competition/annual_reports/2007/en.pdf (accessed 19 June 2009), and the website of its Directorate General for Competition, available at: http://europa.eu.int/comm/competition/index_en.html (accessed 19 June 2009).

51 Harding, C. (2002), 'Business Cartels as a Criminal Activity: Reconciling North American and European Models of Regulation', *Maastricht Journal of European and Comparative Law*, **4**, 393, at 404.

52 For a detailed analysis of these changes, see K. Dekeyser and C. Gauer, as note 10 above.

with prior authorisation from the national judicial authority of the Member State where the inspection takes place.

Secondly, Article 20(2)(e) of Regulation No 1/2003 provides that, during an inspection at the business premises of an undertaking, the inspectors are empowered 'to ask any representative or member of staff of the undertaking [. . .] for explanations on facts or documents relating to the subject-matter and purpose of the inspection and to record the answers'.[53] However, Regulation No 1/2003 does not threaten the individuals thus questioned with any sanctions for a refusal to answer, nor for giving incorrect, incomplete or misleading answers. Article 23(1)(d) of Regulation No 1/2003 only provides for fines on undertakings that 'fail or refuse to provide a complete answer on facts', 'give an incorrect or misleading answer' or 'fail to rectify within a time-limit set by the Commission an incorrect, incomplete or misleading answer given by a staff member'.

As to the defendant companies' rights of defence in antitrust proceedings conducted by the European Commission, they have significantly increased over time.[54] The European Commission combines the investigative and prosecutorial function with the adjudicative function in first instance, but its decisions are subject to an exhaustive review by the EC Court of First Instance.[55] As to the standard of proof which the European Commission has to satisfy to find a violation of Articles 81 or 82 EC and impose a fine, according to Chris Kerse and Nicholas Khan, it 'is a high one, although it would be going too far to say that the infringement must be proven to the criminal standard of 'beyond reasonable doubt'.[56]

---

[53] Under Regulation No 17, the Commission officials could only seek explanations relating to the books and records under examination; see Judgment of the EC Court of Justice of 26 June 1980 in Case 136/79 *National Panasonic v Commission* [1980] ECR 2056, paragraph 15, and Order of the EC Court of First Instance of 9 June 1997 in Case T-9/97 *Elf Atochem v Commission* [1997] ECR II-919, paragraph 23.

[54] *See* Lenaerts, K. and I. Maselis (2001), 'Procedural Rights and Issues in the Enforcement of Articles 81 and 82 of the EC Treaty', *Fordham International Law Journal*, **24**, 1615; Kerse, C.S. and N. Khan, as note 48 above; and Ortiz Blanco,. L. (2006), (ed.*), EC Competition Procedure, 2nd edition*, Oxford: Oxford University Press.

[55] *See* notes 20 and 9 above.

[56] C.S. Kerse and N. Khan, as note 48 above, paragraph 8-038. The standard formula used by the EC Courts is that 'the Commission must produce sufficiently precise and consistent evidence to support the firm conviction that the alleged infringement took place'; see for instance the judgment of the EC Court of First Instance of 8 July 2004 in Joined Cases T-67/00 e.o. *JFE Engineering Corp. v European Commission*, not yet published in ECR, available at http://curia.eu.int/fr/content/juris/index_form.htm, paragraph 179 (accessed 19 June 2009). See

2.3 The EU Framework for Antitrust Enforcement in the EU Member States

Regulation No 1/2003 frames antitrust enforcement in the EU Member States in two ways. First, it allows Member States to provide for criminal enforcement of Articles 81 and 82 EC. Secondly, it restricts the possibilities for Member States to enforce their national competition laws in isolation from the enforcement of Articles 81 and 82 EC.

2.3.1 Member states can criminalise their enforcement of Articles 81 and 82 EC

Article 5 of Regulation No 1/2003 provides that '[t]he competition authorities of the Member States shall have the power to apply Articles 81 and 82 of the Treaty in individual cases. For this purpose, acting on their own initiative or on a complaint, they may take [. . .] decisions [. . .] imposing fines, periodic penalty payments or any other penalty provided for in their national law'.

Member States can thus in their national law provide for administrative or civil fines on companies for violations of Articles 81 or 82 EC, or criminal fines, or fines on individuals, of an administrative, civil or criminal nature, or imprisonment, or indeed 'any other penalty'.

That 'any other penalty' also covers penalties on individuals, including imprisonment, is further confirmed by Article 12(3) of Regulation No 1/2003. Whereas Article 12(1) of Regulation No 1/2003 provides that the European Commission and the competition authorities of the Member States can exchange all kinds of information, and use the information thus exchanged in evidence, Article 12(3) adds the following limitation:

> Information exchanged pursuant to paragraph 1 can only be used in evidence to impose sanctions on natural persons where:
> - the law of the transmitting authority foresees sanctions of a similar kind in relation to an infringement of [Articles 81 or 82 EC] or, in the absence thereof,
> - the information has been collected in a way which respects the same level of protection of the rights of defence of natural persons as provided for under the national rules of the receiving authority. However, in this case, the information exchanged cannot be used by the receiving authority to impose custodial sanctions.

---

further Vesterdorf, B. (2006), 'Burden of Proof in Cartel Cases', paper presented at the Nordic Lawyers Academy Challenges in Nordic Cartel Cases, Helsinki, 4–5 May, and Sibony, A.L. and E. Barbier de la Serre (2007), 'La charge de la preuve et le standard de preuve en droit de la concurrence', *Revue trimestrielle de droit européen*, 205.

This provision confirms what is already apparent from the terms 'any other penalty' in Article 5 of Regulation No 1/2003, namely that Member States can indeed provide for sanctions on natural persons, including imprisonment, for violations of Articles 81 and 82 EC.

By thus allowing Member States to provide for criminal enforcement of Articles 81 and 82 EC, the EU Council, which adopted Regulation 1/2003 unanimously, would appear to have rejected the view, which has sometimes been suggested, according to which Articles 81 and 82 EC would somehow be inherently non-criminal, and that the EC Treaty would thus exclude criminal enforcement of Articles 81 and 82 EC not only at the level of the EU institutions but also at the level of the Member States.[57]

This view appears indeed mistaken. It is of course correct that the text of Articles 81 and 82 EC only mentions 'undertakings'. But, as is apparent from Article 83 EC, the prohibitions on restrictive agreements and abuse of dominant positions by undertakings, as set out in Articles 81 and 82 EC, are only 'principles', and the appropriate regulations or directives to give effect to these principles are to be laid down by the Council. Nothing in the EC Treaty suggests that the Council could thus not allow Member States to provide for penalties for individuals, including imprisonment, to enforce Articles 81 and 82 EC, as it did in Regulation No 1/2003.[58]

The possibility offered by Regulation No 1/2003 for Member States to provide for criminal enforcement of Articles 81 and 82 EC has been used by a number of Member States.[59] Ireland and Estonia have provided only for criminal enforcement, through fines on companies and individuals, as well as imprisonment.[60] In the United Kingdom, non-criminal fines are provided for companies, but also director disqualification for individuals, as well as imprisonment and/or criminal fines for individuals specifically for price-fixing, limitation of supply or production, market-sharing and bid-rigging.[61] In France, Cyprus and the Slovak Republic, the main sanctions provided for are non-criminal fines on companies, but imprisonment

---

57 *See* remarks by Gerard Hogan in Roundtable Debate Session IV – Rights, Privileges and Ethics in Competition Cases, the 31st Annual Fordham Corporate Law Institute Conference on International Antitrust Law & Policy (New York, 8 October 2004), in B.E. Hawk, (ed.) (2005), *Annual Proceedings of the Fordham Corporate Law Institute: International Antitrust Law and Policy*, New York: Juris Publishing.

58 *See* also *Efficiency and Justice in European Antitrust Enforcement*, as note 3 above, paragraph 619.

59 *See* note 5 above.

60 *See* also text following note 76 below on Ireland.

61 *See* also text accompanying notes 67–68 and 78–80 below on the United Kingdom.

for individuals is also provided for, at least in theory.[62] In Denmark and Malta, essentially only fines on companies are provided for, but these have a criminal character. In Malta, directors may be held jointly and severally liable with the company for these fines. In Greece, non-criminal fines on companies (with joint and several liability for managers) are complemented with criminal fines for individuals. In Germany, non-criminal fines are provided for individuals, and derivatively also for companies, as well as imprisonment specifically for bid-rigging. In Austria and Hungary, non-criminal fines are provided only for companies, but also imprisonment specifically for bid-rigging.[63]

2.3.2 Member states cannot criminalise the enforcement of only their national competition laws

The possibilities for Member States to enforce their national competition laws in isolation from the enforcement of Articles 81 and 82 EC are limited in three ways. First, Article 3(2) of Regulation No 1/2003 forbids Member States to prohibit under national competition law agreements or concerted practices which may affect trade between Member States but which do not restrict competition within the meaning of Article 81(1) EC, or which fulfill the conditions of Article 81(3) EC or which are covered by a block exemption regulation applying Article 81(3) EC.[64]

Secondly, it follows from the principle of equivalence, a general principle of Community law developed in the case law of the EC Court of Justice,[65] that the penalties which Member States provide for violations of Articles 81 and 82 EC pursuant to Article 5 of Regulation No 1/2003 must at least be equivalent in effectiveness and dissuasiveness to the sanctions they provide for comparable violations of their national competition laws. If a Member State thus provides for instance imprisonment sanctions to enforce a cartel prohibition under national law, it must also provide for such sanctions to enforce the cartel prohibition in Article 81 EC.

Thirdly, Article 3(1) of Regulation No 1/2003 provides as follows:

---

[62] *See* also text following note 70 below on France.

[63] *See* also text following note 70 and accompanying note 76 below on Austria and Hungary.

[64] On Article 3 of Regulation No 1/2003 and on block exemption regulations, see *Principles of European Antitrust Enforcement*, as note 2 above, sections 1.2.8.2 and 1.2.1 respectively.

[65] *See* inter alia Judgment of the EC Court of Justice of 15 September 1998 in Case C-231/96 Edis [1998] ECR I-4990, paragraphs 34 and 36–37; for a more detailed analysis, see Oliver, P. (2005), 'Le règlement 1/2003 et les principes d'efficacité et d'équivalence', *Cahiers de droit européen*, 343.

> Where the competition authorities of the Member States or national courts apply national competition law to agreements, [. . .] or concerted practices within the meaning of [Article 81(1) EC] which may affect trade between Member States within the meaning of that provision, they shall also apply [Article 81 EC] to such agreements, [. . .] or concerted practices. Where the competition authorities of the Member States or national courts apply national competition law to any abuse prohibited by [Article 82 EC], they shall also apply [Article 82 EC].

Unless the practices concerned do not affect trade between Member States, national competition authorities and national courts cannot apply national competition law without simultaneously applying Articles 81 and 82 EC. This means that they cannot avoid the application of the mechanisms of co-operation with the European Commission and/or within the EU network of competition authorities as provided for in Articles 11 and 15 of Regulation No 1/2003.[66]

Article 3(3) of Regulation No 1/2003 clarifies that, '[w]ithout prejudice to general principles and other provisions of [European] Community law', Article 3(1) and (2) 'do [not] preclude the application of provisions of national law that predominantly pursue an objective different from that pursued by [Articles 81 and 82 EC]'. Recital 9 of Regulation 1/2003 explains that Articles 81 and 82 EC 'have as their objective the protection of competition on the market', and gives 'national legislation that prohibits or imposes sanctions on acts of unfair trading practice' as an example of legislation protecting 'other legitimate interests'.

The three limitations mentioned above can be illustrated by the cartel offence in the United Kingdom. The Enterprise Act 2002, s. 188 provides that an individual is guilty of this criminal offence, sanctionable by imprisonment and/or a fine, if he or she dishonestly agrees with one or more other persons that undertakings will engage in one or more of the prohibited cartel activities, namely price-fixing, limitation of supply or production, market-sharing, and bid-rigging.[67]

First, given that price-fixing, limitation of supply or production, market-sharing and bid-rigging are, when they actually or potentially affect trade between Member States, also prohibited under Article 81 EC, this pro-

---

[66] On these co-operation mechanisms, *see* Schnichels, D. (2004), 'The Network of Competition Authorities: How will it work in practice?', in D. Geradin (ed.), *Modernisation and Enlargement: Two Major Challenges for EC Competition Law*, Belgium: Intersentia, pp. 99–121 and *Principles of European Antitrust Enforcement*, as note 2 above, chapters 1 and 2.

[67] The text of the Enterprise Act 2002 is available at: http://www.legislation.hmso.gov.uk/acts/acts2002/20020040.htm (accessed 19 June 2009).

hibition under United Kingdom law is compatible with Article 3(2) of Regulation No 1/2003.

Secondly, the Enterprise Act 2002, s. 188 does not distinguish in any way between, on the one hand, price-fixing, limitation of supply or production, market-sharing, or bid-rigging that may affect trade between Member States, and thus falls under Article 81 EC, and, on the other hand, prohibited cartel activities that do not affect trade between Member States, and thus only fall under the Chapter I prohibition of the Competition Act 1998, the provision of UK national competition law comparable to Article 81 EC. Unless the UK authorities were to develop an administrative practice of only investigating and prosecuting cases which concern prohibited cartel activities that do not affect trade between Member States, the principle of equivalence is thus fully respected. Indeed, the first prosecution brought by the Office of Fair Trading concerned a worldwide cartel in the marine hose industry.[68]

Thirdly, when a case which concerns prohibited cartel activities that may affect trade between Member States is investigated, prosecuted and punished by the competent UK authorities and courts, it would in my view follow from Article 3(1) of Regulation 1/2003 that they will have to establish that the prohibited cartel activities indeed may affect trade between Member States and are thus contrary to Article 81 EC, and they will have to comply with the mechanisms of co-operation with the European

---

68 In this case, three UK businessmen were convicted by Judge Rivlin at the Southwark Crown Court on 11 June 2008 and sentenced to imprisonment for between two and a half and three years. All three were also disqualified from acting as company directors for periods between five and seven years; *see* Office of Fair Trading press release 72/08 of 11 June 2008, available at: http://www.oft.gov.uk/news/press/2008/72-08 (accessed 19 June 2009). On 1 July 2008, the Judge also made confiscation orders against the defendants totalling just over £1 million as proceeds of crime. Appeals against the sentences have been lodged by the defendants before the Court of Appeal. The prosecution by the United Kingdom Office of Fair Trading followed the arrest of the three defendants in the United States in May 2007, in an operation co-ordinated between the US Department of Justice, the UK Office of Fair Trading and the European Commission. Pursuant to plea agreements entered into with the US Department of Justice, the defendants were sentenced to prison terms in the US of between 20 and 30 months. These sentences were suspended to allow the defendants to return to the UK and plead guilty in the UK courts. According to the US plea deal, if the UK courts sentenced them to less prison time than in the US they would have to return to the US to serve the remainder of their time in US prisons. On 5 May 2008, the European Commission confirmed that it had sent statements of objections to the companies involved in the marine hose cartel, with a view to imposing fines on these companies; *see* MEMO/08/284 of 5 May 2008.

Commission and within the EU network of competition authorities as provided for in Articles 11 and 15 of Regulation No 1/2003.[69]

2.4 Decriminalisation and Criminalisation of Antitrust Enforcement in the EU Member States

Looking at antitrust enforcement in the EU Member States over the last 20 years, one can detect a double tendency of decriminalisation and criminalisation.[70]

2.4.1 Decriminalisation on the one hand

The tendency to decriminalise antitrust enforcement is illustrated by the examples of France, the Netherlands, Austria and Luxembourg. In France, antitrust enforcement under the competition acts of 1953 and 1958 was exclusively criminal. After the first reform in 1977, the competition act of 1986 introduced the current French system, which relies essentially on administrative fines on companies, imposed by the Competition Council, a specialised administrative authority. Criminal sanctions, including imprisonment, are however still provided for in French law. In the Netherlands, the current competition act, which came into effect in 1997, replaced an earlier system of criminal enforcement by a purely administrative system with only fines on undertakings, comparable to the enforcement system at the level of the EU institutions. In Austria, the 2002 competition law reform also replaced a system of criminal enforcement by a system of administrative fines on companies. A specific criminal offence of bid-rigging was however maintained. In Luxembourg, the 2004 competition act abolished an earlier competition regime with criminal enforcement by a new regime with only administrative fines on companies.

These movements to decriminalise antitrust enforcement reflect, I believe, two phenomena. The first explanation is that some of the older competition laws with criminal enforcement which were abolished in these Member States were in fact not comparable to Articles 81 and 82 EC, because they were not based on the prohibition principle. In Luxembourg, for instance, before the 2004 reform, there were in fact no sanctions at all for the mere fact of having concluded and operated a price cartel. Only if a cartel had been investigated, and the undertakings had been ordered to

---

69 *See Efficiency and Justice in European Antitrust Enforcement*, as note 3 above, paragraphs 531–532.

70 *See* also text accompanying notes 59 to 63 above as to the current situation in various Member States.

put an end to it, were the owners, managers and directors of those undertakings threatened with criminal sanctions in case they would continue the cartel notwithstanding the order to put an end to it. Luxembourg can thus hardly be considered to be leading a new trend towards decriminalisation. It rather was the last to follow an earlier trend started by the European Communities and Germany in the 1950s.

Indeed, looking at the whole of Europe over close to a century, specifically with regard to cartels, it would seem that most jurisdictions are historically moving through similar phases in the same direction. In a first phase, the one which Luxembourg only abandoned in 2004, there was no real cartel prohibition, only a system of control of abuse, under which, once an abuse had been established, the undertakings concerned would have been ordered to put an end to this abuse for the future. Non-respect of this specific order for the future may have been punishable with criminal sanctions, including imprisonment. In a second phase, first reached by the European Coal and Steel Community in the early 1950s, and subsequently by Germany and by the European Economic Community in the late 1950s, cartels were prohibited, but the direct effect of this prohibition was softened through a notification system, which allowed temporary immunity from sanctions,[71] and violations of the prohibition were only punishable with fines on undertakings. In a third phase, reached at the EU level through Regulation No 1/2003, the deterrent effect of the cartel prohibition is enhanced through the abolition of the notification system. In a fourth phase, reached long since by the United States,[72] and recently entered into by the United Kingdom,[73] the threat of individual sanctions, in particular imprisonment, is added, so as to increase deterrence for those types of cartel infringements which are most profitable and most difficult to detect, namely secret price-fixing, bid-rigging and market-sharing arrangements.

The second explanation for the observed decriminalisation in some EU Member States over the past 20 years is that, even if some of these Member States had already moved to a system based on the prohibition principle, their criminal enforcement did not work in practice because it was badly conceived. Indeed, as will be argued further in this chapter,[74] criminal

---

71 *See Principles of European Antitrust Enforcement*, as note 2 above, section 1.1.4.4, and Marenco, G. (2001), *Does a Legal Exception System Require an Amendment of the Treaty?*, in C.D. Ehlermann and I. Atanasiu (eds), *European Competition Law Annual 2000: The Modernisation of EC Antitrust Policy*, Oxford: Hart Publishing, pp. 145–184, at pp. 174–175.

72 *See* text accompanying notes 22 to 31 above.

73 *See* text accompanying notes 67 above and 78 below.

74 Text accompanying notes 150 to 164.

antitrust enforcement, in its strongest form, relying on imprisonment, can only work or only makes sense if it is limited to hard-core cartels, complementing other penalties for companies and for lesser antitrust violations, if a dedicated investigator and prosecutor and sufficient powers of investigation are provided for, and if judges or juries are willing to convict, all of which requires a sufficiently broad political or societal consensus that cartels are really bad and thus deserve severe punishment. These conditions would not appear to have been fulfilled in those Member States at the relevant time.[75]

2.4.2 Criminalisation on the other hand

The tendency to criminalise antitrust enforcement is primarily illustrated by the examples of Ireland and the United Kingdom, but also by developments in some other Member States, for example the criminalisation of bid-rigging in Hungary in 2005, or the recent discussions in the Netherlands about introducing criminal penalties for cartels.[76]

In Ireland, since entry into force of the Competition Act 1996, later replaced by the Competition Act 2002, violations of the national law prohibitions equivalent to Articles 81 and 82 EC, as well as violations of Articles 81 and 82 EC, are criminal offences, punishable with fines on companies, and imprisonment and/or fines for individuals. In 2006 the first (suspended) jail sentence was handed down in the heating oil cartel case.[77] A comparable system has been adopted in Estonia. In the United

---

[75] *See* further text accompanying note 150 below.

[76] The introduction of prison sanctions and director disqualification has been discussed in the Second Chamber of the Dutch Parliament. Following hearings in 2004 and 2005, broad support for the introduction of such penalties emerged in a parliamentary debate in June 2006. As a result, the Government announced that it would submit a legislative proposal, but this is still in preparation; see letter of 16 June 2006 from the Minister of Economic Affairs to Parliament, Tweede Kamer 2005–2006, 30 071, No 27; Answer by the Minister of Economic Affairs of 13 September 2007 to the parliamentary question No 2060718300 by Jan ten Hoopen MP; and ten Hoopen, J. (2008), 'Commentaar' in P. Kalbfleisch a.o. (eds), *Trust en antitrust – Beschouwingen over 10 jaar Mededingingswet en 10 jaar Nma*, Netherlands Competition Authority, pp. 175–176. An amendment to the Dutch competition act already adopted in 2007 has given the Dutch competition authority the power to impose administrative fines not only on companies but also on individuals.

[77] Judgment of Justice Delahunt, Dublin Circuit Criminal Court, 6 March 2006; *see* Gorecki, P.K. and D. McFadden (2006), 'Criminal Cartels in Ireland: the Heating Oil Case', *European Competition Law Review*, 631. Other businessmen involved in this cartel were also found guilty and fined. As a result of these convictions, the defendants were also disqualified from acting as a company director or taking a management role for five years; *see Irish Times*, 3 May 2007, at p. 21.

Kingdom, as already mentioned above,[78] the Enterprise Act 2002 has added a criminal cartel offence, limited to hard-core cartels, punishable with imprisonment and/or fines for individuals only, as well as a sanction of director disqualification for individuals,[79] to a system which otherwise relies on administrative fines on companies for breach of Articles 81 and 82 EC and the equivalent prohibitions under national law. As already mentioned above,[80] three businessmen were sentenced in June 2008 to imprisonment for between two and a half and three years in the marine hose cartel case.

The introduction of criminal penalties in Ireland and the United Kingdom has been accompanied by the grant of corresponding criminal powers of investigation to the investigating authorities. In the United Kingdom, for instance, the Office of Fair Trading has been given new powers of covert surveillance for the purpose of investigating the criminal cartel offence.[81]

The introduction of criminal penalties in Ireland and the United Kingdom has clearly been inspired by the US example.[82] That Europe follows the US example in matters of antitrust is, of course, not new. Indeed, the history of antitrust in modern Europe,[83] and in particular the history of Article 81 EC and similar provisions in national law, is very much one of American influence. The prohibition on abuse of a dominant position, first in the ECSC Treaty of 1951 and subsequently in Article 86 of the EEC Treaty of 1957 (now Article 82 EC), was not without precedent: in Germany, for instance, an 'Ordinance against the Abuse of Economic Power' had been enacted in 1923.[84] However, the prohibition on restrictive agreements first laid down in Article 65 of the ECSC Treaty and then also in Article 85 of the EEC Treaty (now Article 81 EC), was 'a fundamental

---

78 Text accompanying note 67.

79 *See* further text accompanying note 145 below on director disqualification.

80 (Text accompanying) note 68.

81 Sections 199–200 of the Enterprise Act 2002, as note 67 above; *see* also Office of Fair Trading, 'Powers for investigating criminal cartels – Guidance' (January 2004), available at: http://www.oft.gov.uk/Business/Legal+Powers/Enterprise+Act/publications.htm (accessed 19 June 2009).

82 *See* Kunzlik, P.F. (2003), 'Globalization and Hybridization in Antitrust Enforcement: European Borrowings from the US Approach', *The Antitrust Bulletin*, Summer, 319; and text accompanying notes 22 and 23 above.

83 *See* note 23 above as to older European precedents.

84 Nörr, K. (1995), 'Law and Market Organization: The Historical Experience in Germany From 1900 to the Law Against Restraints of Competition (1957)', *Journal of Institutional and Theoretical Economics/Zeitschrift für die gesamte Staatswissenschaft,* **151**, 5, at 10.

innovation in Europe'.[85] Before the second world war, cartels were a widespread and highly esteemed institution throughout Europe.[86] The insertion of the prohibition on restrictive agreements in European law, as well as around the same time in German national law, was due to American influence, if not pressure.[87] As Joel Davidow has recently observed: 'In the early years of the 21st Century, it has become evident that US antitrust, once nearly the sole source of influential antitrust enforcement, has become part of a "dynamic duo", along with the European Union. The EU and its Member States have eclipsed the United States in terms of number of professionals employed, sometimes in size of fines and certainly in terms of countries imitating the basic enforcement scheme'.[88] However: 'The United States, even if no longer the world's largest jurisdiction, remains the most influential in terms of policy and theory'.[89] The trend to criminalise antitrust enforcement reflects this influence.

3 IS CRIMINALISATION OF ANTITRUST ENFORCEMENT DESIRABLE?

In this third section, I want to address the question whether, why or under what conditions criminalisation of antitrust enforcement is desirable. The question is addressed in general, irrespective of whether such criminalisation takes place at the level of the EU Member States or of the EU

---

[85] Monnet, J. (1976), *Mémoires*, Paris: Fayard, at p. 413; see however note 23 above as to the older European precedents.

[86] Schröter, H.G. (1996), 'Cartelization and Decartelization in Europe, 1870–1995: Rise and Decline of an Economic Institution', *Journal of European Economic History*, **25**, 129 at 137, who also writes at 140 that Yugoslavia was the only European country where cartels were prohibited at that time.

[87] *See* J. Monnet, as note 85 above, at pp. 356–357 and pp. 411–413; Spierenburg, D. and R. Poidevin (1994), *The History of the High Authority of the European Coal and Steel Community*, UK: Weidenfeld and Nicholson, at pp. 26–28; and, with a detailed description of the strong resistance to be overcome in Germany, Berghann, V. (1986) *The Americanisation of West German Industry 1945–1973*, Oxford: Berg; *see* also Marenco, G. (2002), *The Birth of Modern Competition Law in Europe*, in A. von Bogdandy, P.C. Mavroidis and Y. Mény (eds), *European Integration and International Co-ordination – Studies in Transnational Economic Law in Honour of Claus-Dieter Ehlermann*, UK: Kluwer Law International, pp. 279–304, and *The Optimal Enforcement of EC Antitrust Law*, as note 4 above, sections 5.3.2 and 9.5.

[88] Davidow, J. (2004), 'Recent US Antitrust Developments of International Relevance', *World Competition*, **27**, at 407.

[89] *Idem.*

institutions, or whether it is harmonised at EU level. The question whether it is problematic that antitrust enforcement is criminalised at the level of individual EU Member States without parallel criminalisation at the level of the EU institutions or without EU harmonization will be dealt with afterwards in part 4 of this chapter.

As described above,[90] criminalisation is a phenomenon with different faces. However, I will focus on its strongest variant, namely the introduction of individual penalties, and more specifically imprisonment, as exemplified by Ireland and the United Kingdom.

I will first consider five arguments in favour of imprisonment as a penalty for antitrust offences, then consider for what types of antitrust offences these arguments are valid, and examine whether there are no equally effective alternatives to imprisonment, and finally discuss five conditions which need to be fulfilled for criminal antitrust enforcement to be effective not only in theory but also in practice.

3.1 Five Arguments in Favour of Imprisonment

3.1.1 Effective deterrence with only fines on companies would require impossibly high fines

In a paper presented at the 6th Competition Law and Policy Workshop at the European University Institute (EUI) in 2001, I argued that the minimum level of fines required generally to deter price cartels and other antitrust offences of comparable profitability and ease of concealment would be in the order of 150 per cent of the annual turnover in the products concerned by the violation.[91]

This argument was based on the following hypothetical: I took the figure of 10 per cent of the selling price as an estimate of the average price increase from price-fixing. This estimate had been relied upon by the US Sentencing Commission when drafting its Sentencing Guidelines and appeared to be generally accepted in the American literature – no European studies being available. As the price increase caused by the cartel

---

90 *See* text accompanying note 5.

91 W.P.J. Wils, 'Does the Effective Enforcement of Articles 81 and 82 EC Require Not Only Fines on Undertakings But Also Individual Penalties, In Particular Imprisonment?', paper presented at the 6th Competition Law and Policy Workshop at the European University Institute (Florence, 1–2 June 2001), later published in C.D. Ehlermann and I. Atanasiu, *European Competition Law Annual 2001: Effective Private Enforcement of EC Antitrust Law* (Hart Publishing 2003) pp. 411–452 and in *The Optimal Enforcement of EC Antitrust Law*, as note 4 above, chapter 8, pp. 188–237.

will normally depress demand for the cartel members' products, I assumed conservatively that a price increase of 10 per cent would lead to an increase in profits of 5 per cent of turnover. On the basis of the findings of duration in a number of cartel decisions of the European Commission, and of estimates in the American literature, I assumed, again conservatively, a cartel duration of five years. Finally, I assumed a probability for detection and punishment of 16 per cent, which I considered again a conservative estimate, given that the one existing study in the American literature, by Peter Bryant and Woodrow Eckard, based on a sample of 184 price-fixing cases for the period from 1961 to 1988, had produced an estimate between 13 and 17 per cent,[92] and that European competition authorities have weaker investigative powers than their American counterparts. Assuming a 10 per cent price increase, and a resulting increase in profits of 5 per cent of turnover, a five-year duration and a 16 per cent probability of detection and punishment, the floor below which fines will generally not deter price-fixing would be in the order of 150 per cent of the annual turnover in the products concerned by the violation.[93]

A slight variation on this hypothetical was subsequently used by the UK government in its White Paper setting out its case for the introduction of a criminal cartel offence.[94] The hypothetical was also referred to by the OECD in its 2002 report on hard-core cartels.[95]

Seven years later, would these estimates still appear appropriate? As to the average price increase from price-fixing, the OECD reported in 2002 the results of a survey it had carried out. In the limited data (14 cases) of that survey, the median overcharge was between 15 and 20 per cent.[96] More recently, John Connor has made a survey of hundreds of published social-science studies of hard-core cartels that contained 674 observations

---

[92] Bryant, P.G. and E.W. Eckard (1991), 'Price Fixing: The Probability of Getting Caught', *Review of Economics and Statistics,* 531.

[93] I added that the figure would be even higher if one were to take into account the fact that fines are only paid several years after the gain from the violation is obtained. Indeed, my calculations assumed a zero interest rate. With a more realistic higher interest rate, the minimum fine necessary to achieve deterrence would be even higher.

[94] Department of Trade and Industry, 'A World Class Competition Regime', presented to Parliament by the Secretary of State for Trade and Industry, July 2001, available at: http://www.archive.official-documents.co.uk/document/cm52/5233/523301.htm (accessed 19 June 2009), at 40 (box 7.3).

[95] OECD, 'Report on the nature and impact of hard-core cartels and sanctions against cartels under national competition laws', DAFFE/COMP(2002)7 (9 April 2002), available at: http://www.oecd.org (accessed 19 June 2009), at 19 (note 20).

[96] OECD, as note 95 above, at 9.

of long-run overcharges. His primary finding is that the median cartel overcharge for all types of cartels over all time periods throughout the world is 25 per cent. He also conducted a survey of 24 final verdicts in decided US horizontal collusion cases, revealing an average median overcharge of 21 per cent and an average mean overcharge of 30 per cent.[97] On the basis of these new surveys, I should have taken 20 per cent rather than 10 per cent as an estimate of the average price increase from price-fixing in my hypothetical. Keeping the same conservative assumption as to the price elasticity of demand for the cartel members' products, I would then take ten per cent of turnover as an estimate of the increase in profits resulting from the price-fixing.

As to the average duration of price-fixing cartels, the literature published in the last five years would not alter my conservative estimate of five years.[98]

As to the probability of detection and punishment, it has correctly been pointed out that the detection rate in the US has presumably improved since the period 1961 to 1988 on which Peter Bryant and Woodrow Eckard based their estimate of between 13 and 17 per cent,[99] because of the use of more effective investigative methods, in particular the use of optimized leniency programmes.[100] Some have opined that nevertheless 'there is little reason to believe that the true probability of detection is outside this range'.[101] It would in any event still remain true that the probability is probably lower in Europe than in the US.[102] I believe I would remain very safely on the conservative side by assuming the probability of detection and punishment in Europe not to be above 33 per cent.[103]

---

97 Connor, J.M., 'Price-Fixing Overcharges: Legal and Economic Evidence', American Antitrust Institute (AAI) Working Paper No 04-05, available at: http://www.antitrustinstitute.org/recent2/355.pdf (accessed 19 June 2009).

98 *See* Evenett, S.J., M.C. Levenstein and V.Y. Suslow (2001), 'International Cartel Enforcement: Lessons from the 1990s', *World Economy* 1221, at 1226; J.M. Connor, as note 97 above, at 12; and Levenstein, M.C. and V.Y. Suslow (2006), 'What Determines Cartel Success?', *Journal of Economic Literature*, **44**, 43–95.

99 Note 92 above.

100 *See* OECD, as note 95 above, at 13; and Bush, D., J.M. Connor, J.J. Flynn, S. Ghosh, W. Grimes, J.E. Harrington, N. Hawker, R. Lande W.G. Shepherd and S. Semerano (2004), 'How to Block Cartel Formation and Price-Fixing', Amicus Curiae brief in the US Supreme Court in *Hoffman-LaRoche v Empegran*, 15 March 2004, available at: http://aei-brookings.org/admin/authorpdfs/page.php?id=931 (accessed 19 June 2009), at 28; the point was first made to me shortly after I presented my 2001 EUI paper by Bill Bishop; *see also Principles of European Antitrust Enforcement*, as note 2 above, chapter 5.

101 D. Bush and Others, as note 100 above, at 28.

102 *See* also OECD, as note 95 above, at 13.

103 *See* also Combe, E., C. Monnier and R. Legal (2008), 'Cartels: the Probability of Getting Caught in the European Union', Bruges European Economic Research

Assuming then a 20 per cent price increase, and a resulting increase in profits of 10 per cent of turnover, a five-year duration and a 33 per cent probability of detection and punishment, I would thus still today reach the conclusion that the floor below which fines on companies will generally not deter price-fixing would be in the order of 150 per cent of the annual turnover in the products concerned by the violation.[104]

As I argued in more detail in my 2001 EUI paper,[105] raising the general level of fines to such a high level would be impossible or unacceptable for various reasons. First (and least importantly, as statutory ceilings could be raised), such higher fines are likely regularly to breach the statutory ceilings on the amount of fines which can legally be imposed.[106]

Secondly, and most importantly, such high fines are likely often to exceed the undertakings' ability to pay, with as a result not only incomplete deterrence but also costly side-effects. The fact that the companies that have engaged in a price-fixing cartel have profited financially from the violation offers no guarantee that they will also be able to pay the minimum fine required for effective deterrence. Indeed, in the estimated average case of a price cartel leading to extra profits of 10 per cent of turnover during five years, with a probability of detection and

---

Papers No 12 (March) and Speech by Philip Lowe, Director General for Competition, European Commission at the ICN Annual conference Moscow, 31 May 2007, available at: http://ec.europa.eu/comm/competition/speeches (accessed 19 June 2009), at 2: 'we know that we probably only discover about 10 per cent of the cartels which exist'.

[104] I would again add that the figure would be even higher if one were to take into account the fact that fines are only paid several years after the gain from the violation is obtained; see note 93 above. I would also add that the figure is probably also too low because it ignores the likely effects of overconfidence bias. Indeed, it appears that people consistently tend to overestimate the probability of good things happening to them, and underestimate the probability of bad things happening to them, in particular when the event is question is perceived to be controllable; see Weinstein, N.D. (1989), 'Optimistic Biases About Personal Risks', *Science*, **246**, 1232 and Korobkin, R.B. and T.S. Ulen (2000), 'Law and Behavioral Science: Removing the Rationality Assumption from Law and Economics', *California Law Review*, **88**, 1051, at 1091–1095. Applied to deterrence through antitrust fines, this suggests that companies and individual decision-makers within them will tend to overestimate the gain from the antitrust violation and to underestimate the probability of being caught; see also Denger, M.L., 'Too Much or Too Little', American Bar Association, Section of Antitrust Law, Antitrust Remedies Forum, available at: http://www.abanet.org/antitrust/remedies (accessed 19 June 2009), at 5: 'most cartel participants don't think they will get caught'.

[105] As note 91 above.

[106] *See*, for example, as to fines imposed by the European Commission, the ceiling of 10 per cent of total turnover of the undertaking concerned in Article 23(2) of Regulation No 1/2003, as note 1 above.

punishment of 33 per cent, the cartel members would each have gained over the whole duration of the cartel 50 per cent of their annual turnover in the products concerned by the violation. Even if they had retained these profits until the fine is imposed, these would only pay for one-third of the fine of 150 per cent of annual turnover in the products concerned. It is more likely that these profits would not have been retained but rather would have been paid out in taxes, dividends, salaries and wages.[107]

Even liquidating the assets of the firms concerned is often unlikely to generate enough revenues to pay the fine required for effective deterrence. Indeed, many companies' annual turnover exceeds their assets. A fine of 150 per cent of annual turnover in the products concerned by the violation could thus only be paid out of the assets of large, diversified companies, which have taken part in cartels only for a small part of their activities,[108] or companies with very high asset-to-sales ratios.[109]

If such high fines were really imposed, many of the companies concerned would be forced into bankruptcy.[110] This would, however, entail undesirable social costs, because, in the absence of perfect markets, it would hurt not only managers and shareholders, on whom the bankruptcy may be considered to have a desirable deterrent effect, but also all other stake-holders in the firm: employees, suppliers, customers, creditors and tax authorities.[111]

Even if they stay below the level of inability to pay, the imposition of such high fines is likely to be costly. Very high fines may have undesirable

---

107 Werden, G.J. and M.J. Simon (1987), 'Why Price Fixers Should Go to Prison', *The Antitrust Bulletin*, 917, at 928, note 35, referring to empirical estimates that unions are able to capture most of the monopoly profits earned by US manufacturing firms.

108 When looking at the names of companies found to have been involved in cartels, one often sees the same names coming back, suggesting that companies found to have been involved in a cartel in one market may have been active in cartels in their other markets as well.

109 G.J. Werden and M.J. Simon, as note 107 above, at 928–929.

110 Craycraft, C., J.L. Craycraft and J.C. Gallo (1997), 'Antitrust Sanctions and a Firm's Ability to Pay', *Review of Industrial Organization*, **12**, 171, in an empirical study based on a sample of 386 firms convicted of price-fixing in the US between 1955 and 1993, have estimated that 58 per cent of the firms would not have been able to survive the imposition of an optimal fine without becoming technically bankrupt. Because of data restrictions, the firms in their sample were the larger firms, which means that their result may very well underestimate the extent of the problem of inability to pay.

111 Kraakman, R.H. (1984), 'Corporate Liability Strategies and the Costs of Legal Controls', *The Yale Law Journal*, **93**, 857, at 882.

side-effects. In the absence of perfect markets, very high fines imposed on companies will have an incidence on all the stake-holders in the firm. Bondholders and other creditors will suffer a diminution in the value of their securities. Employees may suffer from cost-cutting campaigns induced by the need to pay the fine. Tax receipts will be reduced. Finally, consumers may end up suffering. Indeed, if the firm competes in a product market characterised by imperfect competition (as will often be the case), the fine may be partly recovered from consumers in the form of higher prices.[112]

3.1.2 Fines on companies do not always guarantee adequate incentives for responsible individuals within the firm

As I also argued in more detail in my 2001 EUI paper,[113] the logic of fining undertakings or companies for antitrust violations is that the threat of the corporate sanction, if sufficiently high, will induce the undertaking or company to try to make its agents respect the law. This shifting of the enforcement function from the authorities to the firm makes sense because in general the firm has a relatively good ability to influence the behavior of its agents. However, in a number of circumstances the firm may not, in reality, be capable of adequately controlling the behavior of its agents, with the result that exclusive reliance on corporate sanctions will not lead to effective deterrence. This situation can arise because firms may not be able to impose sufficiently serious sanctions on their agents. It can also arise when firms are management controlled. Finally, the managers responsible for the violation may have left the firm by the time the violation is detected, and there may be little a company can do to a former employee.

3.1.3 Increased effectiveness of leniency and whistle blowing programmes

Sanctions against individuals have another beneficial effect, in that they provide an incentive for individuals to offer co-operation in cartel investigations, against the interests of their employers.[114]

Leniency (the granting of immunity from penalties or the reduction of penalties for antitrust violations in exchange for co-operation with the competition authorities) has become an increasingly used and increasingly

---

112 Coffee, J.C. (1981), 'No Soul to Damn: No Body to Kick: an Unscandalized Inquiry into the Problem of Corporate Punishment', *Michigan Law Review*, **79**, 387, at 401–402.

113 As note 91 above.

114 OECD, as note 95 above, at 16.

successful instrument in antitrust enforcement.[115] If, as is the case in the United States, Ireland and the United Kingdom, leniency (including immunity) is also available for individuals, and the leniency policies for companies and for individuals are well integrated, in that, when a company is the first to apply for immunity, it can also obtain immunity for its co-operating staff, but that immunity is normally no longer available for a company if an individual has applied for it earlier (and is similarly normally unavailable for an individual if a company has been first and the individual is not part of the company's application), leniency will be more effective, for three reasons.

First, at least to the extent that the companies care for their staff, the higher overall penalty discount available will make it more attractive for companies to apply for leniency.

Secondly, additional races to be the first to co-operate are created between the companies and their staff, as well as between individuals. As Scott Hammond has explained with regard to US Department of Justice's practice of combining corporate and individual leniency programmes:

> the individual amnesty program helps prevent companies from covering up their misconduct. The real value and measure of the Individual Leniency Program is not in the number of individual applications we receive, but in the number of corporate applications it generates. It works because it acts as a watchdog to ensure that companies report the conduct themselves. [. . .] So long as one of its employees has individual exposure, the company remains at great risk. If the company self-reports the conduct under the Corporate Leniency Policy, then the company and all of its co-operating executives will avoid criminal prosecution. However, if the company delays or decides not to report, then the company puts itself in a race for leniency with its own employees. In this example, if the company does not report the conduct first, then the executive may come forward on his own and report the conduct for his own protection, thereby potentially leaving the company out in the cold. [. . .] If the secretary gets nervous, say, after talking to a relative who convinces her that she has real criminal exposure for her own conduct, she may decide to report the conduct.[116]

---

115 *See* Wils, W.P.J. (2007), 'Leniency in Antitrust Anforcement: Theory and Practice', *World Competition*, **30**, 25; Schmidtchen, D., M. Albert and S. Voigt (eds) (2007), 'The More Economic Approach to European Competition Law', Conferences on New Political Economy, **24**, Germany: Mohr Siebeck, 203–254; and *Efficiency and Justice in European Antitrust Enforcement*, as note 3 above, chapter 5.

116 Hammond, S.D. (2004), 'Cornerstones of an Effective Leniency Program', paper presented before the ICN Workshop on Leniency Programs (Sydney, 22–23 November), available at: http://www.usdoj.gov/atr/public/speeches/206611.htm (accessed 19 June 2009), at 12–14.

As Donald Baker has further explained, also describing US practice:

> The same process works between individuals at different companies involved in the suspected conspiracy. There certainly have been cases where an individual was indicted for a one-on-one conversation with someone who worked for a competitor and who then turned the defendant in. Of course, as we saw with the Lysine cartel, an individual who turns herself in to the government may become a government informant and continue to participate in conspiracy meetings, armed with recording devices in order to entrap the other conspiracy members.[117]

Thirdly, the presence of criminal penalties for individuals strongly reduces the risk of perverse effects of leniency policies.[118] It would in particular appear to eliminate the risk that, in situations where the same companies participate in a number of cartels in different markets, or repeatedly form cartels over time, cartel participants might take turns to apply for leniency, every time one of the cartels is (about to be) detected by the competition authority.[119]

Donald Baker has also pointed out that the system of imposing criminal liability on individuals generates not only incentives for whistle blowing based on fear, but also incentives for whistle blowing based on the desire for revenge: 'The desire for revenge is more picturesque, but it is still very much present. In my experience, disgruntled current employees, fired employees, former trade association officials, and even ex-spouses and ex-lovers may be anxious to finger the individuals who they think have done them in'.[120]

As the OECD has pointed out: 'There is an offsetting consideration relating to individual sanctions, however. In many countries, sanctioning individuals requires criminalisation of the conduct. In that context individuals have rights against self-incrimination, which makes it more difficult to obtain evidence from them unless they willingly co-operate. In this sense, criminalisation of cartel conduct for individuals makes voluntary co-operation more possible, because of the threat of personal sanctions, but also makes it more necessary, because a right against self-incrimination

---

117 D. I. Baker, as note 24 above, at 708.

118 *See* 'Leniency in Antitrust Anforcement: Theory and Practice', as note 115 above, at 48–49 and *Efficiency and Justice in European Antitrust Enforcement*, as note 115 above, section 5.2.3.3.

119 *See* 'Leniency in Antitrust Anforcement: Theory and Practice', as note 115 above, at 48, and *Efficiency and Justice in European Antitrust Enforcement*, as note 115 above, paragraph 424.

120 *Idem*.

attaches'.[121] The US experience,[122] though, suggests that the net result is an increase in the effectiveness of investigations.

3.1.4 Imprisonment is a very effective deterrent

There is ample evidence, based in particular on the US experience, that imprisonment is a very effective deterrent for potential antitrust offenders.

In Arthur Liman's words: 'For the purse snatcher, a term in the penitentiary may be little more unsettling than basic training in the army. To the businessman, however, prison is the inferno, and conventional risk-reward analysis breaks down when the risk is jail. The threat of imprisonment, therefore, remains the most meaningful deterrent to antitrust violations'.[123] Or as Joseph Bauer has more recently put it: 'The sight of A. Alfred Taubman, the extremely wealthy chairman of the board of Sotheby's, the world-famous auction house, convicted and sentenced, at the age of 78, to a one-year term of imprisonment and a substantial fine for participating in a price-fixing conspiracy, doubtless sent a message to other business executives about the risks and penalties for this kind of behavior'.[124]

The success of the current criminal antitrust enforcement in the US is shown by several indicators. First, according to Terry Calvani, in the US, 'there is much less domestic cartel activity today than before'.[125] Indeed, a large part of the cartels detected and prosecuted by the US Department

---

[121] OECD, as note 95 above, at 16.

[122] *See* D.I. Baker, as note 24 above, and S.D. Hammond, as note 116 above, as well as text accompanying notes 123 to 131 below.

[123] Liman, A.L. (1977), 'The Paper Label Sentences: Critique', *The Yale Law Journal*, **86**, 619 at 630–631; in the same sense: Baker, D.I. and B.A. Reeves (1977), 'The Paper Label Sentences: Critique', *The Yale Law Journal*, **86**, 619 at 621, and Mukasey, M.B. (1997), 'Comment on Lynch', *Law and Contemporary Problems*, **60**, 71; *see* also Antoine Winckler's remarks in the panel discussion on criminal sanctions at the 6th Competition Law and Policy Workshop at the European University Institute (Florence, 1–2 June 2001), published in Ehlermann, C.D. and I. Atanasiu, *European Competition Law Annual 2001: Effective Private Enforcement of EC Antitrust Law*, Oxford: Hart Publishing, 387, at 404: 'My experience as a legal practitioner is that criminal sanctions are an extremely effective deterrent.'

[124] Bauer, J.P. (2004), 'Reflections on the Manifold Means of Enforcing the Antitrust Laws: Too Much, Too Little, or Just Right?', *Loyola Consumer Law Review*, **16**, 303, at 307.

[125] Calvani, T. (2004), 'Enforcement of Cartel Law in Ireland', in B.E. Hawk (ed.), *2003 Annual Proceedings of the Fordham Corporate Law Institute International Antitrust Law & Policy*, New York: Juris Publishing, 1, at 6.

of Justice in the last years have been international, often even global in membership and geographic spread.[126]

Second, as Scott Hammond has pointed out:

> We [the US Department of Justice] are observing firsthand in some of our investigations how the threat of criminal prosecution in the United States has deterred a significant number of global cartels from extending their conspiracy into the United States. We have uncovered cartels that operated profitably and illegally in Europe, Asia, and elsewhere around the world, but did not expand their cartel activity to the United States solely because it was not worth the risk of U.S. sanctions. I am referring to cartels that had every opportunity to target U.S. consumers, because they sold in the U.S. market. Indeed, in some cases, the U.S. market was the largest and potentially most profitable but the collusive conduct still ceased at the border. Why? The answer, from the mouth of the cartel members and verified by our investigators, is that the executives did not want to get caught and going to jail in the United States.[127]

Third, as William Kolasky has indicated with regard to those international cartels that nevertheless continue to target also US consumers:

> The power of criminal enforcement is illustrated by another characteristic common to those cartels in which the conspirators know that their conduct is unlawful – namely, their efforts to stay away from the United States. International cartels often try to minimize their contacts in the United States by conducting their meetings abroad. This has been particularly true since 1995, when the lysine investigation became public. In fact, co-operating defendants in several recent cases have revealed that the cartels changed their practices and began avoiding contacts in the United States at all costs once the [US Department of Justice Antitrust] Division began cracking and prosecuting international cartels. Some cartel members go so far as to try to keep their cartel activity secret from all U.S.-based employees, even those responsible for carrying out their instructions as to the firm's output and prices.[128]

Fourth, as Margaret Bloom has pointed out:

> Another factor that illustrates the effect of criminal powers is the extent to which international cartels are first uncovered through amnesty applications to the [US Department of Justice]. In these cases, it is the threat of criminal sanctions that drives executives to go first to the [US Department of Justice] – and

---

126 *See* S.D. Hammond, as note 116 above.

127 *See* S.D. Hammond, as note 116 above, at 8–9.

128 Kolasky, W. (2004), 'Criminalizing Cartel Activity: Lessons from the U.S. Experience', fifth lunch talk of the Global Competition Law Centre (Brussels, 29 September), available at: http://www.gclc.coleurop.be/lunchtalk20040929.htm (accessed 19 June 2009), at 11–12.

> only later to the European Commission and other relevant authorities. Without the U.S. criminal sanctions and active enforcement record, how many of these cases would be revealed by leniency applications to the European Commission? It is, of course, impossible to answer this question, but I suspect the answer might well be few.[129]

That imprisonment is a particularly strong deterrent was also confirmed by a study commissioned last year by the United Kingdom Office of Fair Trading on the deterrent effect of its competition enforcement. According to this study, companies perceive criminal penalties as the most important sanction for antitrust violations, followed (in descending order of importance) by disqualification of directors, adverse publicity, fines and private damages actions.[130] This study dates from before the first criminal prosecution brought by the Office of Fair Trading and the conviction of three businessmen to imprisonment of between two and a half and three years in the marine hose case in 2008.[131]

3.1.5 Imprisonment carries a uniquely strong moral message

Corporate managers are not necessarily just maximisers of profits for themselves and their principals. They may feel a moral responsibility to live within the law whether or not they are likely to be caught, and this normative commitment could trump their interest calculus.[132] Indeed, psychological research suggests that normative commitment is generally an important factor explaining compliance with the law.[133]

The public punishment of those who violate the antitrust prohibitions has thus not only a deterrent effect, in that it helps creating a credible threat of punishment for those who would be willing to commit violations on the basis of a profit calculation, but also has moral effects, in that it sends a message to the spontaneously law-abiding, reinforcing their moral commitment to the rules.[134]

Imprisonment is by far the most expressive sanction. Prison sanctions

---

129 Bloom, M. (2005), 'The Great Reformer: Mario Monti's Legacy in Article 81 and Cartel Policy', forthcoming in *Competition Policy International*, **1**, No 1 (Spring).

130 Office of Fair Trading, The deterrent effect of of competition enforcement by the OFT, Report prepared for the OFT by Deloitte, OFT962 (November 2007), at 72.

131 *See* note 68 above.

132 Stone, C.D. (1991), 'Sentencing the Corporation', *Boston University Law Review*, **71**, 383 at 389.

133 *See* Tyler, T.R. (1990), *Why People Obey the Law*, Yale University Press.

134 *See* note 6 above; *see* also Wils, W.P.J. (2006), 'Optimal Antitrust Fines: Theory and Practice', *World Competition*, **29**, 183, at 185–187, and *Efficiency and Justice in European Antitrust Enforcement*, as note 3 above, section 3.1.1.2.

not only send a special message not conveyed by fines, they also send it more effectively, as prison sentences for business people are much more newsworthy than fines and will thus get more publicity and be more noted by other business people.[135]

3.2 For which Types of Antitrust Violations is Imprisonment Desirable?

The above argument that effective deterrence with only fines on companies would require impossibly high fines, and that such fines should be supplemented by imprisonment to achieve effective deterrence, is based on the paradigmatic case of a price cartel.[136] The conclusions reached only apply to those types of violations of Articles 81 and 82 EC, which are comparable to price cartels as to their profitability and ease of concealment. For those types of infringements which are difficult to hide, or which are anyway not very profitable for the undertakings committing them, fines on companies, or fines on companies combined with director disqualification,[137] could be sufficient to achieve effective deterrence.

Secondly, because imprisonment is a much more onerous punishment than fines, the costs of imposing it erroneously are all the greater. These costs include not only the suffering of those unjustly punished, but also the risk-bearing cost to those risking unjustified punishment, the risk of lawful behavior being undesirably deterred, as well as possible negative effects on other people's normative commitment to the law.[138] Prison sanctions should therefore only be imposed in case of clear-cut violations. Alternatively one could conclude that imprisonment should only lie for wilful violations of the law, where there is evidence that the individuals knew that they were violating the law or acted with flagrant disregard for the law, with wilfulness being presumed in cases of clear-cut violations.[139]

Applying these two sets of criteria, it would seem that imprisonment is desirable for horizontal, naked price-fixing, bid-rigging and market allocation schemes. As to all other types of antitrust violations, including vertical

---

[135] G.J. Werden and M.J. Simon, as note 107 above, at 934; G.E. Lynch, as note 6 above, at 47 and 49; and D.M. Kahan, 'Social Influence, Social Meaning, and Deterrence', as note 6 above, at 383–384; see also text accompanying notes 123 and 124 above.

[136] *See* text accompanying note 91 and following above.

[137] *See* text accompanying notes 145 to 147 below on director disqualification.

[138] *See* also R.H. Kraakman, as note 111 above, at 865 and 887, and Blair, R.D. (1985), 'A Suggestion for Improved Antitrust Enforcement', *The Antitrust Bulletin*, 433, at 444, footnote 32.

[139] *See* D.I. Baker and B.A. Reeves, as note 123 above, at 623–624.

restraints, other horizontal agreements and violations of Article 82 EC, it would seem that they are usually easier to detect, as the victims of the violation will very often be aware of it, and that the risk of undesirably chilling lawful behavior is much more substantial, as the borderline between anti-competitive and pro-competitive behavior is often less obvious. For those other types of violations, fines on undertakings, or fines on undertakings combined with director disqualification, may suffice.[140]

3.3 Are there no Equally Effective Alternatives to Imprisonment?

The above argument in favour of imprisonment consists in saying, on the one hand, that hard-core cartels cannot be deterred only with fines on companies, and, on the other hand, that imprisonment constitutes an effective deterrent. But could effective deterrence not also be reached by adding other types of sanctions or remedies to fines on companies?

3.3.1 Fines on individuals

Fines on individuals would not appear to be an equally effective alternative to imprisonment. The main reason[141] is that companies can relatively easily indemnify their agents for any threat of fines or any fines effectively imposed, thus taking away the deterrent effect of the penalty on the individuals concerned. Companies can relatively easily compensate their agents in advance for taking the risk of being fined and/or indemnify them ex post when they have to pay the fine. The crucial advantage of imprisonment is that it is impossible to shift the penalty ex post, and also more difficult to arrange for a premium to compensate the risk in advance.[142]

As Donald Baker has reported a senior corporate executive telling him: 'as long as you are only talking about money, the company can at the end of the day take care of me – but once you begin talking about taking away my liberty, there is nothing that the company can do for me'.[143]

---

[140] The United Kingdom would thus in my view appear to have struck the balance right, in providing for a criminal cartel offence added to fines on undertakings and director disqualification for all types of antitrust violations; see text accompanying notes 68 and 78 above and text accompanying notes 145 to 147 below.

[141] As explained in my 2001 EUI paper, as note 91 above, another reason is that, just as for fines on companies, the level of fines required for deterrence risks being impossibly high.

[142] *See* G.J. Werden and M.J. Simon, as note 107 above, at 931, R.D. Blair, as note 138 above, at 440–441, R.H. Kraakman, as note 111 above, at 876–879, and Stone, C.D. (1980), 'The Place of Enterprise Liability in the Control of Corporate Conduct', *The Yale Law Journal*, **90**, 1, at 45–65.

[143] D. Baker, as note 24 above, at 705.

Fines on individuals may nevertheless have at least some stigmatizing effect. They could thus be considered as a third-best option, to be used when the stronger options of imprisonment and director disqualification are unavailable.[144]

3.3.2 Director disqualification

As already mentioned above, in the UK, the Enterprise Act 2002 introduced not only the criminal cartel offence, but also Competition Disqualification Orders (CDOs).[145] On application from the Office of Fair Trading, the competent court must make a CDO against a director of a company (including a de facto director) if that company commits a breach of competition law (Articles 81 or 82 EC or the corresponding prohibitions in UK competition law) and the court considers that person's conduct as a director makes him or her unfit to be concerned in the management of a company. The maximum period of disqualification under a CDO is 15 years. During the period in which a person is subject to a CDO, it is a criminal offence for him or her to be a director of a company or, in any way, whether directly or indirectly, to be concerned or take part in the management of a company.

Director disqualification would not appear to be as strong a deterrent as imprisonment. Depending on the age of the person concerned, director disqualification may simply be the occasion to move into comfortable retirement, and the company could fully compensate its former director for any financial loss. It can also only be used for directors, not for middle management. On the other hand, when it can be used, director disqualification is certainly more effective than fines on individuals. If the person concerned is not ready for retirement, being barred from taking part in the management of a company may hurt the individual concerned in a way which the company cannot fully compensate financially. Director disqualification may also have a stigmatic effect and send a moral message, not as much as imprisonment would,[146] but certainly more than fines. While

---

[144] Specifically with regard to the enforcement of Articles 81 and 82 EC at the level of the EU institutions, fines on individuals would have an advantage in that they could uncontestedly be introduced under Article 83 EC, provided that they are 'not of a criminal law nature' in the same way as the current fines on undertakings; *see* text accompanying notes 46 to 48 above. It would suffice to amend Regulation No 1/2003; *see* further note 176 below.

[145] Sections 9A to 9E of the Company Directors Disqualification Act 1986, as amended by the Enterprise Act 2002, as note 67 above; *see* also Office of Fair Trading, 'Competition disqualification orders – Guidance' (May 2003), available at: http://www.oft.gov.uk/Business/Legal+Powers/Enterprise+Act/publications.htm (accessed 19 June 2009).

[146] *See* text accompanying note 135 above.

not being an equivalently effective alternative to imprisonment, director disqualification would thus appear to be a useful complement, as well as a defendable second-best.[147]

3.3.3 Private actions for damages

Could the problem of hard-core cartels not being deterred by only fines on companies be solved by adding private follow-on actions for damages? Here, the answer is in my view clearly no.[148]

As explained above,[149] the main problem with fines on companies is that the floor below which fines will generally not deter hard-core cartels would be in the order of 150 per cent of the annual turnover in the products concerned by the violation, and that fines of such a high level would often exceed the companies' ability to pay. This problem exists just as much for damages as for fines, as well as for any combination of the two. Adding private actions for damages against companies to fines on companies also does not bring the above explained advantage of adding individual penalties, namely the increased effectiveness of leniency and whistle blowing programmes.

3.4 Five conditions for criminal antitrust enforcement to be effective not only in theory but also in practice

For criminal antitrust enforcement, and in particular imprisonment, to work as an effective deterrent, it does not suffice to enact legislation creating a criminal offence. The effective operation of such legislation much also be ensured. Indeed, deterrence will only work if there is a credible threat of detection and punishment.

As explained hereafter, for imprisonment to be an effective deterrent for hard-core cartel behavior, four conditions would need to be fulfilled: (1) a dedicated investigator and prosecutor and (2) sufficient powers of investigation must be provided for, and (3) judges or juries must be willing to convict, all of which requires (4) a sufficiently broad political and public consensus that cartels are really bad and thus deserve severe punishment.

Moreover, given that imprisonment can only work or only makes sense if it is limited to hard-core cartels and complements other penalties for companies, it remains important to provide for such other penalties as well as for penalties to deter other antitrust offences than hard-core cartels.

---

147 *See* also text accompanying notes 140 above and 178 and 179 below.
148 *See* also text accompanying notes 168 to 171 below.
149 Text accompanying note 91 and following.

3.4.1 The need for a dedicated investigator and prosecutor

For the threat of imprisonment to be credible, there must be a sufficiently well resourced and sufficiently dedicated body, or bodies, in charge of investigating and prosecuting criminal antitrust offences.

In the US, the Department of Justice Antitrust Division has a National Criminal Enforcement Section in Washington, DC, as well as seven field offices, in Atlanta, Chicago, Cleveland, Dallas, New York, Philadelphia, and San Francisco, dedicated to investigating and prosecuting criminal cases.

The absence of a sufficiently well-resourced and dedicated investigator and prosecutor may to a significant extent explain the ineffectiveness of criminal enforcement in those EU Member States which have decriminalised their enforcement in the last two decades.[150] Indeed, if antitrust offences have to compete with manslaughter and child abuse cases for the attention of a (typically already over-stretched) generalist public prosecutor's office, they are most unlikely to get much priority.

3.4.2 The need for adequate powers of investigation

The success of US criminal antitrust enforcement in recent years is also the result of the strong powers of investigation which the US Department of Justice Antitrust Division has at its disposal.[151]

First, as Terry Calvani has described: 'the Division began using special agents of the Federal Bureau of Investigations ('FBI') to assist in its cartel investigations. FBI agents now routinely staff these investigations. Indeed, agents are actually seconded to the Division field offices where they work together with Division attorneys in jointly investigating cartels. [T]hese FBI agents have brought with them the investigative techniques used to combat serious crime. Antitrust investigators now routinely employ computer forensics, 'wire' witnesses, conduct 'ambush' interviews, etc., in the course of investigations'.[152]

Second, the US Department of Justice has both a Corporate Leniency Policy and an Individual Leniency Policy, under which it can guarantee

---

150 *See* text accompanying notes 70 to 76 above.

151 Apart from the three elements mentioned in text accompanying notes 152 to 156, Donald Baker also mentions the grand jury system, a secretive process favouring the investigators; see D.I. Baker, as note 24 above, at 693, 697 and 708.

152 T. Calvani, as note 125 above, at 7–8. It should be noted that the existence of a leniency programme does not dispense with the need to have other effective powers of investigation. Indeed, leniency can only work if potential leniency applicants know that the competition authorities are also able to detect cartels without co-operation from leniency applicants; see *Principles of European Antitrust Enforcement*, as note 2 above, section 5.2.3, and *Efficiency and Justice in European Antitrust Enforcement*, as note 3 above, section 5.2.3.2.

immunity from prosecution to co-operating companies or individuals. It can also make precisely calculated promises of reduced penalties to those co-operating at a later stage that cannot benefit from immunity.[153] As already explained above,[154] if leniency policies exist both for companies and for individuals, and are well integrated, leniency will be more effective. However, if leniency (including immunity) is not available for individuals, the addition of criminal penalties for individuals will decrease the effectiveness of leniency. At least to the extent that they care about their staff, companies will be less inclined to apply for leniency, as this will expose their staff to punishment. Even if they do not care about their staff, companies may not be able to make useful leniency applications, as their staff will not be willing to co-operate for fear of incriminating themselves. It thus appears essential, when adding criminal penalties for individuals to corporate fines, to provide also for leniency (including immunity) for individuals. This conclusion is confirmed, on the one hand, by the experience of the successful combined application by the US Department of Justice of its Corporate Leniency Policy and its Leniency Policy for Individuals, and, on the other hand, by the example of Germany, where criminal penalties for individuals exist for bid-rigging, without a corresponding possibility for leniency, with the result that the German competition authority, which has an otherwise functioning leniency programme for companies, has never received a leniency application in a bid-rigging case.[155]

Third, as already mentioned above, in the US companies cannot invoke the privilege against self-incrimination enshrined in the 5th Amendment to the US Constitution.[156]

3.4.3 Judges and juries must be willing to convict

For the threat of imprisonment to be credible, it is also essential that judges and juries are willing to convict antitrust offenders and sentence them to prison.[157]

---

153 *See* Wils, W.P.J. (2007), 'Leniency in Antitrust Anforcement: Theory and Practice', *World Competition*, **30**, 25; Schmidtchen, D., M. Albert and S. Voigt (eds) (2007), 'The More Economic Approach to European Competition Law', *Conferences on New Political Economy,* 24; Germany: Mohr Siebeck, 203–254; and *Efficiency and Justice in European Antitrust Enforcement*, as note 3 above, chapter 5.

154 Text accompanying notes 114 to 118.

155 *See* 'Leniency in Antitrust Anforcement: Theory and Practice', as note 153 above, at 55–57, and *Efficiency and Justice in European Antitrust Enforcement*, as note 153 above, section 5.4.1.

156 *See* note 41 above.

157 *See* P.F. Kunzlik, as note 82 above, at 345–346 and N. Green, as note 23 above, at 26–28.

In the US, this is the case today, thanks at least in part to the Sentencing Guidelines.[158]

In the United Kingdom, the first indications from the marine hose case are very encouraging.[159] The three defendants in this case were sentenced to terms of imprisonment of between two and a half and three years.[160] Moreover, in sentencing, Judge Rivlin stated that he had taken into account that this was the first prosecution under the cartel offence and that the conduct had commenced some time prior to it being criminalised. He expressly stated that these mitigating factors would not be available to future defendants and that future sentences for serious cartel offences are likely to be higher.[161]

3.4.4 The need for political and public support

Underlying the three conditions above is a more fundamental fourth one, namely that there needs to be a sufficiently broad political and public consensus that cartels are really bad and thus deserve severe punishment.

In Donald Baker's words:

> When all is said and done, criminal liability ought to reflect the culture and values of the people of a country. The United States has a long tradition of fairly broad and sometimes noisy support of antitrust law and enforcement. After all, this is what created the Sherman Act in 1890 and the felony statute in 1974. Robber barons and cartel conspirators are bad people in the American popular lexicon.[162]

As is well known, Europe does not have the same history.[163] However, we are not condemned to remain stuck in our past. As John Coffee has pointed out: 'the limited empirical evidence on public attitudes toward white-collar crimes suggests that the public learns what is criminal from what is punished, not vice versa'.[164] Leadership, as that which has been shown by the Irish and United Kingdom governments and competition authorities in criminalising cartel enforcement, can thus work.

---

158 D.I. Baker, as note 24 above, at 694. It was not always the case in earlier times; *see* D.I. Baker and B.A. Reeves, as note 123 above.

159 *See* note 68 above.

160 Longer than the prison terms to which they were sentenced in the US pursuant to the plea agreement with the US Department of Justice; *see* note 68 above.

161 Freshfield Bruckhaus Deringer briefing 'Landmark criminal convictions for cartel activity' (June 2008) at 2.

162 D.I. Baker, as note 24 above, at 714.

163 *See* text accompanying notes 82 to 89 above; *The Optimal Enforcement of EC Antitrust Law*, as note 4 above, sections 8.6.7 and 9.5; and Harding, C. and J. Joshua (2003), *Regulating Cartels in Europe*, Oxford: Oxford University Press.

164 J.C. Coffee, as note 7 above, at 1889.

3.4.5 Fines on companies and public penalties for other antitrust violations than hard-core cartels remain necessary

Imprisonment as a penalty for hard-core cartels should only be used in combination with fines on the companies concerned.[165] Indeed, if firms were not responsible for the antitrust violations committed by their agents, serious incentive problems would result. Given that the firm normally benefits from the antitrust violations committed by its agents, it would have an incentive to encourage violations. Even if they risk individual penalties, the firm's agents may be willing to take the risk if they expect to be sufficiently rewarded in terms of salary and promotion (or avoidance of demotion or dismissal). Assigning liability to the firm tends to remove the incentive for both the firm and its agents to commit antitrust violations on behalf of the firm.[166] Firms are instead encouraged to strive for clarity in the messages conveyed to their agents as to the behavior they expect from them.[167]

As argued above,[168] imprisonment appears only desirable for horizontal, naked price-fixing, bid-rigging and market allocation schemes. However, all other types of antitrust violations, including vertical restraints, other horizontal agreements and violations of Article 82 EC, also need to be deterred. As already mentioned above,[169] in the US, apart from the possibility for the Federal Trade Commission to seek disgorgement, deterrence of other antitrust violations than hard-core cartels is left to private treble-damage suits. As has also been observed by some Americans, this could be considered as problematic.[170] Indeed, as I have argued in detail elsewhere, private antitrust enforcement is inherently inferior to public enforcement as a means to achieve optimal deter-

---

165 *See* also text accompanying notes 114 to 120 above, as to the increased effectiveness of leniency and whistle-blowing programmes resulting from the combination of corporate and individual liability, and my 2001 EUI paper, as note 91 above, for other reasons why imprisonment should only be used in combination with corporate fines.

166 Ulen, T.S. (1997), *The Economic Case for Corporate Criminal Sanctioning*, in W.S. Lofquist, M.A. Cohen and G.A. Rabe (eds) *Debating Corporate Crime*, Anderson Press, 117, at 133, and J.C. Coffee, as note 112 above, at 410.

167 DeMott, D.A. (1997), 'Organizational Incentives to Care About the Law', *Law and Contemporary Problems*, **60**, 39, at 47.

168 Text accompanying notes 136 to 140.

169 Text accompanying notes 35 to 37.

170 *See* letter from the Assistant Attorney General, Department of Justice Antitrust Division, as in note 35 above, at 2 ('Our system's extreme weighting of the civil enforcement balance toward private lawsuits as opposed to federal government enforcement is not necessarily ideal.').

rence.[171] The United Kingdom, with its combination of a criminal cartel offence with a system of administrative fines and director disqualification for all types of antitrust violations, would in my view appear to have struck the balance exactly right.

4 IS IT PROBLEMATIC THAT ANTITRUST ENFORCEMENT IS CRIMINALISED AT THE LEVEL OF INDIVIDUAL EU MEMBER STATES WITHOUT PARALLEL CRIMINALISATION AT THE LEVEL OF THE EU INSTITUTIONS, OR WITHOUT EU HARMONISATION?

4.1 Regulation No 1/2003 has been Designed to Accommodate Criminalisation in Individual Member States

The fact that individual Member States, such as Ireland, the United Kingdom and Estonia, have criminalised their enforcement of Articles 81 and 82 EC, without parallel criminalisation at the level of the EU institutions and without EU harmonisation, is not problematic. Indeed, Regulation No 1/2003 has precisely been designed to accommodate criminalisation in individual Member States.

As already explained above,[172] Article 5 of Regulation No 1/2003 leaves each Member State the choice whether or not to provide for criminal penalties to enforce Articles 81 and 82 EC.

Article 12(3) of Regulation No 1/2003, also already mentioned above,[173] ensures that criminal enforcement in some Member States can co-exist with non-criminal enforcement in other Member States. Indeed, whereas Article 12(1) of Regulation No 1/2003 provides that the European Commission and the competition authorities of the Member States can

---

[171] Wils, W.P.J. (2003), 'Should Private Antitrust Enforcement Be Encouraged in Europe?', *World Competition*, **26**, 473, and *Principles of European Antitrust Enforcement*, as note 2 above, chapter 4; see also leading article 'MS.dosh settlement – Microsoft's pay-offs show why regulators are necessary', *Financial Times*, 26 November 2004, p. 12; Kay, J. (2004), 'Antitrust concerns are not so easily dismissed', *Financial Times*, 30 November 2004, p. 13; and Groom, B., European Comment, 'Microsoft's Brussels trouble not over yet', *Financial Times*, 10 November 2004, p. 16: 'It is a comfort that competition policy in Europe is pursued largely by public authorities rather than through private lawsuits. Rival companies can be bought off, but the [European] Commission's role is to safeguard consumers.'

[172] Text accompanying notes 56 to 57.

[173] Text accompanying notes 56 to 57.

exchange all kinds of information, and use the information thus exchanged in evidence, Article 12(3) adds the following limitation:

> Information exchanged pursuant to paragraph 1 can only be used in evidence to impose sanctions on natural persons where:
> - the law of the transmitting authority foresees sanctions of a similar kind in relation to an infringement of [Articles 81 or 82 EC] or, in the absence thereof,
> - the information has been collected in a way which respects the same level of protection of the rights of defence of natural persons as provided for under the national rules of the receiving authority. However, in this case, the information exchanged cannot be used by the receiving authority to impose custodial sanctions.

Without this limitation, the free circulation of information between the competition authorities of all the Member States as well as the European Commission would have caused problems both in the Member States which provide for individual penalties, in particular imprisonment, and in the other Member States as well as at the level of the EU institutions. Indeed, if in Ireland or in the United Kingdom individuals could have been sent to prison on the basis of evidence collected by the European Commission or for instance the Italian competition authority in their administrative proceedings leading only to fines on companies, the rights of defence of the individuals concerned would have been weakened. Indeed, the Irish and United Kingdom courts would probably have refused the use of such evidence. On the other hand, the risk of evidence collected by the European Commission or the Italian competition authority in their administrative proceedings leading only to fines on companies being subsequently used in Ireland or the United Kingdom to send individuals to prison, could have led the EC and Italian courts or legislators to raise the level of the rights of defence in proceedings by the European Commission or the Italian competition authority to the same level at that applying to criminal investigations in Ireland or the United Kingdom. This could have seriously harmed the effectiveness of the investigations by the European Commission or the Italian competition authority.[174]

All these problems have been avoided as a result of Article 12(3), whereas this provision does not create any obstacle to the competition authorities of Ireland, the United Kingdom, Estonia, and any other Member State which may follow their example, exchanging all information between them and using it in evidence to have individuals convicted and sent to prison.

---

[174] *See* further *Principles of European Antitrust Enforcement*, as note 2 above, section 1.2.12.

Article 12(3) of Regulation No 1/2003 prevents information collected in a jurisdiction that does not provide for imprisonment to be used in evidence in another jurisdiction to seek imprisonment. It does not, however, prevent the intelligence being transmitted. The United Kingdom competition authorities could thus for instance, after having received information from the European Commission or the Italian competition authority, start an investigation of their own to collect themselves the same or related information and subsequently use it in evidence to have an individual convicted and sent to prison. This possibility could have as a result that individuals, as well as the undertakings wanting to protect these individuals, may be less willing to co-operate with the investigations of the European Commission or the Italian competition authority. To the extent that co-operation under leniency programmes is concerned, this problem has been anticipated and addressed in the European Commission's Notice on co-operation within the network of competition authorities, which provides that information provided under a leniency programme to the European Commission or a national competition authority will not be transmitted to another competition authority unless the latter commits itself not to use this information, nor any information obtained following that information, to impose sanctions on the leniency applicant or on any of its employees or former employees.[175]

4.2 What would be the Advantages of Criminalising the Enforcement of EU Antitrust Law in all Member States, through EU Harmonisation, as well as at the Level of the EU Institutions?

The fact that Regulation No 1/2003 has been designed to accommodate criminalisation in individual Member States, without EU harmonisation, and without criminalisation of antitrust enforcement at the level of the EU institutions, with the result that criminalisation in individual Member States is not problematic, does not exclude that there may be advantages in criminalising the enforcement of EU antitrust law in all Member States, through EU harmonisation, as well as at the level of the EU institutions.[176]

---

[175] Commission Notice on co-operation within the Network of Competition Authorities, [2004] OJ C101/43, paragraphs 37 to 42; *see* also D. Schnichels, as note 66 above, at 114–115, and *Principles of European Antitrust Enforcement*, as note 2 above, section 1.2.14.

[176] As to the question whether this would require an amendment of the EC or EU Treaties, *see* my 2001 EUI paper, as note 91 above; Zuleeg, M. (2003), *Criminal Sanctions to Be Imposed on Individuals As Enforcement Instruments in European Competition Law*, published in C.D. Ehlermann and I. Atanasiu, *European*

I would personally expect that criminal cartel enforcement for instance in the United Kingdom will prove to be effective, even if enforcement in most other Member States and at the level of the EU institutions continues to rely only on fines on companies, in the same way as US criminal antitrust enforcement has for the past years been highly successful,[177] even if most of the rest of the world did not have similar enforcement. I would however see three or four advantages in criminalising the enforcement of EU antitrust law in all Member States, through EU harmonisation, as well as at the level of the EU institutions.

First, as explained above,[178] Article 12(3) of Regulation No 1/2003 provides, for very good reasons, that the competition authorities in Member States such as the United Kingdom can only use information exchanged in the network of EU competition authorities in evidence in order to have individuals convicted to prison if the information has been collected by the competition authority of a jurisdiction which equally provides for imprisonment. If all EU Member States were to follow the United Kingdom example in criminalising their enforcement of hard-core cartels, either on their own motion or as a result of EU harmonisation, and if also enforcement at the level of the EU institutions could be similarly criminalised, there would be an obvious advantage in that more competition authorities could more effectively work together in investigating criminal cartel offences.

Secondly, more widespread or harmonised criminalisation throughout the EU would enhance the effectiveness of sanctions, allowing for instance individuals suspected or convicted of a criminal cartel offence to be extradited between Member States, or the effect of director disqualifications to be EU-wide.

Thirdly, as explained above,[179] Article 12(3) of Regulation No 1/2003

Competition Law Annual 2001: Effective Private Enforcement of EC Antitrust Law, Oxford: Hart Publishing, 453; *Efficiency and Justice in European Antitrust Enforcement*, as note 3 above, section 6.5; Ladenburger, C. (2008), 'Police and Criminal Law in the Treaty of Lisbon – A New Dimension for the Community Method', *European Constitutional Law Review*, **4**, 20; and the Judgment of the Court of Justice of 23 October 2007 in Case C-440/05 *Commission v Council* [2007] ECR I-9097. In the end, of course, the main issue is whether the European Commission and the EU Member States would want to criminalise the enforcement of EU competition law at the level of the EU institutions and/or, through harmonisation, in all Member States. The day there is a consensus that this outcome would be desirable, it will also be possible to make whatever Treaty changes might be needed.

177 *See* text accompanying notes 123 to 129 above.

178 Text accompanying notes 173 to 175.

179 Text accompanying notes 173 to 175.

prevents information collected in a jurisdiction that does not provide for imprisonment to be used in evidence in another jurisdiction to seek imprisonment, and the European Commission's Notice on co-operation within the network of competition authorities provides that information provided under a leniency programme to the European Commission or a national competition authority will not be transmitted to another competition authority unless the latter commits itself not to use this information, nor any information obtained following that information, to impose sanctions on the leniency applicant or on any of its employees or former employees.

The risk of imprisonment in some Member States, and the exchange of intelligence within the network of competition authorities may however still have an impact on the effectiveness of investigations by the competition authorities in the other Member States or by the European Commission in the absence of leniency applications.[180] Indeed, the risk of imprisonment may lead cartel participants to make even greater efforts to hide the evidence of their behavior, and the possibility of intelligence being transmitted to the competition authorities in for example the United Kingdom may reduce the willingness of individuals, and of the undertakings wanting to protect them, to co-operate outside the framework of leniency with investigations by the European Commission or for example the Italian competition authority. Individuals may for instance be less forthcoming in answering on-the-spot questions during inspections,[181] or companies may be more evasive in their answers to written requests for information.

Fourthly, criminalisation in some EU Member States, and not in others, nor at the level of the EU institutions, could result in those Member States that have criminal enforcement playing a disproportionate role,

---

[180] The ability of competition authorities to detect cartels in the absence of leniency applications is also important for the effectiveness of leniency programmes. Indeed, if companies were to believe that the competition authorities would not be able to detect a cartel on their own, they will have no reason to apply for leniency either; *see* note 152 above.

[181] *See* text accompanying note 53 above as to such questioning under Article 20(2)(e) of Regulation No 1/2003; *see* also Venit, J.S. and T. Louko (2004), 'The Commission's New Power to Question and its Implications on Human Rights', paper presented at the 31st Annual Fordham Corporate Law Institute Conference on International Antitrust Law & Policy (New York, 8 October), as well as remarks by several participants in Roundtable Debate Session IV – Rights, Privileges and Ethics in Competition Cases at the same conference, all in Hawk, B.E. (2005), (ed.) *2004 Annual Proceedings of the Fordham Corporate Law Institute – International Antitrust Law and Policy*, New York: Juris Publishing.

or carrying a disproportionate share of the burden, in the overall task of enforcing EU competition law, in the same way as the US in the last two decades has played a disproportionate role in deterring and punishing worldwide cartels.[182]

Specifically with regard to the role of the European Commission in the overall task of enforcing EU competition law, Peter Kunzlik has made the following conjecture of what might happen if criminal enforcement in Ireland and the United Kingdom is successful, and other EU Member States follow their example: 'the situation might well arise in which cartels will be uncovered and prosecuted more efficiently at the national level than at the European level. In such a scenario the European Commission's view that its proper vocation is primarily in the enforcement of Community competition law against hard-core cartels – a central premise of its own modernization proprosals – may need to be revisited. By the time that the Commission's investigations will have cranked into gear, the national systems may already have taken the initiative. The Commission may in practice lose its central role in European cartel enforcement to quicker, more effective, and better-resourced national competition authorities operating under [systems such as the ones in Ireland and the United Kingdom]'.[183]

In 2007, Commissioner Kroes gave the following answer on behalf of

---

182 *See The Optimal Enforcement of EC Antitrust Law*, as note 4 above, section 8.7.3.3.

183 P.F. Kunzlik, as note 82 above, at 352–353; *see* also *idem*, at 347–348: 'If the approach adopted in [Ireland and the United Kingdom] were to be emulated by other member states then transatlantic cartel enforcement co-operation might become substantially refocused upon the national rather than the European level. This would, in turn, affect the prestige of the European Commission within the European system. It might potentially take back from the Commission, and return to the authorities of the member states concerned, the de facto role as primary collaborators with the U.S. in terms of an important aspect of transatlantic cartel enforcement co-operation'. *See* also Calkins, S. (2007), *Coming to Praise Criminal Antitrust Enforcement*, in C.D. Ehlermann and I. Atanasiu (eds), *European Competition Law Annual 2006: Enforcement of Prohibition of Cartels*, Oxford: Hart Publishing, 343 at 362: 'If criminal enforcement with serious penalties becomes a reality in several national systems, would the Commission, like the US [Federal Trade Commission] with the [US Department of Justice], feel obliged to refer evidence of cartel behavior to another enforcer? Might the Commission wait for national enforcement to end, and then supplement national enforcement by seeking monetary payments – much as the US state or private enforcers follow federal government actions? Or would national courts achieve full relief – leaving the Commission, like the US [Federal Trade Commission], to challenge some mergers and questionable conduct less egregious than cartels?'.

the European Commission to a parliamentary question about the desirability of introducing individual penalties for managers in cartel cases:

> the Commission agrees that individual sanctions on managers may provide for an additional deterrent on the actual actors in a cartel. However, the current Community level enforcement system has been built around sanctions on undertakings, and Council Regulation (EC) No 1/2003 only provides for that type of sanctions. Accordingly, the delineation of the Commission's powers of investigation, the scope of the rights of defence and other institutional and procedural issues are geared towards imposing sanctions on undertakings. This system is not necessarily well suited to sanctions on individuals (e.g. criminal sanctions). The introduction of such sanctions would require far-reaching change to the Commission's investigative system in terms of rights of defence, investigative powers and institutional terms. Such a development is, therefore, unlikely in the foreseeable future. It is important to note that Member States may impose sanctions against individuals for participation in cartels under their respective national laws and that several Member States (Ireland, the United Kingdom and others) already have legislation in place that provides for sanctions against individuals. Their experience in the next years will be crucial to show whether the introduction of such sanctions will pay off for the respective Member States in terms of efficient and effective enforcement. The Commission is convinced that fines imposed on companies under its current system are an effective tool to fight cartels. Set at a sufficiently deterrent level, financial sanctions on companies will have a strong effect on companies and their managers and employees so as not to enter into illegal cartel agreements.[184]

---

184 Answer given by Mrs Kroes on behalf of the Commission (21 June 2007) to written question P-2656/07 by Toine Manders MEP, 'Tackling the formation of cartels', available at: http://www.europarl.europa.eu/QP-WEB/application/search.do (accessed 19 June 2009).

11. Private Enforcement in Europe

Andreas Heinemann*

1 INTRODUCTION

1.1 Starting Point

When we talk about the main topics of competition law development in Europe, private enforcement certainly is one of them. In Europe, private enforcement always has been a subject of strong interest in theory, but of minor importance in practice. There have been some exceptions: It occurred regularly that defendants pleaded the antitrust nullity of contractual obligations (the so-called *Eurodefence* as far as the violation of European competition law is alleged). And in some countries, special types of action have been pursued on the plaintiff's side, e.g. actions for delivery in cases of a refusal to deal. Recently, however, things are about to change. In the wake of the vitamin cartel, actions for damages have been pursued in a couple of EU Member States (and of course in other parts of the world). Generally speaking, compensatory claims have made their entrance into court practice, at least in some European countries. The German Federal Cartel Office (*Bundeskartellamt*) has counted 300 damage claims in antitrust matters in Germany since 2005, with upward tendency.[1]

1.2 Recent Developments

This development has several reasons. Public awareness has increased. Although there have been particularly blatant cartels in the past, the strengthening of sanctions seems to have contributed to this effect. One consequence is that victims of competition law violations do not accept

* Professor of Law, Member of the board of the Europa Institute, University of Zurich, Switzerland.

[1] *See* the indications in *Frankfurter Allgemeine Zeitung* of 7 July 2008, p. 13.

any longer to bear the financial consequences of anticompetitive behavior. A change in legal culture seems to take place in Europe.[2] Moreover, there is a strong political will to strengthen private enforcement. The European legislature has justified Regulation 1/2003 (bringing about a fundamental reform of competition law enforcement) in part with the aim of strengthening the decentralised application of European competition law by private remedies.[3] The ECJ has, in its *Courage* and *Manfredi* judgments, underlined the importance of private enforcement.[4] As a result, some obstacles to private claims have been removed, for example as regards standing, prescription and the exclusion of claims based on the involvement of the claimant in the anticompetitive behavior. As far as Germany is concerned, the amendment of the German 'Law against Restraints of Competition' (*Gesetz gegen Wettbewerbsbeschränkungen: 'GWB'*) by the 7th Cartel Reform from 2005 has substantially alleviated the conditions for private claims.

At present, initiatives of the European Commission have accelerated momentum. In 2005, the Commission presented a Green Paper on Damages Actions for Breach of the EC Competition Rules which explores the main obstacles to private damages claims and proposes different options in favour of a stronger role of private remedies.[5] On this basis, the Commission has published in April 2008 a White Paper which contains specific proposals supposed to remedy the deficiencies of private enforcement in Europe.[6] Some 170 comments have been submitted which go in

---

[2] Most authors welcome this development. For dissenting or at least more cautious views *see* Möschel, W. (2006), 'Erweiterter Privatrechtsschutz im Kartellrecht?' *WuW*, 115; Wils, W (2003), 'Should Private Antitrust Enforcement Be Encouraged in Europe?', *World Competition,* **26**, 473.

[3] *See* Monti, M. (2004), *Private Litigation as a Key Complement to Public Enforcement of Competition rules*, 17 September, SPEECH/04/403, available at: http://europa.eu/rapid/searchAction.do (accessed 19 June 2009).

[4] ECJ, 20 September 2001, C-453/99, *Courage and Crehan* [2001] ECR I-6297; ECJ, 13 July 2006, Joined Cases C-295/04 to C-298/04, *Manfredi* [2006] ECR I-6619.

[5] European Commission, *Green Paper on Damages Actions for Breach of the EC Antitrust Rules*, 19 December 2005, COM(2005) 672 final. *See* also European Commission, *Commission Staff Working Paper – Annex to the Green Paper on Damages Actions for Breach of the EC Antitrust Rules*, 19 December 2005, SEC(2005) 1732.

[6] European Commission, *White Paper on Damages Actions for Breach of the EC Antitrust Rules*, 2 April 2008, COM(2008) 165 final. *See* also European Commission, *Commission Staff Working Paper accompanying the White Paper on Damages Actions for Breach of the EC Antitrust Rules*, SEC(2008) 404.

all possible directions.[7] At this stage, it is open if eventually new legal instruments will be adopted.[8]

1.3 Comparison to US Law

In the US, the ratio of private antitrust suits to administrative procedures is about 10:1 – in favour of private enforcement. The importance of private litigation is due to specific incentives and to procedural alleviations. According to the Clayton Act, s. 4 the victim of anticompetitive behavior is entitled to treble damages. Clients can agree with their lawyers on contingency fees thus increasing the incentives for them to take action. This is particularly important for class actions which are often instigated by lawyers. Class actions make it attractive to sue even if the damage incurred by each single party is very low and would not justify to file a suit for one single victim. American class actions follow the *opt out* principle, i.e. all members of the class are included in the procedure unless they have expressly opposed. As regards civil procedure, pre-trial discovery facilitates access to evidence in the hands of the other party or of third parties. Finally, the constitutional right to a jury trial is held responsible for the fact that the conditions for antitrust responsibility are sometimes applied rather generously and that the amount of damages is fixed rather high.

Given the success of private enforcement in the US, the discussion in Europe has to take into account the framework of US law. However, the view is widespread that the US style litigation culture has paved the way for judicial proceedings which not always serve the interests of the injured parties in the first place, but rather those of their lawyers or other agents.[9] Therefore, a solution has to be found, which removes obstacles to private antitrust litigation, but, at the same time, avoids excessive litigation.

---

7 Available at: http://ec.europa.eu/comm/competition/antitrust/actionsdamages/white_paper_comments.html (accessed 19 June 2009).

8 For the perspectives of the White Paper *see* e.g. Bulst, F. (2008), 'Of Arms and Armor – The European Commission's White Paper on Damages Actions for Breach of EC Antitrust Law', *Bucerius Law Journal*, **81**, 94 et seq.

9 But *see*, *The Next Antitrust Agenda: The American Antitrust Institute's Transition Report on Competition Policy to the 44th President of the United States* (6 October 2008), available at http://www.antitrustinstitute.org/Archives/transitionreport.ashx (accessed 19 June 2009), p. 219 et seq, where private enforcement in the US is defended against the accusation of excessive litigation and overdeterrence.

1.4 Outline

The relevant problems may be classified in questions of substantive law, of civil procedure and of the relationship between private actions and administrative enforcement. Since not all of them can be discussed here, a choice has to be made.[10] In our view, the most important questions concern standing, passing on, the calculation of damages, the access to evidence and the tensions between private enforcement and leniency policy. Some of these points exclusively refer to damage claims, others are relevant for injunctive relief, too, which for victims of an infringement sometimes is the crucial concern. Given the limited space, it cannot be distinguished here between restrictive agreements and the abuse of a dominant position.[11] Therefore, the examples often concern hard-core price cartels.

2 STANDING

2.1 Legal Basis of Competition Law Claims

In some European countries special antitrust claims exist, in other countries resort is had to general civil law. Special antitrust claims exist for example in Germany, Ireland, Italy and Sweden, while in Austria, Denmark, France, the Netherlands, and the UK general tort law (in conjunction with competition law interdictions) is relied upon. It would be preferable to have special rules on antitrust claims everywhere: This would serve, on the one hand, the interests of clarity, that is in the sense that such private law claims exist at all. On the other hand, it would enable the legislator to provide for certain rules which apply specifically to competition law, and which accordingly should not be regulated under general civil law (e.g. details on interest debts, interruption of prescription because of administrative proceedings, binding effect of administrative decisions, etc.).

---

[10] For a comprehensive discussion of all relevant questions see Basedow, J. (2007), (ed), *Private Enforcement of EC Competition Law*; Ehlermann, C.-D. and I. Atanasiu (2003), (eds), *European Competition Law Annual 2001: Effective Private Enforcement of EC Antitrust Law*; Jones, C. (1999), *Private Enforcement of Antitrust Law in the EU, UK and USA*; Komninos, A. (2008), *EC Private Antitrust Enforcement*; Möllers, T. and A. Heinemann (2007), (eds), *The Enforcement of Competition Law in Europe*.

[11] For an analysis of the private enforcement of Article 82 EC *see* the contributions of Ezrachi, A., F. Garcia Cachafeiro, M.-O. Mackenrodt and H. Schmidt (2008), in M.-O. Mackenrodt, B. Conde Gallego and S. Enchelmaier (eds) *Abuse of Dominant Position: New Interpretation, New Enforcement Mechanisms?*

As regards violations of European competition law, the *Courage* decision has led to a controversy on the nature of private remedies. Some authors draw a parallel to the liability of member states according to the principles of the *Francovich* case[12] and qualify the action for damages resulting from the violation of European competition law as a claim directly deriving from community law.[13] On the other hand, the predominant opinion holds the traditional view that such claims are rooted in national law which is simply modified by Community law via the principle of effectiveness (developed by the ECJ in its *Courage* decision).[14] No matter which opinion one shares: Up until now the subject of private remedies has not yet been regulated in European secondary law. Uncertainties in the application of private remedies are the consequence.

2.2 US Law

The risk of private litigation increases if there are no precise rules on standing, i.e. on the question who can take legal action. US law shows that the question of standing in private antitrust litigation is highly problematic. The US Supreme Court ruled in 1977 in *Illinois Brick Co. v Illinois* that indirect purchasers have no standing for compensatory claims based on section 4 of the Clayton Act.[15] This was a direct consequence of the decision in *Hanover Shoe Inc v United Shoe Machinery Corp.*[16] Here the US Supreme Court had decided that the respondent could not defend itself against an antitrust claim on the grounds that the claimant had shifted the overcharge (the increase in price due to the cartel agreement) onto the next market level. Under American law the direct victim of an antitrust

---

12 ECJ, 19 November 1991, Joined Cases C-6/90 and C-9/90, *Francovich/Italy*, [1991] ECR I-5357.

13 *See* e.g. Jones, C., *supra* note 10, at 152; Mäsch, G. (2003), 'Private Ansprüche bei Verstößen gegen das europäische Kartellverbot – *Courage* und die Folgen', *Europarecht*, 825, 841 et seq. In this sense already the Advocate General W. van Gerven, in: ECJ, Case C-128/92, *Banks/British Coal Corporation*, [1994] ECR I-1209; differing van Gerven, W. (2000), 'Of Rights, Remedies and Procedures', CMLR 501 (503).

14 Lettl, T. (2003), 'Der Schadensersatzanspruch gemäß § 823 Abs. 2 BGB i.V. mit Article 81 EG' (2003) ZHR 476; Weyer, H. (2003), 'Schadensersatzansprüche gegen Private kraft Gemeinschaftsrecht', *ZeuP*, 318, 325 et seq); Wurmnest, W. (2003/4), 'Das Gemeinschaftsdeliktsrecht in der aktuellen Rechtsprechung der Gemeinschaftsgerichte', *GPR*, 129, 135.

15 431 US 720 (1977).

16 392 US 481 (1968). For a detailed analysis of these two decisions see Bulst, F. (2006), *Schadensersatzansprüche der Marktgegenseite im Kartellrecht*, 64, et seq.

infringement can thus claim damages even if it from a common sense view is no longer suffering loss, as it has completely passed on the losses to the next market level by selling the products in question at higher prices. In *Illinois Brick* the Supreme Court drew the (negative) conclusion for the standing of indirect purchasers: As the direct purchaser can already claim full compensation, an involvement of the indirect purchaser is no longer possible. Otherwise there would be a duplicating of the claim.

2.3 The Legal Situation in Europe

The question of standing is far from clear in Europe. The ECJ has said in its *Courage* decision that 'any individual' can claim damages for loss caused to him by a contract or conduct liable to restrict or distort competition.[17] However, this is not interpreted in a uniform manner. In this regard, the development in Germany is particularly interesting. Until 2005, the majority of courts only awarded damages when the restriction of competition was directly aimed at the claimant. This rule excluded private claims not only of indirect purchasers but also of direct purchasers in case of industry-wide cartels not directed against a particular enterprise. Under the influence of the *Courage* decision, and because it made not much sense to exempt the most encompassing cartels from civil liability, the law was changed in 2005. According to the new law, anybody 'affected' by a forbidden behavior has claims for injunctions or damages. 'Affected' under the terms of the law are 'competitors or other market participants impaired by the infringement' (§ 33 (1) s. 3 GWB). Nevertheless, some scholars stick to the view that standing should be restricted.[18] This corresponds to tendencies in other European countries. In the UK for example, it is at present not clear if the prejudice of indirect purchasers is not too remote to be covered by damages claims.[19]

As the case law of the US Supreme Court has shown, the question of

---

17 ECJ, 20 September 2001, C-453/99, *Courage and Crehan* [2001] ECR I-6297 n. 26.

18 Bornkamm, J., in E. Langen and H.-J. Bunte (2006), (eds), *Kommentar zum deutschen und europäischen Kartellrecht, Volume 1 – Deutsches Kartellrecht* (10th edition) § 33 GWB n. 36 et seq.; Koch, J. (2005), 'Kartellrechtliche Schadensersatzansprüche mittelbar betroffener Marktteilnehmer nach § 33 GWB n.F', *WuW*, 1210.

19 *See* Beard, D. (2006), 'Damages in competition law litigation in the United Kingdom', in Ligue Internationale du Droit de la concurrence (LIDC), *Should private enforcement (actions for damages) of competition law be encouraged, and if so, through what concrete measures?*, 12 et seq, available at: www.ligue.org/de/homepage/workshops/nat._reporters (accessed 19 June 2009).

standing for indirect purchasers is closely linked to the problem of 'passing on'. Before tackling this question, the special situation of consumers in antitrust law has to be considered.

2.4 Consumers, Consumer Associations, Group Actions

2.4.1 Starting point

In some countries, only enterprises, but not consumers, will be seen as falling within the protection of competition law. The fear is widespread that otherwise the circle of potential claimants would become immeasurably wide. The result is paradoxical: Although competition is intended to bring about the best results for the consumer in the interest of consumer sovereignty, these very consumers are denied standing. This should be changed. Otherwise consumers would depend on the intervention of a competition authority or of enterprises asserting their own claims. Moreover, as regards infringements of European competition law, the exclusion of indirect purchasers or consumers does not seem compatible with the requirements given by the ECJ in its *Courage* decision.[20]

The fear of a vast number of lawsuits does not seem justified. On the contrary, the incentives for consumers to pursue such claims are small. Although the macroeconomic harm of cartel arrangements is immense, the resulting harm to the ultimate consumer can be so fragmented that the pursuit of an independent claim is not worthwhile. Therefore, standing should be granted to consumer associations, not only for cessation claims, but also for compensatory claims.

2.4.2 Proposals of the European Commission in the White Paper

In this sense, the European Commission has proposed two mechanisms of collective redress: On the one hand, representative actions shall allow 'qualified entities', like e.g. recognised consumer associations or trade associations, to sue on behalf of the victims. Normally, these victims have to be identified. However, the Commission mentions also the possibility that – 'in rather restricted cases' – it is sufficient that the victims be

---

[20] This view is also taken by the European Commission in the White Paper (*supra* note 6) at p. 4. In our view, standing should not even be denied *a priori* to 'umbrella' customers (customers of non-participants paying a higher price due to the anticompetitive conduct of other firms) or to 'deadweight loss' customers (customers not buying a product because of the artificial increase in price). However, in these cases, it will normally be impossible to prove quantum and causality. If exceptionally it should be possible to furnish proof, this group of victims should be compensated, too.

'identifiable'. As follows from the accompanying working paper[21] (and the relationship to the 'opt-in collective actions') this seems to mean that representative actions may work on an opt-out basis.

The second mechanism proposed by the Commission are opt-in collective actions 'in which victims expressly decide to combine their individual claims for harm they suffered into one single action'.[22]

2.4.3 Critique

For the reasons already mentioned the proposal for a more effective collective redress deserves support. As regards the second proposal of 'opt-in collective actions', there seems to be no problem because collective actions correspond to a regular joinder of parties generally accepted. More problematic is the proposal of representative actions especially if they are interpreted in the opt-out sense. The fundamental question is if an opt-out system fits to the European context, or if – on the contrary – they are responsible for what is perceived as 'excessive' in the US litigation culture.

A specific example shall be mentioned: According to French law, consumer associations have standing and may sue for damages based on an opt-in system (see the *action exercée dans l'intérêt collectif des consommateurs* in Article L421-1 Code de la consommation and the *action en représentation conjointe* in Article L422-1 in the same statute). The most spectacular case is the cartel on the mobile phone market. The three French operators were fined for a market sharing agreement (the so-called 'Yalta du portable').[23] The French consumer association *UFC-Que Choisir* has asserted claims for about 12,000 clients. In its comment to the White Paper the organisation complains that the costs of opt-in are exorbitant and that only a minor fraction of the victims could be activated. The number of all consumers affected by the mobile phone cartel is estimated at 20 million, so that the rate of active victims is close to zero.[24]

The example shows that an opt-out system would indeed be the only means to achieve total compensation of all victims. On the other hand, an

---

[21] *Supra* note 6, at para 49: 'It is obviously important that qualified entities that are about to bring, or have brought, a damages action are under a clearly set out obligation to use effective mechanisms for informing the victims they represent.'

[22] White Paper (*supra* note 6) at p. 4.

[23] The *Cour de cassation* fixed the fine at 442 million Euro. *See* the judgment No 1020 of 29 June 2007, case 07-10.303, 07-10.354 and 07-10.397.

[24] UFC-Que Choisir, *Réponse au livre blanc sur les actions en dommages et intérêts pour infraction aux règles communautaires sur les ententes et les abus de position dominante* (available at *see supra* note 7), pp. 4–5. See generally Idot, L. (2007), 'Private Enforcement of Competition Law – Recommendations flowing from the French Experience', in J. Basedow (*supra* note 10) 85.

opt-out system is hardly consistent with the right to be heard before the court. Neither does it correspond to the European tradition to oppose the *res judicata* effect to a person who did not join the action. Therefore, it seems more appropriate to introduce collective mechanisms following an opt-in system. Thus, the criticisms by those who evoke the danger of excessive claims can be invalidated. The conditions for the opt-in should be as low as possible: The registration on a website should be sufficient.

2.4.4 Disbursement of damages

The consumer associations should (with the exception of a costs award) not be allowed to retain the monies for themselves and should also not have to surrender it to the state, but rather it should directly benefit the consumer. This could be done by means of a registration system in which consumers have to establish the degree to which they have been affected. In order to limit administrative expenses flat-rate amounts should be possible. Only if the amount for the single consumer is very low, the judge should have the power to decide on a different use of the amount. But even in this case, the money should be used – at least in an indirect way – to the advantage of the consumers, for example by giving it to consumer associations or foundations working in their interest.

2.4.5 Administrative proceedings

Moreover, consumer associations should also have standing in administrative proceedings. In this way the problem of 'buying up' of procedural rights could be resolved. This is, in the first place, significant in connection with merger control. The approval of mergers can be challenged by other enterprises, with the consequence that considerable delays can ensue. Therefore it happens in practice that the would-be merging parties settle with the claimants: in return for payment or the provision of other benefits the claimants withdraw their legal remedies so that the merger can be implemented. Such a practice is problematic because the legality of the merger is not adjudicated on competition-related grounds but rather by an extra-judicial settlement between enterprises frequently of the same sector. If the consumer associations had standing in their own right, the basis for such a settlement between the interested enterprises would disappear: even if the competitors withdrew their claims the association could still maintain its objection.

2.5 Assignment

Collective actions based on the opt-in system are very close to the classical concept of assignment. Indeed, contrary to Roman law, it is possible to transfer a claim (without the consent of the debtor) to another party who asserts the claim in her own name. On this basis, the Belgian company *Cartel Damage Claims (CDC)* has become active in several European countries. The company acquires damage claims against cartel participants and brings them to court in a bundled manner. Thanks to the central administration of the several claims by one professional service provider, the costs of civil procedure stay low. In return, *CDC* is entitled to keep about 15 per cent of what has successfully been claimed.

In the case of the German cement cartel, the Federal Court of Justice (Bundesgerichtshof) has approved this way to proceed.[25] It is not excluded that the assignment approach could solve the problems of cartel damage claims when enterprises are injured. However, this will hardly be a practicable way in cases of scattered damages to the detriment of consumers. Here, only specific collective actions for consumer associations can surmount the judicial abstinence due to costs and risk of taking legal action.

3 PASSING ON

The question of standing for indirect purchasers is closely linked to the problem of 'passing on'. Can the respondent defend himself against a competition claim on the grounds that the claimant had shifted the overcharge (the increase in price due to the cartel agreement) onto the next market level?[26] There are basically four solutions which may be listed as follows:

1. The *passing on* defence is denied; indirect purchasers are excluded.
2. The *passing on* defence is denied; indirect purchasers are entitled.
3. The *passing on* defence is admitted; indirect purchasers are excluded.
4. The *passing on* defence is admitted; indirect purchasers are entitled.

Solution 1 corresponds to US federal law as it is has been interpreted by the US Supreme Court. In *Hanover Shoe*,[27] the US Supreme Court had excluded the passing on defence. This led to the judgment *Illinois Brick*

[25] Bundesgerichtshof, 7 April 2009, case number KZR 42/08 (not yet reported).

[26] *See* on this subject the detailed study of Bulst, F. (2006), *Schadensersatzansprüche der Marktgegenseite im Kartellrecht*. For an analysis of the *passing on* defence with special respect to Article 82 EC *see* Mackenrodt, M. O. 'Private Incentive, Optimal Deterrence and Damage Claims for Abuses of Dominant Positions' in M.-O. Mackenrodt, B. Conde Gallego and S. Enchelmaier (*supra* note 11) 174 et seq.

[27] *Hanover Shoe Inc v United Shoe Machinery Corporation*, 392 US 481 (1968).

in which the Supreme Court denied own claims to indirect purchasers. Otherwise, the same damages could have been demanded twice. The advantage of this solution is that claims are bundled on the level of the direct purchasers where the prejudice is not yet scattered. However, solution 1 leads to an unjust enrichment of the direct purchaser who can claim damages although he passed on his damage on the next market level.[28] For this reason, the case law of the US Supreme Court is very contested. The Antitrust Modernization Commission has proposed to overrule the case law by a statutory provision.[29] It has to be added that the case law of the US Supreme Court only refers to federal law. The states are free to award damage claims to indirect purchasers. Thirty-six states (plus the District of Columbia) have made use of this possibility. From a European perspective, the exclusion of indirect purchasers seems hardly compatible with the 'any individual' requirement of the *Courage* decision.

Solution 2 is followed to some extent in German law. An express rule in the German competition law statute makes it difficult to invoke the passing on defence.[30] On the one hand, private claims become more practicable. On the other hand, there is the danger of multiple damages if the perpetrator is obliged to compensate direct and indirect purchasers for the same prejudice.[31] However, this danger will not always materialize: Frequently, the

---

[28] *See* Antitrust Modernization Commission, Report and Recommendations, April 2007, available at: http://govinfo.library.unt.edu/amc/report_recommendation/toc.htm (accessed 19 June 2009), p. vi: 'Such a system that compensates the uninjured and denies recovery to the injured seems fundamentally unfair'.

[29] *Ibid*, p. 267.

[30] § 33 (3) s. 2 GWB provides: 'If a good or service is purchased at an excessive price, a damage shall not be excluded on account of the resale of the good or service.' The preparatory works show that this text does not categorically exclude the passing on defence. It simply clarifies that even in the case of passing on damage initially occurs. The question if the damages might be compensated by the benefits received is left over to the courts. According to the dominant opinion, the passing on defence will normally be excluded, *see* J. Bornkamm (*supra* note 18), § 33 GWB No 107; Kersting, C. (2008), 'Perspektiven der privaten Rechtsdurchsetzung im Kartellrecht', *Zeitschrift für Wettbewerbsrecht*, 252; Max Planck Institute for Intellectual Property, Competition and Tax Law, *Comments on the White Paper by the Directorate-General for Competition of April 2008* (2008) 12–13 (available at see *supra* note 7). In any event, the competition law infringer bears the burden of proof that damages were compensated through the resale.

[31] There are proposals to cure this problem by a compensation mechanism (*see* Max Planck Institute, *supra* note 30, at 14–15): The infringer cannot invoke the passing on defence. In return, he is – with respect to the overcharge – only liable to the first plaintiff. In a separate procedure, direct and indirect purchasers have to share the amount in dispute according to the prejudice suffered. If all affected persons participate at the compensation phase, the final result will correspond

direct purchaser has no incentive to file a claim against the cartel members, e.g. for the very reason that he was able to shift the loss onto the next commercial level or because he does not wish to harm the business relationship to the supplier. If the direct purchaser waives its own legal action, it is good to have at least the indirect purchaser to sue. On the contrary, if indirect purchasers do not sue, for example because of the fragmented character of their prejudice and the absence of suitable collective mechanisms, there is still a chance that the direct purchasers may take legal action. Therefore, solution 2, although not ideal, may be a good second best solution where barriers to certain groups of claimants are high.

Solution 3 is the worst of all models. If the passing on defence is admitted, but standing to indirect purchasers denied, nobody can claim damages. This scenario contradicts fundamental principles of tort law and should not be followed.

In our view, solution 4 is the most convincing option because it conforms to general principles of compensatory law: Every claimant can demand exactly the damage actually and finally incurred. The perpetrator has to compensate the entire prejudice, but not more than that. Nobody is unjustly enriched. In the White Paper, the European Commission has proposed a model corresponding to solution 4.[32]

However, solution 4 has weak points, too. The first is linked to the rules on the burden of proof. According to general rules, in an action of a direct purchaser against the infringer, the burden of proof for passing on is on the infringer. If he cannot prove that passing on has taken place, he will be sentenced to pay the full amount to his direct client. On the other hand, for actions of indirect purchasers against the infringer, the European Commission has proposed that there should be the rebuttable presumption that the illegal overcharge has been passed on to them in its entirety.[33] So, if the infringer is not able to rebut this presumption, he will be liable to the indirect purchasers, too. Multiple responsibility would be the consequence.[34]

The second shortcoming of solution 4 concerns the situation of indirect purchasers. Solution 4 will only work if collective redress is implemented as suggested above. Otherwise, indirect purchasers would not have sufficient incentives to sue, with the consequence that the infringer would

---

to solution 4. It seems questionable if this complicated mechanism will increase incentives to sue. The question of passing on is simply shifted to the second phase in which the decision on the distribution of damages has to be taken.

32 White Paper (*supra* note 6) at pp. 7–8.

33 White Paper (*supra* note 6) at p. 8.

34 For a proposal to avoid this risk, *see supra* footnote 31.

be unjustly enriched. Therefore, as a transitory solution, the passing on defence should only be recognised, if satisfactory collective mechanisms have been introduced. As long as this is not the case, the passing on defence should be denied.

The overview has shown that there is no panacea for the passing on problem. But no matter which of the different options will be chosen: The most important thing is *that* a legislative decision will be taken: The questions arising from the passing on problem put private enforcement seriously at risk. Private claims need legal certainty. If it is not clear which defences are admitted and which classes of claimants are entitled to the overcharges, private plaintiffs will keep on shrinking from taking legal action.

4 CALCULATION OF DAMAGES

4.1 Multiple Damages

One of the factors responsible for the attractiveness of private enforcement in the US certainly is the availability of treble damages. In Europe, there is a divide in this question between common law and civil law countries. With the exception of Ireland and the UK, no punitive damages are awarded. Even in these countries, punitive damages do not play an important part. Whether punitive damages should be introduced generally in Europe for competition law infringements is highly controversial. The underlying question is if tort law should exclusively aim at the compensation of the victims, or if also the prevention of future violations is intended.[35] Even if a cautious opening to new functions may be found,[36] the predominant view in Europe rejects punitive damages, as they cannot be reconciled with the compensatory principles of damages claims. As a compromise against the background of European circumstances the introduction of double damages has been suggested.[37]

In the White Paper, the European Commission has abandoned the

---

[35] For an in-depth discussion *see* Wils, W. (2009), 'The Relationship between Public Antitrust Enforcement and Private Actions for Damages', 32, 1, *World Competition*, 4.

[36] *See* for example Wagner, G. (2006), 'Prävention und Verhaltenssteuerung durch Privatrecht – Anmaßung oder legitime Aufgabe?', *Archiv für die civilistische Praxis*, **206**, 352.

[37] European Commission, Green Paper (*supra* note 5, Option 16); Monopolkommission (Germany), *Das allgemeine Wettbewerbsrecht in der 7.*

proposal to introduce double damages. In the *Manfredi* judgment, the ECJ has clarified that in the absence of Community rules, Member States are free in this respect.[38] Therefore, the differences between Europe and the US will remain. If private enforcement in Europe is to be improved, there have to be changes in other areas.

4.2 The Determination of Quantum

The typical requirements for a damage claim are:

(a) the competition law violation;
(b) the loss;
(c) causation of the loss by the legal infringement; as well as (in many, but not all countries)
(d) fault.

National legislations in most European countries assume that the loss to be recovered includes the actual losses (*damnum emergens*) as well as loss of profit (*lucrum cessans*).[39] Thus, at least in theory, the legal prerequisites exist to ensure private enforcement of competition law. However, the obstacles are not so much in theory, but in practice, especially when the damage has to be quantified.

In cases where a purchaser has paid too much because of the anticompetitive behavior of his seller, the manipulated price has to be compared to the hypothetical price under competitive circumstances. There are some basic methods which are recognised in many legal orders. According to the 'Before and after' method, the price which was practiced before the implementation of the prohibited behavior is the basis. The 'Yardstick' method, in contrast, refers to comparable markets which have not been affected by anticompetitive practices, e.g. neighbouring, but separate markets for similar products, or separate geographical markets for the

---

GWB-Novelle, Sondergutachten (2004) at No 75 et seq, 126, 131, available at: www.monopolkommission.de/sg_41/text_s41.pdf (accessed 19 June 2009).

[38] ECJ, 13 July 2006, Joined Cases C-295/04 to C-298/04, *Manfredi* (*supra* note 4) note 92 et seq. But *see*, W. Wils (*supra* note 35) at p. 22, who deduces from the principle of *ne bis in idem* that (even in stand-alone actions) the award of punitive damages by a national court is precluded because this would prevent the European Commission imposing fines at a later stage.

[39] As regards violations of European competition law, this follows from the principle of effectiveness, *see* ECJ, 13.July 2006, Joined Cases C-295/04 to C-298/04, *Manfredi* (*supra* note 4) No 95, where, moreover, the duty to pay interests is underlined.

same product. The problem of these methods is that often special economic expertise is needed in order to determine the key figures. The need for an economic expert opinion makes litigation more costly and still less practicable.[40]

Most European countries provide for flexibility regarding the calculation of quantum. If through no responsibility of the aggrieved party the precise calculation presents difficulties, then the courts often have the discretion to estimate the extent of losses incurred.

Nevertheless, more guidance is needed. Therefore, the plans of the European Commission are to be welcomed: The Commission intends 'to draw up a framework with pragmatic, non-binding guidance for quantification of damages in antitrust cases, e.g. by means of approximate methods of calculation or simplified rules on estimating the loss'.[41] In fact, practitioners regularly draw attention to the question of quantum. If a more solid ground could be created here, one of the main obstacles to private litigation would have been removed.

5 ACCESS TO EVIDENCE

The limited status of private claims in Europe is due, among other things, to the difficulty of producing evidence for the four elements mentioned above.[42] All these preconditions have as a rule to be established by the claimant. As regards the proof of a competition law violation, there are some alleviations for follow on actions as, according to Article 16 of Regulation 1/2003, national courts are bound by decisions of the European Commission which already have been adopted or will probably be taken in the future. Moreover, in some Member States, courts are formally bound by rulings of the national antitrust authorities. German legislation goes furthest in this respect: Courts are not only bound by decisions of the European Commission and the German antitrust authority, but also by the findings of the competition authorities of other EU Member States.[43]

---

40 *See* Heizmann, R. and R. Zäch (2008), 'Expertisekosten als neue Hürden für Kartellklagen', in M Leupold *et al.* (eds), *Festschrift für A Bühler*, 3.

41 White Paper (*supra* note 6) at p. 7.

42 For an analysis *see* Zäch, R. and R. Heizmann (2005), 'Durchsetzung des Wettbewerbsrechts durch Private', in *Essays in Honor of S. Soltysinski*, 1059.

43 § 33 (4) s. 1 GWB: 'Where damages are claimed for an infringement of a provision of this Act or of Article 81 or 82 of the EC Treaty, the court shall be bound by a finding that an infringement has occurred, to the extent such a finding was made in a final decision by the cartel authority, the Commission of the European

As regards general rules on evidence, only in Ireland and the UK are there comprehensive duties of discovery. With regard to the evidence question there is therefore a divide between common law and civil law countries although in Scandinavian countries, courts have a certain margin in imposing disclosure, too. It would certainly be too simplistic to say that in common law countries the claimant can file a claim in the hope that the evidence will be revealed by the respondent. But there is at least a certain alleviation of the burden of proof in these countries.[44] In civil law countries by contrast the claimant must undertake intensive preparation of his case. He has to research all the evidence himself. If he realises that he will not be able to produce conclusive comprehensive evidence, he is advised not to persist with the claim.

As the evidentiary difficulties are often unavoidable and result in an unjustified advantaging of the respondent, the European Commission has proposed to create a minimum level of disclosure.[45] The obligation to produce evidence shall be linked to precise conditions:

- The claimant has presented all facts and means of evidence reasonably available;
- they show plausible grounds for a harm caused by the defendant;
- the claimant is unable to produce the requested evidence;
- precise categories of evidence have been specified; and
- the requested evidence is relevant, necessary and proportionate.

Some are afraid that, in spite of these conditions, the rules on disclosure could be used for 'fishing expeditions'. So, here again, we touch upon a subject which is crucial for an appropriate configuration of the framework for private enforcement. In our view, something has to be done in order to remove the information asymmetry typical for antitrust cases. If disclosure obligations are subject to precise conditions – as it is the case in the Commission's proposal – an abuse is excluded, especially if judges stay in control of the procedure. The British example shows that moderate rules on disclosure do not lead to excessive litigation.

Community, or the competition authority – or court acting as such – in another Member State of the European Community'.

44 Therefore, there is a strong incentive to claim before British courts. *See* (particularly with regard to the vitamin cartel) Bulst, F. (2003), 'The Provimi Decision of the High Court: Beginnings of Private Antitrust Litigation in Europe', *EBOR*, 623.

45 White Paper (*supra* note 6) at pp. 4–5.

6 TENSIONS BETWEEN PRIVATE ENFORCEMENT AND LENIENCY POLICY

The co-existence of public and private enforcement is not always peaceful.[46] Tensions become most visible in the area of leniency programs.[47] If whistleblowers run the risk of being sued for damages, incentives to report prohibited practices diminish. Consequently, the question has to be asked how this contradiction can be resolved or at least attenuated. The problem can be tackled in private or in administrative law.

6.1 Reduction of Civil Liability in Favour of Immunity Recipients?

In the Green Paper of 2005, the European Commission had put up for discussion the proposal to provide for a rebate on any damages claim against the leniency applicant and to liberate him from joint liability.[48] This suggestion was inspired by the US-American Antitrust Criminal Penalty Enhancement and Reform Act of 2004 which has introduced the possibility of 'detrebling' and of removing the joint and several liability in favour of whistle blowers. However, the reaction to the Commission's proposal was very sceptical. Therefore, in the White Paper, the Commission (very carefully) 'puts forward for further consideration' the idea to limit civil liability of the immunity recipient to claims by his direct and indirect contractual partners. The option in favour of rebates in damage claims against the leniency applicant is not maintained.[49]

The usual arguments in favour of this proposal are: Without the whistle blower the injured parties would not have known the existence of the prohibited practice, or would at least have gained knowledge only later. Besides, due to the revelation, other infringers can be identified who are liable without restriction. We cannot share this point of view. Pragmatic reflections typical for administrative proceedings and for the fixing of fines are transferred into private law. It does not seem consistent with the com-

---

46 *See* Heinemann, A . (2007), 'Interferenzen zwischen öffentlichem Recht und Privatrecht in der Wettbewerbspolitik', in A. Epiney et al. (eds) *Essays in Honor of R. Bieber*, 681.

47 On the Community level see Commission Notice on Immunity from fines and reduction of fines in cartel cases, OJ 2006, C 298/17.

48 Green Paper (*supra* note 5), p. 10 Option 29 and 30, in conjunction with the Annex to the Green Paper, note 235 et seq.

49 White Paper (*supra* note 6) at p. 10.

pensatory goal of tort law to reduce a damage claim because the tortfeasor has co-operated with a public authority.[50]

6.2 Protection of Confidentiality

Tensions between administrative and private law should be resolved on the administrative level, i.e. by appropriate rules on leniency policy. The European Commission has adopted such rules in the Leniency Notice 2006 providing for the confidentiality of corporate statements. The leniency applicant may request that his statement is given orally, and is recorded and transcribed by the Commission. Only the infringer gets access to the statement. The information may only be used for the purposes of the administrative proceeding pending against him.[51] The information is transmitted to the national competition authorities only if these guarantee the same protection.[52] These rules are adequate: As the confidentiality of corporate statements thus is safeguarded, the information is not available for damages actions.

6.3 Remaining Tensions

However, these rules cannot prevent the administrative proceeding possibly being closed by a decision of the competition authority which may be introduced into a private damage claim against the leniency applicant. This shows that leniency policy is the most prominent example of frictions between public and private enforcement which cannot be completely avoided. The deeper reason is the utilitarian approach of leniency programmes: Sanctions are remitted or reduced although later co-operation cannot undo infringements committed in the past.

7 CONCLUSIONS

The success of private enforcement does not depend on single factors, but on the mix of rules concerning substantive law, civil procedure and

---

50 In this sense *see* also Wils (*supra* note 35) at p. 25. Moreover, *see* the European Commission's Leniency Notice (*supra* note 47), No 39 s. 2: 'The fact that immunity or reduction in respect of fines is granted cannot protect an undertaking from the civil law consequences of its participation in an infringement of Article 81 EC'.

51 In accordance with the Commission Notice on the rules for access to the Commission file, OJ 2005 C 325/7.

52 European Commission, Leniency Notice (*supra* note 47), note 31 et seq.

the relationship between private actions and administrative enforcement. Moreover, the interaction of all these factors as well as the general legal culture including litigation culture has to be taken into consideration. It is not necessary to copy other legal systems in order to achieve a more prominent place for private enforcement. Rather, a mix of measures has to be adopted which gives private parties an incentive to assert their rights. Therefore, if we do not want to introduce treble damages or class actions based on the opt out principle, we have to change other conditions influencing private claims. It is suggested here, that consumers and their associations should get standing, that the rules on the calculation of damages are simplified, that the problem of *passing on* is solved in a convincing way, and that the access of injured parties to evidence is facilitated. If this is done in a balanced way, the concerns of those who predict excessive litigation in Europe will turn out to be baseless. This can be illustrated by the British example: Although the possibility of exemplary damages exists and in spite of disclosure rules similar (albeit not identical) to the US-American discovery rules, no exaggerated litigation can be observed.

Private competition law claims will be considerably strengthened by the ongoing procedures concerning the vitamin and other hardcore cartels. Some national legislators already have adopted rules in favour of stronger private enforcement. The European legislator should take up the suggestions presented by the European Commission in the White Paper on damages actions. A European framework would dissipate the legal uncertainty which exists today due to the underdevelopment of private enforcement in the past. The enforcement of European competition law should be based on harmonised rules, not only in administrative proceedings but also in private law. With clear legal rules, the private enforcement of competition law would quickly lose its special status as a field of law which basically only exists in theory. A better functioning of our economic system would be the consequence.

12. Competition law de lege ferenda

Daniel Zimmer*

In this chapter, I will deal – in brief – with four questions:

1 Where do we stand?
2 Where should we be going?
3 What is the role of economics in competition policy?
4 What has to be done right now?

1 WHERE DO WE STAND? AN ATTEMPT TO DRAW A CONCLUSION

The chapters presented in this book provide an excellent overview of the development of competition policy and law in the past two decades. Looking at them all together, we may draw some conclusions.

The competition principle spreads across the world. From the United States of America, where the legislation against restraints of trade was initiated with the Sherman Act in 1890, the principles of competition law have been brought to Japan and Germany in the late 1940s – certainly not only for the sake of a free and competitive economy, but – in the beginning – also in order to disempower existing economic structures.[1] The European Economic Community, which formed its competition rules in the 1950s, had – with the creation of a common market and the economic advantages of it – already other objectives.[2] The Brazilian legislation dates from the same period. India and other important economies followed

* Professor of Law, University of Bonn, Institute for Commercial Law, Bonn, Germany.

[1] *See* for the Japanese Law Hayashi, S. (2008), 'The goals of Japanese competition law' in J. Drexl, L. Idot and J. Monéger (eds) *Economic Theory and Competition Law*, 68; for the German Law Bock, H.K. and H. Korsch (1957), 'Kartellauflösung und Konzernentflechtung in der westdeutschen Wirtschaft seit 1945', *Wirtschaft und Wettbewerb*, 411.

[2] *See* Gerber, D.J. (1998), *Law and Competition in Twentieth Century Europe*.

in the 1960s. Now, this book has shown that the principle of competition has received another impressive push forward within the past two decades: Modern competition laws have been introduced in many jurisdictions, including a number of countries in Eastern Europe which formerly adhered to principles of socialism. Most recently, China has introduced an antimonopoly law.[3]

Competition laws converge. With respect to their content, competition law becomes more and more alike. It seems fair to say that most countries which have legislation in this field provide a tripartite system, consisting – first – of rules on the coordination of behavior, including, at their core, a cartel prohibition; consisting, secondly, of provisions on the abuse of dominance; and, thirdly, of some kind of a merger control, designed to prevent the creation or deepening of market power by external growth, for example by the acquisition of undertakings. Of course there remain important differences between the legal systems. However, the overall convergence may give a reason for hope for the creation of rules of competition law on an international level.

More and more jurisdictions emphasise the issue of law enforcement. Numerous authorities and legislators strive for an improvement of the private enforcement of competition law. Reforms and reform proposals include an improvement with respect to the incentives to sue. Catchwords are multiple damages; denial of a passing-on defense and admission of private follow-on suits after an administrative proceeding.[4]

The public or administrative law enforcement has been fostered in many legislations by the introduction of effective leniency programs. Some legal systems rely, as we have seen, on effects of criminal sanctions.[5]

All these measures relate to the issue of the effectiveness of competition law: How can we make sure that the competition rules are obeyed? This issue – effectiveness – must not be mixed up with another term: efficiency. Efficiency is, as we know, an economic concept. It deals with the question of the best use of scarce resources in order to reach certain ends. Does competition law have to strive for an improvement of economic efficiency? Asking this question, I enter the second part of my presentation.

---

[3] *See* for the recent developments in Brazilian, Eastern European, Indian and Chinese as well as in Japanese, EU and US law the contributions by de Azevedo, Bejček, Chakravarthy, Huang Yong, Takahashi, Monti and Grimes (in this book).

[4] *See* A. Heinemann 'Private Enforcement in Europe' (Chapter 11 in this volume).

[5] *See* the contribution of W. Wils (Chapter 10 in this volume).

2 WHERE SHOULD WE BE GOING?

The topic of this chapter – Competition law de lege ferenda – relates directly to the issue of the goals of competition law. Like a wanderer who needs to have a destination in order to avoid a foolish march in circles, a competition lawyer needs to have a conceptual orientation about the goals of competition law. Here, however, we raise an intricate question: the goals of competition law seem to belong to the most disputed issues in this field of law.[6]

2.1 One Goal or More?

A first difficulty is raised by the question as to whether competition law serves basically one or – by contrast – more than one goal.[7] Advocates of a multi-goal policy perceive that competition may bring about a variety of benefits – such as economic growth, distributional fairness as well as a protection against economic power. If we recognise the rooting of competition law in the US-American Anti-Trust legislation of the late 19th century, it becomes obvious that this latter aspect – distributional fairness and protection against economic power – may be good explanations for the existence of competition law.[8] In recent decades, however, a different perception has gained an important influence. This concept proposes that competition law serves just one goal: to promote efficiency and thereby enhance welfare.[9] Within this line of reasoning there remains one question to be answered: that is whether the leading motive should be the promotion of total welfare or just of consumer welfare.[10] This appears to be, however, a difference of limited importance. The big issue which has to be discussed in these years is whether competition law is just about efficiency

---

[6] *See* the contributions by Gerber, D.J., A.J. Padilla, D. Zimmer, E. Fox, and H. Schweitzer (2008), in C.-D. Ehlermann and M. Marquis (eds) *European Competition Law Annual 2007: A Reformed Approach to Article 82 EC*; Zimmer, D. (forthcoming), in J. Basedow (ed) *Structure and Effects in EU Competition Law*.

[7] *See* for this discussion Kerber, W. (2008), 'Should Competition Law Promote Efficiency? Some Reflections of an Economist on the Normative Foundations of Competition Law' in J. Drexl, L Idot and J. Monéger (eds) *Economic Theory and Competition Law*, 133, at pp. 152 et seq.

[8] Cf Troesken, W. (2002), 'The letters of John Sherman and the Origins of Antitrust' in *The Review of Austrian Economics,* 15, 275.

[9] *See* Bork, R. H. (1978), *The Antitrust Paradox – A Policy at War with Itself.*

[10] For this discussion, e.g., Neven, D. and L.H. Röller (2000), 'Consumer Surplus v Welfare Standard in a Political Economy of Merger Control', *CEPR Discussion Paper* No 2620.

and, directly connected with this, welfare, or whether it serves a variety of goals which include, but are not confined to efficiency and welfare goals.

2.2 Intermediate or Final Goals?

The issue of goals of competition law has one more dimension: that is whether competition law has to make an effort to reach certain final goals in a direct way, or whether its aim is the pursuit of intermediate goals. There is, of course, a close connection with the previous question: for which goals is competition law aiming? The idea of an intermediate goal fits well with the concept that competition law serves, in the last instance, a multitude of final purposes. Suppose, for example, that the law pursues as an intermediate goal the protection of competition as a process. This idea of serving the competitive process is perfectly consistent with the concept that this intermediate goal – competitive process – serves in the last instance a multitude of purposes, such as welfare as well as distributional and fairness purposes. If we do not say that we go for an intermediate goal such as the protection of competition as a process we get into trouble when trying to reach a multitude of goals as final goals such as welfare, distribution and fairness at the same time. The problem would be that we do not have a criterion to decide upon the balance between those three goals. So a multi-goal concept strongly calls for the construction of one intermediate goal – such as fostering the competitive process – in order to solve the decisional problem which we would have if we tried to realise a multitude of final goals at the same time.

By contrast to the foregoing, things become much simpler if we suppose that the law serves just one final purpose – such as the promotion of welfare by the furtherance of efficiency. If we concentrate on just one final goal, it appears unnecessary to construe on the intermediary level an additional goal such as competition. The implications of such an approach seem clear: 'Competition' would consequently be protected only as far as it promotes efficiency. So the direct orientation towards a final goal of efficiency brings about a reduction of the reach of competition law.

But – is this what the legal systems, the statutes mean by employing the term 'competition'? Some economists have answered the question in the affirmative sense, arguing that they are unable to measure competition in any other way than by calculating effects on efficiency. Here lies, as it seems, an explanation for the success that efficiency-oriented approaches have had in the discussion of the last three decades: the concentration on just one goal – efficiency – seems to make things unambiguous and the results calculable: If we concentrate on the aim to promote efficiency and we find an economist who declares himself capable of calculating the efficiency effects of my decision – for example the decision to prohibit or to clear a certain merger – we will have an obvious and positive criterion: We will prohibit the merger if it reduces efficiency, and we will clear the merger if it enhances efficiency.

In the real world, however, there are some problems with this approach. One major problem is that 'efficiency' is not such a clear and unambiguous concept as it might appear at a first glance. Economists distinguish between productive efficiency, allocative efficiency and dynamic efficiency.[11] Whereas the effects, to give an example, of a merger on productive and on allocative efficiencies may, in certain limits, well be prognosticated by microeconomic calculations, the same seems not to be true for the dynamic aspects of a combination: Economists admit that to date, they are not in the same way able to forecast the effects of a merger on research, development and innovation in a market.[12] So also a decision for a concentration on just one goal of competition policy – such as the promotion of efficiency – would not lead to simple and unambiguous decisional rules.

There would be one more – major – problem with the decision for a one-final-goal concept: This is a problem which stands, for a lawyer, at the very beginning of the analysis: Would a one-goal approach be consistent with the law? If we talk about the currently existing law, the *lex lata*, this question can only be answered for each country, each legislation respectively. As for EU law, it appears clear to me that a one-goal approach would not be in line with the existing law. The structure of Article 81 of the EC Treaty reveals this: Paragraph 1 of this provision prohibits in its paragraph 1 all agreements between undertakings . . . which may affect trade between Member States and which have as their object or effect the prevention, restriction or distortion of competition . . . The provision encompasses all agreements which prevent, restrict of distort competition independent of their effects on efficiency. The issue of efficiencies comes only into play in the third paragraph, on the level of an exception to the principle of prohibition: The provisions of paragraph 1 may, however, be declared inapplicable in the case of any agreement . . . which contributes to improving the production or distribution of goods or to promoting technical or economic progress . . .

The provisions of Article 82 and of the Merger Control Regulation appear to be inconsistent with a one-final-goal approach, as well: both do not relate directly to efficiency, but relate to the legal term of competition.

---

[11] *See* for an assessment of the discussion W. Kerber, *supra* note 7, at pp. 135 et seq.

[12] Cf W. Kerber, *supra* note 7, at pp. 140 et seq.

It can easily be demonstrated that the term 'competition' cannot mean precisely the same as efficiency: A merger to monopoly may bring about the most efficient result – especially on markets with a tendency to so-called natural monopolies, such as network industries. However, the term 'competition' clearly excludes the possibility of a subsumption of a monopoly: If the term shall have any meaning in the sense of the existence of a minimum of rivalry it presupposes the existence of at least two units. So legislations which rely – on a first level – on the term competition seem to pursue this as an intermediate goal. Such a construction does not exclude the possibility that on another level final goals come directly into play. In European Law, this is the case in exceptional provisions on the justification of restraints of competition for efficiency reasons.[13]

The task I have been posed is, however, not to treat the existing law, but Competition law de lege ferenda. I would like to draw attention to one aspect which seems to be of central importance to me. It is the question for the proper role of economics in competition law de lege ferenda.

3 WHAT IS THE ROLE OF ECONOMICS IN COMPETITION LAW DE LEGE FERENDA?

If we talk about the relationship of law on the one hand and economics on the other in the field of competition policy we may refer to various levels of analysis, i.e.:

- Questions of fact (when deciding individual cases)
- Interpretation of existing legal rules (when deciding individual cases)
- Creation of new rules under cost/benefit aspects
- Creation of new rules under policy aspects

We can easily divide these questions into two pairs of questions, by saying: The first and the second one relate to the application of competition law to individual cases, whereas the third and the fourth question concern the task of the creation of new legal rules.

However, this is but one possible 'grouping' of the four questions. I rather suggest another set of pairs. If we look closer at the four levels we may recognise that the first and third level address questions of fact, respectively empirical questions, whereas levels two and four concern questions of competition policy: This is obvious when we look at level 4:

---

13 *See* for the foregoing reasoning D. Zimmer, *supra* note 6.

The creation of new rules under policy aspects; but it is also true for level 2: the interpretation of existing legal rules. As everybody knows, we have to obey certain methodological rules when interpreting legal norms. The underlying policy is a prominent aspect in rule interpretation. This holds true in particular for competition law: In order to understand a provision of competition law we must know and understand its underlying policy.

For reasons which I would like to discuss now, economic expertise may contribute in a very valuable way to the analyses on the levels 1 and 3. By contrast, economic expertise cannot provide answers to the policy questions addressed at the levels 2 and 4.

3.1 Fact Questions (When Deciding Individual Cases)

When authorities such as administrative agencies or competition courts decide upon individual cases, they have to answer – *inter alia* – questions of fact. Economic theory may considerably contribute to this aspect of the decision-making process. I would like to give but three examples:

When defining the relevant product market the authorities relied in earlier times often on a rather simplistic concept of exchangeability of goods. More recently economic theory has developed the hypothetical monopoly test as a general concept and, as its practical implementation, the so-called SSNIP test (for: small, but significant non-transitory increase in price test). This test reflects in a more differentiated manner than the formerly prevailing methods to what degree certain products exert competitive pressure on each other.[14]

Economic theory may explain the competitive effects of certain contractual arrangements, such as exclusive dealing or rebate and bonus schemes. Thus economic expertise can in a very valuable way contribute to a coherent application of the law, thereby preventing an under- or an over-enforcement.[15]

Economic theory has taught us in recent years that mergers among

---

[14] *See* for a description of the methodology Werden, G. (1993), 'Market Delineation under the Merger Guidelines: A Tenth Anniversary Retrospective', *Antitrust Bulletin*, 38, at 517 et seq.; for an analysis of the case practise of the EU Commission see Schwalbe, U. and D. Zimmer *Kartellrecht und Ökonomie*, at pp. 104 et seq; for a modification of the hypothetical monopoly test *see* Ivaldi, M. and S. Lörincz (2005), 'A Full Equilibrium Relevant Market Test: Application to Computer Servers', *CEPR Discussion Paper,* 4917.

[15] *See* Hellwig, M. (2006), 'Effizienz oder Wettbewerbsfreiheit? Zur normativen Grundlegung der Wettbewerbspolitik' in Engel, Ch. and W. Möschel (eds), *Recht und spontane Ordnung, Festschrift für E-J Mestmäcker*, 231 (at pp. 249 et seq).

competitors may have unfavourable effects not just for two, but for three different reasons: First, a merger may lead to a single monopoly. Secondly, a merger may lead to collective market power in the sense that, due to the existence of a retaliation mechanism, firms no longer behave in a competitive way (economists describe this as coordinated effects of a merger). Recently economic theory has focused on a third kind of effects, i.e. so-called non-co-ordinated or unilateral merger effects: Even in the total absence of a coordination of market behavior a merger may lead to a reduction of competitive pressure in the market. The mere disappearance of an independent competitive force from the market can lead to an increase in market prices, if the remaining firms take the exit of the independent competitor into account. In the recent merger control practice economists have provided very valuable analyses with respect to such foreseeable non-coordinated merger effects. One relevant issue of analysis is whether the two parties to the merger used to be relatively close competitors, exercising an important competitive pressure on each other. In this case the elimination of this competitive relationship by the merger will probably lead to a loss in competition also vis-à-vis other firms and result in lower outputs and higher prices in the market.[16]

3.2 Creation of New Rules under Cost Benefit Aspects

One prominent issue in the recent policy debate has been to what degree competition law should consist of, on the one hand, per se rules and, on the other hand, rules of reason, which require economic analyses in each individual case. Discussing possible reforms in the application of Article 82 EC, the provision on abuse of dominance, economists have recently pleaded for a drastic reduction in the number of per se rules. Their argument is that most kinds of business behavior, such as exclusive dealing or bonus- and rebate-schemes, may have, even if they are applied by dominant firms, besides welfare-reducing also welfare-enhancing effects. The balance of welfare gains and welfare losses requires, according to this reasoning, a close economic examination in the individual case.[17]

However, there are also economists who plead for the opposite, for a maintenance or even extension of a system of per se rules. They admit that the effects of certain contractual arrangements may vary from case to

---

[16] *See* for an introduction Ivaldi, M., B. Jullien, P. Rey, P. Seabright and J. Tirole (2003), 'The Economics of Unilateral Effects', *Report for DG Competition*.

[17] *See* the Report by the Economic Advisory Group on Competition Policy (EAGCP) *An Economic Approach to Article 82* (2005).

case, but they point also to the costs and benefits of the entire legal system: Per se rules can provide legal certainty which may result in a reduction of transaction costs. Moreover, clear and simple per-se rules may be applied in a much easier way than rules of reason, thereby reducing the costs of administration and enforcement of competition law.[18]

We recognise that we have just reached, in a certain sense, a meta-level of reasoning: we are discussing rules on rule-making, taking into account also costs and benefits of legal arrangements other than the effects we regularly address when considering competition law, i.e. the effects of competition law on productive efficiency, allocative efficiency and dynamic efficiency. If we adopt this overall perspective, integrating the entire effects of legal rules, including the benefits of general rules and the costs of law administration, we may come to the conclusion that there is not one simple answer to the question of per se rules or rules of reason. Instead, viewed from an economic cost-benefit analysis, we should search for the optimal mix of both types of rules: As far as the benefits of an individual case-by-case analysis exceed the costs of such an analysis, a rule of reason approach appears to be the right kind of rule. On the other hand, as far as the costs of individual analyses exceed the overall gains reached by such case-by-case decisions, simple per se rules are to be preferred. To put it more simply: Even from an economic viewpoint, less economics – in the sense of less economic scrutiny in the individual case – can be the better choice.[19]

3.3 Interpretation of Existing Legal Rules (When Deciding Individual Cases)

Now we turn to issues where economists cannot provide guidance. As indicated earlier, the interpretation of existing legal rules is a legal process, an act of legal craftsmanship. Competition law enforcers such as administrators and judges have to employ legal techniques, in particular techniques on the interpretation of rules. If they failed to comply with the basic methodology on norm interpretation, they would risk ignoring the binding decision of a legitimate legislator – and replace it with their own subjective decision. It goes without saying that this would be impermissible in a political system with divided powers.

Economic theory does not as such provide criteria for the interpretation

---

18 *See* Christiansen, A. and W. Kerber (2006), 'Competition Policy with Optimally Differentiated Rules Instead of Per Se Rules v Rule of Reason', *J Comp L & Econ*, **2**, 215 (emphasising the need to take into account administrative costs when assessing the social costs of a legal rule).

19 *See* Christiansen and Kerber, *supra* note 18.

of a legal rule. Assume that there are two possible interpretations to a legal rule, such as a prohibition of a certain behavior: An extensive interpretation as well as a restrictive interpretation of the prohibition. Economists may inform us about the economic implications of each of these possible interpretations. They may tell us, e.g., that social welfare will be lower under an extensive interpretation and enforcement of the prohibition rule than under a restrictive interpretation. This is an argument that has been brought forward in recent discussions on abuse of dominance: Economists have argued that under a wide interpretation of rules such as Article 82 EC welfare will shrink because of an increase in so-called 'type one errors': An extensive application of Article 82 EC would, according to this reasoning, reduce welfare because it would often result in the prevention of an efficient behavior.[20]

For a lawyer, however, efficiency is not a value in itself. The information that one interpretation will lead, when compared to another, to increased efficiency and thereby to a welfare gain, does not provide a legal argument in favour of this – first – interpretation. There is, however, one exception to this statement: If an accurate legal interpretation of the rule, taking into account its wording, its genesis and its purposes, reveals that the rule is *meant* to enhance efficiency, and that it allows for a consideration of efficiency effects in the individual case, it is appropriate to take the effects of the respective interpretations on efficiency into account when interpreting the rule. In this case the law enforcer does not replace the legislator's intent by his own will; rather he (or she) obeys the law when taking into account efficiency considerations.

So, when interpreting existing rules of competition law it appears crucial to investigate whether and to what degree the legal norm allows an efficiency reasoning in the individual case.

3.4 The Creation of New Rules under Policy Aspects

I return to my topic: competition law de lege ferenda. When taking a decision for a rule of competition law a legislator needs to have one or another concept of competition policy in mind. The point I would like to make in this context is: When deciding upon the policy questions – the question to pursue one or another competition policy – the discipline of economics and in particular the branch of industrial organisation (IO) can – again – provide no answer. Industrial organisation is a positive discipline. It can tell us what happens in a market – in terms of quantities and prices – if

20 *See* the EAGCP Report, *supra* note 17 at pp. 2 et seq.

we employ one or another rule. So economists can – in certain limits – predict the effects of a certain policy decision on total welfare or consumer welfare. However, the discipline of industrial organisation – as a positive discipline – cannot provide an answer to normative questions. It has no answer to the question whether the law should favour total welfare or consumer welfare – or whether it should go further and protect individuals against exploitation by dominant market participants.[21]

Economics can come into play, however, when it comes to an estimation of the effects of one or another policy decision. So the discipline of industrial organisation has an informative function in the legislative process. The policy decision as such has to be taken by the legislator.

4 WHAT HAS TO BE DONE?

It appears evident that there is a need for further discussion on the normative foundations of competition policy.[22] Scholars may contribute to this discussion by developing answers under two different perspectives.

1. What are the normative foundations of the *lex lata* in the respective jurisdictions? Common traces of the various legal systems suggest that the competition laws have – to some degree – a common foundation. A comparative analysis may reveal whether the similarities on the normative level are strong enough to sketch a common concept of competition policy. An answer to this question requires, in particular, thorough analyses of the goals of the existing competition law in various jurisdictions. The structure of these analyses might follow the lines drawn in this book:

(a) Does the *lex lata* pursue just one goal – such as increasing welfare – or is it designed to achieve various goals at the same time, including besides a welfare goal, for example, also the protection of individuals against an abuse of market power by dominant firms?

(b) Are the various competition laws aimed at directly achieving final goals – such as welfare or distribution goals – or do they serve, in the first instance, an intermediate goal – such as fostering the competitive process as such?

(c) As far as competition laws serve intermediate goals (such as fostering the competitive process): is it possible to identify the 'ingredients' of this concept (such as: necessary conditions of the competitive process)?

2. If we arrive at a common understanding of the normative foundations

---

21 D.J. Gerber, *supra* note 6.

22 *See* for a discussion of a central issue in this context W. Kerber, *supra* note 7.

of competition law we might, in the second instance, agree upon conclusions de lege ferenda. A competition policy which is deeply rooted in a number of jurisdictions might serve as a benchmark for codification or reform projects in other jurisdictions, as well. When developing a proposal de lege ferenda it appears important to co-operate with our colleagues in the different branches of economics. The branch of industrial organisation may contribute valuable insights upon the effects of certain legislative decisions on quantities, prices and welfare. Another field of economics – the branch of institutional economics – may help us in analysing another dimension: i.e. how institutions – including legal rules and the practice of their enforcement – create incentives for individuals and organisations (firms) to engage in productive activities.

Index